The Irish *Ulysses*

The Irish *Ulysses*

MARIA TYMOCZKO

UNIVERSITY OF CALIFORNIA PRESS
BERKELEY   LOS ANGELES   LONDON

University of California Press
Berkeley and Los Angeles, California

University of California Press, Ltd.
London, England

© 1994 by
The Regents of the University of California

Tymoczko, Maria.
    The Irish Ulysses / Maria Tymoczko.
        p.   cm.
    Includes bibliographical references and index.
    ISBN 0-520-08027-0 (alk. paper)
        1. Joyce, James, 1882–1941. Ulysses. 2. English fiction—
    Irish influences. 3. Ireland in literature. I. Title.
    PR6019.09U748 1994
    823'.912—dc20   93-26715
                                                CIP

9 8 7 6 5 4 3 2 1

For all those who have taught me about Ireland,
including my many students

Contents

Acknowledgments

This book has taken shape slowly over many years, in part because I am primarily a scholar of medieval literature; I am therefore all the more indebted to many people. Several of the chapters were presented in preliminary form at scholarly meetings, and the organizers of and participants in those conferences contributed to my work. The initial part of chapter 2 was included in "Joyce and His Contemporaries: A Centenary Tribute," a conference held at Hofstra University in October 1982; this paper was later published in *James Joyce Quarterly* as "Symbolic Structures in *Ulysses* from Early Irish Literature" and reprinted in the proceedings of the conference. The principal argument of chapter 4 was presented at the 1983 meetings of the New England Committee for Irish Studies at the University of Connecticut at Storrs and subsequently published in *James Joyce Quarterly* as "Sovereignty Structures in *Ulysses*." Portions of chapter 3 were presented to the annual meetings of the American Conference for Irish Studies at Boston College in 1986, as well as given as addresses at Saint Olaf College, Carleton College, and the University of Minnesota in 1984. A section of chapter 6 was delivered at the annual meetings of the Celtic Studies Association of North America at the University of Cincinnati and the annual meetings of the American Conference for Irish Studies in Dublin in 1987; it was published in the *Irish University Review* as "Molly's Gibraltar and the Morphology of the Irish Otherworld." Sections of chapter 7 have been published as "'The Broken Lights of Irish Myth': Joyce's Knowledge of Early Irish Literature" in *James Joyce Quarterly*. Previously published material is here reprinted by permission of *James Joyce Quarterly* and the *Irish University Review*.

To John V. Kelleher and the late Vivian Mercier I am grateful for readings of the original argument standing at the heart of chapter 2. As my dissertation director, John Kelleher worked closely with me over a number of years and made useful suggestions on my early work on Joyce, sharing generously the conclusions of his own extensive thinking about the problems I was encountering. Vivian Mercier's consideration of my first article on Joyce was the closest reading I have ever had of any piece of my writing. His encouragement and suggestions were enormously helpful, and I regret his untimely death in 1989; the present book would no doubt have profited from his scrutiny and his wisdom.

Many other colleagues have contributed generously to this project, and I will no doubt omit people who deserve notice. I would like to single out Maureen Murphy for her encouragement; Adele Dalsimer for her clarity of perception about the implications of this work; Edgar Slotkin, John Raleigh, and Don Gifford for useful readings of the manuscript; and Chester Anderson for good-humored criticism and interest. Anthony Roche, Dominic Manganiello, and Leonard Orr each contributed specifics to my line of argument; Joyce Flynn, Phillip O'Leary, and Virginia Rohan shared their own closely related research; Janet Dunleavy was helpful with practical advice about publication; the late Brendan O Hehir indulged me in witty and serious discussion of Joyce; Harry Levin read several of the early segments and encouraged me to persist in the project; and Seán Ó Tuama kindly shared with me unpublished material on Joyce. With André Lefevere I have had a running conversation of several years' duration about a shared critical framework. The book would also have been impossible without the discussions in my graduate seminars at the University of Massachusetts at Amherst on topics related to the Anglo-Irish revival and its use of early Irish literary materials. In teaching others one inevitably learns, and the critical reception of my ideas by graduate students has led me to explore various paths and to hone my arguments. Here I would like to single out John Beagan for special notice.

The project would not have been possible without grant support. The research for chapters 7 and 8 was funded by Faculty Research Grants from the University of Massachusetts at Amherst in 1988–89 and 1991–92, and I am grateful to Samuel Conti, who, as Vice Chancellor for Research, ensured that such grants were available; to Bruce McCandless for his counsel; and to Robert Bagg for his support in the process. The research was done primarily at the British Library, both the main facility in Great Russell Street and the newspaper facility at Colindale. To the staff of those libraries I am indebted for their unfailing courtesy and assistance. In 1990 and 1992 I undertook work in Zurich at the Zentralbibliothek, again finding the library staff immensely helpful. I am indebted to Hermann Köstler, Director of the Library; to Jean-Pierre Bodmer, Director of the Manuscript Division; and to Reiner Diederichs and Michael Kotrba. Georg Bührer, Archivist of the Zentralbibliothek, shared his knowledge of the library's past most generously; his warmth and wit made working together a pleasure, and he saved me from many errors. Fritz Senn was, as ever, forthcoming with his own vast knowledge of Joyce, offering resources and hospitality during my trips to Zurich.

Michele Aldrich offered practical intervention when it was time to think about publishing this book, and Bettyann Kevles and Scott Mahler, both editors at the University of California Press, were instrumental in the early stages of working with the press. Edward Dimendberg, the Humanities Editor, was encouraging and patient during the final stages of the manuscript preparation. I am also indebted to Dan Gunter, whose thoughtful and careful copy editing improved the text in many ways, and to Douglas Abrams Arava and Marilyn Schwartz, who saw the manuscript through the production process.

It is with pleasure that I take this opportunity to acknowledge my gratitude to David R. Clark, for many years my senior colleague at the University of Massachusetts at Amherst. Over the years Dave has read my manuscripts, including drafts of several of the segments of this book. Dave has taught me a good deal about Anglo-Irish literature and has encouraged me to pursue scholarship in this area. His faith in my potential as a scholar carried me through many crises of my academic career, while his own graceful blending of excellent scholarship, intellectual curiosity, and a broader vision of life has made such a career seem worthwhile. In short, he has been my mentor and friend.

These acknowledgments would not be complete without thanks to my three children. During the early work my elder son, Dmitri Tymoczko, was also interested in James Joyce: we discussed *Ulysses* often, and he read my early papers on the topic. My daughter, Julianna Tymoczko, served as a valuable research assistant during the polishing phase, doing all manner of tedious things with good cheer and taking responsibility for the bibliography. My younger son, Alexei Tymoczko, kept me going with his humor and his loving concern, and he has taught me something about being "laid-back." All of them were patient under neglect when I was in a work fit, and they encouraged me to persevere even when events of life conspired to put me in a stall. My children also kept my life rooted when my head was preoccupied with writing problems: their growth and their inquiring minds provided the best climate for good work.

Joseph Donohue contributed immeasurably to this book. As colleague he encouraged me throughout this project, modeling his own careful mode of research and writing. He was my companion during the research at the British Library, and we spent many happy hours together in row D under the beautiful blue dome. Joe also gave the manuscript a close reading, saving me from many errors. These collegial contributions, however, were only ancillary to his affection and wisdom, which sustained me during the period the book took shape.

Finally, I am grateful to my birth family, whose working-class and petit-bourgeois life enabled me to appreciate the world of *Ulysses*. My grandparents, aunts, uncles, and family friends provided analogues to Joyce's characters. My father, Robert Fleming, had an intellectual life positioned somewhere between those of Stephen and Bloom, modeling some of the ridiculous and sublime moments of both. My mother, Anne Fleming, had a notable vitality and directness; her own pleasure in being a sexual woman and her frankness about that pleasure prepared me to read and enjoy Molly's soliloquy. Grappling with Joyce's major work has been a time to integrate many parts of my life: a Cleveland working-class youth, ten years of Harvard education, two decades of teaching Irish Studies, a modernist sensibility, and a medievalist's training.

A Note on Texts

Because early Irish literature is not widely known, the primary material compared with *Ulysses* in this volume will be unfamiliar to most readers. There is relatively little critical material, but J. E. Caerwyn Williams and Patrick K. Ford provide an overview of the topic, and suggestions for further reading will be found in the standard bibliographies by R. I. Best and Rolf Baumgarten. In the chapters that follow I presuppose no background on the topic: aspects of Irish literature are introduced as needed, and this book can serve as a good beginning to the subject as it relates to Joyce's writing. Unless noted to the contrary, all early Irish texts and translations quoted below come from publications that had appeared by the time *Ulysses* was published and might thus represent actual materials Joyce knew; their historical value overrides whatever problems they might present as translations per se.

Where appropriate, I have cited the translations gathered in *Ancient Irish Tales*, the useful compendium edited by T. P. Cross and C. H. Slover from translations and editions in early monographs and journals, since this book is so much more accessible at present than are the original journals and editions that Joyce actually had available to him; the normalizations of Cross and Slover are minor and do not affect the substance of the texts. The bibliography prepared by Charles W. Dunn for the 1969 edition of Cross and Slover provides references to the original publications. *Táin Bó Cúailnge* presents special problems discussed in detail below; there is evidence that Joyce worked from Ernst Windisch's German edition and translation of the text, but for the convenience of English-speaking readers I have used modern English translations rather than

Windisch's German or the inadequate English versions available to Joyce and his contemporaries (see Tymoczko, "Translating the Old Irish Epic"). Titles of the early Irish tales discussed in this critical study are usually given first in Irish and then in the standard English translation, which is generally used thereafter; both forms are indexed. Unless otherwise noted all translations of early Irish words and other philological references are taken from the *Dictionary of the Irish Language*, compact edition.

Irish language and literature are generally divided into three major periods: the Old Irish period, from the beginning of the eighth century to the late ninth century; the Middle Irish period, through the twelfth century; and the Modern Irish period thereafter.[1] Most of the stories cited below, as well as the poetics described, date from the Old Irish period, but they were conserved and rewritten by Middle Irish scribes and survive in manuscripts from the twelfth century and later. All the evidence suggests that the Irish literary tradition was remarkably stable—indeed, archaic—throughout the period of documentation. The repertory of tales in the narrative tradition was similar from the Old Irish period to modern times in many respects; in some cases stories that have survived in Old Irish versions continued to be told in Irish-speaking areas until the twentieth century. The persistence of tales over such a long span of time means that there is considerable orthographical variation in names of characters; I have used a standard early Irish spelling for proper nouns throughout the text, though in quotations I have retained the orthography of the source unless otherwise noted. In quotations from Irish sources I have retained marks of length; in general citations of names, however, I have omitted the diacritical marks in accordance with widely established English-language usage.

Though Ireland had the first secular literate class of medieval Europe, Irish tradition was primarily oral. Professionals used texts for mnemonic and other purposes, but the texts per se were not of paramount importance: the living tales were. Tales were composed and passed on orally, and writing was ancillary in the native learned tradition of literary composition. This fact, combined with the vagaries of survival of medieval manuscripts, means that not all of the important medieval tales have survived in early manuscripts: some very old stories, to which there are early

1. Scholars differ somewhat in their datings of these periods; see J. Williams and Ford 9 n. 3.

external references, for example, survive only in early modern texts. *Tó-ruigheacht Dhiarmada agus Ghráinne (The Pursuit of Diarmaid and Grainne)* is such a story, for although there are tenth-century references to it, the earliest full version is a manuscript from the seventeenth century. Other stories that were told in oral tradition in the twentieth century are best represented textually by medieval versions. *Táin Bó Cúailnge* is such an example, for the best texts are from the eighth and twelfth centuries. Still other Irish stories—such as *The Voyage of Saint Brendan*, which was enormously popular all over Europe and translated into a number of medieval vernaculars—do not survive in early Irish texts at all: the normative version is in Latin.

Because of these characteristics of the Irish literary tradition, the Irish narrative patterns discussed most extensively in this study—*The Book of Invasions*, the Sovereignty myth, narratives about the otherworld—are general to the tradition at all periods but may be most easily illustrated by a text from a specific period. Many Irish narratives and aspects of Irish poetics are best represented by Old Irish and Middle Irish texts; paradoxically, early Irish material has often survived where later evidence has not because of the history of political repression in Ireland from the seventeenth to the twentieth centuries. From the mid nineteenth century onward these early texts as well as the living folklore of Ireland enjoyed wide currency in Ireland among English speakers, and during the decades before the Easter Rising in 1916 there was a concerted effort to make the Irish linguistic, literary, and historical heritage known to all Irish people. This is the environment in which Joyce was raised and educated.

In modern critical studies early Irish narrative is usually divided into four major cycles of related tales. The Mythological Cycle is composed of tales related to the pre-Christian Irish deities; the tales are early, but the texts are relatively recent, generally from the late Middle Irish or early Modern Irish period. The Ulster Cycle comprises heroic tales related to the heroes of Ulster, including their tribal conflicts with other groups within Ireland. This cycle is large—more than fifty tales are extant in various degrees of fullness—and early; the texts are principally from the Old Irish and Middle Irish periods and are archaic in various respects. The Finn Cycle has pre-Christian mythological roots yet remained as the most prestigious narrative cycle in twentieth-century folk narrative in both Ireland and Scotland; the texts of this cycle are the most varied of any of the narrative groups, though there are fewer texts that can compete in age with the Ulster Cycle materials. A fourth set of texts, commonly referred to as the Cycles of the Kings, deals with the legendary and historical kings of Ireland; these tales are varied and include mythological motifs on the one hand and traditional accounts of fully historical events on the other. Although W. B. Yeats used the full range of early Irish literature as a background to his own work, he and other members of the Anglo-Irish literary revival were drawn most strongly to the Ulster Cycle. By contrast, in *Finnegans Wake* Joyce has given the most memorable modern refraction of the Finn Cycle, and this is the cycle of Irish literature to which he seems to have been most drawn. Yet he knew and used materials from the entire range of early Irish literature, as the argument presented here will make clear.

I have tried to make all comparisons between texts of Irish literature and *Ulysses* fairly specific: plotting patterns are so susceptible to polygenesis that unless there is a specific or detailed reason to connect an early Irish text with *Ulysses* I have avoided the temptation. As early as 1892 Henri d'Arbois de Jubainville observed in *L'épopée celtique en Irlande* (449) that the plot of a sea voyage with companions from island to island underlies both the early Irish genre of the *imram*, 'voyage', and the *Odyssey*—that in fact the *Odyssey* is an imram. This point has been made recently by Stanley Sultan (42–48) and Hildegard Tristram (221 n. 4) as well. The strongest comparative arguments must go considerably beyond this level; as in the case of Indo-European comparative mythological studies, when proposing specific plotting similarities between early Irish literature and *Ulysses* I have tried to establish points of comparison that involve configurations specific to Irish literature, functional similarities, and telling details, all of which "fingerprint" the material in question as specifically Irish.

Citations from *Ulysses* are from the three-volume *Ulysses: A Critical and Synoptic Edition*, edited by Hans Walter Gabler, unless otherwise specified. For the sake of convenience I use the traditional headings to refer to the episodes in *Ulysses* rather than the episode numbers. However, the more we learn about the other myths that structure *Ulysses*, particularly the Irish mythic substructure, the more this practice should be reconsidered in Joyce criticism and scholarship; it was not for nothing that Joyce removed the episode titles before publishing the book.

Chapter 1

Incipit

MICHAEL: (*to Christy*) And where was it, mister honey, that you did the deed?

CHRISTY: (*looking at him with suspicion*) Oh, a distant place, master of the house, a windy corner of high distant hills.

PHILLY: (*nodding with approval*) He's a close man and he's right surely.

Synge, The Playboy of the Western World

When Stephen Joyce wrote to the *New York Times Book Review* in 1989 defending his decision to destroy certain letters by his aunt Lucia, he asked explicitly for an end to what he considered snooping in his grandfather's private life and implicitly for an end to the psychoanalytic criticism of James Joyce; instead he recommended as useful to readers critical work on "the Dublin-Irish ties that are pervasive and deeply rooted in all my grandfather's major works." Whereas most studies of the Irish elements in Joyce's fiction have centered on the surface realism—elucidating the geographical or historical context of the works, for example (Hart and Knuth; Garvin)—revisionist critical work on Joyce has made it increasingly clear that in all his writings Joyce also utilized plotting elements, mythopoeic imagery, structural features, formal principles, and linguistic resources taken from his Irish heritage. Thus, for example, an early Irish plot focused on fate, violation of taboo, and death serves as backbone of "The Dead," contributing a tone of inexorable disaster (Kelleher, "Irish History"), while a series of names referring to the Old Irish god of the dead is a thematic link binding *Dubliners* as a whole (Nilsen).

Medieval Irish otherworld imagery structures the symbolic node of the climax of *A Portrait of the Artist as a Young Man* (Roche, "'Strange Light'"), and the theme of the kiss, associated with the Irish myth of the Sovereignty, is a leitmotif throughout *A Portrait* (Grayson). It requires a Gaelic lexicon to understand the wordplay of *Finnegans Wake* (O Hehir), even as Irish myth and folklore are reincarnated and metamorphosed through the substance of the text (Benstock, "Finn"; MacKillop).[1]

In *Ulysses* the framework of Irish pseudohistory and Irish Sovereignty imagery sets the relationships of the main characters and provides a second axis of mythic correlatives augmenting the Greek mythos of the book (Tymoczko, "Symbolic Structures"; Tymoczko, "Sovereignty Structures in *Ulysses*"; cf. B. Scott 179–83). At the same time medieval Irish voyage tales double the plotting of the *Odyssey* as mythic determinants behind the wanderings of Bloom (Sultan 42–48.; Tristram 221 n. 4). The affinity of the comic elements in Joyce's later narratives to the Irish comic tradition has been discussed (Mercier, *Irish Comic Tradition* ch. 8), and Joyce himself commented on both the Irishness of the style of *Ulysses* and its debt to medieval Irish tradition in likening his text to the Book of Kells: "In all the places I have been to, Rome, Zurich, Trieste, I have taken [the Book of Kells] about with me, and have pored over its workmanship for hours. It is the most purely Irish thing we have, and some of the big initial letters which swing right across a page have the essential quality of a chapter of *Ulysses*. Indeed, you can compare much of my work to the intricate illuminations" (quoted in Ellmann, *JJ2* 545).

Although literary studies have turned increasingly to issues of intertextuality during the past decades, with the theoretical dictum being that literary works are as much about literature as about life, Joyce's Irish literary discourse has never been systematically delineated. The purpose of this book is to begin the task: to investigate at length Joyce's debt to Irish literature in *Ulysses* and to reclaim Joyce as an *Irish* writer who has much in common with other writers of the Irish literary revival and who is, in fact, in some ways preeminent among them as a writer in the Irish literary tradition.[2] Although Irish elements are found in his earlier works, it is in

---

1. In this study I am using the term *myth* in the broadest sense of "traditional tale," including religious myth, traditional hero tale, and historical legends.

2. *Tradition* in this book refers primarily to Ireland's literary tradition, which has shown a remarkable continuity in the last fifteen hundred years not only in content but in other ways, including its formalism and its sense of the com-

Ulysses that Joyce's Irish poetic emerges in a comprehensive and fully articulated fashion; in turn *Ulysses* sets a pattern for the later extensions of his Irish techniques, styles, and mythic structurings in *Finnegans Wake*. In this regard, as in many others, *Ulysses* is the pivotal text in Joyce's oeuvre. In *Ulysses* Irish mythic correlates and poetics are intertwined with the political dimension of the text; recognition of Joyce's Irish discourse thus requires a reevaluation of his mythic method, the substance of his realism, and the modernist features of his narrative, as well as his involvement with the political questions of his day.[3]

Most of the links between *Ulysses* and Irish literature are elementary—one would say obvious, had they not gone so long unacknowledged. In some ways it is astonishing that the material discussed here has not been part of the critical tradition about *Ulysses* for decades; indeed, in the case of the Irish architectonic structures in *Ulysses*, one of the most scrutinized books of world literature, such an oversight is virtually incredible. This blind spot in the history of Joyce criticism and scholarship is worth reflecting upon. A likely explanation for the oversight has to do with the intellectual framework for the critical tradition on Joyce, a framework begun by Joyce himself when he stressed his own indebtedness to Henrik Ibsen, when he credited his stream-of-consciousness technique to Édouard Dujardin, when he disseminated to Carlo Linati and others schemata elucidating the Homeric parallels in *Ulysses*, when he defined and described *Ulysses* to Frank Budgen, and when he facilitated Stuart Gilbert's landmark study, *James Joyce's "Ulysses."* Joyce's works have been read and discussed primarily within dominant traditions of Western literature—Greek literature, French literature, English literature—and related to the literary programs of the giants of Western literature such as Flaubert and Ibsen. The problem with such conceptual frameworks, as M. C. Escher's fascinating graphic works make vivid, is that they determine what is seen. The central critical frameworks for Joyce—even those established by Joyce himself—have not included Irish literature: hence, no Irish elements have been found by scholars working within these frameworks. It has been principally scholars of Irish literature working

---

ic. Many aspects of this literary tradition have survived the transition from Irish to English and thus characterize Irish literature in English as well as literature in Old, Middle, and Modern Irish.

3. The latter aligns the present work with still other revisionist work on Joyce, including, for example, Manganiello, *Joyce's Politics.*

within an independent tradition of scholarship who have discovered the
Irish substratum of his works.

Another reason that such elements as the Irish symbolic values for the
main characters in *Ulysses* and the significance of their configuration
have not been recognized long since is the dual isolation of the book.
Though there was no Customs exclusion order on *Ulysses* in Ireland after
1932 and though the book was never banned by the official Censorship
Board (M. Adams 31n), it remained isolated from the Irish reading public
by less formal blacklisting, including clerical disapproval. Steeped in Irish
popular history and exposed to Irish narratives, the Irish reading public
is the audience to whom the Irish archetypes and the Irish poetic of *Ulysses* would speak most immediately and to whom these features of *Ulysses*
would be most apparent. But because of the blacklisting of *Ulysses*, Irish
citizens who have been most inclined to read *Ulysses* are usually cosmopolitan and have been influenced by the European and American literary establishment; they, like readers of *Ulysses* in general, come to the
book preconditioned to perceive the established Homeric parallels and
the way in which the book fits into an international literary history. At
the same time the vast majority of the readers and critics of *Ulysses*, Eu-
ropeans and Americans alike, remain isolated from Irish literature, which
has overall not been incorporated into canons of world literature. This
isolation from Joyce's own formative literary traditions has further contributed to the treatment of Joyce as a European writer and to the exclusion of his Irish poetics, themes, symbols, archetypes, and major structural features from critical recognition and discussion.

Theoretical issues about what is meant by world literature, about the
formation and function of literary canons, and about the nature of literary criticism are therefore raised by the critical history of *Ulysses*. This
is paradoxical since in many ways *Ulysses* is at the center of most canons
of modern literature and has received an immense amount of critical attention. The case at hand is an example of criticism as refraction, to use
the formulation of André Lefevere:

Let us take a classic, any classic, in our own literature or in another. Chances
are that we did not first come into contact with it in its unique, untouchable,
"sacralized" form. Rather, for most, if not all of us, the classic in question
quite simply *was* to all extents and purposes its refraction, or rather a series
of refractions, from the comic strip over the extract in school anthologies and
anthologies used in universities, to the film, the TV serial, the plot summary

in literary histories we gallantly tried to commit to memory in those long
dark nights of the soul immediately preceding graduation, critical articles telling us how to read the classic in question, what to think about it and, above
all, how to apply it to our lives. If and when after all that we finally get around
to reading the actual classic, we are often rather surprised by the discrepancy
that appears to exist between our perception of the classic, which is a composite of a series of cumulative refractions we have grown to be quite comfortable with, and the actual text itself. (13)

Ulysses offers a clear instance in which criticism, functioning as a story
about a story, produces a metatext. It is the metatext of *Ulysses*—a non-
Irish metatext—that we have read for the better part of a century. Although
some scholars have recognized and freely discussed parallels between Irish
literature and *Ulysses*, most have not. With the notable exception of writers such as Chester Anderson and Vivian Mercier, even the most distinguished scholars have been hampered by this metatext of *Ulysses*.

In most instances revisionist studies of Joyce that reclaim him as an
Irish author are intended not to replace or set aside established critical
views of *Ulysses* but to supplement them. Joyce characteristically works
on several levels simultaneously, particularly in *Ulysses* and *Finnegans
Wake*—surface naturalism and symbol, mythic correlate and psychological imperative, and so on—with the different levels providing mutual resonance and ironic byplay.[4] Just as we would consider our understanding
of *Ulysses* inadequate without some account of the Homeric parallels, so
a reading of *Ulysses* without an account of the parallels from Irish myth
is a monologic reduction of Joyce's text (cf. Bakhtin). Attention to the
Irish literary elements of *Ulysses* also brings with it a greater appreciation
of the intertextual richness behind Joyce's naturalism, which in turn
serves to illuminate the relation of *Ulysses* to the works of writers of the
Irish literary revival, including the mythic work of W. B. Yeats. Thus, a
study like the present one both reveals elements internal to the text of
Ulysses and situates Joyce in a historical context.

Wolfgang Iser has claimed that the reality of *Ulysses* transcends full
comprehension by a reader because of its complexity:

The reader is virtually free to choose his own direction, but he will not be
able to work his way through every possible perspective, for the number of

4. Herring, *Joyce's Uncertainty Principle*, traces this modality as early as
Dubliners.

these is far beyond the capacity of any one man's naturally selective perception. If the novel sometimes gives the impression of unreality, this is not because it presents unreality, but simply because it swamps us with aspects of reality that overburden our limited powers of absorption. We are forced to make our own selections from the perspectives offered and, consequently, in accordance with our own personal disposition, to formulate ideas that have their roots in *some* of the signs and situations confronting us. (231–32)

Iser goes on to say that it is inherent in Joyce's design and mode of meaning making, of illuminating experience, that no single reader should be able to work through every possible perspective on *Ulysses*; at best one can achieve a partial reading, a partial realization of the signs. By contrast, in *Surface and Symbol: The Consistency of James Joyce's "Ulysses,"* Robert Adams muses that "it is conceivable that a new way of looking at *Ulysses* will be found which will reduce to miraculous harmony all the symbols and references to external reality" (191). Are the Irish elements of *Ulysses* this miraculous thread? Iser has argued, I think rightly, that the hope of any such decoding is illusory (233). Like any reader, in focusing on the Irish intertextuality of *Ulysses* I am reading only some of the signs Joyce has left for us, the signs that as a medievalist and scholar of early Irish language and literature I am most qualified to read. I offer this reading of *Ulysses* with the understanding that it is partial, with no false pretensions to an illusory consistency or comprehensiveness. At the same time it is plain that an awareness of the Irish literary dimension of *Ulysses* does make some of the seeming "errors," discordances, inconsistencies, and departures from realism more transparent: these slippages can be deconstructed to show, among other things, that the Irish discourse in *Ulysses* is one of the patterning principles Joyce has used in his design. Joyce indicates the importance of such "errors" by naming them "portals of discovery" (*U* 9.229). At many points in what follows I hinge my arguments on inconsistencies in the text, showing that a recognition of the Irish elements in *Ulysses* offers a new perspective on long-standing issues in Joyce scholarship, elucidating cultural obscurities even as it enhances an appreciation of the openness in Joyce's construction of the text (cf. Herring, *Joyce's Uncertainty Principle* 77ff.). The Irish signs are central to Joyce's construction of and signification in *Ulysses* and are relevant to virtually any reading of the text.

Although parallels between Joyce's texts and early Irish texts can often be clearly discerned, we must ask how Joyce could have known the Irish literary texts in question. Heretofore, scholars interested in Joyce's use of early Irish material have taken various tacks—showing textual evidence for a literary echo, or asserting that a source is probable, or resting content to delineate a parallel—but a systematic survey of Joyce's knowledge of early Irish literature has remained to be done. The task is undertaken here in chapters 7 and 8. Joyce's multifaceted literary interests, his many literary enthusiasms, and his voluminous reading, particularly in his youth, make it difficult to document his knowledge of early Irish literature. A great range of materials lies open; and since much of his reading Joyce consumed without comment for posterity, it is traced haphazardly, if at all, through the fortunate survival of notesheets or the posthumous reconstruction of his working library at a particular period. Assessments of Joyce's sources for Irish tradition are particularly difficult because Joyce's knowledge of early Irish literature is generally overdetermined: there is usually a plethora of potential sources to be considered, but little evidence to determine which of the many possibilities Joyce depended upon. Materials incorporated into the school curricula, publications of the Irish revival, specialized reading later in life, and informal conversation must all be investigated as possible sources contributing to Joyce's knowledge of Irish literature.

Moreover, though Joyce at various points in his life explored scholarly sources on early Irish literature (probably reading some scholarly journals as well as writers such as P. W. Joyce), his use of literature aimed at the general reader, including periodicals that devoted space to Irish culture and Irish literature, cannot be discounted. Some of Joyce's familiarity with Irish tradition must be attributed to popular culture and generalized knowledge, cultural layers that are always difficult to determine, particularly when they are part of the popular culture and general knowledge of a marginalized culture, as was the case in early twentieth-century Ireland.

To return for a moment to the established critical metatext of *Ulysses*, one can note another aspect of the failure of Joyce criticism to recognize the relationship of his work to Irish literary tradition. It is finally too simple to suppose that Irish literature has been ignored in investigations of Joyce's work because Irish literature has not been incorporated into the canons of Western literature. Joyce's Irish contexts have been missed in part because critics have also failed to consider the Irish popular cultural context of his writing, a popular culture that included refractions of a great deal of the early Irish literary repertory. This popular cultural context is omitted only at great cost to an adequate appreciation of Joyce's range of meaning, his artistic achievement, and the mechanisms by which he relocated twentieth-century narrative. In this regard Joyce is a paradigm for many writers currently being incorporated into revised canons—women, racial and ethnic minority writers, writers from varied socioeconomic strata, writers with minority language backgrounds, colonial and postcolonial authors—whose marginalized cultures illuminate and drive their work. The question of Joyce's knowledge of early Irish literature, therefore, is again paradoxical, for the work of this eminently canonical writer presents affinities with those whose discourse has, for whatever reasons, been marginalized.[5]

The structures from early Irish literature in *Ulysses*—or *Finnegans Wake* for that matter—are pervasive and fundamental, but they are rarely elaborated in a detailed manner. As with the elements from Greek mythology or the parallels in *Ulysses* with Dante and Shakespeare, the correspondences with Irish tradition are most often general, partial, and suggestive rather than exhaustive. As a whole they do not necessitate that Joyce did specialized research on or possessed recondite knowledge of early Irish literature, though recognition of those same structures may require specialized training and research on the part of a modern critic or scholar. The allusive quality of Joyce's mythic method contributes to the difficulty in determining Joyce's sources for this material: although Joyce rarely makes "errors" that rule out knowledge of, say, scholarly publications, he also rarely gives specific details that can be used as telling evidence for the identification of a particular source text. The very generality of Joyce's use of Irish mythos is usually consonant with any number of publications that he could plausibly have known.

Joyce was exposed to material related to Irish tradition by several types of sources that reinforced each other; it is in this sense that his knowledge is usually overdetermined. At Joyce's disposal were certain facets of early Irish history and literature that had already by the time of his youth been incorporated into the background culture of English-speaking Ireland as part of the school curricula. In this category we must

5. For other approaches to Joyce as a postcolonial or minority-culture writer, see the studies by Jameson and Deane 92–107. See Herr for a study of other aspects of Joyce's relationship to popular culture, as well as a theoretical discussion of his use of these elements as a reference point.

put Joyce's knowledge of *Lebor Gabála Érenn* (*The Book of Invasions*), which he probably learned about when still in school. *The Book of Invasions* was, in any case, part of daily contemporary discourse in Ireland; thus, the metaphors of Milesian and Fir Bolg pepper *Ulysses* as they did the speech of Joyce's contemporaries. He owes much as well to the Irish literary revival. By the time *Ulysses* was written, most of the major works of the Irish literary revival had been published, reviewed, discussed, assimilated; since as a literary movement the Irish revival is characterized by the use of Irish myth and symbol, the works of these writers served their readers as an introduction to the literary heritage of Ireland. Thus, for example, the otherworld imagery widely used by writers such as A. E. and Yeats would have served Joyce as ample introduction to this aspect of early Irish literature and Irish folklore.

One of the uncertain aspects of determining Joyce's knowledge of early Irish tradition results from the fact that Irish culture was in Joyce's day, and indeed still is, oral to a very great extent. Just as one cannot investigate eighteenth-century French literature without acknowledging that information circulated and was shared orally in coffeehouse and salon, so one cannot ignore the importance of conversation and oral sources in Joyce's Irish circles. The text of *Ulysses* itself exemplifies how certain ideas about early Irish literature were retailed in conversation, as we see, for example, in the passage where Haines tells Mulligan about the theory that ancient Irish myth had no concept of hell (10.1077–85). A certain familiarity with early Irish history and literature was widespread, perhaps inevitable, even among those who had no textual sources at their disposal, because of oral transfer and circulation of Irish cultural materials; this familiarity must be accounted for in a determination of Joyce's sources. Questions such as these are pursued in chapters 7 and 8. It should be noted that the chapters on Joyce's sources are self-standing and may be read first by the skeptical reader, but for the sake of general readability these technical aspects of the argument have been placed last. The chapters are, however, an important part of the argument: this study is not simply about James Joyce or *Ulysses* but about an author and his relationship to culture. Thus, the final two chapters are in part a model for a methodology, presenting one paradigm for assessing the impact of popular and oral culture upon an author.

It might be objected that if Irish literature and myth are central to the structure and technique of *Ulysses*, Joyce would have been more explicit about this fact: he would, for example, have provided us, albeit indirectly, with an Irish analogue to Gilbert's study of the Homeric elements. This is not altogether an easy objection to answer. One possible response is that Joyce molded his narrative on Irish tales, motifs, images, narrative genres, and styles intuitively rather than deliberately. A similar position has in fact been taken by Vivian Mercier, who concludes that Joyce wrote within the Irish comic tradition without being entirely conscious of the fact (*Irish Comic Tradition* 236). It is certainly possible for a writer to be in a literary tradition without being familiar with all of its texts; but in Joyce's case there is evidence of his extensive familiarity with the content of the Irish literary tradition. The climate of cultural nationalism, the self-conscious use of Irish traditional materials by members of the Irish literary revival, and the extent to which awareness of Irish stories, genres, and literary techniques had entered popular culture all speak for Joyce's conscious use of Irish elements to be found in his works. Moreover, a preconscious awareness on Joyce's part of literary motive and technique doesn't really fit what is known about Joyce as an artist.

Though Mercier may underestimate Joyce's deliberate cultivation of Irish literary tradition, his major premise that Joyce worked within that tradition should be sustained. Some of the elements of the Irish literary tradition came to James Joyce as a birthright, in part in virtue of being the son of John Stanislaus Joyce. The importance of this lineage was signaled in Joyce's later life when he commissioned his father's portrait, later hanging it in his flat (*JJ*2 565n). Whatever his failings, John Stanislaus Joyce was a storyteller; and what can be gleaned of his stories places him in the Irish narrative tradition. His son Stanislaus remembers that the father prided himself on knowing Dublin better than the Dubliners, for all that he was a Cork man (*MBK* 81). He would take walks with people, telling stories about people, places, and events that the walk called to mind (*JJ*2 44–45). This melding of placelore, oral history, and narrative entertainment is typical of Irish literature; it is an example of the *senchas*, the 'lore' or 'learning', that the Irish poet, the *fili*, was to preserve and to promulgate in narrative. Specific narrative threads in Joyce's work have also been traced to stories of John Stanislaus Joyce (Garvin 50, 87–90). No doubt some of the traditional Irish imagery, symbolism, and narrative repertory that are reused in James Joyce's literary works must be traced back in their first instance in Joyce's life to his father as well.

Joyce's father was also a witty man; after his father's death, Joyce said that the humor of *Ulysses* was his father's. This is no light tribute; insofar as the wit and humor of *Ulysses* are typical of Irish literature, we may conclude that this element came to Joyce through oral tradition, as it had been preserved and passed down for millennia in Celtic culture as a whole. We may judge from the portrait of Simon Dedalus in Joyce's works, as well as from anecdotes preserved about John Joyce, that his humor was more than a little tinged with satire and irony, aspects of the Irish comic tradition that his son inherited as well. Simon in *A Portrait* is also named as storyteller (241), and from him the son hears "of Irish politics, of Munster and of the legends of their own family, to all of which Stephen lent an avid ear" (62). In this regard it is certainly not accidental that *A Portrait of the Artist* begins with the father's voice telling a story to the boy and ends with the young man's invocation of the mythical father: the young writer about to try his wings traces his vocation to the primordial narrative of the father, where the father represents as well the boy's patrimony of art in the largest sense. Stephen's first consciousness is of his father as storyteller; and in a measure the father passes on the profession of storyteller to the son at the end of the book, not unlike the early Irish poet who was responsible for training his successor. These hints of the *literary* relationship between father and son suggest that Joyce participated in a living tradition linking him to early Irish literature, but it was a tradition that had crossed the linguistic boundary and was carried in English rather than Irish. Insofar as elements of the Irish literary system came to Joyce as a birthright, he had a position in the Irish literary tradition shared by few of his contemporaries writing in English. This position is one of the elements that differentiates him from most other members of the Irish literary revival writing in English, including Yeats.

It must be remembered that although Joyce did not foster a critical introduction to the Irish myth in *Ulysses* as he did with the Homeric myth, he has in fact left clues embedded internally in the narrative to the Irish mythic structuring of *Ulysses* as well as to sources of his own knowledge of the myth. In the text there are explicit references to the Sovereignty myth, to Kathleen ni Houlihan, to the historical scheme of *The Book of Invasions* (including the Milesians and the "Clan Milly"), to Slieve Bloom, and in fact to most of the central literary elements discussed in this book. The references to Henri d'Arbois de Jubainville, R. I. Best, and Julius Pokorny are not mere decor; they are in part Joyce's wry mode of footnoting and acknowledging his debt to these writers. Stephen—a portrait of the artist as a young man—is presented as someone who knows Irish and whose stream of consciousness includes many aspects of Irish literary tradition. The signs of the Irish intertextuality and Irish structuring are there for anyone to read; it is the inability of most readers of *Ulysses* to read the signs that creates the problem.

There are external signs of the Irish literary dimension of *Ulysses* as well. I find it significant that Joyce's relatives—his grandson quoted above, his brother Stanislaus elsewhere (*Recollections* 19)—take for granted the Irish strand of his writing; it suggests that there was a private, familial awareness of Joyce's use of and dependence on Irish myth and Irish poetics. And perhaps the greatest irony of all is that Gilbert's study itself points to the debt of *Ulysses* to Irish literary tradition: he includes a synopsis of *The Book of Invasions*, noting explicitly the Greek and Spanish elements in Irish pseudohistory and citing specific references in Joyce's text to Irish pseudohistory (65–68). It was presumably Joyce himself who alerted Gilbert to these materials, as well as to aspects of the art and social position of the fili relevant to *Ulysses*, all of which Gilbert duly relays to his readers (69–71). These materials have been available *in potentia* to the critical tradition for decades, but neither Gilbert nor his successors could see the significance of the information Joyce had provided, any more than they knew how to read the signs of the Irish literary echoes internal to *Ulysses*.

As an indicator of the importance of his Irish upbringing and his Irish culture to Joyce, the aesthetic of literary forms developed in *A Portrait of the Artist* has in it a timely reminder:

The lyrical form is in fact the simplest verbal vesture of an instant of emotion, a rhythmical cry such as ages ago cheered on the man who pulled at the oar or dragged stones up a slope. He who utters it is more conscious of the instant of emotion than of himself as feeling emotion. The simplest epical form is seen emerging out of lyrical literature when the artist prolongs and broods upon himself as the centre of an epical event and this form progresses till the centre of emotional gravity is equidistant from the artist himself and from others. The narrative is no longer purely personal. The personality of the artist passes into the narration itself, flowing round and round the persons and the action like a vital sea. . . . The dramatic form is reached when the vitality which has flowed and eddied round each person fills every person with such vital force that he or she assumes a proper and intangible esthetic life. The personality of the artist, at first a cry or a cadence or a mood and then a fluid and lambent narrative, finally refines itself out of existence, impersonalises itself, so to speak. The esthetic image in the dramatic form is life purified in and reprojected from the human imagination. The mystery of esthetic like that of material creation is accomplished. The artist, like the God of the creation, remains within or behind or beyond or above his handiwork, invisible, refined out of existence, indifferent, paring his fingernails. (214–15)[6]

Joyce's statement about "the dramatic form" is often cited out of context and generalized to represent his attitude toward the relationship of the artist and any literary work. Yet Joyce is explicit that in a narrative—an epic—like *Ulysses*, the personality of the artist is of vital importance: "The personality of the artist passes into the narration itself, flowing round and round the persons and the action like a vital sea"; only in drama does the artist become "refined out of existence" "like the God of the creation." In Joyce's narrative works it is an *Irish* personality at work, flowing round the narrative like a vital sea, and the works mediate between one formed by *Irish* culture and Joyce's audience formed by the dominant English and European cultures. Thus, the many currents of Joyce's Irishness must be examined again and again for their ecological impact on his works.

Hugh Kenner has suggested that one reason Joyce described *Ulysses* in Homeric terms and was explicit about the Greek mythos while the book was in progress was that the Homeric scheme turned the book "into something that could be talked about"; still later the Homeric structure helped critics and readers alike manage the amorphous text with its genre innovations:

"I am now writing a book based on the wanderings of Ulysses," [Joyce] told Frank Budgen at their second meeting (summer 1918). "The Odyssey, that is to say, serves me as a ground plan. Only my time is recent time and all my hero's wanderings take no more than eighteen hours." It is hard to think of three sentences better contrived to turn an unwritten book into something that could be talked about. Later, if you were a critic struggling simulta-

---

6. Cf. Joyce's 6 March 1903 entry in the Paris Notebook: "There are three conditions of art: the lyrical, the epical and the dramatic. That art is lyrical whereby the artist sets forth the image in immediate relation to himself; that art is epical whereby the artist sets forth the image in mediate relation to himself and to others; that art is dramatic whereby the artist sets forth the image in immediate relation to others" (*CW* 145).

neously with the queer book and with the need to describe it for readers who had not seen it, you would find the parallel more manageable than the text. Joyce . . . knew the value of informed articles. (*"Ulysses"* 22–23)

The Greek myth provided bewildered readers with a point of reference and a point of departure; it universalized a book that was on its surface very localized. If this is the case, then there is, of course, another very good reason Joyce did not foster a vade mecum for the Irish myth in his book. Such a scheme would have helped most of Joyce's international readers—and it is the international audience that *Ulysses* most appealed to—not at all. In fact, rather than locating the book for them, the revelation of the unfamiliar Irish literary and mythic substratum would have served further to *dis*locate the book from the international readership. Thus, an insistent revelation of these aspects would have been counterproductive to Joyce's purpose to have *Ulysses* be accepted as part of world literature; one might even speculate that Joyce had reasons to conceal the Irish literary substructure.

The humor of *Ulysses* has been touched upon as particularly Irish; a premise in the following argument is the coexistence of the comic and the serious in Irish culture. In Irish literature, conversation, and culture, serious points are made with jokes, often satirical or ironic jokes; and the habit is one of long standing, as we can see from the following ninth-century poem:

> Ro-cúala
> ní tabair eochu ar dúana;
>   do-beir a n-í as dúthaig dó,
>   bó.
>
> I have heard
> that he gives no steeds for poems;
>   he gives what is native to him,
>   a cow.
>
> (Murphy, *Early Irish Lyrics* 90–91)[7]

This is a political poem criticizing a prince or noble, making the point that the man who should be generous, an aristocratic patron of poetry, is instead stingy and churlish. Rather than make the political point in a tendentious manner, the poet elegantly uses figurative speech: the low-

---

7. Murphy prints his literal translation as prose; I have lineated it here.

class nature of the man is indicated by accusing him of giving an agrarian animal rather than the noble horse as a reward for art. The point is emphasized by rhyme and by the short fourth line of the epigram: it suggests metrically, through the form of the verse itself, the paucity of the poet's reward. The line falls short of the expected metrical requirement (one syllable where eight are normal), just as the poet's gift falls short of what he might expect in a normal transaction between poet and patron. This very short poem thus presupposes a great deal of background about how the culture works and should work, as well as familiarity with how literature works and should work. The poem is funny, elegant, condensed, formal, but it is also political, ideological, serious, even biting. This is the way of Irish tradition: the intertwining of humor and serious discourse within highly compressed and formal literary structures.

Ulysses takes its place naturally in this framework; and Irish tradition, with its double consciousness about humor, can most easily be used to situate Joyce as a political writer.[8] Joyce came of age as a writer in an environment in which art was highly politicized. After the fall of Charles Stewart Parnell in 1890, many Irishmen turned in disgust from the realm of politics as narrowly conceived to a broader cultural nationalism. It was during the years before Joyce left Ireland that such organizations as the Gaelic Athletic Association and the Gaelic League captured the imagination of the nation; that the Irish Literary Society and the Irish Literary Theatre began the work of developing and promoting an Irish literature and drama; that popularizations and translations of early Irish literature became widely available; that writers of the Anglo-Irish literary revival such as A. E., Yeats, and Augusta Gregory began to take their material from Irish literature.[9]

The development of this Irish cultural consciousness and its determined goal of differentiation from English culture affected Joyce profoundly. In the last decade of the nineteenth century the term "West Briton" was coined, and thereafter "West Britonism" became a slogan

8. In *John Bull's Other Island*, written for the Irish National Theatre Society in 1904, Shaw has his famous dictum "Every jest is an earnest in the womb of Time" (611). Shaw's humor is also a vehicle for his politics, though in ways quite different from those of Joyce.

Cf. Mercier, *Irish Comic Tradition* 244–48, on the melding of humor and seriousness in Irish literature.

9. For a fuller discussion of the issues touched on here, see W. Thompson, *Imagination of an Insurrection* ch. 2, and Hunt, *Abbey* esp. 11.

that could be used as a weapon, as we see in the interaction between Miss
Ivors and Gabriel Conroy in "The Dead" (*D* 187ff.). The call to differentiate Irish life and culture from those of England went deep during the
period; in the political sphere they led to the rise of the concept of Sinn
Féin, 'We Ourselves', and ultimately to the political actions organized by
the party of that name. In the literary sphere the concern about West Britonism was strong as well, resulting in a search for an Irish literature, including an Irish formalism. Joyce's own literary innovations, particularly
those in *Ulysses*, are closely related to such concerns for an Irish literature. A major thesis of this book is that Joyce is responding to the political
ambience of Ireland even in *Ulysses*,[10] and that much of his ideological
discourse uses the Irish literary elements in the book, particularly his manipulations of Irish mythos, Irish formalism, and Irish humor, as the vehicles of its expression.

To claim that Joyce is serious and political in *Ulysses* is not to say that
he is polemical or solemn, any more than the early Irish epigram quoted
above is polemical or solemn. At the turn of the century, particularly the
years between 1900 and 1907, there was a raging controversy in Ireland
about the role of art, with many people, including Arthur Griffith and
Maud Gonne, taking the position that art should be used primarily for
political purposes and that such political art should be overtly polemical.
It is well documented that this view of art disgusted Joyce, and he takes
the Irish Literary Theatre and many of the central cultural figures to task
over the point in his 1901 broadside "The Day of the Rabblement" (see
*JJ*2 88–90; *CW* 68–72). The controversy was particularly heated just before Joyce departed from Ireland in 1904, and hindsight alone allows a
clear assessment of the direction that literature in Ireland was taking in
1904. Many of Joyce's most vitriolic statements about the role of politics
in art reflect the situation of the Irish literary revival in the years immediately before his 1904 departure, when the writers made their closest
rapprochement to the political movement. This was the period when
Yeats collaborated with Augusta Gregory on *Cathleen ni Houlihan*—

---

10. I am, of course, not the only person to make this argument. See, for example, Ellmann, *Consciousness of Joyce* ch. 3, and Manganiello, *Joyce's Politics*.
Manganiello's work also has excellent brief summaries of the political developments in Ireland that are the background of Joyce's work. These concerns can be
traced to the present through the works of Austin Clarke, Flann O'Brien, Thomas
Kinsella, and Seamus Heaney, among others.

"political claptrap" Joyce thought it (*MBK* 187)—and it is the period when the Irish theatrical movement moved away from Ibsenism, indeed from internationalism as a whole, to specialize in a drama that was Irish in the most narrow sense: Irish peasant dramas and mythic revivals. But in October 1903 the Irish National Theatre Society staged J. M. Synge's *Shadow of the Glen*, the play that brought the split in the dramatic movement between "Art for Art's Sake or Art for Propaganda," to use Maud Gonne's words (MacBride 332). Yeats's position in that controversy, his appeal from the stage to the disgruntled audience for "life" in its unpredictability against the principles and assertions that political parties substitute for life, led to Annie Horniman's decision to give Yeats a theater (Hone 194). The controversy over Synge's play is thus the event that marks not only the founding of the Abbey Theatre but also the beginning of Yeats's move away from nationalist politics and from art for politics' sake. But these developments would not yet have been clear at the time Joyce left Ireland in October 1904 looking for a more congenial place to do his art: the Abbey itself did not open until December of the same year, and in any case it took a while for the new drift to express itself. One could argue, in fact, that only the riots over Synge's *Playboy of the Western World* in 1907 made the rupture quite clear.[11]

Most of Joyce's statements about politics and art must be given their proper historical context, a context in which literature in Ireland was under extreme pressure to be a tool of political revolution. Most of his dicta are a response to the inflexible demands to subordinate art to politics that he experienced during his coming of age as an artist in Ireland, and they reflect an ambience in which others besides Joyce projected difficulties in an artist's being able to work in Ireland.[12] To conclude from these statements by Joyce that his work has no meaning, particularly ideological or political meaning in the broadest sense, is to misrepresent the situation. In this regard Joyce's 1902 essay on James Clarence Mangan offers clarification: "Finally, it must be asked concerning every artist how he is in relation to the highest knowledge and to those laws which do not take holiday because men and time forget them. This is not to look for a message but to approach the temper which has made the work . . . and to

---

11. On the development of the Abbey, see Hunt, *Abbey*; Ellis-Fermor, *Irish Dramatic Movement*; and the recent reappraisal by Frazier, *Behind the Scenes*.

12. See, for example, "Can a Literary Man Exist in Ireland," *Leader*, 30 Apr. 1904; "The Future Irish Novelist," *Leader*, 28 May 1904.

see what is there well done and how much it signifies" (CW 75). The Irish literary dimension of *Ulysses*, like the elements from Greek myth, is a major vehicle for the way Joyce signifies in his work, the way he encodes and communicates meaning. It is a vehicle by which he, like an early Irish poet/seer, comments on the values and standards of life.

A word on terminology: What is meant by *Irish* in this book? This is a question that might be asked about any book about Irish literature, and it is rarely easy to answer. In Ireland in the past twelve hundred years, literature has been spoken and written in many languages: Irish, of course; Latin; Old Norse; Old French; Middle Welsh; and English. Although a language may bring with it some aspects of a literary system— generic convention, for example, and meter—these are not the sole determinants of whether a literary piece is part of a *national* literature. When we use the term *Irish*, are we speaking of nationality or of language? How are these distinctions to be made? Irish culture (in the national sense) is a divided culture—divided by language, sectarian concerns, politics. Irish literature (again in the national sense) is also a divided literature—divided as any literature is by ideological and sectarian loyalties, but, more important, divided linguistically. In modern times the linguistic divide has been primarily between literature in Irish and literature in English. Joyce was conscious of Ireland's having a divided tradition; he writes, for example, in his essays on Mangan, "[Mangan] inherits the latest and worst part of a tradition upon which no divine hand has ever traced a boundary, a tradition which is loosened and divided against itself as it moves down the cycles" (CW 185; cf. CW 81–82). Joyce's awareness of Ireland's divided tradition and Ireland's linguistic dispossession is made clear in *A Portrait of the Artist* in the scene between Stephen and the English dean of studies at the university:

[Stephen] felt with a smart of dejection that the man to whom he was speaking was a countryman of Ben Jonson. He thought:

—The language in which we are speaking is his before it is mine. How different are the words *home*, *Christ*, *ale*, *master*, on his lips and on mine! I cannot speak or write these words without unrest of spirit. His language, so familiar and so foreign, will always be for me an acquired speech. I have not made or accepted its words. My voice holds them at bay. My soul frets in the shadow of his language. (189)

Still later Stephen acknowledges to Davin (203), "My ancestors threw off their language and took another. . . . They allowed a handful of foreigners to subject them." In *A Portrait of the Artist* Stephen's consciousness of personal and familial dispossession (e.g., 87) recapitulates the national dispossession; ontogeny recapitulates phylogeny.

Throughout the following discussions I assume an awareness of Ireland's divided literary tradition that involves making the distinction between an Irish literature (in the national sense) that originated in and was recorded in Irish (in the linguistic sense), and an Irish literature (in the national sense) that originated in and was recorded in English. Irish (in the national sense) literature in the Irish language naturally grows out of the Irish (in the linguistic sense) literary system, just as Irish (in the national sense) literature in English grows out of the English (in the linguistic sense) literary system. The former (Irish literature in the Irish language) is frequently referred to as "Gaelic" in the critical literature; but as I am dealing with early Irish literature as well as Modern Irish literature, and referring primarily to texts in Old Irish and Middle Irish, *Gaelic* will not do, since that is a term for Modern Irish (not to mention Scottish Gaelic). Thus, of necessity, here I am using the term *Irish* as the linguistic referent for literature in the various stages of the Irish language, and *Anglo-Irish* is used to denote Irish (in the national sense) literary texts and traditions in the English language. The term *Anglo-Irish* is not to be construed here as in any way pejorative or as carrying with it invidious ideological or sectarian connotations.[13] Some linguistic overlapping remains (between *Irish* in a linguistic sense and *Irish* in a national sense), but context should make the meaning clear.

Mercier, in discussing Anglo-Irish literature (using *Anglo-Irish* as I am here), has speculated on the vigor of this literature and traced it to the archaism of Irish literature in both languages.

For all the limitations which it imposes, archaism must be acknowledged as chiefly responsible for the vigour not only of Anglo-Irish comic literature but of Anglo-Irish literature as a whole. Whereas the writers of other Western countries have lately striven to re-establish contact with primitive modes of thought and feeling through the study of mythology, anthropology, and psychoanalysis, the Anglo-Irish writer has the past always at his elbow—in cold storage, so to speak—preserved in the Gaelic language and literature, in bi-

---

13. See the discussion by Richard Wall of the same terminological problem. In opting for the use of "Anglo-Irish," Wall notes that this was also the term used by Joyce (9).

lingual folklore, in Gaelic modes of thought and feeling and speech which have become part of the rural Anglo-Irish dialects. (*Irish Comic Tradition* 241)

Mercier continues with a discussion of the strengths of Anglo-Irish literature, deriving them from the contact with Irish tradition:

Colleagues and students frequently ask me, in jest or in earnest, why the greatest figures in twentieth-century "English" literature are Irishmen, meaning usually Joyce and Yeats. I can suggest at least four reasons to those who are in earnest. Their Irish background gave (or at any rate offered) Joyce and Yeats these four priceless gifts: contact with a living folklore and thus with myth; contact with a living folk speech; a traditional sense of the professional, almost sacred prestige of poetry and learning; a traditional sense of the supreme importance of technique to a writer, coupled with the realization that technique must be learnt, by imitation, study, and practice. (*Irish Comic Tradition* 241–42)

These strengths of Anglo-Irish literature are a leitmotif in this book, and parts of this discussion are in ways an expansion of Mercier's generalized observations as they apply specifically to *Ulysses*.

The appearance of a study of this sort in which are unveiled Irish literary parallels to and sources of some of Joyce's architectonics, generic conventions, and styles in *Ulysses* should not really be surprising. In Victor Bérard's view the poet of the *Odyssey* invented nothing: "The Hellene is, first and foremost, a skillful arranger" (trans. Gilbert and qtd. in Gilbert 81–82).[14] Joyce is kin to Bérard's Homer. Within *Ulysses* Joyce has left many clues about the Irish literary elements that he has arranged and rewritten; at the same time he has mainly left a deceptive silence about the Irish intertextuality external to the text. Deception is a theme threaded through all of Joyce's work, as Kenner has noted:

Deceiving the reader becomes . . . a way of establishing something about this book, about books, about life. For we are deceived, rather frequently, and there have even been canonical deceptions the righting of which constitutes much of the history of *Ulysses* criticism. (*Joyce's Voices* 87)

The present study is another such righting, and a long overdue one it is.

---

14. Cf. Kenner: "Joyce writes nothing that is not already written. Like the Homer of Samuel Butler's imagination he does not like inventing, chiefly because he thinks human beings seldom invent" ("*Ulysses*" 50).

Chapter 2

The Irish Architectonics
of *Ulysses*

Symbolic Structures from
The Book of Invasions

HILDA: Oh, it was so gloriously thrilling! I couldn't have
believed there was a builder in the whole world that could
have built such a tremendously high tower. And then, that
you yourself should stand at the very top of it, as large as
life! And that you shouldn't be the least bit dizzy! . . .

HILDA: Why don't you call yourself an architect, like the
others?

SOLNESS: I haven't been systematically enough taught
for that. Most of what I know, I've found out for myself.

HILDA: But you succeeded all the same.

Ibsen, The Master Builder

Symbolic structures in *Ulysses*—the phrase conjures up images of a wily,
battle-scarred veteran of Troy afoot in Dublin, a woman weaving and unweaving a tapestry of thoughts, a son looking for (or perhaps not looking
for) a father, bronze-by-gold sirens, a surly nationalist of a cyclops, and
all the rest of those determinations that go back to Joyce's old chapter
headings for *Ulysses* and Stuart Gilbert's study, symbolic elements linked

by the architectonics of the *Odyssey*.[1] Gilbert's book was immensely useful in helping general readers and critics alike to understand *Ulysses* in the early decades after the publication of the book, but the view of *Ulysses* that Joyce fostered and Gilbert disseminated has in many ways narrowed critical investigation and interposed itself between readers and the text. The Homeric parallels popularized by Gilbert have served to restrict critical reception of *Ulysses* in no area more than that of its symbolic structures and its architectonics.

The commonly accepted symbolic values for Bloom, Stephen, and Molly all come from European tradition as a whole: there is nothing particularly Irish about them. The established approach to the symbolism and architectonics of *Ulysses* reflects the predilection of the critical establishment to see Joyce as a European writer rather than an Irish one; accordingly, his cosmopolitan spirit is stressed, his disdain for the Anglo-Irish literary revival and Irish nationalism celebrated. We are told that Joyce's books "are of Irishmen and by an Irishman, but not for Irishmen" (Levin, *James Joyce* 6). I do not wish to dispute Joyce's cosmopolitan spirit or the established symbolic interpretations of Bloom, Stephen, or Molly; instead, I would like to suggest that these values are incomplete. We must reconsider the notion that Joyce's books are not "for Irishmen," particularly in light of the advice Joyce gave Arthur Power in 1921 while finishing *Ulysses*: "You are an Irishman and you must write in your own tradition. Borrowed styles are no good. You must write what is in your blood and not what is in your brain." When Power objected that he was tired of nationality and wanted to be international, like all the great writers, Joyce countered, "They were national first, and it was the intensity of their own nationalism which made them international in the end" (Power, *From the Old Waterford House* 64–65; cf. *JJ2* 505). European elements of Joyce's symbolism and architectonics in *Ulysses* are correct so far as they go, but the European values for Leopold Bloom, Stephen Dedalus, and Molly Tweedy Bloom are harmonics. The dominant of the symbolism behind their identities and their relationships is Irish and comes from Irish tradition.

It has become a somewhat procrustean commonplace to observe that Joyce's writings meld nineteenth-century realism and the symbolist re-

---

1. For the argument that Stephen is trying to "get clear" of all fathers, see Kenner, "*Ulysses*" 10–19.

action to realism. To generalize somewhat, if we accept the prevailing critical view that the symbolism in *Ulysses* is European, particularly Greek, then the Irish elements in the book presumably must be naturalistic. But if Joyce's writings are to be set in the context of Irish tradition, the question of this balance of symbolism and realism in *Ulysses* must be reopened. Why is the Irish Ulysses—Leopold Bloom—a Jew? Why is his "son" a Greek named Stephen Dedalus? Why is his wife, Molly, from Gibraltar? In what sense are these three characters in James Joyce's tradition, of his "blood" rather than his "brain"? The explanations of these apparent anomalies not covered by the Homeric parallels are also commonly made in terms of European symbol systems or an ingenuous realism. It is said that Bloom was modeled on specific Jews whom Joyce had met in Dublin or elsewhere (*JJ*2 197, 230, 374–75, 430; Hyman 167–92), and critics point out that the character evokes the legend of the Wandering Jew.[2] As a Jew, Bloom is seen as a universal metropolitan hero "equally at home and ill at ease in any city of the world" (Levin, *James Joyce* 84). Stephen Dedalus, by contrast, is at once rational Greek, master artisan, Christian martyr, and emblem of Dublin. His name is "the wedge by which symbolism enters" *A Portrait of the Artist* (Levin, *James Joyce* 46), and that symbolism carries over into *Ulysses* as well. Finally, Molly's youth in Gibraltar captures the ironic Irish presence in the British army; her Mediterranean origin infuses passion and profusion, fertility and sensuality, into the clammy climate of Dublin.

Let us consider the realism in all this. Not one of these characters has a typical Irish name, not one is from the oldest native families of Ireland—families whose clan is signaled by "mac" or "ó." Why do the main characters of *Ulysses*, particularly Bloom as the Irish Everyman, not come from modern Irish stock with common Irish names? Why is each alienated in some way from Irish culture?[3] Is this constellation of characters plausible in any naturalistic sense? Hugh Kenner notes the incongruity in Bloom's coming from an immigrant family in a "country whose

2. This legend was widely known in Anglo-Irish circles, for it formed the basis of Charles Robert Maturin's popular three-volume novel *Melmoth the Wanderer*, published in 1820. Maturin, a relative of Speranza and Oscar Wilde, was curate of St. Peter's, Dublin. An edition of *Melmoth* with a biographical essay about the author appeared in 1892, and Joyce refers to Maturin in *Finnegans Wake* 335.34–35.
3. For some thematic values of the characters' alienation, see the discussion in Hyman 178–80, as well as the references cited there.

citizens characteristically emigrate" ("*Ulysses*" 71; cf. Hyman 183). In the text of *Ulysses* Joyce even signals the difficulty of accepting Leopold Bloom as an immigrant and a Jew in a realistic sense with Deasy's bigoted joke that Ireland is the only country never to have persecuted the Jews "because she never let them in" (2.442). We might pursue this problem by asking why Bloom's "Jewishness" causes relatively little comment within the framework of the book, the scene with the Citizen notwithstanding, and why Bloom knows relatively little about Jewish culture. Indeed, Bloom is so ignorant about "the faith of his fathers" that Jewishness becomes the decor rather than the substance of his world.[4]

These are some of the problems of the "realism" of *Ulysses*, particularly if it is to be viewed as the Irish element of the book. The fact that these questions are so seldom raised should remind us of how strongly readers and critics of Joyce's work are influenced by the prevailing European symbolic interpretations of the identities of the main characters of *Ulysses* even when the symbolic values contravene naturalism.

i. The *erigenating hierarchitectitiptitoploftical* framework of *Ulysses*: Joyce's refraction of *The Book of Invasions*

If Joyce is to be taken seriously as an Irishman, the possibility that his primal symbol systems may be Irish must be considered. In particular, we must examine native Irish literature for correlates to his work when realism breaks down, as it does in the case of the configuration of the main characters in *Ulysses*. Taken one by one, Joyce's main characters in *Ulysses* are plausibly explained in terms of the shared symbolism of European literary tradition. As a *system*, however, Joyce's characters have no parallel in European literature; taken together, the three main characters point to a more unified source than European literature can provide. The interface of Stephen, Bloom, and Molly is Irish because Joyce's constellation of characters in *Ulysses*—a Greek, an ersatz Jew, and a lady from Spain—is based on the mythic structures of *Lebor Gabála Érenn* (*The Book of the Taking of Ireland*), generally known in English as *The Book of Invasions*.

---

4. A discussion of the actual background of Irish Jews is found in Hyman.

The Book of Invasions contains the pseudohistory of Ireland: the traditional history of Ireland before A.D. 432, the usual date for the coming of Patrick and the beginning of written history in Ireland. Its prototype was probably composed in the seventh century to fill in the gap for Ireland in such standard late Roman universal histories as those by Origen and Eusebius. Though the story apparently was originally restricted to the account of the postdiluvian history of the Milesians, supposed ancestors of the Goidelic stock in Ireland, it was opened up at an early period to include bits of cosmogony and old myth. Eventually it came to contain the "history" of Ireland since the Creation, giving accounts of several conquests of Ireland before and after the Flood and culminating in the invasion of the sons of Mil.[5]

The Book of Invasions and its associated kinglist became the matrix for the rest of Irish history and literature; and as the organizing referent for Irish tradition, it stands in initial position in the great twelfth-century manuscript the Book of Leinster, a compendium of Irish narratives and histories, genealogies, and learned poetry. By the seventeenth century the contents of *The Book of Invasions* were presupposed or distilled in most native Irish historical materials from the Annals of the Four Masters to Geoffrey Keating's *History of Ireland*. In 1861 Eugene O'Curry felt obliged to spend little time explaining *The Book of Invasions* to his English-speaking Irish audience; he notes in his *Lectures on the Manuscript Materials of Ancient Irish History*, "The Milesian history is pretty generally known, and has been much canvassed by the writers of the last 150 years" (446). In the nineteenth century the story of the Milesians was promoted by scholars and popularizers alike, from precursors of the Anglo-Irish literary revival like Standish O'Grady to writers of school history books. Elements of *The Book of Invasions* are still part of popular history among the Irish and Irish-Americans as well.

The relevant features of *The Book of Invasions* for the symbolism and the architectonics of *Ulysses* can be summarized as follows.

There are six invasions of Ireland. The first two groups of invaders are wiped out and leave essentially no survivors. The third, fourth, and fifth—those of

---

5. *The Book of Invasions* survives in four recensions, which have been edited in two series: R. A. S. Macalister and John MacNeill, eds., *Leabhar Gabhála, The Book of Conquests of Ireland, The Recension of Micheál Ó Cléirigh*; and R. A. S. Macalister, ed., *Lebor Gabála Érenn, The Book of the Taking of Ireland*, 5 vols.

Nemed, the Fir Bolg, and the Tuatha De Danann, respectively—come from
Scythian Greek stock. The Nemedian invasion is eventually abandoned because of opposition and difficulties from the Fomorians, a chaotic and op-
pressive race of marauders. The Nemedian invasion is succeeded by that of
the Fir Bolg, who are in turn overcome by the Tuatha De Danann. Though
these three groups are related genealogically, their characters and experiences
differ widely. The Fir Bolg are subjugated and become laborers in Greece,
while the Tuatha De Danann become skilled in lore, crafts, and hidden
knowledge. The Tuatha De Danann become allies of the Athenians before
departing for Ireland.

Meanwhile the Goidels—descendants of Noah, of course, and genealogically related to their predecessors in Ireland—are involved in building the
Tower of Babel. After that architectural disaster, they establish a language
school, becoming language teachers with a specialty in Hebrew and Irish
(which is constructed from all the languages that come into existence after
Babel). They are invited to Egypt at the time of the pharaohs because of their
erudition. Their leader, Nel, is given Scota, the daughter of the pharaoh, as
wife. The Goidels become sympathizers of Moses and aid the Israelites in
their flight from Egypt. Moses is grateful for their help and offers the Goidels
a place in the Promised Land should they care to accompany the Hebrews.
However, the Goidels decline Moses's offer. After some years the Goidels are
expelled from Egypt in revenge for aiding the Israelites. They undertake various travels (including a second sojourn in Egypt, during which their leader
Mil marries the pharaoh's daughter). Eventually they go to Spain, where they
make conquests, settle down, and take wives. While in Spain the Goidels see
Ireland from a high tower and decide to go there. After various struggles with
their predecessors in Ireland (the Tuatha De Danann), the Goidels (or Milesians) defeat the Tuatha De and arrange a settlement with them—the Milesians get the upper half of Ireland, and the Tuatha De get the half below
ground.[6]

The Book of Invasions is in itself a fascinating subject. It depends on the
medieval circular map of the world (which explains the somewhat bizarre
geographical course of the Milesians and the contiguity of Spain and Ireland), the medieval tradition of the seven wonders of the world (which
included the Roman pharos at Corunna from which the Milesians sight
Ireland), and much more. It also cheerfully assumes that Ireland is the

---

6. Because the story survives in four recensions and countless retellings, details vary from text to text. The summary here is a schematic based on the outline
common to most versions.

second Promised Land and that the Irish language is second only to Hebrew in its purity and sacredness.[7]

There is ample evidence that James Joyce knew the main lines of *The Book of Invasions*. In the text of *Ulysses* there are direct references to the Milesians, including a reference to Milesius (12.1310), an allusion to the Milesian facility in Hebrew and a synopsis of the passages in *The Book of Invasions* related to the language school of Fenius Farsaigh (17.748ff.), and a naming of the Milesians as the Clan Milly (14.371), as well as a reference to Balor (12.197–98). In addition to the internal evidence in *Ulysses*, there are references to the framework of *The Book of Invasions* in Joyce's other writings. *The Book of Invasions* figures explicitly in *A Portrait of the Artist*, for example, when Stephen sees Davin as a "rude Firbolg" and Thomas Moore, the national poet, is described as "a Firbolg in the borrowed cloak of a Milesian" (180); and *Finnegans Wake* is larded with allusions to the story (e.g., 15.5ff., 86.15, 130.4, 144.12ff., 219.11, 309.11, 381.03ff., 601.36).[8]

The Book of Invasions stands as the epitome of an early Irish narrative whose sources were overdetermined for Joyce.[9] Even had Joyce read nothing about *The Book of Invasions*, he would have been familiar with the main outlines of the story from oral sources; discourse about Milesians and Tuatha De Danann, Fir Bolgs and Fomorians, was part of daily life.[10] The popular periodicals of Joyce's youth are full of allusions to *The Book of Invasions* and summaries of its pseudohistorical scheme. In addition to popular and oral sources, Joyce had several written sources for his material related to *The Book of Invasions*. In 1920 Joyce's library included William Francis Collier's *History of Ireland for Schools* (Ellmann, *Consciousness of Joyce* 105; Gillespie #111), a school history that opens with a summary of *The Book of Invasions*; it is likely that Joyce chose to own Collier's school book as he was writing *Ulysses* precisely because he had

---

7. For a discussion of some of these elements, see Kelleher, "Humor in the Ulster Saga" 35–38.

8. References are found elsewhere in Joyce's critical writing as well; see, for example, CW 166.

9. John Kelleher writes, "It would be as pointless to try to determine where Joyce got his knowledge of *Lebor Gabála*, or how much of it he knew or in what detail, as it would be to attempt to ascertain how an American writer learned about the first Thanksgiving, Pocahontas, and George Washington's cherry tree" (quoted in French 281).

10. Oliver Gogarty had accused Joyce himself of having Fir Bolg melancholy and needing to be roused to Attic joy (*JJ2* 118).

used this book early in life during his schooldays and wished to have it as a reference while he worked.[11] Joyce had also read at least one scholarly source on the topic, Henri d'Arbois de Jubainville's *Irish Mythological Cycle and Celtic Mythology*, R.I. Best's translation of which had been serialized in 1901–2 in the *United Irishman*, which Joyce read regularly (see below ch. 7); d'Arbois de Jubainville's study includes a close and detailed examination of the materials in *The Book of Invasions*. Still another likely textual source is P.W. Joyce's *Concise History of Ireland*, which Gilbert cites (65), presumably at James Joyce's behest; this volume, initially published in 1893, was in its twenty-fourth edition in 1920 and contains material similar to the author's *Illustrated History of Ireland*, which James Joyce owned in 1939, again presumably because he had known versions of P.W. Joyce's history since his youth.[12]

The Book of Invasions is used only in a partial way in *Ulysses*, in the manner that Joyce uses mythic structures in general. In his discussion of early Irish mythological elements in "The Dead," John Kelleher cautions,

Everyone of course knows that Joyce was fond of weaving into his work parallels with myth, saga, and epic. It is, however, a mistake to assume, when such a parallel is identified, that it must be complete. It rarely is. Even *Ulysses* does not reflect the entirety of the *Odyssey*. In *Finnegans Wake* wonders can be done with a mere hint of resemblance. Usually Joyce is content with a few salient indications as, for example, in the well-known sketch-parody of Dante's *Divine Comedy* in the story "Grace." The same, I think, holds for "The Dead" and "The Destruction of Da Derga's Hostel." The shadowy similarity between Gabriel Conroy and Conaire Már is enough for Joyce's purposes which by their very nature must be suggestive rather than explicit. ("Irish History" 421)

The parallels between Joyce's text and his mythic prototype are general and sketchy rather than complete and detailed in part because of his mythic method itself: though most retellers of mythic stories use the surface content of myth, manipulating the mythic material so as to fore-

---

11. I am indebted to John Kelleher for this suggestion. See below, ch. 4, for a specific element Joyce took from Collier.

12. For Joyce's ownership of a 1921 edition of P.W. Joyce's *Illustrated History*, see Connolly 21 #163. Kelleher suggests that Joyce probably read P.W. Joyce's *Child's History of Ireland* during the years between Clongowes and Belvedere (quoted in French 281).

ground thematic material, Joyce uses myth as an architectural substructure to the realistic surface of the story. In the terms developed by Mieke Bal in her *Narratology*, the myth in Joyce's narratives does not enter the *story* at all; it enters on the level of the *fabula*, whereby the sequence of the mythic events can be equated to the sequence of narrative events in *Ulysses*, or whereby the relation of actors in Joyce's narrative can be equated with a configural grouping in a myth. In this process, the myth itself is condensed and reduced before entering Joyce's creative process; the fabula of the myth intersects with the fabula of Joyce's narrative. Ipso facto, therefore, Joyce's use of myth appears to be minimalist, as Kelleher has observed.[13] By using a myth as a subtext—by using the fabula of a myth rather than a mythic story—Joyce develops a mythic method with great flexibility. In virtue of his method he is, for example, able to conflate different mythic narratives and different mythic systems; he can also suggest a myth and undermine it simultaneously.[14] This technique characterizes Joyce's use of *The Book of Invasions* in *Ulysses* as it does his use of other myths; he refers to main elements in the early Irish story rather than give point-by-point correspondences. Though the references to *The Book of Invasions* are incomplete, condensed, and schematized, they are not insignificant: in the Irish story we find the unified source for the constellation of main characters in *Ulysses*, the constellation of Greek, Jew, and Mediterranean woman. *The Book of Invasions* provides the scaffold for the relations of the central characters in Joyce's book and supplies typologies for Joyce to work with in developing his cast.

Leopold Bloom can be seen as a counterpart to the Goidels, the Irish invaders who could have been Jews because they are invited by Moses to share in the Promised Land: " 'Come with us, with thy whole people,' said Moses, 'if you will, and remain permanently with us, and when we reach the land that God hath promised us, you will get a share in it' " (Macalister and MacNeill 198–99). The Goidels are confederates of Moses but

---

13. Bal distinguishes between three levels of a narrative: the "deep structure" (10), or the *fabula*, in which a series of logically and chronologically related events are caused or experienced by actors (5); the *story*, which is a certain manner of presenting the fabula (5); and the *text*, in which a narrative agent tells a story (117).

14. The technique is unlike that of many other twentieth-century mythic retellings in which the myth appears on the surface, as it does, for example, in Anouilh's *Antigone* or Giraudoux's *La guerre de Troie n'aura pas lieu*.

not Hebrew, sympathetic to Moses but not among the chosen people. The Goidels share Hebrew history but choose deliberately to go in different directions. In the same way Bloom has Jewish sympathies and through his father the potential of being a Jew, but his actual experience and identity are not Jewish. Because under religious law Jewish descent comes through the mother's line and Bloom's mother and maternal grandmother both have Irish names, Bloom appears not to be a Jew. Bloom is not circumcised, he has been twice baptized as a Christian by official clergy, and in the cabman's shelter Bloom tells Stephen explicitly that "in reality" he's not a Jew (16.1085).[15] Bloom's mixed identity—his Jewish sympathies and ancestry combined with his Irish actuality—mirrors the early history of the Goidels in *The Book of Invasions* more than it does the actual experience of any Irish Jew at the turn of the century. It is possible, moreover, that Bloom's preoccupation with Egyptian and Turkish things (e.g., 4.192ff., 15.297ff.) is intended to reflect the Goidelic sojourns in Egypt in *The Book of Invasions*; Bloom's preoccupation with Egypt also brings to mind the pharaoh's daughter who becomes one of Mil's wives.

In the Stephen Dedalus of *Ulysses* we can see a representative of the Irish invaders with a Greek heritage, particularly the Tuatha De Danann. As noted in the summary, in *The Book of Invasions* the Tuatha De Danann are known for their learning and skill, including their magical skills. The Tuatha De Danann "learned druidry and many various arts in [the northern islands of Greece] . . . till they were knowing, learned and very clever. . . . They considered their men of learning to be gods" (Macalister and MacNeill 142–43). Like the Tuatha De, Stephen Dedalus is schooled in ancient knowledge; like them he has the richness of Western culture and its secret mysteries at his disposal; like them he can be arrogant and aloof as a divinity. The attitude of the Tuatha De Danann toward artists, considering "their men of learning [or *artists*] to be gods," has an amusing parallel in Stephen's own aesthetic theory; following Flaubert, Stephen believes that in drama "the artist, like the God of creation, remains within or behind or beyond or above his handiwork, invisible, refined out of existence, indifferent, paring his fingernails" (*PA* 215). The identification of Stephen and the Tuatha De Danann is mediated as well by an

---

15. For a full discussion of the question of Bloom's religion and ethnic affiliations, see Steinberg 27–49.

Athenian alliance of the Tuatha De Danann since in some versions of the classical myth Daedalus is an Athenian. The chief hero of the Tuatha De Danann is Lug, the *samildánach*, the 'many-skilled'; and Stephen, too, is many skilled. Teacher, bard, singer, potential journalist—Stephen has many arts and on Bloomsday is urged to take up the professions of singer and newspaperman even as he is acknowledged as an emerging literary man.

Molly appears to represent the recurrent Spanish connections in Irish pseudohistory. In her is embodied Mediterranean sensuality—but a sensuality that is Ireland's legitimate heritage in the framework from *The Book of Invasions*. Of the many characters in *The Book of Invasions*, Molly calls to mind Tailltiu in particular, the daughter of Magmor, king of Spain, who is wife to Eochaid son of Erc, king of the Fir Bolg. When Eochaid son of Erc is defeated, Tailltiu marries Eochaid the Rough, son of Dul of the Tuatha De Danann. Later Tailltiu becomes foster mother of Lug, the young hero of the Tuatha De Danann, and her memory comes to be celebrated with games at the site of her grave.[16] Tailltiu is also credited with clearing one of Ireland's plains: "Tailltiu [came] after the fighting of [the first] battle of Mag Tuired to Coill Chuan [Cuan's Wood]; and the wood [was] cleared at her command, so that it was a clovery plain before the end of a year, and she inhabited it afterwards" (Macalister and MacNeill 150–51).[17]

Tailltiu—a character mentioned by Joyce in *Finnegans Wake* (83.23) and most probably familiar from his youth—has a dwelling place that brings to mind Molly's love of flowers and nature, a love of lushness appropriate to both women because of their Mediterranean origins. Note, too, that both Bloom and Molly toy with the idea that Stephen might move into their home—become, as it were, their "foster son." Whatever her erotic fantasies about the situation, we might say that Molly, like Tailltiu, almost becomes "foster mother" of a multitalented youth. Taill-

---

16. Tailltiu is the modern Telltown; under the Gaelic Athletic Association the old Telltown games had been revived, and they continue to be observed to the present. The irony of the nationalists' choice to celebrate the memory of a woman who goes from husband to husband cannot have escaped Joyce. Note also that Tailltiu's "sensuality" here is part of her function as a Sovereignty figure (cf. chapter 4 below).

17. I have silently normalized the spelling of proper nouns in this quotation.

tiu and the Spanish wives obtained by some of the Goidels after their conquest of Spain might have suggested to Joyce that Mediterranean passion
enters Irish tradition through the distaff side—a possible explanation for
all the women with vigorous sexual appetites who people medieval Irish
literature. In terms of the scaffolding of *Ulysses*, we should also observe
that Molly enjoys dalliance on hilltops and heights and places from which
she has a large vista. Her final thoughts of the day are memories in which
her embraces with Mulvey on the rock of Gibraltar fuse with memories
of her lovemaking with Poldy on the hill of Howth. This scene should
remind us of the Spanish tower from which the Goidels spot Ireland in
The Book of Invasions.

The identification of the central characters in *Ulysses* as types from
The Book of Invasions explains some of the puzzles about Bloom, Stephen, and Molly noted in the critical literature. Phillip Herring ("Toward
an Historical Molly Bloom" 507, 521 n. 31), for example, has commented that Molly and Leopold have a curiously parallel heredity and
that by religious law she is more Jewish than he. It is obviously the subtext of *The Book of Invasions* that explains the unlikely case of having
both Bloom and Molly be of Jewish ancestry: because Molly is also identified with the Milesians in Joyce's use of the pseudohistorical scheme, her
having potential Jewish ancestry is consistent with the Irish mythic underpinnings, even if it is a rather notable statistical anomaly in Joyce's
realism. In a similar way, Bloom's famous "blooper," "All that long business about that [*sic*] brought us out of the land of Egypt and into the
house of bondage *alleluia*" (7.208–9), takes on a new meaning as an
ironic Milesian commentary on Irish pseudohistory rather than as a simple error of a man who is ignorant of Jewish ritual: the Milesians have
left the bondage of pharaoh only to end in the house of British imperialism.

In *Surface and Symbol* Robert Adams has suggested that a departure
from or absence of surface realism points to a symbolic purpose in the
text; Adams concludes that "Bloom's Jewish character was a symbol into
which Joyce tried to project, not only his social reflections about modern
man, but some rather intimate and complex psychic responses of his
own" (106). However, the absence of surface realism in Bloom's Jewishness not only indicates Joyce's symbolic intent but also reifies Bloom's
identity as an ersatz Jew, like that of the Milesians as a whole; he thus
signals the Irish mythic system behind the Joycean text. In the same way

the lack of verisimilitude in Molly's portrait is usefully reconsidered in light of the Irish architectonics of *Ulysses*.[18]

It has also been observed that when Stephen Dedalus leaves Bloom's garden in episode 17, he walks out of the Joycean world. He vanishes. The point should not escape the reader: it is a radical relocation of Joyce's interests and priorities to replace Stephen Dedalus with Leopold and Molly Bloom, to leave the reader with those two protagonists in possession of the fictive world, inhabitants of the reader's Dublin. This shift, which has in its nature something of a revolution, is an enactment of the progression of *The Book of Invasions*, a text presenting wave after wave of invasion, wave after wave of possession and dispossession of the land of Ireland. In *The Book of Invasions* in particular there is a confrontation of the Tuatha De Danann and the Milesians; the result of that confrontation is that the Milesians take possession of Ireland, driving their predecessors underground. The Tuatha De walk out of the world of men and retreat to the hollow hills, an exit as sudden and total as that of Stephen from *Ulysses*. The feature of replacement here is, particularly in light of its mythic counterpart, part of the meaning in *Ulysses*.

Recognition of the framework from *The Book of Invasions* illuminates more than the relations of the three major characters; it is also a factor in Joyce's portrait of the Citizen in the "Cyclops" episode of *Ulysses*. Joyce's treatment of this character has been cited to show his disdain for the Irish cultural revival and for the cruder forms of insular nationalism. The Citizen was modeled on the founder of the Gaelic Athletic Association, Michael Cusack (*JJ*2 61; cf. Groden 132–39), but *The Book of Invasions* adds resonance to the character, for the Citizen can be identified as the representative of still another wave of invaders, the Fir Bolg. In Irish typology the Fir Bolg are short, dark, ugly, crude people. They were laborers in Greece, and in Ireland, after the conquests of the Tuatha De

18. Although these issues will be addressed at length in chapter 6, it is appropriate to comment here on the seeming incongruity of Molly's "Spanish" origin and her lack of a Gibraltar accent. Phillip Herring has observed that Molly speaks with an Irish brogue, thus claiming that her language undercuts the surface realism. This seeming error is again related to the Irish mythos behind *Ulysses*: with the shearing of realism Joyce here is conveying to his audience that Molly is both Spanish *and* Irish; her sensuous Mediterranean nature is subsumed within her Irishness. Herring also argues that Molly has "no understanding of her mixed heritage"; but we should understand that Molly's mixed ethnicity is not intended as a surface, but as a symbol of her Milesian identity from *The Book of Invasions*. See Herring, "Toward an Historical Molly Bloom" 516.

Danann and the Goidels, they become the unfree, subjugated, nonnoble populace. The Fir Bolg typology—current in Joyce's time and still in force today—is one element behind Joyce's construction of the Citizen.

Not only is the Citizen crude in person and thought, but he is chaotic as well. Kenner points out that Joyce could associate the nationalist movement with destruction and chaos, particularly with the 1916 destruction of Dublin: "When the biscuit-tin, by heroic amplification, renders North Central Dublin a mass of ruins we are to remember what patriotic idealism could claim to have accomplished by Easter 1916" ("*Ulysses*" 139; cf. 92–96). The most chaotic figures in early Irish literature are the Fomorians (or Fomoiri), who are responsible for the failure of the Nemedian invasion and who fight against and for a time oppress the Tuatha De Danann; this battle between the Fomorians and the Tuatha De Danann is a reflex of the Indo-European pattern of the battle of the gods of order with the gods of chaos (Gray 1–10; Sjoestedt 19; Mac Cana, *Celtic Mythology* 60). The Fomorians are often conflated with the Fir Bolg in the ancient texts; each group opposes the Tuatha De Danann in a battle at a location called Mag Tuired, and each group is defeated by the Tuatha De. This conflation is apparent in Joyce's treatment of the Citizen, who is as unattractive as the Fir Bolg and as chaotic as the Fomorians; the conflation is partly reflected in the Citizen's being simultaneously an ordinary-sized person in the narration and a gigantic figure in the parodies paralleling the action of the episode.

The most chaotic figure of all the Fomorians is Balor, the one-eyed figure who can turn men to stone with his gaze and who is killed in the Second Battle of Mag Tuired by Lug.

An evil eye had Balor the Fomorian. That eye was never opened save only on a battle-field. Four men used to lift up the lid of the eye with a polished handle which passed through its lid. If an army looked at that eye, though they were many thousands in number, they could not resist a few warriors. It had a poisonous power. Once when his father's druids were concocting charms, he came and looked out of the window, and the fume of the concoction came under it, so that the poison of the concoction afterwards penetrated the eye that looked. (*AIT* 44)

Elsewhere the Fomorians in general have only one eye (cf. Sjoestedt 16). As a group, therefore, the Fomorians can be compared to the race of Cyclopes; and we should remember that it is the narrator as much as the

Citizen whose (single) eye is mentioned: "I was just passing the time of day with old Troy of the D. M. P. at the corner of Arbour hill there and be damned but a bloody sweep came along and he near drove his gear into my eye" (12.1–3). While he represents two groups in *The Book of Invasions* at one and the same time—crude Fir Bolg and chaotic, one-eyed Fomorian—the Citizen also owes something to the specific characterization of Balor; and the one-eyed quality of the Fomorians, best elaborated in the descriptions of Balor, provides the surface linkage between the Irish mythic prototypes and the Homeric Cyclopes.[19]

Given this mythic background for the Citizen, we should expect Stephen Dedalus rather than Bloom to oppose the character, since Dedalus seems to represent Lug in particular and the Tuatha De Danann in general. It is the Tuatha De who fight both the Fir Bolg and the Fomorians at the two battles at Mag Tuired, and Lug slays Balor. Thus, it is suggestive that Joyce originally intended Stephen to be part of the "Cyclops" episode (Groden 133–37; cf. 149). Because Bloom was apparently intended as the Citizen's victim from the very start (Groden 132), the mythological structure of *The Book of Invasions* may offer some clue to Joyce's original plans for the chapter. As it stands, Joyce has bent the early Irish myth by having Bloom rather than Stephen oppose the Citizen, but *The Book of Invasions* explains in part why there is a typological as well as a personal contrast between Bloom and the Citizen: they represent the opposition of their races within Ireland.

In sum, *The Book of Invasions* helps to explain why the central characters in *Ulysses* are all outsiders though they stand as universalized representations of Dubliners, for the invasion theory of Irish history in *Lebor Gabála* is predicated on the notion that there are no aboriginal inhabitants of the island. In this scheme, everyone is an outsider, descended as it were from immigrants. From the perspective of Irish pseudohistory, the cultural alienation of Stephen, Bloom, and Molly mirrors the heritage of all the island's inhabitants as descendants of invaders: to be Irish is to be an immigrant. Thus, within an Irish *mythic* framework, if not an Irish

19. Henri d'Arbois de Jubainville, *Irish Mythological Cycle* 123, takes the view that in Irish literature there is no counterpart to the Cyclops, but Rees and Rees (66) note that the theme of the one-eyed enemy pervades Irish literature. Ingcel in *The Destruction of Da Derga's Hostel* is an example both of a one-eyed enemy and a chaotic figure (*AIT* 104ff.).

naturalistic context, the main characters of *Ulysses* are typical of their country. Irish myth, therefore, underscores the modernist alienation that pervades the book.

In this light we see the ultimate irony of Deasy's joke about Ireland's having no Jews as well as the irony of the Citizen's xenophobia and his virulence against the Jews in particular (12.1140ff., 12.1666). *The Book of Invasions* provides a framework in which the Goidels of Ireland and their descendants should have a natural sympathy and affinity for the Jews, for the Goidels might well have joined Moses's band and shared in Jewish history after aiding the Israelites in Egypt. Indeed, from this mythic perspective the Goidels might well be called an "Israelitish" race, a term Joyce applied to the Irish;[20] and the views of the tolerant characters in *Ulysses* are all sentiments that Joyce himself espoused, believing that the Irish least of all have a claim to purity of race (discussed at greater length below). Against the mythic framework of *The Book of Invasions*, the Citizen betrays his non-Goidelic and base ancestry through his anti-Semitic views.[21]

Bloom and the Goidels, Stephen and the Tuatha De Danann, Molly and Tailltiu, the Citizen and the Fomorians/Fir Bolg—taken one by one, each correspondence between *Ulysses* and *The Book of Invasions* is of little moment. Taken together they carry weight. Ireland's pseudohistory, which had shaped Irish concepts of time and identity for over a thousand years, found its way into *Ulysses* and informs the relations of Joyce's main characters. *Ulysses* is a roman à clef, though no one key fits it exactly. To the *Odyssey* and *Hamlet* and the *Divina Commedia*, the books that are most widely acknowledged to have contributed to the architectonic structure of *Ulysses*, we should now add a fourth: *The Book of Invasions*. One of the keys to *Ulysses* is Irish, a key unlocking many of its textual puzzles, its mode of signification, its meaning.

ii. *That greekenhearted yude*: Hebrew and Greek in *Ulysses*

It is well known that Joyce subscribed to Victor Bérard's theory of the Phoenician origin of the *Odyssey*, elaborated in Bérard's two-volume

---

20. Cf. Hyman 180–82.
21. Joyce believed that anti-Semitism was a touchstone of bigotry; see the discussion in Manganiello 56.

publication, *Les Phéniciens et l'Odyssée* (1902–3). Bérard maintains that the *Odyssey* is a Greek account of the wandering of a Phoenician merchant-adventurer, a Hellenized Phoenician tract on the geography of the Mediterranean world and on navigational instruction. Bérard's analysis includes a linguistic component, and he accounts for various names and words in the *Odyssey* by providing Semitic etymologies or loan-transfers. About the *Odyssey* Bérard concludes: "The poem is obviously the work of a Hellene, while the 'log' is clearly the record of a Semitic traveller. The poet—Homer, if you will—was a Greek; the seafarer—Ulysses, as we know him—was Phoenician" (trans. Gilbert 82). Joyce probably became acquainted with Bérard's theories in Zurich while he was writing *Ulysses* (*JJ2* 408), and they influenced his own manipulation of the Homeric parallels in *Ulysses*. It is thus Bérard's views on the *Odyssey* that Gilbert quotes again and again as he draws the parallels between *Ulysses* and the Homeric poem, for Bérard's metatext of the *Odyssey* was one of the main refractions of the Greek text that Joyce relied on in constructing *Ulysses*. In general critics have viewed Joyce's interest in Bérard as idiosyncratic, the sort of eccentricity that is tolerated in a great artist. According to the conventional interpretation of Joyce's mythic substructure in *Ulysses*, the value of Bérard's theory lies in its ability to provide a link between the Greek plot of *Ulysses* and Joyce's Semitic hero, for the Phoenicians, as Bérard indicates, were Semites. Bloom can be both Ulysses and a Wandering Jew under this construal of the *Odyssey*.[22]

It is not generally recognized in Joyce scholarship that a theory similar to that of Bérard had also been proposed for the settlement of Ireland.[23] At the end of the eighteenth century, Charles Vallancey had claimed that the original explorers and settlers of Ireland were Phoenician and that the Irish language itself was to be derived from the Semitic language of the Phoenicians. Vallancey elaborated on these views in a series of publications including *An Essay on the Antiquity of the Irish Language* (1772), *A Grammar of the Iberno-Celtic or Irish Language* (1773), *A Vindica-*

---

22. A summary of Bérard's views is found in Gilbert, esp. 76–84. For the argument that *Ulysses* is indebted to Bérard in rather thoroughgoing ways, see Seidel. See also Groden 75–94; Rose and O'Hanlon xxix–xxxi.

23. Seidel (17) is an exception, but he fails to pursue the implications of the similarities between Vallancey's theories and those of Bérard for the construction of *Ulysses*.

tion of the Ancient History of Ireland (1786), and *Prospectus of a Dictionary of the Language of the Aire Coti or Ancient Irish* (1802). Though Vallancey's views of Ireland's settlement are extreme, Phoenician contact with Ireland may be historical, for it is generally agreed that Ptolemy's geography of Ireland derives from that of Marinus of Tyre and thus perhaps from Phoenician sources (Dillon and Chadwick 19). Vallancey's linguistic views about Irish are now considered quaint, but at the end of the eighteenth century the family group of the Celtic languages was still in doubt, largely because of the initial mutations in Celtic languages as well as the Irish word order; it was not yet widely agreed that Irish was Indo-European, and many people grouped Irish with the Semito-Hamitic (Afro-Asiatic) family of languages.[24]

Vallancey's theories were therefore accepted widely in his day in Ireland, and they addressed various timely issues about Irish culture. In his works, particularly in his *Vindication*, Vallancey depends on material from the *The Book of Invasions* to construct his thesis about Phoenician exploration, and in the seventh chapter of this work, entitled "Phenian History," he actually attempts to correlate episodes in *The Book of Invasions* with the various episodes in the *Odyssey*, giving Irish etymologies or cognates in some cases for the names of the Homeric sites (e.g., Scylla and Charybdis); these arguments are to some extent anticipated by *The Book of Invasions* itself, where an episode parallels Ulysses's use of wax in the ears of his men as a means of resisting the Sirens (Macalister 2: 20–21, 2: 40–43; Macalister and MacNeill 206ff.). Vallancey's *Prospectus* opens with a brief argument that the Phenian (leg. Fenian, i.e., Irish) and Phoenician languages are related; the bulk of that work is a lexicon of Irish words, comparing their meanings with the meanings of supposed cognates from Hebrew, "Hindoostanee," Arabic, "Chaldee," and other languages. All of these arguments dovetail to a remarkable extent with those of Bérard. A reader today will dismiss Vallancey as fanciful, but he was a man of his time: a nascent (if wrongheaded) comparative philologist and a traditionalist in holding to the Mediterranean theory of the origin of Western culture. It is worth noting that ideas not unrelated to those of Vallancey and Bérard have recently been revived by Martin Ber-

---

24. For a brief history of the controversy about the linguistic affiliations of Irish and the development of the argument that Irish is an Indo-European language, see Dillon, "Archaism of Irish Tradition" 1–2, and Aitchison 27–28, as well as references cited by these authors.

nal in his *Black Athena*, in which he argues that the intellectual hege-
mony of the Indo-European proposition has led to the denial and suppression of evidence that points to the debt of Greek culture to the cultures
of the Mediterranean world, to the Egyptians and the Phoenicians in particular. The popularity of Vallancey's ideas in Ireland throughout the
nineteenth century and into the twentieth may be attributed to the val-
orization of Irish culture that results from an antiquity greater than the
classical civilization of Greece; the theory was also attractive as a means
of euhemerizing and rationalizing the traditional pseudohistory of Ireland.

To have been aware of Vallancey's theories in Ireland at the turn of the
century, it was no more necessary to have read Vallancey's publications
than at present it is necessary for a literary critic to have read Derrida in
order to know something about deconstruction. Vallancey's theories had
been taken up in various general histories of Ireland in the nineteenth century, and they were still current during Joyce's youth in Ireland, even at
times discussed in the popular press (e.g., *All Ireland Review* 30 Mar.
1901). Joyce cites Vallancey by name in his 1907 Trieste lecture entitled
"Ireland, Island of Saints" (CW 156), and he held views deriving from
those of Vallancey, for in the same lecture Joyce takes the position that
Irish is an outgrowth of Phoenician,[25] that the Greeks learned about the
Irish from the Phoenicians, and that the religion and civilization of Ireland, "later known by the name of Druidism," were Egyptian in origin
(CW 156). There are also oblique references to Vallancey and his theory
of the Phoenician origin of the Irish in the "gran Phenician rover" of *Finnegans Wake* (197.31). It is possible that Joyce had read some of Vallancey firsthand, even perhaps while he was writing *Ulysses*, since the Zentralbibliothek in Zurich where Joyce worked almost daily from 1915 to
1919 contains both Vallancey's *Essay on the Antiquity of the Irish Language* and his *Grammar of the Iberno-Celtic*. Joyce's interest in Bérard
during this period may have sent him back to Vallancey as well, though
it is clear from the Trieste lecture that his initial exposure to Vallancey
had occurred before 1907, most likely before he left Ireland in 1904.

In *The Book of Invasions*, the foundation of Ireland's traditional history, the connection between the Israelites and the Goidels had been established, including the proposition that the Irish language has affinities

---

25. Nonetheless, he also maintains that Irish is Indo-European (CW 155).

to Hebrew. Joyce was therefore predisposed to be attracted to Bérard's theories by his own cultural background, which included both *The Book of Invasions* and the theories of Vallancey, theories that are themselves derivative in part from *The Book of Invasions*. It is one of those famous Joycean coincidences that Bérard's theory links Semite and Greek, a linkage found in *The Book of Invasions* as well, and that both the *Odyssey* and the settlement of Ireland could be traced to Phoenician travels. That Vallancey had already begun to correlate the adventures in *The Book of Invasions* and the *Odyssey* is suggestive, and it is tantalizing to think that Joyce may have known this material firsthand.

The importance of Vallancey's theory of the Phoenician origin of the Irish for the construction of *Ulysses* is obvious. Not only do Vallancey's theories dovetail very nicely with those of Bérard, thus fitting with Joyce's conceptualization of the *Odyssey*, but the two theories in tandem become a historico-literary rationale for Joyce's enterprise of merging Irish myth and Greek myth. The similarity between *The Book of Invasions* and the *Odyssey* within a framework set by the critical theories of Bérard and Vallancey would in turn have legitimated Joyce's own fusion in *Ulysses* of mythic elements from both texts. The theories of both Bérard and Vallancey serve to link Joyce's three primary mythic systems: the Greek story, the story of the Wandering Jew, and the architectonics from *The Book of Invasions*. Paradoxically, in forging a link between the Phoenicians and the *Odyssey*, Bérard was also forging a link between the Irish and the *Odyssey*. But a special value to Joyce of Bérard's theory of the *Odyssey* was that, like the Homeric parallels in *Ulysses*, it could be talked about in an international context and therefore facilitated the critical reception of *Ulysses*; because of their limited circulation outside of Ireland, neither Vallancey's theory nor the mythic matter in *The Book of Invasions* could serve that function.

Though all these theories and pseudohistories related to the Mediterranean and to Ireland are important for Joyce's imaginative construct behind *Ulysses*, his choice of typologies from *The Book of Invasions*, particularly his decision to make the main character in *Ulysses* "a Jew," was not simply literary, a function of his sources and his mythic method. The question of national traits was of great interest to Joyce. He felt personal affinities to the Jews, and he felt that in general the Irish and the Jews were similar and their destinies alike. In his letter to Carlo Linati accompanying a scheme of classical and anatomical correspondences for the book, Joyce referred to *Ulysses* as "an epic of two races (Israelite-Irish)" (*Letters* 1: 146).[26] These apparently naturalistic observations were perhaps in part a conventional product of the "two peoples" rhetoric of Irish nationalist politics, in which Irish suffering under the English was frequently compared to the Israelites' bondage and captivity.[27] This political trope is encoded in Bloom's "blooper" regarding the exodus "out of the land of Egypt and into the house of bondage," and a full example of the discourse is given in the text of *Ulysses* when professor MacHugh recites John F Taylor's speech supporting the Irish language movement (7.791–870).[28]

At the same time Joyce's views on race have a larger cultural context, a context formulated by Matthew Arnold, who believed that the world moves between the two poles of Jew and Greek; these polarities are discussed in several places in his work, particularly the chapter entitled "Hebraism and Hellenism" in *Culture and Anarchy*, which Joyce owned in 1920 (Ellmann, *Consciousness of Joyce* 99; Gillespie #17). Joyce himself held this view (cf. *JJ2* 395), and Bloom and Dedalus are representations of these two types. By suggesting the affinities, indeed the union, of Hebraic Bloom and Hellenistic Dedalus through the convergence of their thought, as well as through classical parallels and the Irish substructure, Joyce is suggesting that Ireland is heir to the whole range of human experience, valuation, and potential. Elsewhere such temperaments might be opposed, but in Ireland they are fused: "Jewgreek is greekjew" (15.2097–98). The binding structure from *The Book of Invasions* helps to explain why Joyce believed that in Ireland, at any rate, those two temperaments could be reconciled: Ireland's populace can be seen as heirs to both typologies because of successive waves of invasions and generations of intermarriage.

But this view may be supported also by the history of the Milesians themselves. In summarizing *The Book of Invasions*, Gilbert stresses that several of the invasions of Ireland have connections with Greece, and he

26. On these points, see also *JJ2* 373, 382, 395, 515, 521.

27. For a discussion of the "two peoples" theme in Irish politics, see Kenner, "*Ulysses*" 137–39, and Hyman 162, who gives examples.

28. It may be, of course, that the political trope is itself based on the *Book of Invasions* scheme, which Irish audiences would have recognized but which most Joyce scholars do not. John Garvin (66–70) claims that Joyce rewrites the speech to emphasize Egypt and the Jews and hence, we might add, the connection with *The Book of Invasions*.

notes that "Irish chroniclers had a strongly rooted belief in the Grecian origins of the Irish race" (65). A second reading of Stephen, as related to the poles of Jew and Greek, emerges from the framework established by *The Book of Invasions*. This second reading is also hinted at in *A Portrait of the Artist*, where an embryonic manipulation of the mythos of *The Book of Invasions* suggests an implicit racial contrast between Davin as Fir Bolg (180) and Stephen. Stephen's own race is not named explicitly in *A Portrait of the Artist*, but Stephen thinks in racial terms, musing about "his race" (e.g., 183, 238, 253; cf. 202, 221). Because the normal second term of contrast with Fir Bolg in Irish nationalist rhetoric is Milesian, in this reading Stephen, like Leopold and Molly in *Ulysses*, is also a Milesian. The juxtaposition of these two schemes from *The Book of Invasions* suggests that Joyce is saying that the privileged race in Irish pseudohistory has *within* its own heritage both Hebraic and Hellenic qualities, an identity that is dubletted by the successive waves of invasions altogether, thus underlining the reconciliation of "jewgreek" and "greekjew" that we find in *Ulysses* (15.2097–98).[29]

A doubled rewriting of the *The Book of Invasions* in *Ulysses* is not in the least improbable; indeed, Joyce manipulates Greek myth in exactly this manner. In *A Portrait of the Artist* Stephen can be read not only as Daedalus the artificer but also as Icarus; he is both simultaneously, and the multiple readings add resonance and interest to the mythic subtext. In *Ulysses* Molly is both Calypso and Penelope; multiple mythic perspectives take Joyce's mythic parallels beyond the technique of simple mythic retelling, deepening the semiotic values of the mythic subtexts and adding ambiguity and openness to the Joycean text. Joyce is able to manipulate myth in this fashion precisely because he uses only the deep structure of the myth, the fabula. It gives him tremendous flexibility: he can, for example, invoke expectations using the mythic subtext (Stephen as Telemachus is searching for his father) and then undercut those same expectations (Stephen is trying to stay clear of all fathers). By working the myth against itself in this fashion, Joyce establishes a productive ironic gap in his text that can be used for any number of purposes: intellectual and aesthetic delight in a new reading of an old myth, political

29. Kelleher lays out the contrast between Davin, who "is described as a Fir-bolg—dark, a serf, one who knows the secret ways of Irish life," and Stephen, who is to be understood as "a Milesian—fair, free, bravely open" (quoted in French 281).

or aesthetic signification, humor or parody. The double readings of myth contribute to Joyce's complex tone and facilitate the textual elements of humor that nonetheless do not undercut other more serious readings.

In *Finnegans Wake* Joyce refers to the "mixed racings" of the Irish (117.22), and his theories about the mixture of Celtic and Viking races in Ireland permeate his last book. But as early as 1907 he held these views, writing in his Trieste lecture "Ireland, Island of Saints and Sages" that

our civilization is a vast fabric, in which the most diverse elements are min-gled, in which nordic aggressiveness and Roman law, the new bourgeois con-ventions and the remnant of a Syriac religion are reconciled. In such a fabric, it is useless to look for a thread that may have remained pure and virgin with-out having undergone the influence of a neighbouring thread. What race, or what language . . . can boast of being pure today? And no race has less right to utter such a boast than the race now living in Ireland. (CW 165–66; cf. CW 161–62)

This is obviously a political statement, one that radically repudiates the bitter sectarianism and cultural oppositions that have characterized Irish history of the past four centuries. It is also a theme elaborated in *Ulysses* through the mythic structuring from *The Book of Invasions*, a structure that resonates with Bérard's theory of the *Odyssey*, with Arnold's theory of Hellenism and Hebraism, and with Vallancey's theory of the Phoeni-cian origin of the Irish.

iii. An Irish *met him pike hoses*

A most celebrated aspect of Celtic thought is the belief in reincarnation. Diodorus Siculus, like other classical writers, reports on this view among the early Celts: "Among [the druids] the doctrine of Pythagoras had force, namely, that the souls of men are undying, and that after achieving their term of existence they pass into another body" (quoted in Nutt, *Celtic Doctrine of Re-birth* 108.)[30] Since Irish texts—particularly the Ulster

---

30. A convenient collection of the classical references to Celtic beliefs in me-tempsychosis is to be found in Nutt, *Celtic Doctrine of Re-birth*, 107. These statements by classical writers have engendered a lively interpretive debate among scholars in the modern period, a debate that began in the nineteenth century and has continued to the present. An assessment of this literature is beyond the scope of the present work, but a brief summary of current critical views of Celtic beliefs

Cycle, which Kenneth Jackson has called "a window on the Iron Age"—
frequently presuppose cultural patterns corresponding to those of Gaul,
it is not surprising that in early Irish literature the motif of metempsychosis is common.

Metempsychosis, the word that reverberates through *Ulysses* like the
thunderclap in *Finnegans Wake*, refers not only to the rebirth of Ulysses,
Penelope, and Telemachus but also to the rebirth of Ireland's avatars from
The Book of Invasions: in *Ulysses* the types of Hebraic Milesian, Greek
Tuatha De, and Spanish female reappear in contemporary Dublin. The
motif of metempsychosis permits Joyce's characters to represent simultaneously characters from the *Odyssey*, *The Book of Invasions*, *Hamlet*,
and the other mythic schemes that Joyce has used partially or wholly in
Ulysses; Bloom is at once Ulysses, Milesian, the Wandering Jew, and
Hamlet's father. In the repertory of mythic elements that Joyce uses in
Ulysses, metempsychosis is in fact the mainspring; it coordinates and
drives all the mythic systems of the book. Metempsychosis is the philosophical center of the reanimation of all mythologies in *Ulysses* and the
rationale for Joyce's complex mythic compression; serving to bind the
parallel mythic systems, metempsychosis is in fact the center of Joyce's
mythic architectonics and mythic method in *Ulysses*.[31] Critical discussions of metempsychosis in *Ulysses* have generally related the principle
to the Greek mythos in the book; the motif can be seen as providing a
Pythagorean and Neoplatonist context for Joyce's work.[32] The Celtic belief in reincarnation is less well recognized, yet a close consideration of
Joyce's treatment of the motif of metempsychosis in *Ulysses* indicates that
Joyce utilized an Irish rather than a Greek conception of metempsychosis.

By 1904 Celtic beliefs in reincarnation had been widely discussed in
critical studies and disseminated in popular literature as well. The foremost treatment of the topic from the period is Alfred Nutt's volume entitled *The Celtic Doctrine of Re-birth*, published in 1897 as the second
volume of Kuno Meyer's edition of *The Voyage of Bran*. Though Nutt's

---

about reincarnation, metempsychosis, and life after death, including a discussion
of the attribution to the Celts of the Pythagorean theory of metempsychosis, can
be found in Mac Cana, *Celtic Mythology* 123; Piggott 102–4; and Dillon and
Chadwick 152–53. See also Nutt, *Celtic Doctrine of Re-birth*, and references
cited in these sources.

31. Metempsychosis is also central to *Finnegans Wake*, though its subordination to Viconian cycles alters its role in the later work.

32. Gilbert sets a Buddhist context for this feature of Joyce's text.

study is comprehensive and rather scholarly, it was issued as part of a popular series of books published by David Nutt, a series that also included Alfred Nutt's *Cuchulainn, the Irish Achilles* and Eleanor Hull's *Cuchullin Saga in Irish Literature*.[33] The topic had also been taken up by d'Arbois de Jubainville in *The Irish Mythological Cycle*, with which Joyce was familiar from his reading of the *United Irishman*. The Irish and Celtic views on reincarnation were, in fact, well known in the Dublin of Joyce's youth; most discussions of early Irish literature included at least a brief consideration of the topic, the popular press ran articles on the subject, and Celtic ideas about reincarnation fascinated and influenced writers of the Anglo-Irish literary revival including A. E. and Yeats.

The Celtic material on reincarnation, particularly the classical references, had given rise to a critical debate on how to construe the evidence. For example, in *The Celtic Doctrine of Re-birth* Nutt takes the position that early Celtic views on reincarnation are very close to the Archaic Greek material on the subject (133), particularly the Orphic materials that underlie the Pythagorean doctrines. Nutt says that in Irish stories "the personality subsists in its entirety whatever be the form under which it manifests itself" (72), though in some stories reincarnation involves memory of the past life and in others it does not. Nutt acknowledges that "the Irish doctrine, if doctrine it may be called, has no apparent connection with any belief in a soul as distinct from the body, or in a life led by the soul after the death of the body" and that the Irish myths are "innocent of metaphysical colouring" and are "the outcome of no religious or philosophical impulse" (96); overall, however, he stresses the similarity between Greek and Irish views of metempsychosis. In his interpretation, therefore, an Irish version of the motif of reincarnation would be rather similar to a Greek example.

By contrast, in *The Irish Mythological Cycle* d'Arbois de Jubainville distinguishes rather sharply between Irish views of metempsychosis and Greek views, particularly the Pythagorean conceptions. D'Arbois notes that for the Pythagoreans metempsychosis "is a punishment and the common lot of the wicked" (197); for the Celts "it was a privilege and not a punishment."[34] Here d'Arbois's observation is consistent with the fact

---

33. David Nutt, a London publisher, also published volumes issued by the Irish Texts Society as well as Douglas Hyde's *Beside the Fire*.
34. All quotes from this volume are taken from Best's translation.

that in Irish tales only special persons are subject to metempsychosis; it is not the lot of common mortals. He continues that for the Greeks, "the souls of the just are not encumbered with a body: pure spirits, they live in the atmosphere around, free, happy, immortal" (197). The distinctions that d'Arbois makes about the two types of metempsychosis are germane to a reading of *Ulysses* and suggest that Joyce was influenced by his reading of d'Arbois de Jubainville in the elaboration of the concept of reincarnation in *Ulysses*. Following d'Arbois de Jubainville's analysis, metempsychosis in *Ulysses* is a Celtic metempsychosis: it is not as a punishment that the Milesian/Wandering Jew/Hamlet's-ghost-of-a-father/Ulysses reappears as Leopold Bloom in Ireland at the end of the nineteenth century. Rather, this reincarnation is a privilege and an affirmation of eternal verities, eternal values, eternal types, eternal—archetypal, Jung would say—situations. The Irish quality of the metempsychosis in *Ulysses* is also demonstrated by Joyce's attitude toward the body: the body is no encumbrance to the reincarnated figures of *Ulysses*. Bloom and Molly, in particular, have a kind of joyousness about the body that is notably lacking in Pythagorean conceptions.

In his analysis of the differences between Greek and Celtic ideas of reincarnation, d'Arbois de Jubainville goes on to say:

Thus the lofty idea of justice which dominates the doctrine of Pythagoras is absent from the Celtic conceptions. . . . Pythagoras, who is already a modern, sees in the other life a sanction for the laws of justice respected or violated in this. But a more ancient doctrine than that of Pythagoras makes no distinction between justice and success, considering as just all that happens in this world, and seeing in the second life of the dead but a continuation of the joys and sorrows experienced in the first. This is the Celtic doctrine.

This conception of immortality differs widely from ours, whose philosophic nature, making a distinction between justice and the success of this world, includes the hope of a reparation beyond the grave. The Celtic race has not this hope. (198–99)

This analysis of Celtic ideas about reincarnation relates to the moral stance of *Ulysses*. Joyce works in the modernist tradition that can be traced back to Flaubert and others who refuse a bourgeois normative perspective on their material; but Joyce's choice of a Celtic framework for the reincarnation of his figures is a factor in the nonjudgmental treatment of Stephen, Bloom, and Molly. The characters and character types do not reappear in *Ulysses* either because they have sinned or because they have won reincarnation: the return of these figures is inevitable because they represent the resurgence of eternal human verities. In the Celtic tradition of reincarnation, there is no ultimate balance or reckoning for the characters, no absolute scale on which they are judged. A Balor has as much chance of reincarnation as a Milesian chief.

Joyce himself alerts us to this aspect of reincarnation through the discussion between Buck Mulligan and Haines regarding Stephen's idée fixe about Hell. Mulligan has claimed, "They drove his wits astray . . . by visions of Hell. . . . He can never be a poet" (10.1072–74), to which Haines responds: "Eternal punishment . . . I see. . . . It's rather interesting because professor Pokorny of Vienna makes an interesting point out of that. . . . He can find no trace of hell in ancient Irish myth. . . . The moral idea seems lacking, the sense of destiny, of retribution. Rather strange he should have just that fixed idea" (10.1076–84). This is a complex interchange, containing a great deal of information for the reader. On the one hand we are informed that Stephen is at odds with his Irish tradition because of the Christian concepts of retribution and judgment with which he is obsessed; he will not be a poet, certainly not an Irish poet, until he frees himself from these fixed ideas.

But on the other hand there is a metatextual sign here, guiding a reading of the theme of metempsychosis. The views, anachronistically attributed here to Julius Pokorny, go back to his predecessors, including d'Arbois de Jubainville, which were in circulation in 1904, though not at Pokorny's instance, and to which Joyce had been exposed to as early as 1902 by his reading of Best's translation of d'Arbois de Jubainville's *Irish Mythological Cycle* in the *United Irishman*.[35] The textual reference to Pokorny emphasizes the fact that there is no hell or retribution driving me-

---

35. See also, for example, the views of Windisch cited by Nutt, *Celtic Doctrine of Re-birth* 95–96.

In 1904 Julius Pokorny was seventeen and professor of nothing. Though Pokorny, who was privatdozent of Celtic philology at Vienna between 1914 and 1921 (Thornton, *Allusions in "Ulysses"* 237; cf. Gifford 281) did hold the views ascribed to him in *Ulysses*, he did not publish them until after Joyce's book had appeared; Joyce apparently knew of Pokorny's position from oral sources either in Ireland in 1912 (cf. Senn, "No Trace of Hell" 255–56) or in Zurich.

The reference to Pokorny in *Ulysses* is condensed, signaling explicitly to the reader Pokorny's influence on Joyce and implicitly the views of d'Arbois de Jubainville and others who had anticipated Pokorny. Joyce was no doubt receptive to Pokorny's views later precisely because he had been exposed to similar ideas in earlier days.

tempsychosis in the Joycean universe of *Ulysses*; though the character
Stephen may be obsessed with visions of Hell, Joyce as author of *Ulysses*
is not.

The question of metempsychosis, identity through ever-changing
forms, has a global or communal reflex as well as a personal one.[36] Much
of the action of *Ulysses* takes place as the characters walk about Dublin.
The path captures, in part, a walk Joyce took with his friend Byrne on
the eve of his departure from Dublin in 1909 (*JJ*2 290), and it also mirrors the sea journeys of Ulysses as he attempts to return to Ithaca. But
the motif of a sea journey is not confined to the *Odyssey*: it is a commonplace in much of world literature (in part for naturalistic reasons), it
structures the Irish genre of the imram, which Joyce may have used (Sultan 42–48; Tristram 221 n.4; see as well the discussion in ch. 6, below),
and it is also found in *The Book of Invasions*. The invasion framework
of Irish history and the insular geography of Ireland necessitate a great
deal of journeying in Irish pseudohistory, and the Milesians in particular

36. In Joyce's work the theme of metempsychosis is extended to questions of
identity as well, and this extended form of the concept of metempsychosis is the
fundamental presupposition behind the idea of biography as narrative in *A Portrait of the Artist*, in which, as Joyce says in his sketch of the same name (Scholes
and Kain 60), "the past assuredly implies a fluid succession of presents, the development of an entity of which our actual present is a phase only." The point is
embedded in a conversation between Stephen and Cranly in *A Portrait of the Artist*, in which Stephen claims, "I was not myself as I am now, as I had to become"
(240). This aspect of metempsychosis is taken up again in *Ulysses* when Stephen
counsels himself (9.89), "Hold to the now, the here, through which all future
plunges to the past." In *Ulysses* Stephen also muses about his own personal identity under such conditions, its change and stability over time as he thinks about
a debt he owes A. E. (9.205–12):

> Wait. Five months. Molecules all change. I am other I now. Other I got
> pound.
> Buzz. Buzz.
> But I, entelechy, form of forms, am I by memory because under ever-
> changing forms.
> I that sinned and prayed and fasted.
> A child Conmee saved from pandies.
> I, I and I. I.
> A. E. I. O. U.

Bloom takes up similar thoughts, his words anticipating those of Stephen (8.608):
"I was happier then. Or was that I? Or am I now I?" Cf. 9.376–85, where Stephen
incorporates the ideas into his aesthetic argument.

On themes in *Ulysses* related to metempsychosis, including the flux of being,
see Kain, *Fabulous Voyager* ch. 14.

spend a long time in boats upon the sea. In the Irish story as in the Greek, the characters are not merely at sea; they have a goal for the journey's end, to wit, Ireland. The counterpart of that journey's goal in *Ulysses*, the ultimate goal of Bloom's travels, is 7 Eccles Street; thus, Bloom's home has both Ithaca and Ireland as its mythic counterparts.

In a symbolic sense, therefore, the journey in *Ulysses* is a journey to Ireland, and the Ireland aimed at is the New Ireland of Arthur Griffith's state as much as it is the geographical island or the old Ireland of *The Book of Invasions*. Entelechy, form of forms. The book is a sort of journey undertaken to a reincarnation of Ireland and for a reincarnation of Ireland; *Ulysses* is in part about the old Ireland becoming renewed, and the metempsychosis of Ireland is as much an operative in *Ulysses* as is the metempsychosis of mythic characters.

iv. Conclusion

Recognition of the connection between *The Book of Invasions* and the constellation of the main characters in *Ulysses* sheds light on a critical bone of contention: the level of irony and satire in *Ulysses*. Ellmann has detailed Joyce's concept of Ulysses and shown how Bloom fits these ideas: like Ulysses, Bloom is intelligent, prudent, sensitive, and of good will. His broadmindedness, love of life, curiosity, and kindliness mark him as special. Kenner speaks of Bloom as "the hidden hero" and shows that Bloom has the traits of a Homeric chieftain (Kenner, *"Ulysses"* ch. 5; cf. *JJ*2 360–64, 368–69, 371–73). Nonetheless, if *Ulysses* is seen primarily within the framework of classical myth and European symbolism, the constellation of Jewish father, Greek son, and Spanish wife is at best bizarre and at worst a travesty. If only the Homeric parallels are considered, the text can be seen as primarily satiric or mock heroic: Molly becomes "faithful Penelope with a difference," and Bloom is "a legendary hero fallen upon evil days" (Levin, *James Joyce* 68, 73). Levin notes "the Homeric overtones do contribute their note of universality . . . but in doing so they convert a realistic novel into a mock-epic" (*James Joyce*, 71).[37]

37. Cf. Kain, *Fabulous Voyager* 36–37. Note, however, the possibility that Joyce's work reflects back on the classical epic itself, suggesting that "Homer's heroes were not quite so heroic as he painted them, and that Penelope like Molly Bloom, was no better than she should be" (Mercier, *Irish Comic Tradition* 213–

However, when the characters take their place in the context of Irish pseudohistory as well as Greek myth, the constellation of the main characters is perfectly clear; indeed, it is appropriate and natural. And Molly, following in the footsteps of Tailltiu and other women in early Irish literature and myth, should not be expected to limit herself to one man. The great female figures of Irish literature are forthright in their sexuality rather than physically chaste.

Paradoxically, Joyce's use of the Irish framework from *The Book of Invasions* is part and parcel of his insistence that Ireland must be European if Ireland is to be renewed, a viewpoint that was echoed in contemporary Irish politics. In the words of Thomas Kettle, Joyce's friend, "If Ireland is to become a new Ireland she must first become European" (see *JJ*2 62–63; cf. *Exiles* 43). The import of Joyce's use of *The Book of Invasions* is that through its history of invasions Ireland has inherited the best from Egypt and Israel, Greece and the north of Europe, Belgium and Spain. Ireland's people and culture are the distillate of Europe and the Mediterranean world. In *Ulysses* this ideal is presented in a modern idiom; the Irish myth of *The Book of Invasions* is revived in the context of detailed, contemporary realism and a modern discourse. Joyce suggests the applicability of that myth to twentieth-century life: the myth is alive, universal, to be taken literally. Joyce suggests that Ireland's populace will tend toward the characteristics embodied in the main characters of *Ulysses*: Greek, Hebrew, sensual Mediterranean. Implicitly we can see Joyce's nationalistic statement—albeit a statement repugnant to most Irish nationalists. Joyce, the old Parnellite and later admirer of Griffith, puts forth a position reminiscent of both: to cease being "an unfortunate priestridden race" and to escape the straitjacket of colonial morality—British Victorianism—Ireland needed spiritual "home rule," a return to her own past and her heritage. Paradoxically, to achieve this end she could turn to a Continental outlook.

Used as it is in *Ulysses*, *The Book of Invasions* suggests that cosmopolitanism is Ireland's heritage as well as her goal—a heritage obliterated by the twin conquests of Christianity and the Sassenach. The Irish mythic parallels for *Ulysses* imply that neither an inward-turning insular men-

---

14). Mercier also suggests that Joyce may have known an account of Penelope's infidelity. See also Herring, *Joyce's "Ulysses" Notesheets* 67 n.10, and Herring, "Bedsteadfastness of Molly Bloom" 49–61. Ellmann makes a similar point (*JJ*2 360).

tality nor a stifling sexual asceticism is natural to Ireland. In holding these positions, Joyce stands apart from the studied insularity of most other Irish revival authors and their insistence that the peasantry of Ireland preserved a noble and natural moral purity that would redeem a corrupt, English-speaking world.[38] In turning to *The Book of Invasions* for his typologies of Irish character and experience, Joyce gives his perspective on the Irish literary revival: that the best of Ireland never was and never can be inward turning. Ireland must reach out beyond Ireland and beyond England to the wisdom and experience and morality of all Europe and the wider world.

Joyce had a vision for Ireland that may yet be relevant: to transcend the crabbed, insular, prejudiced, political framework; to reach out to the world; to overcome priestly, puritanical morality; to assert the artistic and the rational and the moral rather than merely the pedestrian. These desiderata might be accomplished, he says, by reasserting the Greek and the Jewish and the sensual Mediterranean elements of the Irish heritage—in other words, by the Irish owning themselves as Irish, not as Anglo-Saxons or West Britons. Irish mythic elements in *Ulysses* are part of Joyce's attempt to create "at last a conscience in the soul of this wretched race" (*Letters* 2: 311; cf. *PA* 253). In 1906 Joyce wrote to his brother Stanislaus, "If the Irish programme did not insist on the Irish language I suppose I could call myself a nationalist" (*Letters* 2: 187). *Ulysses*, written more than a decade later, is as nationalist as anything by Hyde or Gregory, Yeats or Synge: through an exploration of the Irish architectonics of his work, Joyce can be situated in the context of the Irish literary revival both in terms of his reuse of Irish literary material and in terms of the nationalist implications of his thematics.

Consonant with his aesthetic theories, Joyce does not present these views didactically. He "seeks a presentation so sharp that comment by the author would be an interference" (*JJ2* 84; cf. 60). Bloom and Molly and Stephen speak in their own voices, the voices of Ireland's traditional history and myth. It is Molly who denigrates priestly morality in favor of nature and Bloom who has compassion and a large political outlook, who hates xenophobia (the great vice of both classical literature and the Irish heroic age). Joyce does not comment on these issues in his authorial voice. Instead, he "abandons himself and his reader to the material" (*JJ2*

38. Cf. W. Thompson 10ff.

84). Art, rather than nationalist polemic, is Joyce's goal. Whatever nationalist message there is to be found in *Ulysses,* "the nation might profit
or not from his experiment, as it chose" (*JJ*2 66). By and large, Ireland
has chosen not to profit from *Ulysses.*

Joyce's method of inscribing ideology in *Ulysses* is also consonant with
the aesthetic theory that Stephen develops in *A Portrait of the Artist:* "The
feelings excited by improper art are kinetic, desire or loathing. Desire
urges us to possess, to go to something; loathing urges us to abandon, to
go from something. These are kinetic emotions. The arts which excite
them, pornographical or didactic, are therefore improper arts. The esthetic emotion . . . is therefore static. The mind is arrested and raised
above desire and loathing" (205). Encoding archetypal perceptions about
culture and humanity that transcend the views of any particular age, mythos is one of the stable or, we might say, static aspects of culture; a
mythic poetics such as that used by Joyce is therefore a static poetics.
Through his mythic architectonics and his reanimation (or reincarnation)
of mythos, particularly Irish mythos, Joyce offers his observations about
Ireland; he does not engage in polemics calculated to incite the kinetic
emotions of desire or loathing, and his art becomes neither pornographic
nor didactic. It is ideological nonetheless, for the mind is seized, arrested,
by eternal verities about Ireland, its people, its ideals. The mythic structures *predicate* features about Ireland and, in fact, life in general; the linguistic (and mythic) mode of predication is static, but the predicates in
turn have implications in the historical and political context in which
Joyce writes. Joyce leaves the working out of these implications to the
reader; it is not the artist's role to frame a (kinetic) program of action,
though he may provide the rationale for the same.[39]

After Joyce's death, his brother Stanislaus recollected Joyce's methods
of literary creation (*Recollections of James Joyce* 19): "In all Joyce's work,
the architectonic plan is dominant. He did not set to work until he had
the plan clearly in mind."[40] The architectonic structure of *Ulysses* has
been perceived primarily in terms of its Homeric parallels and secondarily

---

39. For other aspects of Joyce's politics, the ideological aspects of *Ulysses,* and
the interaction of Joyce's politics and aesthetics, see Manganiello and Ellmann,
Consciousness of Joyce 73–95.

40. In part Stanislaus describes his brother this way as a counter to Matthew
Arnold's claim that the Celt has no patience for architectonics in art ("On the
Study of Celtic Literature" 345).

in terms of *Hamlet*. But Stanislaus Joyce, who was more versed in Irish tradition than were most of his brother's Continental companions, wrote of *Ulysses* in 1941, "Whoever studies it in detail will find that a number of generations of Irish history have been superimposed one on another" (*Recollections of James Joyce* 19). This is an almost perfect description of the ways in which elements from *The Book of Invasions* and the mythic theme of reincarnation have been intertwined in *Ulysses*.

An architectonic structure is the work of an *architecton*, a "master builder." Structures, buildings, towers are recurring images in Joyce's work. In *Finnegans Wake* a controlling metaphor is the Tower of Babel (Stewart 201–2), and in *Ulysses* we also find the recurrent image of the tower. On the surface of the text there are the Martello tower in which Stephen and Mulligan live, O'Hara's tower in Gibraltar (under whose shadow Molly and Mulvey dally), and the towering hill of Howth. In the mythic substructure there are the Tower of Babel that the Goidels help construct, as well as the pharos in Spain from which Ireland is sighted. The inhabitants of the Dublin in *Ulysses* are preoccupied with towers: from the tower climbed by the two Dublin vestals out to see the sights of Dublin—a tower they fear will fall but that affords a sight of the (sterile) promised land dominated by the onehandled adulterer (7.918–1075)—to the tower of sand built by those terrors of the beach, Tommy and Jacky Caffrey (13.40ff.). These towers are symbolic correlates of the verbal Tower of Babel that Joyce creates in *Ulysses* by conjoining, conflating, and compressing disparate mythic systems and literary traditions. As a Babel of mythic structures from different linguistic sources, *Ulysses* anticipates the construction of *Finnegans Wake*. Like his Goidelic ancestors in *The Book of Invasions*, Joyce became a master builder, dedicated to the fusion of languages and cultures, myths and literary systems, and the unification of diverse human experience, following blueprints that he created himself.

Chapter 3

Irish Nationalism
and *Ulysses* as Epic

JOYCE: I have only one request to make of *you*—

CARR: And I have only one request to make of *you*—
why for God's sake cannot you contrive just once to wear
the jacket that is suggested by your trousers??
(It is indeed the case that JOYCE *is now wearing the other*
halves of the outfit he wore in Act One.)

Tom Stoppard, Travesties

The Irish literary revival was haunted by the desire for a national epic. From *Ulysses* we see that this was a pressing issue in 1904; in the scene in the National Library literary discussion turns to the very topic, and Mr Best remarks: "Our national epic has yet to be written, Dr Sigerson says. Moore is the man for it" (9.309–10). There had been a number of attempts and experiments with epic form among the revivalists, including refractions of early Irish epics such as Aubrey De Vere's *Foray of Queen Maeve*, which appeared in 1882. The desire for a national epic had also motivated translators of early Irish literature; this impetus culminated in Mary Hutton's 1907 translation entitled *The Táin*, a 495-page version of *Táin Bó Cúailnge* and associated tales in blank verse, complete with Homeric epithets, formulaic phrases, and formal division into "books."[1] De-

1. The thirst for a Celtic epic is also shown in James Macpherson's interpretations of the extant Scottish ballads as fragments of a lost early epic; his own extended "epic" productions were molded by these genre ideals. On these and related points, see Tymoczko, "Strategies."

spite these efforts, Sigerson's comment that the Irish national epic had yet to be written implies that all previous attempts had in some way failed to meet the goal, either for formal reasons or for reasons of quality. Sigerson's statement also suggests that a national epic was not to be found in early Irish literature: the medieval heritage was not perceived as including an epic that the nation could compare to the *Iliad*, the *Aeneid*, or even *Beowulf*. Thus the task remained for the modern age.

What would it have meant to write the Irish national epic at the time of the Irish literary revival? For the nationalists—as for ourselves—*epic* was a value-laden term, a valorizing approbation as much as it was the name of a literary genre. The *Oxford English Dictionary* gives the following definition: "Pertaining to that species of poetical composition . . . represented typically by the Iliad and Odyssey, which celebrates in the form of a continuous narrative the achievements of one or more heroic personages of history or tradition." This definition presupposes as a standard the classical tradition of long verse narrative, elevated and weighty in tone, heroic in content. Though the definition is based on classical epics, as medieval literature was explored and reabsorbed in the nineteenth century, the canon of celebrated epics was extended to include heroic verse tales such as *Beowulf*, *The Song of Roland*, and the *Nibelungenlied*, which came to be seen as the cornerstones of their respective national literary traditions. The *OED* continues: "The typical epics, the Homeric poems, the Nibelungenlied, etc., have often been regarded as embodying a nation's conception of its own past history, or of the events in that history which it finds most worthy of remembrance. Hence by some writers the phrase *national epic* has been applied to any imaginative work (whatever its form) which is considered to fulfill this function." Irish nationalists not surprisingly desired such an epic—either medieval or modern—for the prestige it would confer on their national literature and for the centering of the literary tradition it would provide both at home and abroad.

Early Irish literature was seen as wanting in a national epic in part because of its form. Although the topic is complex, it can be noted briefly that early Irish hero tales are generally short and they are grouped in cycles. Thus most of the Irish tales do not meet the minimal definition of epic as being composed of continuous narrative; where long narrative exists, as in *Táin Bó Cúailnge*, it is almost always demonstrably pastiche. Irish heroic literature, moreover, is not in narrative verse; the narrative line is carried in prose, with (typically) several varieties of prose textures within an individual work. Short poetic passages (usually of short-line verse of several formal types) are inset into the prose. The content of Irish hero tale—often scatological or pornographic, grotesque or paltry—was equally problematic for the literary revival. *Táin Bó Cúailnge*, about a cattle rustlers' raid on an adjacent tribe in Ireland, stands as a notable example: far from recording a noble or dignified enterprise, the story involves grotesque and scatological descriptions of battle, adultery, and pandering. Moreover, since the sympathies in *Táin Bó Cúailnge* are with Ulster as it is invaded by the other four provinces of Ireland, the enemy is referred to as "the men of Ireland"; the story is therefore virtually worthless as the raw material for an Irish national epic of a conventional sort. Finally, the highly variable tone of Irish heroic literature, mixing the heroic or the exalted with grotesque or macabre humor and hyperbole, presents difficulties.

The problems of adapting the early material were so severe that the process of translating the early texts was inhibited, and the early material was reclaimed in severely circumscribed ways (Tymoczko, "Strategies"; "Translating the Old Irish Epic"; "Translating the Humour"). Many stories were simply suppressed or radically abridged in translation; when sagas were translated, elements of the contents were expurgated or the form assimilated to established genres such as verse epic or folktale. Humorous sagas fared least well; they were either repudiated or eliminated from the translation record altogether. Largely for these reasons, *Táin Bó Cúailnge* was not translated in its entirety into English until 1976, more than seventy years after a full German translation appeared. Thus, not only was early Irish hero tale difficult to present as a national epic in its own right, but it also offered very poor models for those who would write modern Irish epics because it did not present a native Irish poetics that could be received into the European canon and embraced by the modern age. Revivalists could neither reuse the content nor write "in the style of" the early material without colliding with the dominant poetics and canons of Western literature as a whole and of English literature in particular. Sigerson's call went unanswered because of the problematic nature of writing a modern epic in a tradition where no regulation epics had existed, where there was neither dominant Western epic form nor epic style. Sigerson's challenge presented a double bind: to write to meet the received definition of epic was to give up the game and repudiate the national tradition; to write within the national tradition was to produce a work that would not meet the criteria of epic or command the respect of international audiences.

Whatever their professed stand on the need for a national literature or on Irish nationalism, the Anglo-Irish writers of the Irish literary revival were in the main committed to an English poetics. English poetics had formed their literary sensibilities as English speakers and as people educated in an English educational system. In their works they employ English genres, English prosody, and English standards of narrative. Anglo-Irish precursors of the Irish revival such as Ferguson write in the style of Tennyson, Yeats begins as a nineteenth-century English romantic, and many of the principal writers of the revival use drama, not a native Irish genre at all, as their main form. English poetics determines both the form of original writings and the form of literary translations. Despite the surface concern with Irish subject matter, formally the Anglo-Irish literary revival is a branch of English literature, and the Anglo-Irish writers show themselves to be West Britons in their poetics.

The interest of the Irish literary revival in a national epic and the question of Anglo-Irish poetics are obviously germane to Joyce's choice of form in *Ulysses*. *Ulysses* has often been hailed as a modern epic, a determination invited both by its title and by the Homeric parallels that Joyce judiciously disseminated. Yet I suggest that if one were to have sat down to write the *Irish* national epic in English at the turn of this century, transposing an Irish poetics and content into English, it would have come out rather like *Ulysses*. It would have involved a compromise between established European guidelines for the genre and native formal principles for hero tale. The content would have balanced Irish themes, perspectives, plotting, and tone with those sanctioned by classical models. Joyce's *Ulysses* can be seen as his solution to these problems. In this chapter I sketch out several ways in which *Ulysses* is an epic reflecting Irish poetics, with the argument concentrating on three principal features of *Ulysses*: the gaps in the narrative, the stylistic variation, and the comic elements.

i. Moving down the cycles: *Ulysses* and the discontinuous narrative of Irish oral tradition

Like canonical epics, *Ulysses* is long and weighty (two pounds, eight ounces in the Gabler reading edition), but unlike traditional or canonical epics, it is composed of episodes rather than continuous narrative, each of which claims approximately one hour of June 16, 1904.[2] Joyce stressed the episodic structure of his narrative in his references to *Ulysses*, naming the chapters and writing to Carlo Linati, "Each adventure is so to say one person" (*Letters* 1: 147). Of the names of the episodes Hugh Kenner has written, "Their usefulness points up one of the salient peculiarities of *Ulysses*: the identity each of its eighteen episodes assumes, by contrast with the relatively anonymous chapters of normal novels. 'Episode,' a word Joyce used consistently, suggests something more bounded than a chapter" (*"Ulysses"* 23). The episodes are separated by significant gaps in which things vital to an understanding of the day's events are left unspoken. Transitions are not supplied between the episodes; we have the narrative equivalent of the cut rather than the dissolve (Kenner, *"Ulysses"* 15) as we move from discrete episode to discrete episode.

There are, moreover, other gaps in the narrative as well, and about these hiatuses or skips Kenner comments: "There is much that the Blooms do not say to each other, much also that the book does not offer to say to us. Pondering such instances, we may learn how largely *Ulysses* is a book of silences despite its din of specifying, and may notice how eloquent is the Blooms' rhetoric of avoidance and also the author's. Some of the most moving things the book has to say are things never said" (*"Ulysses"* 48). Kenner cites as an example the gap during which Molly and Leopold discuss their plans for the day (*"Ulysses"* 48–49; cf. Kenner, "Rhetoric of Silence"); during this hiatus Molly tells the time when Boylan will come to visit her and Leopold says he will be out in the evening, seeing *Leah* at the Gaiety. Later allusions to the conversation tell the reader it has happened, but the event itself is omitted from the narrative. Leopold thinks to himself as the funeral cortege makes its way through Dublin:

Could I go to see *Leah* tonight, I wonder. I said I. Or the *Lily of Killarney?* Elster Grimes Opera Company. Big powerful change. Wet bright bills for next

---

2. Joyce distributed Homeric schemata to Carlo Linati in 1920 and Valéry Larbaud in 1921, among others, indicating the time occupied by each episode as well as the classical mythic parallels signaled by the titles of the episodes (Ellmann, *JJ*2 519–21; Kenner, *"Ulysses"* 23–25). For a comparison of these schemata, see Ellmann, *Ulysses on the Liffey* appendix. Kenner, *"Ulysses"* 24, describes each episode as a "space-time block of words."

week. *Fun on the Bristol*. Martin Cunningham could work a pass for the Gaiety. Have to stand a drink or two. As broad as it's long.

He's coming in the afternoon. Her songs. (6.184–90)

The time at which Boylan will come is made clear for the reader in "Sirens," where Bloom thinks to himself, "At four, she said" (11.188). The gap is intentional; Joyce knows what has transpired, taking care to alert the reader as well, and yet omits the material. As Kenner observes, "The text has details to sustain our sense of the probable. Joyce clearly did think out such a scene, and very pointedly did not write it" (*"Ulysses"* 48).

The conversation between Molly and Bloom occurs within an episode, but there is a similar gap between episodes 12 and 13 in which Bloom and some of the other mourners pay their respects to Paddy Dignam's widow, leaving her a monetary gift; again the event itself is omitted from the narrative, but it is both anticipated and recollected by Bloom. It is this errand that sets the meeting place between Bloom, Martin Cunningham, Jack Power, and Crofton at Barney Kiernan's Pub; and it is while waiting for them that Bloom has his confrontation with the Citizen. On the beach afterward, Bloom refers back to the visit lightly as he recollects his day: "Long day I've had. Martha, the bath, funeral, house of Keyes, museum with those goddesses, Dedalus' song. Then that bawler in Barney Kiernan's. Got my own back there. . . . But Dignam's put the boots on it. Houses of mourning so depressing because you never know. Anyhow she wants the money" (13.1214–27). Again Kenner points out that the narrative gap is artistically contrived by Joyce and the events deliberately effaced: "By featuring this errand a little more, both before and after it happened, Joyce could have made easier not only the reader's lot but also his own; he wouldn't have had to contrive subsidiary links—Joe Hynes's money, Nannetti's errand to London—to give 'Cyclops' some look of entrainment with the rest of the book" (*"Ulysses"* 102).[3]

In some ways it is difficult to approach these features of *Ulysses* anew because critical analysis of the gaps and the episodic structure of *Ulysses*

---

3. See Kenner's discussion of the psychological undertones of this errand for Bloom (*"Ulysses"* 102–3). A whole series of gaps is correlated with the characters' use of the Dublin tram system; see the examples in Hart and Knuth 18, 24–38; cf. Kenner, *"Ulysses"* 14–15.

has shaped contemporary views of narrative itself and much of contemporary narratology. The gaps have resulted in theories about the unspoken elements of a text and certain features of reader reception theory.[4] The gaps and narrative silences in *Ulysses* are seen as characteristically Joycean, and critics have demonstrated that they have a variety of functions in the narrative.

The sources to which these features of *Ulysses* are attributed are varied. Kenner, for example, connects the episodic structure of *Ulysses* and Joyce's conception of the episodes as "adventures" with the organization of Charles Lamb's *Adventures of Ulysses*, a refraction of the *Odyssey* known to Joyce from his boyhood. Lamb's chronological and episodic version is organized around Ulysses's adventures, features that Kenner sees as decisive for Joyce's narrative: "Encountered by Joyce at twelve, this version so impressed itself on his exceptional memory that he seems to have read versions of the Greek text as though they were expansions and rearrangements of Lamb. When he planned *Ulysses* the 'adventure' was his unit, and the core of the book consists of twelve episodes in chronological order, each based on one adventure, each independently elaborated and bounded" (*"Ulysses"* 23–24).[5] Although it may be true that Lamb influenced Joyce's treatment of the Homeric parallels, it is disingenuous to maintain that Lamb is the driving influence on the formal organization of Joyce's narrative. Lamb omits the Telemachia and the descent to Hades (cf. Kenner, *"Ulysses"* 24), and since Joyce restored those elements of Homer's epic, it is clear that he was not strangled by Lamb's narrative arrangement in his own formal treatment of the myth.[6]

The gaps and the episodic structure of *Ulysses* link Joyce's epic more to the episodic composition of the cycles of Irish heroic literature than to the structure of other classical or medieval heroic texts. However much Joyce might have been influenced by Lamb's *Adventures of Ulysses*, it is inconceivable that he should have failed to appreciate the formal alternatives embodied in Irish heroic literature on the one hand and in classical epic on the other, and that he should have failed to be aware that in choosing an episodic structure with the types of gaps *Ulysses* presents,

---

4. See, for example, Kenner, *"Ulysses"*; Iser chs. 7 and 8; Schutte and Steinberg 160.
5. Cf. Litz, *Art of James Joyce* 1.
6. Gilbert avoids the issue entirely by claiming that "the structure of [*Ulysses*] as a whole is, like that of all epic narratives, episodic" (3).

he was choosing to write in the form of Irish hero tale. Though it would be simplistic to look at the episodic structure and the gaps in *Ulysses* solely from the perspective of influence theory, in order to understand adequately the many levels on which the episodic structure and the narrative gaps function, it is essential to realize that in *Ulysses* they are an aspect of the intertextuality between Joyce's narrative and Irish hero tale.

Irish hero literature is organized into "cycles" of relatively short, discrete narratives; bridges between the stories generally do not exist, and it is often difficult even to establish chronological relations between many of the tales. *Serglige Con Culainn* (*The Sickbed of CuChulainn*), the source of Yeats's *Only Jealousy of Emer*, offers an example of the difficulty of integrating stories chronologically with others; in the story CuChulainn lies abed for a year of his life after being wounded by women from the otherworld:

"Wilt thou not be carried to Dun Delgan, thy stronghold, to seek for Emer?" said Loeg.

"Nay," said [CuChulainn], "my word is for Tete Brecc"; and thereon they bore him from that place, and he was in Tete Brecc until the end of one year, and during all that time he had speech with no one. (*AIT* 179)

Where does this story fit in the narrative of the early Irish Ulster Cycle? During which year of his life was CuChulainn intended to be imagined as in bed silent? Nowhere is there a medieval synchronism telling us how to fit this episode into the progression of CuChulainn's life. It is left to the individual members of the audience—if they are so inclined—to integrate this material with the other narrative episodes of the cycle and to reconcile the events of the various stories into a coherent chronology.[7]

---

7. The problems of chronology in the early Irish texts apparently did at times trouble some of the medieval readers of the manuscripts, for, though they may be later scribal accretions, in some medieval texts there are synchronisms, attempting to establish the chronology of the different episodes of the heroic cycle. In the case of *Loinges Mac nUislenn* (*The Exile of the Sons of Uisliu*), we are offered a synchronism after Fergus and the Ulstermen go in exile: "To the Ulstermen the exiles showed no love: three thousand stout men went with them; and for sixteen years never did they allow cries of lamentation and of fear among the Ulstermen to cease: each night their vengeful forays caused men to quake and to wail" (*AIT* 245). This passage is intended to reconcile the fact that Fergus is at once foster father of CuChulainn and yet part of Medb's forces when CuChulainn opposes the Ulster exiles at the age of seventeen: it is an attempt to mesh the action in *Compert Con Culainn* (*The Birth of CuChulainn*) and *The Exile of the Sons of Uisliu*, an older story that was being integrated to the CuChulainn form of the

Typically each early Irish story gives a single perspective on the heroes, one that may vary in significant ways from those of other sagas. There is, for example, a difficulty in reconciling the dominant form of the Ulster Cycle in which CuChulainn is chief hero with *Scéla Mucce Meic Dathó* (*The Story of Mac Datho's Pig*), where Conall Cernach is the main champion of Ulster and there is no reference to CuChulainn. At other times there are outright inconsistencies between texts, for example, in the genealogy and birth tale of the Ulster king Conchobor or in the generational level of the sons of Uisliu.[8] Characters may also be presented with fundamentally different characterizations; thus, Conchobor is generally a noble, just king, but in *The Exile of the Sons of Uisliu* he is treacherous, lying, jealous, and tyrannical. Examples such as these could be multiplied from every cycle of early Irish literature.

In early Irish literature the variations in perspective, the absence of chronological integration, and the inconsistencies embedded in the texts reflect the fact that the medieval texts derive from an oral literary tradition; they derive from temporal and geographical multiforms of the cycles and of the stories, variations typical of oral literature that have been recorded in the medieval manuscripts. The inconsistencies may have been tolerated by the medieval learned classes because the manuscripts were intended as compendia of lore, perhaps reflecting the range of variants that could be used as the learned classes saw fit in different political or cultural contexts. But thus fixed, the material has survived for posterity as "texts"; as a consequence, modern readers of Irish hero tales must relate, integrate, and in some cases reconcile the various traditions preserved and the various facets of the heroes revealed in individual stories.

In medieval Irish literature, as in oral traditional literatures in general, every creation of a story is a re-creation; every telling of a tale is metonymic of the tradition as a whole.[9] Oral traditional tales are not self-contained in the way that written stories typically are, and they presuppose that the audience is familiar with the content and form of the literature; this is what

---

Ulster Cycle. For an early discussion of the variant texts of *The Birth of Cu-Chulainn*, see Nutt, *Celtic Doctrine of Re-birth* 39–47; on the synchronism of *The Exile of the Sons of Uisliu* with the CuChulainn form of the Ulster Cycle, see Tymoczko, "Animal Imagery" 159–60.

8. On some aspects of the inconsistent versions of Conchobor's genealogy, see Nutt, *Celtic Doctrine of Re-birth* 72–74; Tymoczko, "Animal Imagery" 154–55, discusses the generational variation in the presentation of the sons of Uisliu.

9. On these aspects of oral literature, see, for example, Lord and Foley 193ff.

"traditional literature" is by definition. An oral traditional literature like Irish literature presupposes an audience that understands both the cultural context from which the tale grows and the metonymic nature of any given oral performance. That early Irish literature grows out of such a context is revealed in part by the presence of many unspoken assumptions behind the texts—for example, that the audience understands the relationship between this world and the otherworld, that the audience knows the tribal and genealogical matrix into which characters fit, that the audience will understand the economic basis of the culture and the forms of the honor culture, or that the audience knows the narrative framework of the cycle in which the individual tale takes its place.

The result is another notable feature of early Irish literature: the quantity of material that is introduced but not explained, material that gives the stories a somewhat cryptic quality to the uninitiated modern reader. In *Aided Óenfir Aife* (*The Death of Aife's Only Son*), for example, CuChulainn's son dies and in his honor the Ulstermen keep the calves from their mothers for three days: "Then his cry of lament was raised, his grave made, his stone set up, and to the end of three days no calf was let to their cows by the men of Ulster, to commemorate him" (*AIT* 175). This ending is metaphorically apt as a conclusion to a story about the failure of a boy to reach his parent and receive nurture from his tribe, but the audience must understand that early Irish culture is a cow culture, that wealth is measured in terms of herds, that the Ulstermen are putting in jeopardy what they hold dearest, and that unmilked cows and hungry calves set up a bawling that will serve as a suitable keening for the dead lad. When in *Echtra Nerai* (*The Adventures of Nera*), Nera enters the otherworld on Samain (Halloween) and returns bearing primrose and garlic and golden fern (*AIT* 251), the audience is to understand that time in the otherworld is inverted with respect to this world: winter here is summer there. Nera can therefore prove he has been to the otherworld by returning to his people with summer fruits. Every tale has such intrusive elements, elements that are introduced but not explained, because the traditional audience understood the presumptions and explanation would have been superfluous.[10]

10. Unfortunately, such presumptions are seldom identified in the notes accompanying modern editions and translations aimed at general audiences who do not understand the presuppositions of the texts.

All of these features of early Irish literature cause difficulties for modern readers, and they were particularly problematic for the Irish cultural nationalists who attempted to reclaim early Irish literature in the nineteenth and early twentieth centuries. In English translations of the Ulster Cycle and also in Anglo-Irish retellings of the materials, authors and translators struggle with all these generic and textual features. Early adaptations, retellings, and translations attempt to reconcile the inconsistencies, to establish synchronisms, to establish a uniform perspective, to provide transitions, to fill gaps in the narrative of the Ulster Cycle, and to explain (or explain away) the unfamiliar content. Links between stories are supplied, transitions invented, chronological order and consistency established, a uniform perspective imposed, objectionable material suppressed, and canonical epic form imposed, with the result that such refractions are much closer to traditional European epic narratives (and further from Joyce) than are the early Irish originals.[11]

Despite all these difficulties, the Irish literary revival privileged and romanticized early Irish literature. Joyce reflects the atmosphere of the time and simultaneously treats the attitudes ironically in *A Portrait of the Artist*, where Davin is described as having learned Irish stories in his youth from oral tradition: "His nurse had taught him Irish and shaped his rude imagination by the broken lights of Irish myth. He stood towards this myth upon which no individual mind had ever drawn out a line of beauty

---

11. Standish O'Grady, a seminal figure in the adaptation of Irish literature to English poetics, begins the process of integrating the narrative material of the Ulster Cycle. In the second volume of his *History of Ireland*, for example, he retells *Táin Bó Cúailnge* and other early tales in a style that has elements of nineteenth-century retellings of romances: the Ulster heroes are described as knights, supernatural elements (at times with Christian overtones) are added, and the whole is told in a pseudo-archaizing language in the lineage of William Morris's medieval publications. At the same time, a novel-driven aesthetic is apparent: O'Grady adds to his narrative internal states, feelings, and motivations where the Irish texts, like most medieval stories, are eloquently silent; circumstantial detail, rationalization, and sequential ordering suggest nineteenth-century realism; added dialogue gives a nineteenth-century balance between the narrator's voice and other textual elements; and so on. Augusta Gregory also works along these lines in *Cuchulain of Muirthemne* when she eliminates the episodic structure of the medieval narratives, synchronizes the chronology of the early stories to suggest a consistent cycle, translates the poetry as prose, normalizes the style to folk narrative, and eliminates the senchas. Both authors remove sexual and grotesque elements that would offend late Victorian taste and screen out most of the humor. In their versions of the tales the main characters are presented almost uniformly as seemly and noble, whereas the early texts have a problematic heroic.

and to its unwieldy tales that divided themselves as they moved down the cycles in the same attitude as towards the Roman catholic religion, the attitude of a dullwitted loyal serf" (181). Kelleher reminds us that this is a romantic account, since by the nineteenth century the medieval tales were known primarily through scholarly publications or through a few popular retellings to which no Irish nurse would have had access ("Irish History" 419–20). What we can glean from the passage is that Joyce knew enough about early Irish narrative to know that it comprised discrete tales organized into cycles and to characterize its narrative texture as unwieldy—an apt description (from the perspective of modern English poetics) for tales that present modern readers with the problems just discussed. Joyce's characterization of early Irish literature in *A Portrait* suggests that the episodic yet cyclical structure of *Ulysses* refers back in part to the early Irish narrative tradition and that some of the "unwieldy" features of the narrative of *Ulysses* likewise have antecedents in the literary tradition of Ireland.

The inconsistencies and the variations in perspective found in early Irish literature are, for example, related to features of *Ulysses* that have been discussed in the critical literature. Each of Bloom's adventures in the chapters of *Ulysses* offers a variant perspective on the hero and the action, and these variants have a variety of aspects. At times there is a sort of parallax, the doubling of reference to the same events as perceived by different characters (Kenner, *"Ulysses"* 75–82); at other times the variation in perspective is a function of the diversity of style (Iser 179–95). Variation also results from the mythic functions assigned to characters; Kenner has observed that characters change their Homeric roles when passing between "playlets" (*"Ulysses"* 27); accordingly, the perspective on Molly shifts as she changes from Calypso to Penelope. Whatever the reasons for the shifts in perspective, the narrative texture of *Ulysses* presents in this regard analogues to the oral variants and variation in perspective of the early Irish heroic tales.

Using these means, Joyce invites us to reconsider perspective as a determinant of the definition of reality, a point that Wolfgang Iser makes in his discussion of the emergence of the character of Bloom in "Circe":

The figure of Bloom becomes ever more dominant. And this figure is shown from a variety of quite astonishing angles. . . . What Bloom is seems to depend on the perspective from which he is viewed, and his mirror image depends on his environment at the time. It is not surprising then that in the

course of the night Bloom becomes Lord Mayor of Dublin and, indeed, the
illustrious hero of the whole nation. . . . The emergence of Bloom's hidden
selves is not to be viewed as a symptom of repression, or as a way around the
censorship imposed by the superego, but rather as an attempt to realize the
potential of a character which in everyday life can never be anything more
than partially realized.

This potential becomes richer and richer with the great variety of forms
that the hitherto familiar character of Bloom adopts. And, conversely, if one
wished to identify the Bloom of everyday life, one would be obliged more and
more to pare down this rich virtual character. The everyday Bloom is merely
a collection of individual moments in the course of his life—a collection
which is infinitely smaller than that of the unlimited possibilities of the Bloom
that might be.

. . . Whatever Bloom reveals of himself is revealed because he is in a particular situation; the forms of his character arise out of changing contexts of
life, and so each form is bound to a particular perspective—indeed, this is
the only way in which the potential can be realized. (216–17)

These functions of the variation in perspective invite still another comparison with the type of variation exhibited in the oral multiforms of
early Irish literature. Iser is suggesting that each realization of Bloom is
metonymic of the virtual Bloom, a point not unrelated to John Foley's
suggestion that each realization of an oral tale is metonymic of the virtual
oral tradition.[12] The relationship of the part to the whole that we grasp
in Joyce's method of characterization is not unlike that of oral tradition.

Related to the gaps, the narrative hiatuses, and the implicit assumptions in early Irish literature is also a feature of *Ulysses* that Richard Ellmann has termed "the blurred margin": "Joyce's surface naturalism in
Ulysses has many intricate supports, and one of the most interesting is
the blurred margin. He introduces much material which he does not in-

12. See, for example, 192–93, where Foley discusses the function of the stock
epithet: "The aspect named could be taken as a symbol sufficiently active to evoke
not a partial characterization but rather the totality of a character's identity—
pars pro toto, as it were. Since we know that a hero achieves his traditional identity . . . by the accumulation of his actions or deeds, so that mention of a single
adventure can bring to life the entirety of a hero's accomplishments, why could
not a single attribute command as its referent not a single idiosyncrasy but a
whole personality complete with its mythical history? . . . This diction is explo-
sively dynamic; . . . the seemingly humble phrase accesses whole worlds of reference. . . . All these and more can be called up into the narrative present merely
by plugging into the traditional association of ideas, a network built up over generations."

tend to explain, so that his book, like life, gives the impression of having many threads that one cannot follow" (*JJ2* 377). Richard M. Kain elaborates on the same feature, seeing *Ulysses* as

an immense structure containing allusive trifles, loose ends, errors intentional and accidental—in short, a magnificent but flawed creation . . . like life itself. . . . Almost every event has its penumbra of details, partially recognized or unknown, whether on the naturalistic or symbolic levels, or . . . on both levels simultaneously. Thus it matters little that the book can never be fully comprehended, for the very infinitude of motifs and allusions creates an atmosphere of significances. ("Motif as Meaning" 75–76)

From the point of reader reception, these unexplained materials in *Ulysses* are not unlike the implicit presuppositions of early Irish narrative— the assumption of knowledge of the accepted belief system, the historical scaffolding, the economic substratum of the narrative, and so forth—discussed above. The unexplained assumptions in the early texts also create a sort of "blurred margin," evoking a similar response in the modern reader though originating in a vastly different poetics. This aspect of Joyce's narrative is related to his inclusion of lore of all sorts (a point discussed in chapter 5), and it is a feature that Gilbert (probably at Joyce's behest) has connected with the practices of the Irish poets:

It is interesting to note that the Irish sagas came, at an early stage, to be written in *prose*; such orally preserved prose sagas were recited by the *file* or professional minstrels in Ireland as early as the seventh century. . . . These prose narratives were "detailed and elaborate," and the minstrels of the period must have possessed remarkable powers of memory, far exceeding those necessary for the reciters of epic poems. It is significant that *Ulysses* is both detailed and elaborate in its narration of facts and its numerous historical and literary echoes. Like his predecessors Joyce was gifted with a prodigious memory, and had none of the modern aversion from elaboration and a detailed treatment of narrative. (70–71)

In *Ulysses* Joyce recapitulates the episodic organization of Irish tales into cycles with his gappy narrative, and he provides a blurred margin in *Ulysses* parallel to the knowledge assumed of a traditional Irish audience. Though these features in *Ulysses* grow out of radically different artistic purposes and function in radically different ways from similar features of Irish hero tale, nonetheless the narrative texture of *Ulysses* is remarkably akin to the early texts, having both analogues and antecedents in early

Irish literature to important Joycean narrative techniques. Joyce exploits these features in his narrative for various purposes, including the restructuring of the novel and expression of the twentieth-century interest in perspective and style. At the same time in his narrative method Joyce looks backward to early Irish narrative tradition.

Iser, writing about gaps in Henry Fielding's narrative, observes, "The gaps, indeed, are those very points at which the reader can enter into the text, forming his own connections and so creating the configurative meaning of what he is reading" (40). To twentieth-century readers of early Irish literature, the gaps, the variation in perspective, the inconsistencies, and the unexplained background knowledge at times are all still troublesome, yet they may also be seen as opportunities and challenges to enter into the texts, to create configurative meaning. These were invitations that most of Joyce's contemporaries shirked. The gappy structure of early Irish narrative cycles and the reader response required to approach this oral literature present similar challenges to the challenges of *Ulysses*. Because many of the distinctive qualities of early Irish narrative result from the oral base of the tales, it is possible that Joyce was sensitized to such narrative possibilities by his own position in a living, if attenuated, Irish storytelling tradition and his own literary relation with his father. But we may also speculate that some of Joyce's techniques in *Ulysses* were engendered in part by his own attempts to make configurative meaning of the unfamiliar narrative texture of medieval Irish literature and his own reader response to the early narrative of his native tradition.

ii. Stylistic variation in *Ulysses*:
Prose modes and poetic structures

Joyce's attachment to the stylistic experimentation and diversity of *Ulysses* is well known. In 1921 he wrote to Harriet Weaver, "The task I set myself technically in writing a book from eighteen different points of view and in as many styles, all apparently unknown or undiscovered by my fellow tradesmen, that and the nature of the legend chosen would be enough to upset anyone's mental balance" (*Letters* 1: 167). His stylistic variation met with strong negative reactions from Pound and others as he was writing *Ulysses*, and Pound wrote after the receipt of "Sirens," "A new style per chapter not required." Joyce nonetheless persevered with his intentions (cf. *JJ*2 459–62, 471), and he wrote to Miss Weaver: "I understand that you may begin to regard the various styles of the episodes with dismay and prefer the initial style much as the wanderer did who longed for the rock of Ithaca. But in the compass of one day to compress all these wanderings and clothe them in the form of this day is for me only possible by such variation which, I beg you to believe, is not capricious" (*Letters* 1: 129).

Many critics have discussed aspects of the narrative complexity that result from the stylistic variation in *Ulysses*, and some of the functions of this element of Joyce's work have been illuminated. Iser observes of "Oxen of the Sun" that

one has the impression that the different views presented by the different styles exclude rather than supplement one another. With each author [parodied], the theme takes on a different shape, but each treatment seems to assume that it is offering *the* reality. . . . By parodying the styles, Joyce has exposed their essentially manipulative character. . . . With his historical panoply of individual and period styles, Joyce exposes the characteristic quality of style—namely, that it imposes form on an essentially formless reality. . . .
    . . . While the theme of this one chapter is love, the theme of *Ulysses* itself is everyday human life, and the stylistic presentation of this varies from chapter to chapter, because it can never be grasped as a whole by any one individual style. Only by constantly varying the angle of approach is it possible to convey the potential range of the "real-life" world. (192–93, 194; cf. 200–227)

Joyce's stylistic shifts thus function to convey an essential modernist view, yet at the same time Joyce's tenacious attachment to the stylistic diversity and experimentation in *Ulysses* is explained partially by the intertextual reference it makes with the stylistic diversity of early Irish heroic narrative prose, which has as one of the most notable features stylistic variation, a variation that was at odds with the canonical form of Western epic. Insofar as Joyce was writing within the generic conventions of Irish epic, however, such stylistic variety was de rigueur, and the mixture of poetic and prose types to be found both in *Ulysses* and in early Irish texts merits special attention.

At least three types of prose can be identified in early Irish hero tales: an idiomatic and syntactically direct prose used for the narrative and the dialogue, a formulaic prose used for descriptions behind which we see the traces of oral formulaic verse (Slotkin), and an alliterative prose used for certain ornate passages. The syntactically direct prose varies in a number of parameters, including tone and register, particularly in dialogue that delineates character and establishes hierarchical relationships of the characters. The poetry includes both stanzaic rhymed verse and alliterative cadenced lines seriatim in stanzas of irregular length. Because narrative verse was not part of native Celtic poetics, poetry in the early Irish narratives is all spoken, generally taking the form of dialogue, though it may also be used for spoken prophecy, ceremonial greeting, description, and other "lyrical" purposes.[13] A celebrated example of spoken verse elements in a prose narrative occurs in the ninth-century *Exile of the Sons of Uisliu* when the unborn infant Deirdre screams out from her mother's womb at a gathering of the assembled Ulstermen.

Then they brought the woman before them, and thus spoke to her Fedlimid, her husband:

> What is that, of all cries far the fiercest,
> In thy womb raging loudly?
> Through all ears thou piercest with that clamor;
> With that scream, from sides swollen and strong:
> Of great woe, for that cry, is foreboding to my heart;
> That is torn through with terror, and sore with grief.

Then the woman turned, and she approached Cathbad the druid, for he was a man of knowledge, and thus she spoke to him:

> Give thou ear to me, Cathbad, thou fair one of face,
> Thou great crown of our honor, and royal in family;
> Let the man so exalted be set still higher,
> Let the druid draw knowledge, that druids can obtain.
> For I want words of wisdom, and none can I express;
> Nor to Fedlimid a torch of sure knowledge can stretch:
> As no wit of a woman knows what she bears,
> I know naught of that cry that sounds forth from within me.

And then said Cathbad:

> It is a maid who screamed wildly just now,
> Fair and curling locks shall flow round her,

---

13. It should be understood that in Celtic tradition as a whole verse was also used for lore (Irish *senchas*)—as a mnemonic for such things as genealogy and law. Though Celtic tradition has no epic verse, the old Indo-European epic-gnomic verse tradition is represented by such forms.

Blue-centred and stately her eyes;
And her cheeks shall grow like the foxglove.
For the tint of her skin, we commend her,
In its whiteness, newly fallen like snow;
And her teeth are faultless in splendor;
And her lips are red like coral:
A fair woman is she, for whom heroes, that fight
In their chariots for Ulster, shall be doomed to death.

(*AIT* 240)

The distribution of the poetry in the early prose narratives is generally uneven, with some tales having a great deal of poetry and others having little or none at all; even within a single tale the distribution of poetry may be very uneven. The FerDiad section of *Táin Bó Cúailnge*, for example, is almost half dialogue poetry, while in other sections of the *Táin* poetry is not to be found. At times the verse is quoted *in extenso*, but in some cases only a single line or a couplet of the poem is quoted in the medieval text. Thus, in *Aided Con Culainn* (*The Death of CuChulainn*), when CuChulainn's charioteer Loeg is mortally wounded, the text includes only the initial line of his death poem:[14]

Then Lugaid flung the spear at Cu Chulainn's chariot, and it reached the charioteer, Loeg mac Riangabra, and all his bowels came forth on the cushion of the chariot.
Then said Loeg,
"Bitterly have I been wounded," etc. [*sic*]

(*AIT* 336)

It is possible to tell when a poem in an early Irish text is quoted in full and when only a fragment of a poem is quoted because poems in Irish tradition end where they begin: they come full circle, either by repeating the entire first line, or by repeating the opening word or syllable, or by repeating the opening phoneme or phonemes. Such a closing is called a *dúnad*, 'closing, shutting; stoppage'. In the manuscripts the ending of a poem is often further delineated by the repetition in the margin or after

---

14. Scholars have assumed that such fragmentary poems were so well known that it was superfluous for the scribe to write them out in extenso, or that for some other reason in the scribe's opinion the material was not worth wasting vellum on.

the poetic text of a phrase, word, or syllable reiterating the dúnad, thus marking the poem as complete.[15]

A curious feature of the poetry in Irish hero tales is that it often does not fit smoothly in its prose context. It may be redundant with the prose, repeating the action in a different key, as it were, rather than advancing the narrative, or it may even be somewhat inconsistent with respect to the prose. In *Imram Brain maic Febail* (*The Voyage of Bran Son of Febal*), for example, a woman is reported to sing fifty quatrains to Bran, but the text gives only thirty verses (cf. *AIT* 588–91). Similarly, in *The Exile of the Sons of Uisliu* Noisi has dark hair in the prose, but in one of the final lyrics spoken by Deirdre he is described as having hair with "yellow beauty" (V. Hull 63, 67). Scholars have debated about these inconsistencies and redundancies, and it is generally agreed that the poetry is exiguous (an assessment backed up by linguistic analysis), reflecting a slightly different oral variant than that recorded in the prose. Thus, the poetry and the prose can be seen as giving two perspectives on the same tale or the same episode.

Frequently there is a sizable poem at the end of a story, sometimes taking the form of a kind of epilogue. A particularly striking example of a verse "epilogue" occurs at the end of the early version of *The Exile of the Sons of Uisliu*, in which before her death Deirdre speaks two very beautiful love poems that have a great deal of nature imagery in them:

Deirdre lived on for a year in the household of Conchobar; and during all that time she smiled not a smile of laughter, she took not her sufficiency of food or sleep, and she raised not her head from her knee. And if any one brought before her entertainers, she used to speak thus:

Though troops brave and fair to see,
    May return home and ye await them;
When Usnech's sons came home to me in Alba,
    They came more heroically.

With abundant mead my Naisi stood:
    And near our fire his bath I poured;
On Anli's stately back wood;
    On Ardan's an ox or a goodly boar.

15. For a discussion of the dúnad, see Murphy, *Early Irish Metrics* 43–45. See examples in Meyer, *Bran* 2: 285–91.

Though ye think the mead sweet
   That warlike Conchobar drinks,
I oft have known a sweeter drink,
   Often on the edge of a spring.

Our board was spread beneath the tree,
   And Naisi kindled the cooking fire;
Meat, prepared from Naisi's game
   Was more sweet to me than honey.

              (*AIT* 246)[16]

The fact that Irish hero tale consists of a mixture of several types of poetry and prose instead of the uniform poetry of canonical epics caused a great deal of interference in the perception and reception of the stories as native epic throughout the nineteenth century and into the twentieth; the record of this interference can be traced extensively in the translations of the Irish revival as well as in critical assessments of the time.[17] Initially the prose matrix of early Irish narrative was interpreted as an indication of the lateness of Irish tradition; only gradually was it realized that the mixture of prose and verse is more likely archaic, since it appears in early Sanskrit writings as well.[18] Gilbert, probably taking his cue from Joyce, presents prose as a characteristic feature of Irish narrative at an early period (70).

The intertextual links between *Ulysses* and the system of prose and poetic types in Irish heroic texts form a complex pattern. Like medieval Irish epic literature, *Ulysses* is in prose, thereby coinciding with the form of the novel. But like Irish heroic literature and unlike a more conventional form of the novel, the prose of *Ulysses* varies stylistically. Joyce does not confine himself to imitating the Irish stylistic range; instead, he

16. In the case of this story, though not in all others, there is a final paragraph of narrative prose following the poetic epilogue; nevertheless, it is the poetry that sets the tone of the end of this tale. For other examples of verse at the ends of tales, see *AIT* 48, 133, 332.

17. Various strategies were adopted by translators and critics to assimilate the Irish stylistic variation to other forms more acceptable to English poetics; Irish material was presented in translation, for example, as prosimetrum, folktale, or verse epic (Tymoczko, "Strategies"). Rarely was the form simply transposed into English, though in literal German translations such as Windisch's translation of *Táin Bó Cúailnge* the form is clear.

18. See Dillon, "Archaism of Irish Tradition" 9–10, as well as references cited there for a discussion of the archaism of Irish form.

transposes into English the Irish *principle* of stylistic variation and the incorporation of a variety of prose types, borrowing some prose types from Irish literature (as I argue in the next chapter) but extending this modality in terms of modern English prose possibilities by using newspaper prose, the developmental repertory of English styles, the "*Peg's Paper*" style of "Nausicaa," and so forth.[19]

Joyce is faithful to the form of Irish epic narrative not only in his use of various styles and types of prose but also in his insertion of poetic elements into the prose texture of *Ulysses*, thereby reproducing a number of the features of the verse in early Irish narrative. Page upon page of Joyce's text has snippets of verse—from Mulligan's doggerel,

> I hardly hear the purlieu cry
> Or a Tommy talk as I pass one by
> Before my thoughts begin to run
> On F. M'Curdy Atkinson,
> The same that had the wooden leg
> And that filibustering filibeg
> That never dared to slake his drouth,
> Magee that had the chinless mouth.
> Being afraid to marry on earth
> They masturbated for all they were worth.
>
> (9.1143–52)

and nursery rhymes, both straightforward and parodied,

> THE CHIMES
>
> Turn again, Leopold! Lord mayor of Dublin!
>
> (15.63–64)

to quotations from Yeats,

> And no more turn aside and brood
> Upon love's bitter mystery
> For Fergus rules the brazen cars.
>
> (1.239–41)

---

19. Mercier, *Irish Comic Tradition* 212; cf. Gilbert 76, who says the chapter is written in the style of *Every Girl's Magazine*. Joyce does in fact also parody certain Irish prose styles, particularly the alliterative adjectival style that became popular after the twelfth century. To be precise, he parodies the translation style of these passages, as Mercier, *Irish Comic Tradition* 212, has observed.

Songs also account for a great deal of the verse in *Ulysses*.[20] In thinking about his daughter and wife, for example, Leopold muses:

On the *Erin's King* that day round the Kish. Damned old tub pitching about. Not a bit funky. Her pale blue scarf loose in the wind with her hair.

All dimpled cheeks and curls,
Your head it simply swirls.

Seaside girls. Torn envelope. Hands stuck in his trousers' pockets, jarvey off for the day, singing. Friend of the family. *Swurls*, he says. Pier with lamps, summer evening, band.

Those girls, those girls,
Those lovely seaside girls.

(4.434–46)

Generally these poetic elements in *Ulysses* have been taken as naturalistic reflections of the role of poetry and song in Irish culture, as of course in part they are; but song and poetry have been central elements of Irish narrative for more than a millennium, and these features of Joyce's text are also links to the poetics of early Irish narrative. Because the most common word for 'poem' in early Irish is *láid*, also translated as 'song' since poetry was recited to musical accompaniment, the early Irish poems inserted into narratives are often referred to as "songs" in translations of the medieval texts; in *Ulysses* the poetry and verse found in the narrative are also often literally songs.

As mentioned above, songs and poems in the early stories are often quoted only partially or alluded to by their opening lines, and the examples of songs already quoted from *Ulysses* show that poems and songs are also seldom quoted in full in the Joycean text. Joyce's narrative is realistic in this respect, for rarely does a full poem or song pass through a person's thoughts; more typically a phrase or a few bars go through the mind. Moreover, Joyce does not need to provide his audience with the complete text because the words of popular songs and Yeatsian lyrics alike were familiar to his readers as a whole and to his Irish audience in particular. Joyce's treatment of the poetic elements is therefore analogous to the early Irish scribal practice of quoting only a line or two of many poems alluded to in the narrative, poems like the poetic elements of *Ulys-*

---

20. On the role of songs in Joyce's work, see Hodgart and Worthington, *Song*; and Z. Bowen, *Musical Allusions.*

ses that were apparently so well known or so trite that the scribe felt it unnecessary to write them out in full.

The poetic elements in *Ulysses*, like those in early Irish literature, are primarily "spoken," either in conversation or in the narrative representation of performance of songs. But in *Ulysses* the "speaking" of a poetic element may also be interiorized as part of the stream of consciousness, the inner dialogue. There is no purely narrative verse in native Irish tradition, and the role of poetry in *Ulysses* mirrors this situation in not carrying the narrative line any more than poetry does in early Irish stories.[21] The verse in *Ulysses*, however, does frequently act as a commentary on the narrative line, offering a sort of parallax view of the situation, as in M'Coy's conversation with Bloom:

— My wife too, he said. She's going to sing at a swagger affair in the Ulster Hall, Belfast, on the twentyfifth.
—That so? M'Coy said. Glad to hear that, old man. Who's getting it up?
Mrs Marion Bloom. Not up yet. Queen was in her bedroom eating bread and. No book. Blackened court cards laid along her thigh by sevens. Dark lady and fair man. Letter. Cat furry black ball. Torn strip of envelope.
Love's.
Old.
Sweet.
Song.
Comes lo-ove's old . . .
— It's a kind of a tour, don't you see, Mr Bloom said thoughtfully. *Sweeeet song.* There's a committee formed. Part shares and part profits. (5.151–63)

Here M'Coy's question "Who's getting it up?" reminds Bloom of his wife's plans to meet with Boylan that afternoon and their sexual relations, euphemized in the line "Love's old sweet song." The song comments on the action, adding to the conversation an emotional element that Bloom represses even from himself, providing a doubled perspective that is not unlike the parallax in the doubled prose and poetry in some early Irish tales.

Finally, like many early Irish stories, *Ulysses* ends with a "lyrical" coda, Molly's soliloquy, the longest poetic element in the book and the final note. Marked off from the rest of the text in the first edition by a

---

21. Z. Bowen comments "nothing in the plot or themes depends for its existence on song or musical allusion alone" (*Musical Allusions* 65).

large black dot at the end of episode 17, Molly's soliloquy was regarded by Joyce as the "clou" that finished the whole (*Letters* 1: 170) and simultaneously as a kind of epilogue (cf. *Letters* 1: 172). Like the poems that end some early Irish stories, forming a kind of poetic appendix, Molly's interior monologue sets the final tone of *Ulysses*; reminiscent of the Deirdre poems cited above, Molly's monologue celebrates past events in a lyric mode, particularly at the very close of the episode. Neither character's lyric, however, advances the plot of its respective story; instead, these lyric elements determine meaning and mood. Joyce may have structured the ending of *Ulysses* partly with such Irish analogues as models.

The Irish dúnad, the proper closing to a poem, has been discussed, and it is clear that Joyce uses such a structure to close "Penelope," ending the chapter as he began it:

Yes because he never did a thing like that before . . .
    . . . and his heart was going like mad and yes I said yes I will Yes. (18.1, 18.1608–9)

Joyce explained to Frank Budgen that this circularity mirrored Molly's identification as earth goddess and eternal woman: "*Penelope* is the clou of the book. . . . It begins and ends with the female word *yes*. It turns like the huge earth ball slowly surely and evenly round and round spinning, its four cardinal points being the female breasts, arse, womb and . . ." (*Letters* 1: 170). Although this explanation may be accepted as an intention Joyce could talk about, the circularity also gives the most poetic chapter of *Ulysses* a traditional Irish poetic close. The type of dúnad given to Molly's interior monologue is technically called *saigid*, 'attainment'; it is the most common form of ending in the Old and Middle Irish period, the linkage of beginning and ending of the poem by the reiteration of a whole word. In oral tradition such a device is mnemonic and, in conjunction with the alliteration that binds the end of one stanza to the beginning of the next, serves to preserve a poem intact and ordered. By marking Molly's soliloquy with a dúnad, Joyce emphasizes that the chapter is a lyric element, and he gives the episode poetic structuring. Joyce's correspondence indicates clearly that he was at some pains to choose the perfect word for the end of the book, and thus we have an indication that the crafting of the dúnad was of some importance to him (*Letters* 1: 169; cf. *JJ*2 712).

Though the final episode of *Ulysses* ends with the dúnad called 'attainment', a weaker sort of dúnad binds the end of the book to the beginning, forming a "poetic" whole of the entire structure of Ulysses. The book ends as it begins, on the letter and sound of s:

> Stately, plump Buck Mulligan came from the stairhead . . .
> . . . and his heart was going like mad and yes I said yes I will Yes. (1.1, 18.1609)

Joyce's ending is similar to the weakest dúnad in early Irish poetics, comindsma, 'riveting together'; in this type of dúnad the opening consonant and vowel of the first word are generally the last sounds of the poem, but occasionally only a single phoneme is repeated. Critics have noted this phonological circularity, comparing the entire book to a snake that bites its tail,[22] but the link with Irish poetics has been missed in the critical literature. By providing a dúnad for Ulysses as a whole, Joyce sets a pointe finale to his entire creation, closing the poetic world, indicating that it is fully bounded with nothing missing. Thus, to attempt to extrapolate beyond the time of the text, to speculate on the future of Molly and Leopold, whether about events of the next morning or the long-term future as some critics have done,[23] is to violate the poetic wholeness and boundedness of the Joycean world, emphasized here by the dúnad patterned on Irish poetics.[24]

Joyce's mixture of prose with poems, songs, and lyric elements of all types in Ulysses can be classed as a prosimetrum. As such, the book fits neither the form of the conventional European novel nor the mold of European epic; rather, it stands as a radical challenge to both genres. But the same mixture of formal types that differentiates Ulysses from the dominant European narrative genres links it to the dominant narrative pattern of early Irish hero tales; thus, in his basic generic typology Joyce

22. See, for example, Ellmann, Ulysses on the Liffey 162.
23. As John Henry Raleigh does at length, 244–62, both about the next day and more distant events in time.
24. The dúnad structures of the final episode of Ulysses and of the book as a whole anticipate the circularity of the prose in Finnegans Wake, but there are significant differences as well. In Finnegans Wake the circularity brings the reader back to the point of departure; nothing definitive has changed, and the book begins again. In the final episode of Ulysses, however, the final yes of the text terminates a development of Molly's thought that leaves her and the reader in a very different place from the point of departure. The same is true of the dúnad of the book as a whole; we have a sort of mystic sameness and difference, a closure and yet a mantic recognition of both similarity and difference.

affiliates his work with the early Irish tradition of heroic literature. These formal intertextual links to Irish hero tale are eloquent. If we can speak of a national spirit reflected in literary creation, then metempsychosis is as much a part of Joyce's form as it is of his content. Though *Ulysses* is in prose as Irish epics are, the Irish poetic structure of the dúnad makes *Ulysses* a kind of poem. Thus, Joyce marks *Ulysses* as the product of an Irish poet and asserts through the formal structures his own identity as a fili, the Irish poet who was equally the storyteller, an identification suggested, probably at Joyce's instigation, in Gilbert's study of *Ulysses* (70–71). Yet the poetic signals make *Ulysses* a sort of narrative poem and hence a covert analogue to the *Odyssey* and to Greek epic as a whole. Joyce conflates the structures of prose and poetry in his narrative, giving us prose with the opening and closing signals of poetry, collapsing the distinction of these two formal types in the creation of his epic, thus riveting together Greek and Irish form as he rivets together Greek and Irish myth.[25]

iii. Epic and mock epic

Though Joyce obviously enjoyed and fostered the view of his book as a modern counterpart to classical epic, he also found it an incomplete reading. He complained that people missed the humor in the work: "The pity is the public will demand and find a moral in my book, or worse they may take it in some serious way, and on the honor of a gentleman, there is not one single serious line in it" (*JJ*2 523–24). It may be doubted that there is nothing serious in *Ulysses* or that Joyce was a gentleman, but Joyce's words indicate that there is a great deal of humor in *Ulysses*.[26]

Relatively early in the critical history of *Ulysses*, the view was developed that the book was a mock epic. Harry Levin stands as an early advocate of this position: "The relation of the *Odyssey* to *Ulysses* is that of parallels that never meet. The Homeric overtones do contribute their note of universality, their range of tradition, to what might well be a triv-

---

25. Following a rather different line of argument, Litz, *Art of James Joyce* 65, comes to a similar conclusion that Joyce destroys the conventional distinctions between poetry and prose.

26. There have been many studies of the comic elements in *Ulysses*. L. Thompson, *Comic Principle*, Z. Bowen, *"Ulysses" as a Comic Novel*, and Hayman, "Forms of Folly in Joyce," offer perspectives on the comic elements that are in some ways related to the argument I am developing here.

ial and colorless tale. But in so doing, they convert a realistic novel into a mock-epic" (*James Joyce* 71; cf. 71–73). This view of *Ulysses* has formed a continuous strand of the critical response ever since. It is congenial to those who see Joyce's work growing out of the line of nineteenth-century realism and naturalism inherited from Flaubert and Zola, Ibsen and Hardy, and it fits with Joyce's desire to show the hemiplegia of Dublin in *Dubliners* (*Letters* 1: 55).[27] This interpretation, which sees Joyce as struggling with the chaos and tawdriness of modern life, follows T. S. Eliot's analysis of the purpose of Joyce's mythic method: "In using the myth, in manipulating a continuous parallel between contemporaneity and antiquity, Mr. Joyce is pursuing a method which others must pursue after him. . . . It is simply a way of controlling, of ordering, of giving a shape and a significance to the immense panorama of futility and anarchy which is contemporary history" ("*Ulysses*, Order, and Myth" 201).

These two polarities—epic and mock epic—have been perennials of critical debate and pedagogical practice regarding *Ulysses*. More recent criticism has tried to reconcile the views of *Ulysses* as both epic and mock epic—in such attempts, for example, as Kenner's analysis of Bloom as a hidden Homeric hero ("*Ulysses*" ch. 5). John Gross has also attempted to stop the quarrel by insisting that everyone is right: the two views can coexist because the book is big enough to be both epic and mock epic:

As everyone knows, Joyce partly uses the *Odyssey* to show up the unpoetic and unheroic aspects of modern life; as most readers probably come to recognize, he is equally concerned with the underlying continuities between past and present. The comparison between Bloom and Ulysses is more than a mock-heroic joke, and it cuts both ways, enhancing Bloom's dignity and reminding us that *Ulysses*, too, had his flesh-and-blood infirmities. (63)

Although this position is essentially sound, it seems to beg some questions about the genre of *Ulysses*—questions that find at least partial answers in early Irish literature.

Joyce's approach to writing an Irish epic in *Ulysses* must be understood in light of his view of comedy and his relationship to the Irish comic tradition. Joyce attributed the humor in his epic to his father, and when John Stanislaus Joyce died, the son said, "The humour of *Ulysses* is his"

27. See, for example, Wilson 150.

(*JJ*2 22). A deeper investigation of Joyce's relation to Irish tradition, however, indicates that the situation is far from this simple. Joyce never explicitly acknowledged the importance of Irish tradition as a formative element in his thought, but in *The Irish Comic Tradition* Vivian Mercier has linked Joyce's practice to the Irish tradition of parody, a major comic form fully established in Ireland by the twelfth century. Mercier takes the view that Joyce was not fully conscious of his participation in the Irish literary tradition: "Though [Joyce] was so much more in the true bardic tradition than many minor figures of the Anglo-Irish Literary Revival, I doubt whether he ever became fully aware of this fact" (*Irish Comic Tradition* 235; cf. 236). But the father in Joyce's statement of debt can also be read as a sign of a larger inheritance: the humor and wit embodied in *Ulysses* derive from Joyce's patrimony, his birthright; the father is a signum for the cultural tradition that produced the son and that John Stanislaus Joyce epitomized.

Because the Irish comic tradition is complex and can be dealt with only in summary fashion in this context, I rely here on Mercier's excellent study *The Irish Comic Tradition*. Mercier's study has the virtue of including both halves of Ireland's dual linguistic and literary tradition; he compares Irish material with Anglo-Irish, showing continuities where appropriate. Although Mercier has concentrated on establishing the debt of Joyce's parody to the Irish comic tradition by devoting a chapter to the topic, Mercier's scheme is also useful as an overview of Joyce's entire comic repertory and its relation to Irish tradition, facilitating comparison where appropriate with comic texts in Irish. In fact, Mercier deals with Joyce throughout his book. Comic elements are pervasive in the Irish literary tradition: virtually no piece of secular literature (and little of the ecclesiastical literature) from the early period is devoid of humor, and the literature is characterized by a mixed tone. In Mercier's scheme Irish humor is distinguished by its absurdity and fantasy, and macabre and grotesque humor also play prominent roles.[28] Wit and wordplay, including riddling and punning, are also important elements of the Irish comic tradition discussed by Mercier, and he stresses that the tradition is known for its invective, satire, and parody as well.

28. Note that Mercier concentrates on aspects of Irish comic tradition that distinguish it from English literature; his analysis could profitably be expanded with a greater account of absurdity, understatement, and overstatement or hyperbole.

Mercier sees the fantastic humor in Irish literature as reflecting a taste for marvels and magic when these features are pushed to the edge of the ludicrous. Early Irish humor alternates between overstatement and understatement: exaggeration and hyperbole on the one hand, a dry or tongue-in-cheek quality on the other. Both types push the normal bounds of narrative into the realm of fantasy; such fantastic exaggeration can be seen in the "heptad of Fergus":

Three hundred, three score and five persons in Conchobar's household—that is, the number of days in the year is the number of men that were in Conchobar's household. Among them was a partnership—namely, a man to victual them every night, so that the first to feed them on that night, would come again at the end of the year. Not small was the feeding, to wit, a pig and a deer and a vat (of ale) for every man. There were, however, men within whom, as is told, that did not suffice, for instance, Fergus mac Róig. If true it be, noble was his size—i.e., the heptad of Fergus was not often met with any other [*sic*], to wit, seven feet between his ear and his lips, and seven fists (= 42 inches) between his eyes, and seven fists in his nose, and seven fists in his lips. The full of a bushel-cup was the moisture of his head when being washed. Seven fists in his penis. A bushel-bag in his scrotum. Seven women to curb him unless Flidais should come. Seven pigs and seven vats (of ale) and seven deer to be consumed by him, and the strength of seven hundred in him. It was needful for him then to feed the household for a week (seven days) more than anyone. (Stokes, "Tidings of Conchobar Mac Nessa" 26–27)

The elaborate detail and the perfect symmetry of both the arrangement of Conchobor's house and Fergus's anatomy combine with hyperbole and a dry tone to produce fantastic humor in the passage. As exemplified in this passage, absurdity is an essential element of much Irish literature. Here the passage is highly stylized and there are two symmetrical schemata—the matching of days of the year and the number of Conchobor's men on the one hand, and the sevenfold description of Fergus on the other. But the schemata are incompatible: if Fergus feeds the household for a week, then not all Conchobor's men will be pressed into service during the year. The inconsistency of the two schemata based on the numbers 365 and 7 throws the fantasy of the passage into relief and pushes the humor toward absurdity.[29]

---

29. Absurdity in early Irish literature is pervasive enough to have been parodied by the twelfth-century author of *Aislinge Meic Conglinne* (*The Vision of Mac Conglinne*).

Fantastic humor often results from the exploitation of marvelous characters in early Irish literature, as we see in the case of Fergus. The tendency also extends to comic descriptions of deities (cf. Mercier, *Irish Comic Tradition* 19ff.). A celebrated passage of this sort in early Irish literature is the description in *Cath Maige Tuired* (*The [Second] Battle of Mag Tuired*) of the Dagda, the 'good god' of Irish mythology, one of the most powerful yet most humorous figures of the early literature:

Then Lug sent the Dagda to spy out the Fomorians and to delay them until the men of Ireland should come to the battle. So the Dagda went to the camp of the Fomorians and asked them for a truce of battle. This was granted to him as he asked. Porridge was then made for him by the Fomorians, and this was done to mock him, for great was his love for porridge. They filled for him the king's cauldron, five fists deep, into which went four-score gallons of new milk and the like quantity of meal and fat. Goats and sheep and swine were put into it, and they were all boiled together with the porridge. They were spilt for him into a hole in the ground, and Indech told him that he would be put to death unless he consumed it all; he should eat his fill so that he might not reproach the Fomorians with inhospitality.

Then the Dagda took his ladle, and it was big enough for a man and woman to lie on the middle of it. These then were the bits that were in it, halves of salted swine and a quarter of lard. "Good food this," said the Dagda. . . .

At the end of the meal he put his curved finger over the bottom of the hole on mold and gravel. Sleep came upon him then after eating his porridge. Bigger than a house-cauldron was his belly, and the Fomorians laughed at it. Then he went away from them to the strand of Eba. Not easy was it for the hero to move along owing to the bigness of his belly. Unseemly was his apparel. A cape to the hollow of his two elbows. A dun tunic around him, as far as the swelling of his rump. It was, moreover, long-breasted, with a hole in the peak. Two brogues on him of horse-hide, with the hair outside. Behind him a wheeled fork to carry which required the effort of eight men, so that its track after him was enough for the boundary-ditch of a province. (*AIT* 39)[30]

Immediately following this passage, the Dagda attempts to copulate with the daughter of his enemy—with ensuing difficulty because of the bulge

---

30. The humor here turns in part on the reader's knowledge that the puddled dirt floors of Irish cottages often contained holes where animals could be fed; the Dagda is therefore bestialized by the Fomorians in this passage. On the survival of this practice to the modern period, see Evans 62.

Joyce may have known this description from Hyde, *Story of Early Gaelic Literature* 64–66, a volume that Joyce quotes in *Ulysses* 9.96–99.

of his belly.[31] The Dagda is clearly a humorous figure in this text—humorous within the world of the tale as well as humorous to the audience—but the description is not parody: the Dagda's sexual prowess is established earlier in the text by his coupling with the Morrigan, the war goddess (*AIT* 38), a coupling that portends victory for his side. The text is an example of fantastic humor in which the genial father-god of the otherworld, the possessor of the caldron of plenty and the primeval progenitor, is seen to be akin to paltry human beings both insofar as he is the grateful (over)consumer of the otherworldly plenty and the subject himself of sexual dysfunctions like those of the audience.

That the passage represents an essentially comic view of the fantastic characters of the otherworld rather than parody can also be seen by comparing this description with another of the Dagda in *Mesca Ulad* (*The Intoxication of the Ulstermen*):

"Here in front of them to the east, outside," said Crom Deroil, "I saw a large-eyed, large-thighed, noble-great, immensely-tall man, with a splendid gray garment about him; with seven short, black, equally-smooth cloaklets around him; shorter was each upper one, longer each lower. At either side of him were nine men. In his hand was a terrible iron staff, on which were a rough end and a smooth end. His play and amusement consisted in laying the rough end on the heads of the nine, whom he would kill in the space of a moment. He would then lay the smooth end on them, so that he would reanimate them in the same time."

"Wonderful is the description," said Medb.

"Great is the person whose description it is," said Cu Roi.

"What, then; who is he?" said Ailill.

"Not hard to tell," said Cu Roi. "The great Dagda son of Ethliu, the good god of the Tuatha De Danann. To magnify valor and conflict he wrought confusion upon the host in the morning this day; and no one in the host sees him." (*AIT* 229)

The Dagda's description here is amusing, but it is also clear that he is a wonderful figure (*ingnad*, 'strange, wonderful, remarkable, unusual') with the power of death and resurrection in his potent phallic club. These early Irish texts offer a dual vision in which awe and amusement can coexist.

---

31. The sexual passage between the Dagda and the young woman was omitted from Stokes's 1891 edition and translation of the text; it was published without translation by Thurneysen in 1918 ("Zu Irischen Texten" 401–2). A modern edition and translation appears in Gray 46–49.

Mercier identifies as typical of the Irish comic tradition two other types of humor, the macabre and the grotesque, which he characterizes respectively as helping the audience to accept death and to overcome the awe of life and reproduction (*Irish Comic Tradition* 49). Macabre and grotesque humor, like the fantastic humor discussed above, may be connected with absurdity: "The macabre and grotesque do not become humorous until they have portrayed life as even more cruel and ugly than it is; we laugh at their absurd exaggeration, simultaneously expressing our relief that life is, after all, not *quite* so unpleasant as it might be" (Mercier, *Irish Comic Tradition* 1). Medieval Irish literature is full of examples of macabre and grotesque humor. Death, wounds, and sex are all part of the comic scene that shows the immense hero Mac Cecht lying wounded on a gory battlefield in *Togail Bruidne Dá Derga* (*The Destruction of Da Derga's Hostel*):

Now when Mac Cecht was lying wounded on the battlefield, at the end of the third day, he saw a woman passing by. "Come hither, O woman!" said Mac Cecht.

"I dare not go thus," said the woman, "for horror and fear of thee."

"There was a time, O woman, when people had horror and fear of me; but now thou shouldst fear nothing. I accept thee on the truth of my honor and my safeguard." Then the woman went to him.

"I know not," said he, "whether it is a fly, or a gnat, or an ant that nips me in the wound." It really was a hairy wolf that was there, as far as its two shoulders in the wound! The woman seized it by the tail, dragged it out of the wound, and it took the full of its jaws out of him. "Truly," said the woman, "this is 'an ant of ancient land.'"

Said Mac Cecht, "I swear what my people swears, I deemed it no bigger than a fly, or a gnat, or an ant." And Mac Cecht took the wolf by the throat, and struck it a blow on the forehead, and killed it with a single blow. (*AIT* 125)

Here fear of death is defused by the woman's fear for her own chastity, Mac Cecht's wounds notwithstanding; Mac Cecht's ability to survive the ravening wolf, which he unceremoniously dispatches with a bop on the head, contributes to the effect.[32] Macabre humor is common in early Irish literature, where the heroic topics of single combats and battles provide ample material for jokes about blood, wounds, and death. Sexuality is

---

32. Joyce probably knew a version of this passage since he uses *The Destruction of Da Derga's Hostel* as a mythic substructure in "The Dead"; cf. Kelleher, "Irish History."

also a ubiquitous source of humor since women figure largely in early Irish literature and the sexual potential of their encounters with heroes is fully realized.

All these types of humor also characterize *Ulysses*, and the inclusion of such elements is a major reason the book has been viewed as mock epic. The description of Bloom in the bath presents the same type of fantastic humor as that of Fergus quoted above; overstatement and exaggeration mixed with a little ironic blasphemy cause laughter, yet behind the humor Bloom is presented as a cosmic figure in the eternal waters:

Enjoy a bath now: clean trough of water, cool enamel, the gentle tepid stream. This is my body.

He foresaw his pale body reclined in it at full, naked, in a womb of warmth, oiled by scented melting soap, softly laved. He saw his trunk and limbs riprippled over and sustained, buoyed lightly upward, lemonyellow: his navel, bud of flesh: and saw the dark tangled curls of his bush floating, floating hair of the stream around the limp father of thousands, a languid floating flower. (5.565–72)

In this comic mystical vision Bloom, like Fergus, has taken on monumental proportions; his body floats like the earth upon the waters in creation myths, a sanctified body cum giant flower—lemon yellow like his soap—while the moving water swirls around his limp penis, "the father of thousands." The beauty of the language reminds the reader of the essential import of the vision, but the hyperbole of the imagery is humorous.[33]

Joyce's presentation of his epic character is thus typical of Irish literary tradition. The description of Bloom's culinary delectation, so often seized on in the critical literature on *Ulysses*, is a good example: "Mr Leopold Bloom ate with relish the inner organs of beasts and fowls. He liked thick giblet soup, nutty gizzards, a stuffed roast heart, liverslices fried with crustcrumbs, fried hencods' roes. Most of all he liked grilled mutton kidneys which gave to his palate a fine tang of faintly scented urine" (4.1–5). Hardly heroic fare, one might say, and the food becomes a commentary on Bloom's character, making him seem less than promising as an epic

33. Cf. Ellmann, *Ulysses on the Liffey* 71–73, 110–16, who discusses inflation and deflation (magnification and "parvication") as basic techniques in both "Aeolus" and "Cyclops."

hero.³⁴ Yet the tongue-in-cheek presentation of Bloom's appetites closely re-
sembles both the passage on Fergus's prodigious appetites and the passage
on the Dagda's love of the humble porridge. Absurdity does not necessarily
render heroism impossible or even unlikely in Irish literature.

Ulysses is also full of macabre and grotesque passages; indeed, many
of the parts of the book that most outraged moral purists and censors
have these qualities. Probably the most infamous is the passage showing
Bloom defecating:

He kicked open the crazy door of the jakes. Better be careful not to get these
trousers dirty for the funeral. He went in, bowing his head under the low
lintel. Leaving the door ajar, amid the stench of mouldy limewash and stale
cobwebs he undid his braces. . . .

Asquat on the cuckstool he folded out his paper, turning its pages over on
his bared knees. Something new and easy. No great hurry. Keep it a bit. Our
prize titbit: *Matcham's Masterstroke.* . . .

Quietly he read, restraining himself, the first column and, yielding but resisting, began the second. Midway, his last resistance yielding, he allowed his
bowels to ease themselves quietly as he read, reading still patiently that slight
constipation of yesterday quite gone. Hope it's not too big bring on piles
again. No, just right. So. Ah! (4.494–510)

Bloom on the cuckstool shows us mortality, but mortality becomes funny
because of Joyce's play on the word *column*. Reading and defecating fuse
as one experience of columns, and when the two fuse literally—"He tore
away half the prize story sharply and wiped himself with it"—the entire
episode ends on a comic note, allowing us to reclaim our bodily functions, even those that involve death (consumption/eating) and fertility
(production/defecation). In Mercier's terms the passage is both macabre
and grotesque. In a similar way sexuality almost always has a comic side
in *Ulysses*, as it does in Irish literature as a whole. When Molly reminisces
about Poldy's having insisted upon seeing her drawers on a public street
before they were married (18.293–325), we laugh at his impatience, his
disregard of consequences, the potential for mishap, his all-too-human
foibles when sexually attracted, like the heroes of early Irish literature led
astray by their urges and appetites. Here and throughout *Ulysses* the sex-

---

34. We must tread lightly on the question of Bloom's diet insofar as the Homeric heroes eat the innards in ceremonial sacrifices.

ual passages remove the awe from the coupling of human bodies, even those of the primordial mother and father.

We could continue on through the other levels of Mercier's analysis of the Irish comic tradition, giving examples of Irish wit, wordplay, and riddling, as well as Irish irony, satire, invective, and parody, and marshaling close parallels from *Ulysses*. Suffice it to say that Joyce exploits all the resources of the Irish comic tradition. The textual examples cited here of early Irish humor are not significant per se, and I do not argue that Joyce knew all the passages in question, though he might well have done. One could substitute or multiply examples from any of the cycles of early Irish literature or indeed from virtually any period of Irish literature and much of the Anglo-Irish literary tradition as well to make the same points. Thus, any exposure to Irish literature—from the material Joyce found in the *United Irishman* to stories he read when studying Irish—would have reinforced the living tradition of Irish humor carried by his father and would have contributed to the particularly Irish sense of the comic found in Joyce's later work.

Ellmann has argued that Joyce makes unexpected junctures in his work:

One of his unexpected fusings takes place between beauty and its opposite. . . . Dublin is dear and dirty; so are the mind and body. In theory we grant these combinations, but in practice seem to hold the units apart. Joyce never does. What other hero in the novel has, like Stephen Dedalus, lice? Yet the lice are Baudelairean lice, clinging to the soul's as well as the body's integument. What other hero defecates or masturbates like Bloom before our eyes? Joyce will not make it easy for us either to contemn or adore. (*JJ*2 5–6)

These juxtapositions hold true of the heroic tradition in Ireland as well, which offers a sophisticated view of heroic culture and heroic values, continually asking that the audience reevaluate heroism by presenting tarnished heroes (Tymoczko, *Two Death Tales*, introduction). In *The Story of Mac Datho's Pig* the great Ulster heroes are by turns revealed to be cowardly, stuttering, impotent, limping, or foolish. And in *Táin Bó Cúailnge*, if not in the realistic novels of Ellmann's acquaintance, Ellmann's rhetorical question about Stephen's lice finds a concrete answer, for in the earliest version of that tale the great CuChulainn begins his day by picking the lice off his clothing: "Cúchulainn was squatting haunch-deep in the snow, stripped and picking his shirt" (Kinsella, *Táin* 116).

CuChulainn's lice, like those of Stephen, are spiritual as well (*PA* 174, 234; *SH* 194; cf. Herring, *Uncertainty Principle* 157; cf. *JJ2* 5–6), for he is the hero who in various tales kills his son, betrays his wife with another woman, lets men go past him on the occasion of the *Táin* while he has a tryst with a woman, suggests retreat from the territory of his enemies after a drunken incursion, and gets his head rubbed in dung by CuRoi (*AIT* 172–75, 176–98, 223, 329; Kinsella, *Táin* 72).

These strange juxtapositions come about because the essence of the comic tradition in Irish literature is to mix humor, wit, and satire with serious material. Medieval Irish literature in particular, but most of the later Irish tradition as well, is characterized by its mixed tone. Rarely is a tale purely comic or purely tragic. There are exceptions, to be sure, but in most early Irish tales tragedy and comedy go hand in hand. The most tragic stories—like *The Death of Aife's Only Son* or *The Death of CuChulainn*—have humorous episodes. The most humorous tales—like *Fled Bricrend (The Feast of Bricriu), The Intoxication of the Ulstermen,* or *The Story of Mac Datho's Pig*—take heroes and heroism seriously or convey an implicit warning. Jokes can have a serious edge and serious things can be laughed at in early Irish literature, including the gods. Irish tradition is archaic in many respects,[35] and Mercier (*Irish Comic Tradition* ch. 9) has detailed the archaism of the Anglo-Irish comic tradition in particular. The mixed tone of Irish narrative is another such archaism, the product of a literature not schooled in classical genres and an Aristotelian aesthetic.

The importance of humor to Irish tradition had been partially obscured for English speakers, particularly members of the Ascendancy, during the nineteenth and early twentieth centuries, because of the dominant critical view of Celtic literature promulgated by Matthew Arnold in "On the Study of Celtic Literature." Though Arnold praised Celtic literature and recommended that it be included in university curricula, at the same time he gave it a definition based on a very slender knowledge of Welsh and no knowledge of Irish literature in the original. One of the characteristics he most valued and most recommended was "Celtic melancholy" (361 and passim)—seeing the Celts on the whole as a gentle, if emotional, elegiac folk with a fine attunement to "natural magic." This

---

35. See, for example, Dillon, "Archaism of Irish Tradition"; Jackson, *Oldest Irish Tradition*; and Robinson.

romantic view of Celtic literature in turn influenced how early Irish literature was read and translated in Ireland as well, distorting the reception of the humor in early Irish texts considerably. The notion of "Celtic melancholy," particularly insofar as Irish texts are concerned, is a product of English criticism rather than a quality notable in the early Irish literary texts themselves; but it was a critical view that affected the tone of most Anglo-Irish writers of the Irish literary revival, writers who were themselves often guided by Arnold's critical refraction of Celtic literature as well as by nationalist ideological constraints that privileged melancholy and tragedy.[36]

More than most other writers of the Irish literary revival, Joyce uses humor and maintains the mixed tone of early Irish narrative. But humor is not the only face of Joyce's writing. Ellmann has written of *Ulysses (JJ2* 360), "The many light-hearted cross-references [to the *Odyssey*] have lent support to the idea that *Ulysses* is a great joke on Homer." Though *Ulysses* includes all facets of the Irish comic tradition, humor is not the whole story, as Ellmann remarks:

Jokes are not necessarily so simple, and these [references to the *Odyssey*] have a double aim. The first aim is the mock-heroic, the mighty spear juxtaposed with the two-penny cigar. The second, a more subtle one, is what might be called the ennoblement of the mock-heroic. This demonstrates that the world of cigars is devoid of heroism only to those who don't understand that Ulysses' spear was merely a sharpened stick, as homely an instrument in its way, and that Bloom can demonstrate the qualities of man by word of mouth as effectively as Ulysses by thrust of spear. (*JJ2* 360)[37]

Joyce's use of jokes as a vehicle for a serious aim is typical of Irish tradition. The converse is also true. Writing about Joyce's correspondence, Ellmann cautions that "his remarks are bitter, but they are also funny. It is easy to forget, in the midst of his descriptions of his troubles in letters, how repugnant to his personality 'Celtic' melancholy remained" (*JJ2*

---

36. Arnold, who knew Welsh tradition somewhat better than he did Irish, may have based his generalization on the elegiac tone of much of Welsh poetry from the early period, though by no means is this the sole note to be found. This view of the Celtic literature is ironized by Joyce in "A Little Cloud" (cf. Herring, *Joyce's Uncertainty Principle* 58–62, 153).

37. Mercier, *Irish Comic Tradition* 213–14, makes a similar point; cf. also Herring, *Joyce's "Ulysses" Notesheets* 67 n. 10, and Herring, "Bedsteadfastness of Molly Bloom" 49–61.

218).[38] Joyce is closer to the spirit of native Irish literature in his mixed tone both in his letters and in *Ulysses* than virtually any other Anglo-Irish writer of the period.[39]

Joyce shows his appreciation of the comic in his literary theory as well as his practice, defending comedy as superior to tragedy:

All art which excites in us the feeling of joy is so far comic and according as this feeling of joy is excited by whatever is substantial or accidental in human fortunes the art is to be judged more or less excellent: and even tragic art may be said to participate in the nature of comic art so far as the possession of a work of tragic art (a tragedy) excites in us the feeling of joy. From this it may be seen that tragedy is the imperfect manner and comedy the perfect manner in art. (CW 144)

Thus, in *Ulysses* the comic elements are not intended merely to be funny but to raise joy. *Ulysses* is also comic in the medieval sense of having a happy ending; like Dante's *Commedia*, *Ulysses* is designed to bring hope as much as to amuse.[40]

To summarize, then, Joyce shows the full range of Irish comic devices: fantastic, grotesque, macabre humor; wit, wordplay, and punning; satire and parody. His mixed tone—comic and serious, bitter and funny—his refusal to limit himself to either a heroic or a mock-heroic vision, his ability to embrace both views: all these qualities mark Joyce's writing, particularly in *Ulysses*, as part of the Irish literary tradition and show that in *Ulysses* he produced an epic with the tone of early Irish heroic literature. Moreover, Joyce developed an aesthetic theory that formalized the importance of comedy and hence justified important aspects of his nation's literary heritage.

iv. Conclusion

Among his Irish contemporaries, Joyce is one of the few to have chosen *The Book of Invasions* as the basis for a literary refraction of Irish mythic literature. On the face of it the story holds little promise: a rather dry succession of invasions, it is also among the least plausible of medieval

38. Cf. S. Joyce, *Recollections of James Joyce* 14–15, 26.
39. Since Joyce, of course, this has become a familiar mode in Irish writing, as the work of Flann O'Brien or Austin Clarke illustrates.
40. See Dante's "Epistle to Can Grande," quoted in B. Clark 47.

Irish narratives. Yet in retrospect it is clear why Joyce turned to this tale in writing his version of the national epic. As the organizing principle for the chronology of Irish history and Irish myth, *The Book of Invasions* stands at the center of Irish tradition; it gives a relatively simple framework for the national history of Ireland, providing typologies for the population. Unlike the Ulster Cycle or the Cycles of the Kings, its referent is universal, all of Ireland, for it primarily purports to tell the history of the invasion that furnished the ancestors of all the leading clans of Ireland. Because of its containment and clear outline, *The Book of Invasions* was more useful for an epic than was the Finn Cycle. Though the Fenian material held much potential for Joyce, it was not right for his attempt at a modern epic because of its amorphousness, its greater regionalization, and its multifariousness, the very features put to good use in *Finnegans Wake*. Although *The Book of Invasions* includes wars and conflicts, it is not principally a celebration of the heroic deeds and ethos of the warrior class, as so much of early Irish literature is; the story is thus a framework for an epic that is potentially other than a glorification of war. In telling the story of Ireland's past, *The Book of Invasions* also connects Ireland with Europe and the Mediterranean world, thus contributing to Joyce's coordination of multiple mythic patterns. Moreover, *The Book of Invasions* was known by virtually all the Irish of Joyce's time. For all these reasons, it becomes clear why Joyce based his attempt at a national epic on this material.

Ulysses has been problematic for readers and critics alike since the book appeared, in large part because it violates formal expectations for all the standard European genres. These violations of generic expectations made it hard for the initial readers of *Ulysses* to construe the book, hard to configure its meaning. The gaps in the narrative structure, the blurred margin, the variations in style and form, and the hyperbolic or humorous elements have also fueled critical debate about such polarities as novel or epic, epic or mock epic, modern or postmodern. As early as 1923, Eliot, in his discussion of Joyce's mythic method, encapsulated aspects of the problem: "I am not begging the question in calling *Ulysses* a 'novel'; and if you call it an epic it will not matter. If it is not a novel, that is simply because the novel is a form which will no longer serve; it is because the novel, instead of being a form, was simply the expression of an age, which had not sufficiently lost all form to feel the need of something stricter" ("*Ulysses*, Order, and Myth" 201). Some seventy years and countless novels later, Eliot's zeitgeist solution will not serve, and it is necessary to turn to other quarters for a solution to the puzzle.[41] Although there is danger in falling into a *post hoc, propter hoc* argument in a study of this sort, simplicity is always a desideratum in a theory, so long as the theory accounts for the phenomena in question. In this case the generic configuration of Irish heroic literature provides an elegant template for Joyce's generic experiments in *Ulysses*, a template that does not undermine most other investigations of Joyce's form but rather provides a pattern that integrates what has often been scattered critical response. The sheer number of points of contact between the narrative form of *Ulysses* and the form of early Irish narrative is telling.

Joyce elevated comedy above tragedy in his literary theory. This theoretical view suits Irish literature, but it does not facilitate the writing of epics, which in Western literature are more often associated with serious matter than with comedy. The comic tone, or even a mixed tone, is minimal in our canon of epics. Among the earliest epics the *Odyssey* is one of the few to be comic in the sense of having a happy ending, though even at that precious few of its characters come out well, and it is not primarily amusing or humorous in its tone. In terms of possible models for writing an Irish epic at the turn of the century, the discussion of epic in the library scene of *Ulysses* provides some illumination: "Our national epic has yet to be written, Dr Sigerson says. Moore is the man for it. A knight of the rueful countenance here in Dublin. With a saffron kilt? O'Neill Russell? O, yes, he must speak the grand old tongue. And his Dulcinea? James Stephens is doing some clever sketches. We are becoming important, it seems" (9.309–13). Considering the importance of the comic in Irish tradition, it is no wonder that an Irish *Don Quixote* comes to mind when the Irish national epic is imagined. Joyce here may be signaling that just as the Irish have a Spanish origin in *The Book of Invasions*, so too their national epic would have a Spanish flavor: like *Don Quixote* it would be full of humor and burlesque, mixing the comic and a serious worldview. We could look at *Ulysses* as a modern Irish analogue to the Spanish epic, a comparison Joyce may have had in mind given his structural and the-

---

41. For other, more recent approaches to the problem of Joyce's genre, see Litz, "Genre of *Ulysses*"; Kenner, *"Ulysses"* 2–4; Gifford 1–3.

matic use of *The Book of Invasions* as well as his commitment to the view
that the Irish were a Spanish race. A full exploration of this possibility,
however, lies beyond the scope of the present study.[42]

Joyce attempted to disguise and make palatable his attempt at an Irish
epic by constructing it like a series of Chinese boxes: remaining faithful
to contemporary Ireland through surface realism, gaining justification as
a canonical epic through accessible classical parallels and his title, building on the Irish heroic narrative tradition through the subtext of *The
Book of Invasions*, Irish narrative techniques, and Irish tone, and passing
the whole off as a novel. The man who felt that "an Irish safety pin is
more important than an English epic" (*JJ*2 423) could be counted on to
continue the Irish narrative tradition in his version of a modern Irish epic.
Joyce's juncture of the Irish and classical epic traditions at their points of
greatest similarity was decisive in his ability to make the enterprise succeed.

The problems posed by the form of *Ulysses* are precisely those of Irish
epic. When *Ulysses* appeared, it was anomalous both as a modern novel
and as a modern epic for many of the same reasons that Irish hero tale is
anomalous as epic: for its odd characters, its scatology and sexuality, for

---

42. In a 1911 essay entitled "Irish Books," John Eglinton (W. K. Magee) had
speculated about the idea of a modern Irish epic in the mold of Cervantes's work:
"If a masterpiece should still come of this literary movement . . . we have a fancy
that appearances in modern Ireland point to a writer of the type of Cervantes
rather than to an idealising poet or romance writer. A hero as loveable as the great
Knight of the Rueful Countenance might be conceived, who in some back street
of Dublin had addled his brains with brooding over Ireland's wrongs, and that
extensive but not always quite sincere literature which expresses the resentment
of her sons towards the stranger. His library would be described, the books which
had 'addled the poor gentleman's brain.' . . . We can conceive him issuing forth,
fresh-hearted as a child at the age of fifty, with glib and saffron-coloured kilt, to
realise and incidentally to expose the ideals of present-day Ireland. What scenes
might not be devised at village inns arising out of his refusal to parley with landlords in any but his own few words of Gaelic speech. . . . His Dulcinea would
be—who but Kathleen ni Houlihan herself, who really is no more like what she
is taken for than the maiden of Toboso, . . . an old woman, . . . not a friendly
and buxom wench, whose partiality for strapping young foreigners, whether
Danish, Saxon or Scotch, has had a great deal to do in bringing about the present,
by no means desperate, situation of modern Ireland" (87–88; see also Gifford
214; Thornton, *Allusions in "Ulysses"* 171–72). It is possible that Joyce knew
about Eglinton's idea from a conversation prior to the publication of the essay, as
represented in *Ulysses*.

For a comparison of *Ulysses* and *Don Quixote*, see Z. Bowen, *"Ulysses" as a
Comic Novel*, esp. 83–102.

its mixture of the heroic and the comic, for its anomalous form, its variation in styles, its mixture of prose and poetic structures, its gaps, its blurred margin. The question of "epic or mock epic?" is one that only someone outside Irish tradition would think to ask about either early Irish hero tale or *Ulysses*. One is tempted to say "neither" or "both," but the real answer is that *Ulysses* is an *Irish* epic. The irony of *Ulysses* is that as a national epic this most Irish of modern narratives was no more acceptable to the Irish literary revival or to cultural nationalists than the early Irish hero tales had been.

Chapter 4

Sovereignty Structures
in *Ulysses*

SERGIUS: Louka: do you know what the higher love is?

LOUKA: (*astonished*) No, sir.

SERGIUS: Very fatiguing thing to keep up for any length of time, Louka. One feels the need of some relief after it.

Bernard Shaw, *Arms and the Man*

The architectonic structures in *Ulysses* taken from early Irish literary tradition are not limited to those from *The Book of Invasions*; a second set of symbolic structures in *Ulysses* pertains to the Sovereignty of Ireland, one of the oldest and most pervasive patterns of Irish myth, a pattern that had also been exploited before Joyce by the Anglo-Irish literary revival. In *Ulysses* the symbolic structures related to the Sovereignty interlock with those from *The Book of Invasions*, underscoring and extending their meanings. Because the Sovereignty is a female figure, this second set of mythological elements from early Irish literature naturally clusters around Molly Bloom.

Molly has been such a focus of critical inquiry that no attempt can be made here to treat her comprehensively. Accordingly, this discussion is not intended as an "even-handed" account: many aspects of Molly's character and position in the narrative will be set aside. Rather, the goal is to offer a compensatory treatment, to address issues about Molly that have long been neglected, and to focus on the mythic and structural aspects of her character.¹ For the sake of convenience, the material here is organized into four sections. After a brief survey of goddess figures in early Irish literature, there is a detailed consideration of the parallels between Molly Bloom and Sovereignty figures elsewhere in Irish literature. The chapter then turns to the significance of the mythic structures for understanding the character of Leopold Bloom. The discussion concludes with the implications of Joyce's mythic structuring of Molly—implications for *Ulysses* as a narrative, for the place of *Ulysses* in the tradition of Irish literature, and for the ideological dimension of *Ulysses*.

i. A survey of the Irish goddesses

Female figures play a large role in early Irish myths and sagas and are often associated with fertility and the well-being of the landscape.² Some of the female mythic characters are territorial goddesses whose names are coded in the landscape: Anu, for example, gives her name to the double mountain in Kerry known as *Dá Chích Anann*, 'The Two Paps of Anu'. A striking aspect of certain early Irish mythic females is their connection with war: they may be leaders of armies or frankly supernatural characters like the Morrigan, a war goddess who can metamorphose into a carrion crow. Still another common figure is the goddess associated with a river or well; the Boann is probably the most well known example of this type of goddess. Though there is no Celtic goddess of love, most of the female figures in the early literature display a vigorous sexuality, illustrating their connection with love in its functional and ritual aspects rather than in its personal aspect. The most distinctive Irish goddess is the Sovereignty, whose union with the rightful king was thought to result in the fertility and prosperity of the land. Her union with the sacral king was signaled by her metamorphosis from hag to beautiful young girl. Before turning to Joyce's application of Irish Sovereignty materials in *Ulysses*, I will briefly survey these types of goddess figures in early Irish tra-

---

1. The discussion of Molly by B. Scott in *Joyce and Feminism*, 156–83, serves as a guide to recent criticism about Molly. Scott's discussion draws together the materials in a fresh way and begins also to demonstrate Joyce's debt to early Irish literature in his portrait of Molly. An earlier survey of the Molly criticism from a very different perspective is found in Mark Shechner, *Joyce in Nighttown* 196–97; cf. Herring, "Bedsteadfastness of Molly Bloom" 57–59.
2. For a more extensive discussion of the Celtic goddesses, see Mac Cana, *Celtic Mythology*, and Ross, *Pagan Celtic Britain* 265–301.

dition. This overview is intended to indicate the extent to which the figure of the Sovereignty has deep historical and mythological roots, the way in which it permeates Celtic tradition and informs the Irish world view.

One of the most important innovations of insular Celtic myth seems to be the concept of the mother of the gods, a notion reflected in the term *Túatha Dé Danann*, 'the tribes of the goddess Danu'. The idea of a great mother is not particularly Indo-European in character; it may be a legacy of the pre-Indo-European peoples of the British Isles, deriving from the Neolithic people and their descendants who became assimilated with, and left lasting cultural marks on, the Celts in the British Isles.[3] Goddesses were also important in Celtic traditions on the Continent, where they figure frequently in Gaulish statuary as triads of *matres* or *matronae*. The Gaulish goddesses are clearly associated with agrarian practices, fertility, and health (Georges Dumézil's third-order concerns);[4] frequently they are portrayed with emblems such as infants, textiles, fruits, and grain products that illustrate their connection with these aspects of life. A common Gaulish figural representation also shows a goddess as consort of a ruler god, and in some of these instances it appears that the goddess is the embodiment of the tribe or the district over which her male companion has dominion. These iconographic representations of goddesses have textual parallels in early Irish literature, where there is a series of imperious, strong-minded, alluring, and sexually active women.

A striking and significant aspect of the females in early Irish literature is their connection with war. As leaders of armies or warriors themselves, or as frankly supernatural characters who can metamorphose into carrion crows delighting in battlefields, many female figures in early Irish literature are imposing characters associated with violence and destruction. Such connections with war would appear to be inconsistent with fertility associations, but the great mother, especially when she is associated with the earth, is at once the source of life and the repository of life after death.[5] Moreover, the welfare and fertility of a people depend on their security against external aggression, and the warlike aspect of

---

3. Evans, *Irish Folk Ways*, discusses the debt of Irish culture in general to Neolithic culture, showing how it influences various facets of Irish traditional life; survivals of religious myth are therefore not to be ruled out.

4. For a summary of the ideas of George Dumézil, see Littleton.

5. For the distinction between the fertility and chthonic aspects of the earth mother, see Hillman 35–45, as well as references cited there.

supernatural females may represent such military resistance of the territory. Warlike action can thus have a protective aspect.

The Morrigan most clearly illustrates the goddesses' associations with war. Her name may mean 'phantom queen', and she appears on battlefields, often in the shape of a crow or raven. The Morrigan is a fateful goddess; she claims, for example, to be able to set a term on Cu-Chulainn's life in *Táin Bó Regamna* (*The Cattle Raid of Regamna*) (*AIT* 213), and she speaks a prophecy of doom at the end of *The Second Battle of Mag Tuired* (*AIT* 47–48). But the Morrigan has connections with fertility as well. She is a mother (albeit of a sinister son who must be killed before his destructiveness gets out of hand), and in early Ireland there was a place named *Dá Chích na Morrígna*, 'The Two Paps of the Morrigan', a parallel with the Munster site noted above (Stokes, "Rennes Dindšenchas" 15: 292–93). Moreover, in *The Second Battle of Mag Tuired* the Morrigan copulates with the Dagda, thereby seeming to ensure victory for his side (*AIT* 38–39).[6]

Many of the Irish mythic females are associated with the land, and there is ample evidence that some were originally territorial goddesses. The clearest example is the triad of goddesses Eriu, Fotla, and Banba, who bear the three names of Ireland itself and who embody the island, welcoming the Milesians when they invade Ireland in *The Book of Invasions* (*AIT* 17–18). It appears that there were goddesses of this type representing the individual provinces of Ireland, and perhaps individual tribes as well.[7] Several of these figures have survived in Modern Irish folklore.

Celtic goddesses also are associated with or embodied in rivers. They are frequently pictured as guardians of springs or wells, and many of the principal rivers of Europe and the British Isles are named after Celtic river goddesses. The Seine, for example, is named after the goddess Sequana, and at its headwaters was a major sanctuary in her honor where an immense number of votive offerings was submerged. In Ireland the Boyne bears the name of the Boann, consort of the Dagda, a ruler god of the

6. The Morrigan's name can also be interpreted as 'great queen'. For a discussion of the name and other aspects of this goddess, see *DIL* s.v. "Morrígan," as well as discussions of the Morrigan in Ross and in Mac Cana, *Celtic Mythology*. The story of the Morrigan's son Meche is found in Stokes, "Rennes Dindšenchas" 15: 304–5.

7. See Mac Cana, "Aspects of the Theme."

Tuatha De Danann. The evidence indicates that river goddesses are simply one specific manifestation of the fertility goddesses and the mother
goddesses: water is, of course, associated with both health and fertility.
We see this link specifically in the goddess Matrona, 'the divine mother',
who gave her name to the river Marne.

Although there is no Celtic goddess of love equivalent to Aphrodite,
the female figures and the goddesses in Irish literature often "display a
vigorous sexuality"; love in its functional and ritual aspects of union and
procreation, rather than love as an emotional or personal experience, is
highlighted in Irish myth (Mac Cana, *Celtic Mythology* 85). Union is frequently the explicit point of a story, and the concern may be to determine
which one of several competing royal men will be joined to the female
figure. As is apparent from this brief treatment, fertility is the leitmotif
of the Irish myths about goddesses, and it is linked to the rule of the rightful sovereign, the sacral king.[8] It was believed that during the time of a
good king there would be plenty; during the time of an evil king, the land
would fail. A good deal of evidence suggests that actual historical kings
were believed to be wedded to the local territorial goddess and hence to
the land that she embodied. As Proinsias Mac Cana notes (*Celtic Mythology* 94), the goddess "symbolized not merely the soil and substance
of [the] territory, but also the spiritual and legal dominion which the king
exercised over it." War, failure of animal, vegetable, or human fertility,
and unfavorable weather were all taken as signs that there was an improper union of king and goddess.

In a number of early Irish stories, a goddess appears who is called explicitly *In Flaithius*, 'The Sovereignty'. In these stories the goddess ensures
the rule of a king or his successors by granting a drink (or drinks) of ale
or other beverage. The stories are associated with the motif of the transformation of the Sovereignty from hag to beautiful young woman, and
R. A. Breatnach has claimed that metamorphosis is the hallmark of the
Irish form of the Sovereignty myth (335): that though other cultures have
developed myths in which king and goddess are joined, the feature of the
puella senilis, the hag changed to young girl by the new union, is particularly Celtic. In the most well known of these stories, *Echtra Mac
nEchach Muigmedóin* (*The Adventure of the Sons of Eochaid Muigme-*

---

8. Mac Cana, *Celtic Mythology* 117–21, has a brief discussion of the Celtic
institution of sacral kingship.

don), Niall and his four brothers are subjected to a number of tests to determine who is most suited to be king (*AIT* 508–13). At the last the young men go out hunting and become lost after their successful hunt. When they eat their meat, they become thirsty. One by one they go to find water, and each encounters a hideous hag by a well who says she will grant the water only in exchange for a kiss. All refuse to kiss her except Niall, who volunteers to lie with her, whereupon she is transformed into a beautiful girl. She identifies herself as the Sovereignty of Ireland, and Niall is recognized thereafter as the rightful king.

Because Ireland was politically fragmented through most of its history, a tribal society rather than a national one, there is a proliferation of goddess figures in the early literature, each with similar functions and characteristics, rather than a single goddess who can serve as the mythological prototype for the image of the goddess in the Irish collective unconscious. Moreover, the mythological tradition of female figures continued to be influential in later Irish tradition, with the two aspects of the Sovereignty, hag and beautiful woman, becoming distinct literary prototypes after the seventeenth century. Breatnach has traced the continuity of the tradition of representing Ireland as a young, beautiful woman from the medieval period to the eighteenth-century *aisling* ('dream, vision, apparition') poetry.⁹ In the aisling poems the poet has a vision or dream of a beautiful woman who comes to appeal or lament to him. The woman in the aisling represents Ireland, and her misery is associated with Ireland's political bondage; she is often portrayed as languishing for her rightful spouse— associated at this period with the exiled Stuart line.

A link between the languishing women of the aisling tradition and women who are vigorous in their sexual demands can be seen in the eighteenth-century text *Cúirt an Mheadhón Oidhche* (*The Midnight Court*), by Brian Merriman. In Merriman's poem the dream framework is fused with the medieval court-of-love convention; in this context the women of Ireland bring their complaint that they languish for husband and child. They make their humorous but imperious demands for more sexual fulfillment and better sexual arrangements, for the young men to marry young women rather than to wait to marry until they are old or to prefer the old but rich spinster and widow.

The aisling tradition passed into Anglo-Irish through translations and

9. See also Corkery 126–42; J. Williams and Ford 217–19.

the ballad tradition. The folk poem "Róisín Dubh" was translated into English as "Dark Rosaleen" by James Clarence Mangan in 1837, and Diane Bessai ("'Dark Rosaleen'") has shown that Mangan's translation of a love poem fuses an allegorical interpretation of the poem with aisling elements to produce an emblem of Ireland with strong nationalistic overtones:

> O my dark Rosaleen,
>   Do not sigh, do not weep!
> The priests are on the ocean green,
>   They march along the deep.
> There's wine from the royal Pope,
>   Upon the ocean green:
> And Spanish ale shall give you hope,
>   My dark Rosaleen!
>   My own Rosaleen!
> Shall glad your heart, shall give you hope,
> Shall give you health and help, and hope,
>   My Dark Rosaleen.
>
> Over hills, and through dales,
>   Have I roamed for your sake;
> All yesterday I sailed with sails
>   On river and on lake.
> The Erne, at its highest flood,
>   I dashed across unseen,
> For there was lightning in my blood,
>   My dark Rosaleen!
>   My own Rosaleen!
> Oh! there was lightning in my blood,
> Red lightning lightened through my blood,
>   My Dark Rosaleen!
>   . . . .
>   I could scale the blue air,
>   I could plough the high hills,
> Oh, I could kneel all night in prayer,
>   To heal your many ills!
> And one beamy smile from you
>   Would float like light between
> My toils and me, my own, my true,
>   My dark Rosaleen!

My fond Rosaleen!
Would give me life and soul anew,
A second life, a soul anew,
My Dark Rosaleen!

(Colum 269–71)

In Mangan's translation the sexual elements of the original are muted in favor of romantic adoration. In the original Irish the last stanza quoted above runs:

Dá mbeadh seisreach agam threabhfainn in aghaidh na gcnoc
is dhéanfainn soiscéal i lár an aifrinn do mo Róisín Dubh;
bhéarfainn póg don chailín óg a bhéarfadh a hóighe dom
is dhéanfainn cleas ar chúl an leasa le mo Róisín Dubh.

This is translated more literally by Thomas Kinsella as follows:

If I had six horses I would plough against the hill—
I'd make Róisín Dubh my Gospel in the middle of Mass—
I'd kiss the young girl who would grant me her maidenhead
and do deeds behind the *lios* with my Róisín Dubh![10]

(Ó Tuama and Kinsella 308–11)

Mangan's interpretation fuses Marian emblems of the virgin queen and the lover's eagerness for martyrdom, giving spiritual longing where the Irish poet has more carnal things in mind. Mangan's English translation became a nationalist byword, signifying "total adherence to a cause that is never won and a hope that is never questioned" and appealing on an emotionally intimate level (Bessai, "'Dark Rosaleen'" 80). In addition, the poem represents a stage in the establishment of rose imagery as emblematic of Ireland in Anglo-Irish literature, imagery that permeates the poetry of Yeats and that can be found in Joyce as well.[11]

The other face of the Sovereignty, that of the old hag, also had an extensive literary development in later Irish and Anglo-Irish tradition.[12] The

---

10. A *lios* (or *liss*) is translated 'a courtyard, ring-fort'.

11. On the rose imagery in Joyce's works, particularly *Portrait*, see Seward, *Symbolic Rose* 187–221. Seward focuses almost exclusively on the international aspects of rose symbolism in Joyce's works rather than the Irish nationalist valences.

12. For a more extensive treatment of this topic, see Bessai, "Who Was Cathleen Ni Houlihan?" as well as the references she cites.

most significant presentation of this figure in English for our purposes
here is the "Shan Van Vocht," whose name is found in a ballad with that
title. The name is from the Irish *an seanbhean bhocht*, 'the poor old
woman'. The figure of the Poor Old Woman appeared originally in a satiric Irish song about the marriage of a young man to a wealthy old
woman, but the Irish tune was reused and its refrain adapted at the end
of the eighteenth century for a patriotic song in English celebrating the
French landing of 1796. In the English song, the old woman is only a
name rather than a character per se; however, her name conjures up a
typology that had been established elsewhere in the literature (Bessai,
"Who Was Cathleen Ni Houlihan?" 117). The political message of this
ballad is clear; in it the voice of the old woman predicts the coming of
the French, the decay of the Orange, the rising of the yeomen, and the
freedom of Ireland. The yeoman will "swear that they'll be true / To the
Shan Van Vocht" (Colum 98–99). The song was widely popular throughout the nineteenth century. A figure related to the Shan Van Vocht is
Cathleen Ni Houlihan. The name originated in a love song but came, like
the aisling women, to represent Ireland. By the end of the eighteenth century there were two variants of an Irish poem celebrating Cathleen. Both
were translated by Mangan, who worked from the literal translations of
his predecessors; one of the poems he worked with, both in the original
and in his translation, suggests that Cathleen is an ugly hag who would
become transformed if she were joined with "the king's son" (Bessai,
"Who Was Cathleen Ni Houlihan?" 119ff.).

The Sovereignty mythos had been given still other literary filters before
Ulysses appeared. In 1901–2 Yeats seized upon the tradition of Ireland
as the poor old woman and remolded it for his play *Cathleen ni Houlihan*. In one speech by the title character, Yeats deliberately fuses two
names for the mythic type he is treating: "Some call me the Poor Old
Woman, and there are some that call me Cathleen, the daughter of Houlihan" (ll. 277–79).[13] Yeats's old woman is more a "pathetic mild old
woman" than a disgusting or gross hag, as many of her antecedents had
been (Bessai, "Who Was Cathleen Ni Houlihan?" 115, 119, 125–25). It
was the perfect role for Maud Gonne, a "daughter of Ireland" and "servant of the Queen" whose imagination had already been stirred by the

---

13. This quotation and all subsequent citations of Yeats's plays are from *The
Variorum Edition of the Plays.*

iconography of the Sovereignty.[14] In Yeats's play the old woman is explicitly associated with the heroes of Ireland's patriotic past:

Many a man has died for love of me. . . . There was a red man of the O'Donnells from the north, and a man of the O'Sullivans from the south, and there was one Brian that lost his life at Clontarf by the sea, and there were a great many in the west, some that died hundreds of years ago. (ll. 199–214)

Yeats's play is associated with a revival in the twentieth century of the early Irish heroic ethos, and it can be seen as a kind of call to arms. By fusing Irish patriotic history with themes of the dispossession, the folk ideal, Christian martyrdom, and a heroic thirst for fame, *Cathleen ni Houlihan* set the stage for the Easter Rising. Yeats later wondered in "The Man and the Echo," "Did that play of mine send out / Certain men the English shot?" The answer is almost certainly yes. In *Cathleen ni Houlihan* the Sovereignty has become a kind of war goddess.[15]

In Yeats's play, as in Mangan's "Dark Rosaleen," the Sovereignty is sexually pure. She says, "With all the lovers that brought me their love I never set out the bed for any" (ll. 247–48). Chaste herself, she leads the men who follow her to chastity. In the play Michael turns from an earthly bride to the old woman even before Cathleen's epiphany. For Yeats, Ireland in her guise as woman demands chastity in her followers. Yeats's characterization fit his times: it suited Victorian and Catholic morality and a nationalism that courted those values. The results of this presentation of Ireland can be seen in the actual life of Patrick Pearse, who gave up family, love, and marriage, and died for his country. The most striking feature of Yeats's Cathleen is, of course, her transformation at the end:

PETER: Did you see an old woman going down the path?

PATRICK: I did not, but I saw a young girl, and she had the walk of a queen.

(ll. 345–48)

In the transformation we see the influence of medieval Irish literature, in particular the influence of stories like that of Niall, in which the hag metamorphoses into a beautiful woman.

To summarize, then, the early Irish mythological figures survived and

14. See MacBride, *Servant of the Queen*, for this iconography in Maud Gonne's autobiography.

15. R. Clark discusses the development and mutual influences of the war goddesses and the Sovereignty in Anglo-Irish literature.

were adapted in later Irish literary tradition, particularly in the aisling poems; still later they were used by Anglo-Irish writers, most notably Yeats in his *Cathleen ni Houlihan*.[16] The two faces of the Sovereignty, hag and young woman, both continued in the tradition, leading to such figures as Mangan's Dark Rosaleen on the one hand, and to hags such as the Shan Van Vocht, the Poor Old Woman, and Cathleen Ni Houlihan on the other. By the end of the nineteenth century the revival of interest in Ireland's medieval literary heritage and the attempts to reclaim that heritage through the publication, translation, and adaptation of texts meant that these female types had become part of the cultural consciousness of the nation. Because of the mythic heritage of Ireland and the nationalist literary revival of that heritage in English, the semiotics of female figures in Irish and in Joyce's Anglo-Irish tradition is distinct from the semiotics of female figures in other English-speaking areas or in Continental tradition. Lack of awareness of these semiotic values of women has been a serious limitation of the critical orthodoxy regarding Joyce's women.

The question of Joyce's early Irish sources for his Sovereignty imagery is complex since the imagery was so well established in the Ireland of his youth. It can nonetheless be documented that he was acquainted with a number of publications that would have familiarized him with stories about the Irish goddesses and other euhemerized female figures of early Irish literature. Many of the early stories related to the female mythological characters are summarized in the general histories of Ireland as well as in d'Arbois de Jubainville's *Irish Mythological Cycle and Celtic Mythology*. Augusta Gregory's *Cuchulain of Muirthemne* and her *Gods and Fighting Men* are other sources in which Joyce would have found the main lines of much of early Irish literature, including an outline of the goddess figures. There is also evidence that Joyce read some scholarly sources for early Irish tradition in 1901–2, when he was studying Modern Irish, and by the time he wrote *Ulysses* he was familiar with *Táin Bó Cúailnge*, which features the figure of Medb, a sexually vigorous and imperious female.

Joyce knew Mangan's reworkings of the aisling tradition as well; his enthusiasm for Mangan is well known, and he writes of both Mangan's

---

16. For more detailed treatments of the topic, see Breatnach; Corkery 126–42; Bessai, "Who Was Cathleen Ni Houlihan?"; and Bessai, " 'Dark Rosaleen.' "

"Kathleen-Ni-Houlahan" and "Dark Rosaleen" as poems he appreciated (CW 79–80). Joyce was familiar with the aisling tradition in general, as references in *Finnegans Wake* indicate (e.g., 179.31). He was also sensible of the emotional and political overtones of the Sovereignty imagery used by Mangan, as he indicates in his 1902 lecture; indeed, Joyce analyzes Mangan by himself using Sovereignty imagery:

In the final view the figure which [Mangan] worships is seen to be an abject queen upon whom, because of the bloody crimes that she has done and of those as bloody that were done to her, madness is come and death is coming, but who will not believe that she is near to die and remembers only the rumour of voices challenging her sacred gardens and her fair, tall flowers that have become the food of boars. (CW 82; cf. CW 185–86)

This assessment of Mangan's Sovereignty imagery shows that Joyce was critical of the political views behind the Irish nationalist use of the figure; it is clear that Joyce believed that the old Gaelic nationalist ideal was beyond reviving. Joyce also knew Yeats's refraction of the myth of the Sovereignty, *Cathleen ni Houlihan*, but found it of little appeal. Stanislaus Joyce reports that his brother "was indignant that Yeats should write such political and dramatic claptrap" (*MBK* 187). It is significant that in *Ulysses* it is the Citizen, rather than Stephen or Bloom, who embraces the symbols of Yeats's play. This is Joyce's comment on the nature of Yeats's audience for the play and the type of mentality that would welcome that particular manifestation of Gaelic nationalism.

ii. *Petticoat government*: Molly Bloom as Sovereignty

Joyce had used Sovereignty imagery before writing *Ulysses*. Janet Grayson has shown that *A Portrait of the Artist as a Young Man* is structured around the motif of the kiss, "on each occasion . . . offered by a temptress, all of whom are aspects of the land, Ireland—correspondences Joyce takes pains to develop" (121–22). The kiss becomes symbolic of submission to Ireland and to Ireland's history, both of which Stephen rejects lest his life as an artist be compromised. Yet, ironically, as Grayson suggests, Stephen will become no artist until he learns "to love the old girl, imperfect though she may be" (125). It is as if Stephen cannot become the artist-as-priest until he is willing to kiss, just as only a young man willing to kiss the Sovereignty will become the sacral king. Here the connection of becoming an artist with kissing or accepting a woman symbolic of Ireland shows that the Sovereignty functions as the poet's muse—a development implicit in some of the aisling poems and explicit in Yeats's work, particularly in his treatment of Red Hanrahan (Bessai, "Who Was Cathleen Ni Houlihan?" 129). In Joyce's work the motif of kissing also figures in *Exiles*, where a kiss "is an act of homage" and "an act of union" (*E* 41) and where the woman also represents Ireland. The language in Joyce's play suggests the sort of political overtones that Sovereignty imagery has always evoked in Ireland; the phrase "an act of union" is particularly suggestive.

Arguing that Sovereignty imagery pervades much of Joyce's work, Hugh Kenner sees in Joyce's tendency to use doubled female figures a legacy of this Irish mythological pattern. Kenner maintains that the doubling of females may have evolved from Joyce's brooding over the metamorphosis scene in Yeats's *Cathleen ni Houlihan*. According to Kenner, Joyce rejects the transformation of the hag to young woman: "The look of a queen, that is what Joyce rejects. He sees the old woman who beckons to young men to go off and die, and not marry, and he will let no fine talk deflect attention from that" ("Look of a Queen" 118). Kenner contends that many of Joyce's women, from Gretta Conroy to ALP, have a devouring aspect and that in *Ulysses* there are several examples of this typology, including the Church and Stephen's mother. In the dyad Molly/ Milly, Kenner sees one example of Joyce's tendency to double his female protagonists. Kenner overstates the devouring nature of Joyce's female figures by reading them solely in the context of English literature, but it is clear nonetheless that Sovereignty imagery is explicit in *Ulysses*.

The figure of the Shan Van Vocht appears prominently at the opening of *Ulysses* in the person of the poor old woman selling milk who comes to the Martello tower. The old woman in *Ulysses* fits the pattern of the Sovereignty—the hag who has a drink to offer, as in *The Adventure of the Sons of Eochaid Muigmedon*. The fact that she sells milk is both a touch of realism and mythically apposite. In the twentieth century milk is a staple of the Irish diet as it has been since time out of mind: because Irish culture was traditionally pastoral, dairy products have held a larger place in the Irish diet than in the diet of most other European nations. In early Irish culture dairy products were called "white meats" (e.g., *AIT* 553ff.), and the prominence of dairy products in the Irish diet was an object of mockery for English travelers in Ireland in the seventeenth and

eighteenth centuries. At the same time the mythic importance of milk is
seen in the magic cows that play such central roles in early Irish literature
and Modern Irish folklore, as well as in the many early Irish goddesses
who seem to have special dominion over cows. One such example of a
goddess associated with milk is found in *Táin Bó Cúailnge*, where the
Morrigan, disguised as an old woman milking a cow, offers a drink to
CuChulainn.[17]

In *Ulysses* the old woman represents peasant Ireland—the revivalist
ideal of many of Joyce's contemporaries—but a peasant Ireland that appears to be beyond reviving. The crone herself has lost her country's native language; and when Haines the Englishman speaks Gaelic to her, she
takes it to be French. With her "old shrunken paps," distributing "rich
white milk, not hers" (1.397–98), Joyce's poor old woman is also asexual
and infertile. Joyce does not have her metamorphose; she is bound for
the grave, not a second life. For Joyce, Gaelic Ireland is dead, and its symbol, the Shan Van Vocht, is only the butt of jokes, unable to compel young
men to pay for their milk with farthings, never mind their lives.

On Bloomsday Stephen is obsessed with the Shan Van Vocht.
Throughout the day his thoughts turn repeatedly not only to Mangan's
ballads but to Yeats's *Cathleen ni Houlihan* as well. For Stephen the Shan
Van Vocht has become "a crazy queen, old and jealous" whose message
to him is "Kneel down before me" (1.640). She metamorphoses into the
nightmare of Gummy Granny, who demands of him "odd jobs" (1.640),
murder and self-destruction:

OLD GUMMY GRANNY: *(thrusts a dagger towards Stephen's hand)* Remove
him, acushla. At 8:35 a.m. you will be in heaven and Ireland will be free. *(she
prays)* O good God, take him!

(15.4736–39)

She, like Yeats's Cathleen ni Houlihan, devours young men, causing them
to consume each other and in the process consuming them herself, send-
ing them to their deaths. Fused with images of Stephen's own dead
mother, in part because both are associated with a very conventional type
of Irish nationalist Catholicism, the old woman has become "the old sow
that eats her farrow" (15.4582–83; cf. *PA* 203) and, like Death itself,
"the corpsechewer" (15.4214). These images echo the early Irish iconog-

17. See C. O'Rahilly 196–97; cf. Tymoczko, *Two Death Tales* 87–88.

raphy of the war goddesses who can metamorphose into ravens and scald-crows, the scavengers of the battlefield; in addition, Stephen's aphorism about "the old sow that eats her farrow" is a multilingual pun on one of the traditional names of Ireland, Banba, which is homophonous with *banb*, 'young pig'.[18]

If Joyce directly rejects the image of *Cathleen ni Houlihan* and the Poor Old Woman, he relies on other aspects of the Sovereignty in early Irish literature for his treatment of Molly Bloom. Molly has long been recognized as a goddess figure and has been identified with a "Gaea-Tellus" type.[19] The Gaea-Tellus model for Molly fits with the Joycean exegetical tradition based on classical myth, and it is signaled in the text itself (17.2313). Only relatively recently has the character of Molly as classical earth mother begun to give way to a mythic conception of Molly that shows some Celtic configurations, including those of the Celtic goddesses associated with the land. This aspect of Molly's nature is suggested in Joyce's note to "Ithaca" that reads "her rump = promised land" (Herring, *Joyce's "Ulysses" Notesheets* 463), which establishes her as an earth goddess in terms that recall the theme of Ireland as the second promised land, a central theme of *The Book of Invasions*.

The importance of history and pseudohistory in Irish literature has already been touched on, but it must be emphasized that historicization is the hallmark of Irish mythology. Though *The Book of Invasions* was composed to parallel such classical histories as those of Origen and Eusebius, gradually it accreted bits of cosmogony and old myth and eventually became the organizing referent for all of early Irish tradition. The process of historicization was both the salvation and destruction of early Irish mythology. On the one hand, because the material was euhemerized, much of Celtic religious mythology survived Ireland's conversion to Christianity. On the other hand, euhemerization has irrevocably marked and distorted all of early Irish narrative: the old myths were remolded as history; the mythic time frame of the old gods was coordinated with the progress of Judeo-Christian history; the character of the gods became obscured. Since virtually all of the old hero tales and tales of the gods were

18. Joyce here anticipates the type of linguistic play that characterizes *Finnegans Wake*.

19. For a discussion of this typology and a bibliography of the critics who have investigated it, see B. Scott 158–59 and the reference cited there.

located at points on the Christian-Latin time line of history, there are euhemerized mythic figures in all the major cycles of early Irish literature.

Molly Bloom thus takes her place in the long line of Irish euhemerized
goddesses. Indeed, the way Molly's character is poised between mythic
and realistic components itself recapitulates almost perfectly the presentation of most of the great female figures of early Irish literature, particularly as presented in the sources Joyce would have known. The female
figures take their place fully in a historical context, yet their characters
are informed by mythic patterns. The most striking and well known example of this sort is Medb of Cruachan, the queen of Connacht and
leader of Ulster's enemies in *Táin Bó Cúailnge*. Many aspects about
Medb—from her name, which means 'the intoxicating one' (connecting
her with the ale of sovereignty), to her wide onomastic connections, to
her history in one text of having a long series of husbands[20]—indicate that
she is the euhemerized Sovereignty of Tara who has been translated to
Connacht, yet she is localized in one specific temporal period and treated
as a historical figure in the text of *Táin Bó Cúailnge* itself.

Celtic myth provides many parallels to Molly's urination and menstruation, symbols that are central to the linked destructive and procrea-
tive powers of Celtic mother goddesses. Charles Bowen ("Great-
Bladdered Medb") has argued that menstruation and urination in early
Irish literature are both centrally connected with the powers of the Celtic
mother goddesses. The blood of menstruation, the literal demonstration
of female fertility and the female life force, is one reason the goddesses
were connected with bloody war. Bowen connects urination, by contrast,
with the life-bringing powers and creative fertilization of water—rain,
rivers, and amniotic fluid. Bowen sees this water symbolism as linking the
territorial or Sovereignty goddesses with the Celtic river goddesses. The
dual symbolism of blood and urine is found at the end of *Táin Bó
Cúailnge*, where Medb fills three lakes with her *fúal fola*, literally her 'urine of blood' or her 'bloody urine' (C. O'Rahilly 133).

These elements of blood and urine are also central to the portrait of

---

20. See O'Neill; an alternate title for the text is *Ferchuitred Medba* (*Medb's
Portion of Men*). Medb of Cruachan also has a double, Medb Lethderg, 'Medb
redside' or 'Medb halfred', of whom it is stated explicitly, "She it was who would
not allow a king in Tara without his having herself as a wife." For these points
as well as a general survey of Medb as a Sovereignty figure, see Ó Máille.

Molly in *Ulysses* since Molly produces a large volume of mixed menstrual flow and urine (18.1104–48), and they connect Molly with the Irish river goddesses. Frank Budgen pointed in this direction as early as 1934, when he described Molly's monologue in terms of a river: "Marion's monologue snakes its way through the last forty pages of *Ulysses* like a river winding through a plain, finding its true course by the compelling logic of its own fluidity and weight" (*Making of "Ulysses"* 262). It is not simply that the monologue represents "the displacement to language of her urinary and menstrual flow," a kind of mental punning on the body, as Mark Shechner (217) would have it. Rather, Molly's bodily flow and fluid language are both part of her mythic nature as Joyce has delineated it in *Ulysses*; they are counterparts and complements to the earth-goddess aspects of her portrait. The circularity of Molly's soliloquy, which begins and ends with "Yes," is more than a counterpart to her nature as earth goddess, a sign of her as the "huge earth ball slowly . . . spinning" (*Letters* 1: 170); this circularity is also one facet of Molly as a river deity. Joyce matured and perfected the image of Molly as river goddess in the figure of ALP in *Finnegans Wake*; but as in *Finnegans Wake* the circularity of Molly's speech should be related to the continuous cycle of the waters running from cloud to rain to river to sea to cloud again.

The associations of the goddesses' urine with fertility may explain why one early Irish text stresses women's urination as a measure of sexual potency. In *Aided Derbforgaill* (*The Death of Derbforgaill*) the women of Ulster have a contest urinating on a phallic pile of snow; the one whose urine penetrates most deeply is deemed to have the greatest sexual potency. The winner of the contest, Derbforgaill, arouses so much jealousy among the other women that they disfigure her, causing her eventually to die of shame (Marstrander, "Deaths of Lugaid"). Molly's urination and her sexual nature, like Derbforgaill's, are interconnected by Irish iconography. All these considerations indicate that what appears to be a touch of naturalism in *Ulysses*—Molly's chamberpot sequence, complete with the emphasis on the volume of her urine and the beginning of her period—has its place in the mythic framework of Joyce's early Irish prototypes. It is probably significant that toward the end of his life Yeats also drew on these same mythic elements, particularly the Derbforgaill story; in "Crazy Jane on the Mountain" Yeats uses early Irish prototypes to represent the full-bodiedness that twentieth-century Ireland has lost, and he refers to CuChulainn's wife as "Great bladdered Emer." Molly, like

Derbforgaill in the Irish story and Yeats's Great bladdered Emer, is a heroine of micturition.[21]

Molly's urinary capacity is only one of the Celtic mythological components related to her sexuality. Bonnie Kime Scott has observed (180–81) that Molly, like all the Sovereignty figures, has had a succession of lovers, and like them she is not apologetic about her sexual appetites. Whether or not we accept David Hayman's view that Bloomsday is special because it marks Molly's first affair within marriage ("Empirical Molly" 113ff.),[22] it is obvious that sexuality is a vital part of her character. Robert Adams suggests that it would be grotesque to suppose that she would "be content with one sexual contact in ten years," since she "exists in an atmosphere of sexual provocation" and the whole tenor of her thought is against the assumption of a single lover (37–41). Adams attributes some of the textual disarray with respect to Molly's actual sexual contact to the fact that Joyce was a jealous man "who used the object of his jealousy as a model." It seems, however, that in this instance the break in the mimetic surface of *Ulysses* is as likely to be related to Joyce's mythic prototypes for Molly as to his psychological dispositions toward his wife: this is again one of Joyce's "portals of discovery" (9.229). That the list of Molly's possible lovers ends "and so each and so on to no last term" (17.2141–42) is a signal to the reader that this woman has the immortal status of the Sovereignty and that her series of potential lovers extends through the eternal time frame of the gods, just as she herself through metempsychosis and shapeshifting will persist.[23]

Like her predecessors in Irish literature, Molly engages in sexual acts for their own sake. No more than her Irish mythic foremothers is Molly interested much in sentiment and romantic love; like them, she neither exhibits guilt about her sexual acts nor expects to curtail her behavior. Sexuality is of Molly's essence, just as sexuality is essential to the Sovereignty goddess. Medb is again an accessible example of this mytholog-

21. We might ask in fact whether Yeats's image of "Great bladdered Emer" and his more frank treatment of sexuality with respect to Crazy Jane was influenced by *Ulysses* and his perception of Joyce's treatment of Irish tradition or whether Yeats and Joyce are simply drawing independently on the same literary heritage. I incline to the former alternative.

22. See also the supporting arguments in references cited by Hayman, as well as Kenner, "Molly's Masterstroke" 23ff.

23. For another view of this listing as the narrator's imagination brooding on Molly's affairs, which take on "truly epic proportions," see McCarthy 613–16.

ical dimension of Irish female types: without apology Medb tells her consort Ailill that she requires a husband with no jealousy, for, she says, "I was never without [one] man in the shadow of another" (C. O'Rahilly 138). Medb, like Molly, also thinks about sleeping with even more men than she does—offering her "friendly thighs" throughout *Táin Bó Cúailnge.*[24] This Irish paradigm for Molly, which includes the vigorous sexuality of early Irish goddesses, resolves the paradoxes of her character as both earth mother and "thirty-shilling whore."

In the earlier discussion of Molly's flow, I noted that Shechner (219) sees Molly's monologue as being a linguistic and mental reflection of her physical menstruation; thus, he sees the roses and crimson sea in her musings (18.1601ff.) as correlates of her own menstrual blood. Perhaps more to the point, the crimson images and the menstrual blood of the soliloquy link Molly to the war goddesses of Irish literature, for women's capacity to bleed and not die, their shedding of menstrual blood, is a prime source of their terror to men.[25] But Molly is associated with war in more direct ways as well: as a daughter of a soldier in an Irish regiment of the British army, her connections with war are manifest. She is proud of being a soldier's daughter (18.881–82), and she has been brought up in a military environment.[26] She loves seeing soldiers on parade, and her first lovers are young soldiers. It is a brilliant touch of naturalism that Joyce should explain both her military connections and her Spanish origin by having her father in service with the British troops in Gibraltar, as many Irishmen actually were. Molly's connections with war are rather muted, however: she appreciates the more harmless aspects of the military, such as its pageantry and the handsome bodies of the young men in service. In these aspects of Molly's characterization we perhaps see Joyce's pacifism attenuating what he may have felt to be a requisite part of the Irish delineation

24. See Kinsella's translation.

25. Irish goddesses are at times associated with the color red, and the appearance of the Morrigan in *The Cattle Raid of Regamna* is a particularly striking example: "They saw before them a chariot harnessed with a chestnut horse. The horse had but one leg, and the pole of the chariot passed through its body, so that the peg in front met the halter passing across its forehead. Within the chariot sat a woman, her eye-brows red, and a crimson mantle around her. Her mantle fell behind her between the wheels of the chariot so that it swept along the ground" (*AIT* 211–12).

26. Herring, "Toward an Historical Molly Bloom" 504, 517, emphasizes the military nature of Gibraltar.

of mythic female figures.[27] Note that Molly is also literally daughter of 'a soldier of Spain'—or, as the Irish would say, daughter of *Míl Espáine*, hence a Milesian. Here Joyce is creating an image involving verbal realism that links naturalism, mythic symbolism of the Sovereignty and the war goddesses, and symbolism from *The Book of Invasions*.

Despite her connections with the military, Molly's primary associations, like those of most Irish mythological women, are with fertility. She delights in the produce of the earth, in flowers and fruit—aspects that link her to Tailltiu of *The Book of Invasions* specifically and to the Celtic mother goddesses in general. Her union with Bloom, marked by the transfer to him of the seedcake during their lovemaking, associates her, like many Irish goddesses, with grains.[28] Bonnie Kime Scott notes also that Molly intends to give Bloom eggs in the morning and that eggs are symbols of fertility (181). The emphasis on Molly's breasts throughout *Ulysses* may be related to the importance of milk in Irish culture and to the Irish interest in the goddesses' paps. She is obviously "a good milker"—she had a "great breast of milk" when she was nursing Milly (18.570–71), Bloom himself has tried her milk and found it good enough to want to milk her into the tea (18.578), and he appreciates "her large soft bubs, sloping within her nightdress like a shegoat's udder" (4.304–05). Finally, though Molly's concern with nutrition may be related to Joyce's Aristotelian concepts of women (Voelker 39–40),[29] it also fits the pattern of Celtic mother goddesses, who are patrons of agrarian concerns of all types and thus intimately connected with nourishment.

In assessing Molly's fertility we cannot ignore the fact that she is menstruating every three weeks (18.1151). She is potentially fertile inconveniently often, having roughly the shortest menstrual cycle that still falls

27. Shechner (221–22) and others have noted that Molly is the agent of Joyce's vengeance, embodying the cutting edge of his wit: her condescension cuts a swath through the corn of Dublin, and her judgments are the means by which the suitors are slain. These aggressive aspects of her character also connect her with the war goddesses.

28. See Máire Mac Neill, passim. A number of female figures have names that specifically link them with cereals, including *Eithne*, 'kernel', and *Gráinne*, 'grain, seed'.

29. In general the philosophical predisposition Voelker outlines can be nicely integrated with the mythological framework of mother goddesses. See below, for example, on the mythological dimension of Molly's stationary quality, and cf. Voelker 38.

within the normal range. The fact that she has borne only two children despite her frequent ovulation should not suggest that she is infertile. It seems to be her choice not to have had more children, for she has the sense she could choose to bear another child at any time (18.166). The small number of her children coupled with her frequent fertile periods can most easily be explained by realism. Molly is a modern woman who *chooses* to limit the number of her children through the use of birth control; ALP and HCE make the same choice in *Finnegans Wake*. Molly's assertion of reproductive choice may relate to a controversial aspect of *Ulysses*: the "disrupted" sexual relations between Molly and Bloom. Although it is true that Molly no longer finds sexual relations with her husband fully satisfying, we can perhaps best understand their sexual patterns in the historical context of 1904, when coitus interruptus was the most available, most dependable, and most widely practiced form of birth control short of abstinence. This reading of the sexual relations between Molly and Bloom fits with the fact that Joyce nowhere says they don't have intercourse;[30] instead, he specifies the limits of their relations: "there remained a period of 10 years, 5 months and 18 days during which carnal intercourse had been incomplete, without ejaculation of semen within the natural female organ" (17.2282–84). It is Molly who has apparently claimed to Blazes Boylan that she and her husband do not have sexual relations, but she is glad that Bloom will not be accompanying them to Belfast since she fears her deception will be revealed: "its all very well a husband but you cant fool a lover after me telling him we never did anything of course he didnt believe me" (18.354–56). Her decision not to have children results in coitus interruptus with her lover as well as her husband (18.154–55; cf. 18.168), and at the end of the book she is relieved that she has started her period, knowing that she's not pregnant (18.1123) despite the fact that she let Boylan finish it off in her the last time they made love.

There are also mythological parallels to Molly's practice of birth control, for in Irish myth, as in myth and folklore worldwide, women are sometimes credited with the ability to control conception voluntarily.

---

30. Cf. Hayman, "Empirical Molly" 115, who notes that their sexual arrangements do not preclude coitus interruptus, cunnilingus, manual stimulation, and the nightly buttock kiss.

Thus, for example, in *Tochmarc Emire* (*The Wooing of Emer*) Cu-
Chulainn elicits the agreement from Aife that she will bear him a son, the
implication being that the ability to do so or not is within her control
(*AIT* 167). Note also that the fertility of the Sovereignty in early Irish
literature is not always demonstrated by her bearing many children herself. As Mac Cana has observed ("Aspects of the Theme" 7: 88, 95, 98),
it is primarily in her role as the mother of a sovereign or the founder of
a lineage that the procreation of the goddess is stressed. In stories emphasizing union or the relations of the Sovereignty with a spouse—as we
might argue *Ulysses* does on a realistic level—childbearing per se is less
significant.

Like the Sovereignty goddesses, Molly is also queenly and imperious.
She lies in bed while her husband serves her, and she cuckolds him in his
own bed. Bonnie Kime Scott (181) has pointed out that Molly also demands tributes: another book and lotion for her eternal youth. When we
see Molly in the context of Irish literature rather than English or Continental literature, there is no reproaching her for these qualities. They are
part of her typology.

Clearly Molly is a recumbent figure, and Celtic and classical models
converge in their prototypes for this recumbency, for there are earth goddesses in both traditions. The Celtic Sovereignty goddesses are sometimes
literally identified with specific districts that bear their names; they are
tied to a place. Molly's beddedness and stationary physical location are
thus appropriate qualities for a Sovereignty figure. Moreover, since rivers
flow in beds, Molly's location melds both earth-goddess and river-
goddess imagery, and again she prefigures ALP in this regard. Nonetheless, Molly's preference is *not* to be at home—her fondest memories are
of walking out in the world (cf. B. Scott 170). In this respect she is not
unlike Celtic territorial goddesses, who were mobile in their human form
and walked about in their territory, though it was not given to every mortal to see them on such occasions. The readers of *Ulysses* are in the position of ordinary mortals with respect to the Sovereignty: we hear reports of Molly's appearances in the world, but it is not ours to encounter
her on such an occasion. In fact, aside from the chamberpot episode, we
see her out of bed only once: as the flash of a white arm distributing largesse to a beggar (10.222, 250–53, 542). The activity is appropriate for
a euhemerized fertility goddess, and this veiled glimpse of a woman pow-

erful enough to rearrange the furniture of her house (as a goddess might rearrange her territory) is like the epiphany of a divinity.[31]

I have elaborated on the parallels between Molly and early Irish literature to show that Joyce's character fits thoroughly in the framework of Irish literary tradition as well as in the framework of Irish myth and Irish archetypes. The parallels are so deep and so pervasive that they cannot be the result of fortuitous likeness or polygenesis. Although the comparisons between Molly and women in early Irish literature have been somewhat detailed, they are by no means exhaustive. Much remains to be done. A review of the criticism of *Ulysses* shows that virtually every aspect about Molly has been investigated save the ways she is a product of Irish literary history and Irish symbology—the ways she should be referred to Irish literature as much or more so than to life or to other literary systems.

Aside from the reluctance of most orthodox Joyceans to consider Joyce's Irish literary heritage seriously, the neglect of Molly's Irish mythic background results from the fact that sexuality in *Ulysses* is expressed in modern forms rather than early Irish ones. Because the forms of sexual encounter are different, the connection between Molly and the sexual females in early Irish literature is somewhat effaced. Here it is well to remember one of Joyce's earliest aesthetic statements, delivered in his lecture "Drama and Life" in 1900: "The forms of things . . . are changed. . . . But the deathless passions, the human verities which so found expression then, are indeed deathless, in the heroic cycle, or in the scientific age" (*CW* 45). We have become more comfortable with female sexuality in the years since *Ulysses* was published, yet it is worth noting that Molly's frank thoughts about penises or her enjoyment of obscenity are modern counterparts to the medieval characters' direct solicitations of their lovers; they are also manifestations particularly appropriate for narrative in the form of interior monologue. Joyce merges Irish mythic structures and convincing mimesis smoothly in his portrait of Molly in *Ulysses*.

The sexual elements of early Irish literature would have particularly appealed to Joyce, and he no doubt enjoyed renewing them in modern guise. He loathed the tenets of sexual purity preached by the church, by

31. For the argument that Molly has herself rearranged the furniture in honor of Boylan's visit, see Honton.

Victorianism, and by contemporary feminists (B. Scott 33), and we can surmise that he disliked the emphasis on chastity in Yeats's *Cathleen ni Houlihan*. Joyce's attitude toward sexuality in general distinguishes him from most of the other writers of the Anglo-Irish revival. In fact, the sexual aspects of early Irish literature were an embarrassment to most of the major figures of the Irish revival and were one element leading to the suppression and distortion of early Irish literature in English translations.

The mythic components related to the Sovereignty interlock with the architectonic structures from *The Book of Invasions*. Molly's identification with Tailltiu is particularly apt since Tailltiu clearly is a Sovereignty figure. Wife of successive kings, foster mother to a third king, situated in a plain profuse with flowers, Tailltiu draws together a number of the Sovereignty characteristics. We have also seen that Molly is identified with Ireland as the second promised land and that she is a daughter of Mil Espaine. Molly's one surviving child is named Milly, and it is amusing to find that the Milesians are called "Clan Milly" in the text of *Ulysses* (14.371), a term found also in Collier's *History of Ireland for Schools* (10–11), which was part of Joyce's personal library in 1920. It is no accident that the symbol systems pertaining to the Sovereignty and *The Book of Invasions* reinforce and amplify each other: that is the way of a vigorous, coherent tradition. An author writing in a tradition of this kind will tap its power on several levels simultaneously, just as Joyce has done in *Ulysses*.

iii. King and goddess:
Bloom, *unconquered hero*

If Molly is a Sovereignty figure, Bloom cannot simply be considered a henpecked, mealymouthed husband: his waiting on her, his serving her breakfast in bed, his running errands for her and bringing her offerings are things one might expect of the mortal consort of a goddess. Molly is an earth goddess, associated with dominion as Celtic Sovereignty figures are; thus, when Bloom kisses her rere on returning to her domain, her bed, he does not act very differently from Ulysses himself, who kisses the earth after landing at Ithaca. The Sovereignty framework thus provides a perspective on the relationship between Molly and her husband as well as an alternate reading of Bloom's character. Still, the question must be put directly: is Bloom the rightful spouse for a Sovereignty goddess? The reader, echoing Bloom's own question (11.732, 13.1209), must ask why Molly chose Bloom.

In exploring the Sovereignty theme in *A Portrait of the Artist*, Grayson observes (124) that the chosen male frequently has a marked name and that Stephen Dedalus's special name is consonant with Joyce's development of this theme in *A Portrait*. In *Ulysses* Joyce again signals the hero's status by conferring on him a special name, choosing *Bloom* for the name of Molly's husband. Molly is explicit about the fact that the name is pleasing to her (18.841), and for an English speaker the presumption must be that this is the case because of the connection with flowers and fertility. So it is, and Bloom's name is, moreover, a piece of verbal realism; he is essentially connected with flowers, for his father's Hungarian name, *Virag*, 'flower', was merely changed to the equivalent English signifier, with the signified remaining stable. As it turns out, Molly's "fib" to Mulvey that she was to be married to the son of a Spanish nobleman named Don Miguel de la Flora (18.773–74) prefigures her marriage to Bloom; her statement is prophetic, another instance of verbal realism inasmuch as the name *de la Flora* may be read as an alternative to *Bloom*, signifying her "destined" spouse.

As an essential bloom, Bloom can also presumably recognize his kind, and he wins Molly with his words as much as his deeds: "yes he said I was a flower of the mountain yes so we are flowers all a womans body yes that was one true thing he said in his life" (18.1576–77). Bloom perceives that Molly is a flower (cf. 8.910), and she conceives of herself in the same way (18.1602); thus, there is an element of recognition in their mating, similar to the recognition that is associated with Sovereignty stories like *The Adventure of the Sons of Eochaid Muigmedon*. In their essences as well as through the magic of words, Bloom and Molly are alike, fitting mates.

Let us digress a moment to consider Molly-the-flower-of-the-mountain. If she is a flower, what sort of flower is she? Joyce here invites us to penetrate the signs he has left and the rhetorical question implicit in the text: she is a flower, a dark flower, a woman who would love "to have the whole place swimming in roses" (18.1557–58), a woman who wears roses in her hair ("a red yes") (18.1603), a woman "in her roses" (cf. 5.285). In Irish tradition the semiotics of the flower imagery suggests that Molly is to be construed as a rose—as, in fact, *the* rose, the Dark Rosaleen. The references to roses throughout *Ulysses* confirm Molly as a Sov-

ereignty figure and tie Molly to Mangan's "Dark Rosaleen," to the Anglo-
Irish symbolism that derives from Mangan, and to the earlier Irish
"Róisín Dubh"; and Joyce's humorous view of Molly, like his humor
throughout *Ulysses*, does not invalidate this identification. Though full-
blown on Bloomsday and no longer "the *little* dark rose," *róisín dubh*,
Molly's floral nature is a semiotic concomitant of her Sovereignty status;
and Bloom's name, as well as his ability to recognize her nature, is a sign
that he is her rightful spouse. With the rose imagery Joyce lightly, playfully, but traditionally evokes established political and literary symbolism
for female figures representing Ireland and for their male partners.[32]

These aspects of Bloom's name are essential but do not exhaust the
meaning of the name *Bloom*. Within Irish tradition there is yet another
level of significance, for the name holds a place in Irish mythology and
toponymy, with *Bloom* being the English eponym of Slieve Bloom, the
prominence in the midlands of Ireland called *Sliabh Bladhma* in Irish.
This place name is twice mentioned in the text of *Ulysses*, and in one of
those instances it is identified with Leopold Bloom specifically: "Boys are
they? Yes. Inishturk. Inishark. Inishboffin. At their joggerfry. Mine. Slieve
Bloom" (4.138–39; cf. 12.1833). This well-known mountain had figured
in Anglo-Irish refractions of the mythic literature; thus, in Standish
O'Grady, for example, "Eire" the great queen of Ireland has her throne
on "Slieve Blahma" (*History of Ireland* 1: 70). Joyce might also have
found information on Slieve Bloom in P. W. Joyce's works. For example,
in *Origin and History of Irish Names of Places* Slieve Bloom is said to
be named after "Bladh, [one] of Brogan's sons," a Milesian who, P. W.
Joyce suggests, might also have given his name to Lickbla, "Bladh's flag-
stone" (*Liag Bladhma*), in Westmeath. P. W. Joyce also notes that "Ar-
derin ['the height of Ireland'] in the Queen's County is the highest of the
Slieve Bloom range; and the inhabitants of the great central plain who
gave it the name, signifying the height of Ireland, unaccustomed as they
were to the view of high mountains, evidently believed it to be one of the
principal elevations in the country" (373). Since James Joyce refers to

---

32. Molly's pleasure in flowers of all kinds, with its Aristotelian overtones and
its fertility associations, acts at the same time as a naturalistic envelope for her
symbolic association with roses and her flower nature. In the multiple levels of
this aspect of the text is encapsulated Joyce's manipulation of the modes of realism and symbolism, his use of the mythic, the philosophical, the political, and
the historical.

P. W. Joyce's volume in the broadside "Gas from a Burner" (CW 244), it is quite possible that he knew these particular entries related to Slieve Bloom, but it is also possible that his knowledge derived from other sources, including oral ones.

Thus, not only is Bloom associated with flowers through his name and essential nature, but he is also the namesake of a primordial Milesian in whose territory the eponymous goddess of Ireland resides. The toponymic associations for Bloom's name fit with the heroic elements in his characterization; moreover, in his identification with placelore and the land, Bloom anticipates the placelore associated with the male figures of *Finnegans Wake*. Thus, in virtue of his name Leopold Bloom is the destined consort for the Sovereignty, having suited in another incarnation Eriu herself (cf. J. Williams and Ford 218).

While Bloom's name suggests his fitness to be consort of Molly-as-rosy-Sovereignty, it is essential to consider the larger lines of his character and to compare them to other consorts of Sovereignty figures in Irish tradition. Here Ailill, the spouse of the Sovereignty figure Medb, serves as a useful parallel. Though Ailill is somewhat burlesqued in *Táin Bó Cúailnge*,[33] he is a character of some standing elsewhere in the early tales. In the "Pillowtalk" introduction to the twelfth-century version of *Táin Bó Cúailnge* Medb makes it clear that she, not Ailill, chose their union and that she believes he is the right man for her because of his qualities. She tells him:

I demanded a strange bride-gift such as no woman before me had asked of a man of the men of Ireland, to wit, a husband without meanness, without jealousy, without fear. If my husband should be mean, it would not be fitting for us to be together, for I am generous in largesse and the bestowal of gifts and it would be a reproach for my husband that I should be better than he in generosity, but it would be no reproach if we were equally generous provided that both of us were generous. If my husband were timorous, neither would it be fitting for us to be together, for single-handed I am victorious in battles and contests and combats, and it would be a reproach to my husband that his wife should be more courageous than he, but it is no reproach if they are equally courageous provided that both are courageous. If the man with whom I should be were jealous, neither would it be fitting, for I was never without

33. Similarly, Medb is the butt of medieval misogyny in the text, particularly in the twelfth-century version.

[one] man in the shadow of another. Now such a husband have I got, even you, Ailill mac Rosa Ruaid of Leinster. You are not niggardly, you are not jealous, you are not inactive. (C. O'Rahilly 138)[34]

The qualities Medb values in her spouse in this early Irish passage are relevant to an assessment of Bloom's character and his relation to Molly, for there are close parallels in *Ulysses*.

In the critical literature on Bloom both his generosity and his bravery have been discussed at length: Bloom has been described as the Homeric hero and the hidden hero (see Kenner, *"Ulysses"* ch. 5), but the same characteristics demonstrate that he is worthy to be a Celtic king. Like Ailill he shows he is without meanness by giving a sizable contribution to the Dignam family and by offering to take Stephen in, thus exhibiting the Celtic heroic virtues of generosity and hospitality. And his lack of fear—or perhaps his courage, in a post–Stephen Crane sense—is shown in Barney Kiernan's pub and in Nighttown. Bloom's lack of jealousy is a primary reason he is laughable and unheroic (or worse) within dominant Western standards (cf. French 61), a problem summed up by Bloom himself: "I am a fool perhaps. He gets the plums, and I the plumstones" (13.1098–99). Yet it is this attitude that is most easily understood in the context of Irish intertextuality. The comparison with Ailill suggests that Molly's infidelities and Bloom's tolerance of them need to be seen in a mythic context rather than in the framework of petit-bourgeois morality. Molly, like Medb, has chosen her marriage because her spouse has a character appropriate to her. Her phrasing of the matter, however, is less blunt, more Victorian, than that of her medieval counterparts: "I saw he understood or felt what a woman is and I knew I could always get round him" (18.1578–80).

Like Ailill, Bloom should be viewed as a man without jealousy, achieving equanimity in the face of his wife's adultery in part because the impetus to union—particularly in a Sovereignty figure—is natural: "As as natural as any and every natural act of a nature expressed or understood executed in natured nature by natural creatures in accordance with his, her and their natured natures, of dissimilar similarity" (17.2178–80). Just as Ailill tolerates Medb's having always "one man in the shadow of an-

---

34. Joyce would have known versions of this passage both from reading Gregory's *Cuchulain of Muirthemne* and from the quotation of the passage in Maud Gonne's speech on Medb, which was printed in the *United Irishman* 5 Oct. 1901.

other," so Bloom will tolerate Molly's involvements with men—on whatever level they occur—"to no last term" (17.2142), because such liaisons are particularly *de naturae* of Irish female mythic figures such as Medb and Molly.

Medb has selected Ailill as a mate who is "without meanness, without jealousy, without fear"; Bloom also fits Medb's requirements and therefore, like Ailill, could be a candidate for her consort. In selecting a mate with the same characteristics as those desired by Medb, Molly establishes her own mythic nature and at the same time valorizes Bloom's character. Leopold Bloom does appear to be the right man to be joined to a Sovereignty figure, and it is thus perhaps less surprising that throughout *Ulysses* he is periodically referred to as a king or prince (15.1471ff., 18.3, 18.931; cf. 11.359, 11.523, 11.1000). Despite the humor and fantasy on the literal level of the text, these references can be considered examples of *the author's* verbal realism pointing to the mythic pattern behind Bloom. Bloom is a rightful king, albeit a modern, domestic representation of one whose kingdom has shrunk to the size of a semidetached villa. Hence, he rightly commands the fruits of the earth—eggs for breakfast—which the goddess will deliver, and the Sovereignty returns to him despite other dalliances she might enjoy.

In early Irish stories the Sovereignty figure usually initiates, invites, and arranges the union with the male, which is sealed with a kiss or sexual intercourse, or both. In *Ulysses* it is thus fitting that Molly initiates sexual contact with both Bloom and Boylan (cf. Honton 26–27). Bloom and Molly both acknowledge that she took the lead in their union, and she is explicit on the point in her monologue: "I got him to propose to me . . . I gave him all the pleasure I could leading him on till he asked me to say yes and I wouldnt answer first only looked out over the sea and the sky I was thinking of so many things he didn't know . . . and then I asked him with my eyes to ask again" (18.1573–1606). In keeping with the mythological prototypes that Joyce is following, neither Molly nor Poldy has memories of their wedding ceremony itself in *Ulysses*. In her memory, the day that marks their union is their day of lovemaking on Howth Head, the day of their breathtaking kiss: "the sun shines for you he said the day we were lying among the rhododendrons on Howth head in the grey tweed suit and his straw hat the day I got him to propose to me yes first I gave him the bit of seedcake out of my mouth and it was leapyear like now yes 16 years ago my God after that long kiss I near lost my breath yes he said I was a flower of the mountain" (18.1571–76). For Leopold, too, that was the decisive day:

Coolsoft with ointments her hand touched me, caressed: her eyes upon me did not turn away. Ravished over her I lay, full lips full open, kissed her mouth. Yum. Softly she gave me in my mouth the seedcake warm and chewed. Mawkish pulp her mouth had mumbled sweetsour of her spittle. Joy: I ate it: joy. Young life, her lips that gave me pouting. Soft warm sticky gumjelly lips. Flowers her eyes were, take me, willing eyes. Pebbles fell. She lay still. A goat. No-one. High on Ben Howth rhododendrons a nannygoat walking surefooted, dropping currants. Screened under ferns she laughed warmfolded. Wildly I lay on her, kissed her: eyes, her lips, her stretched neck beating, woman's breasts full in her blouse of nun's veiling, fat nipples upright. Hot I tongued her. She kissed me. I was kissed. All yielding she tossed my hair. Kissed, she kissed me. (8.904–16)

These passages entwine the flower imagery, the initiation, and the theme of the kiss all associated with Sovereignty figures.

In *Ulysses* the emphasis on kissing as the seal of union between the Sovereignty and her consort is an extension of the Sovereignty theme as it is used in *A Portrait of the Artist.* Stephen cannot kiss the old girl and hence will never be a poet. Bloom, by contrast, has a touch of the artist about him and is a passionate and ready kisser of women. He has patience even with old, unattractive women: Bloom's seemingly ridiculous relationship with Mrs. Riordan should be read in the light of Joyce's Sovereignty imagery. In Molly's interior monologue, not only is their kiss on Howth Head remembered fondly, but the memory itself brings the "transformation" of her attitude toward her husband: her *Yes* is the assent of the Sovereignty. Stephen's obsession with the devouring Shan Van Vocht and his inability to kiss contrast with Bloom's willingness to embrace women, Bloom's ability to bring about their transformation, and Bloom's obsession with the fertility of the women in his world.[35] These differing attitudes toward the Sovereignty and toward women are key in Joyce's shift of focus from Stephen Dedalus to Leopold Bloom in *Ulysses* and

35. Even the menstrual blood of women, which can potentially be connected with war and destruction, is attractive rather than repellent to Bloom; it becomes a sign of their fertility.

part of the significance of the work, involving a transfer of both the author's and the reader's identification to the older and more "all round" protagonist.

Bloom is also a fit spouse for Molly because of his sexual eagerness, which itself has antecedents in early Irish literature. Though the goddess may initiate sexual contact with her prospective partner, in the early Irish *Adventure of the Sons of Eochaid Muigmedon*, for example, Niall can be seen as a fit consort for the Sovereignty because of his sexual readiness: he does more than what the Sovereignty invites him to do by lying with her in addition to kissing her.

So then Niall went seeking water and happened on the same well. "Give me water, O woman," said Niall.

"I will give it," she answered, "but first give me a kiss."

"Besides giving thee a kiss, I will lie with thee!" Then he threw himself down upon her and gave her a kiss. But then, when he looked at her, there was not in the world a damsel whose figure or appearance was more loveable than hers! (*AIT* 511)

If early Irish literature is filled with sexually potent females, it has as well its share of vigorous men like Niall. One example is the Dagda, who copulates with the Morrigan and thus helps to ensure victory in *The Second Battle of Mag Tuired*. The Dagda can be a humorous figure whose distended belly causes problems when he tries to copulate with his enemy's daughter, but he is also known as Eochaid Ollathair, 'Eochaid the Great Father', and his fearsome club both kills and restores life. Fergus mac Roich is another male with prodigious sexual prowess. His name means 'manly strength [or 'potency'] son of great horse'; in "the heptad of Fergus" already quoted he is described as having a penis as long as seven fists and a scrotum the size of a bushel measure, generally requiring seven women to satisfy his sexual desire (Stokes, "Tidings of Conchobor Mac Nessa" 27). Fergus mac Roich also copulates with Medb in *Táin Bó Cúailnge*; and though he loses his sword in the process (!), he is apparently a fitting match for that powerful woman. Fergus's sexual potency is appropriately commemorated in contemporary Irish folk tradition, for the six-foot-long phallic stone at Tara was known to the country people as "the Penis of Fergus" up to the present century (Petrie 225).

Like the Dagda and Fergus, Bloom may be absurd or even burlesqued at times, but that should not defiect us from recognizing his stature any more than we should underestimate the Dagda because the latter can raise a laugh. The estimation of Bloom's character, therefore, must be made not only within the context of Irish myth but also within the parameters of the narrative patterning of Irish myth, including its double consciousness about humor. Like Niall, Bloom was an eager suitor, and Molly remembers fondly his courtship antics, which went far beyond the things she incited him to do (18.294ff.): pestering her for bloomers, threatening to kneel in the public street so as to get a view under her skirt, and so forth. On 16 June 1904, Bloom is a fully mature and vigorous sexual male. His skirt chasing and sexual fantasies are modern expressions of sexual appetites and sexual presence. Like Fergus, he enjoys more than one woman a day—albeit through correspondence and fantasy rather than in the flesh. His penis makes several appearances in the book and even in its limp state is crowned "father of thousands" (5.571). Irony and verbal realism, which are finely balanced in all Irish myth, are reproduced in the Joycean text as well.

If Molly is a great mother figure, Bloom seems her equal as a father figure. He is a literal father to Milly, a foster father to Stephen, a potential "father of thousands," a man with a lot of spunk (18.168). Here again his Jewish associations are useful, for they call to mind the term *patriarch*. Bloom is the male fit to match Molly, the great father to her great mother. Bloom's sexual preoccupations and his intrigues with Martha or Gerty are thus not simply pathetic; they indicate within a surface of realism that Bloom, like Molly, is sexually potent. Though Molly's sexuality is the more striking note in the book, he is her fitting mate. She rightly says that if she chooses to bear another child, it will be by him (18.166–68).

Feminist critics have noted that Bloom has some womanly qualities and have argued that he could be considered androgynous; these qualities can probably be attributed primarily to Joyce's mimesis.[36] However, some features of Irish tradition involve the inversion of Western gender markers and hence might lead to seeming "androgyny" in literature, if not in reality. Perhaps because the Sovereignty pattern is so pervasive in Irish literature, sexual advances in the stories are most commonly attributed to women: women in general are the sexual initiators and solicitors. There

---

36. See, for example, Unkeless, "Leopold Bloom as a Womanly Man"; Herr (149) sounds a cautionary note on this interpretation.

is also a corresponding inversion in mythological stories associated with the motif of the metamorphosis of the lover from hideous object of fear to attractive beauty. Such metamorphosis is generally associated with women in early Irish literature (i.e., the motif of the *puella senilis*), but elsewhere in Western tradition the motif is more commonly associated with the male sexual partner, as in the "animal groom" cycle of tales, including AT 425C, "Beauty and the Beast," where the male lover takes a variety of hideous forms. In Freudian readings this motif has been associated with the psychic acceptance of sexuality in its physical forms and the transference of love from parent to spouse.[37] Whereas in Indo-European tradition as a whole male figures generally symbolize these dimensions of sexuality, in early Irish literature female figures carry these roles. Similarly, early Irish tradition inverts the dialectic of desire. An example of this inversion occurs in the treatment of the motif "red as blood, white as snow" (Z 65.1), which is applied almost invariably worldwide to women or children; in Irish tradition, however, the motif has been adapted as a suitor test, with men becoming the objects of desire.[38] Inversions such as these form a psychic network within which Irish writers write and Irish audiences read. They may appear as "androgyny" in some contexts (particularly from the viewpoint of dominant Western tradition); such inversions are a factor in Joyce's characterizations of Leopold and Molly Bloom and contribute to the readings and misreadings of these characters by critics who do not understand the intertextual matrix of Irish literature within which Joyce wrote.

Claims about Joyce's intrapsychic (or personal) reasons for his presentation of males and females need to be reconsidered in this light. Thus, Shechner's theories in *Joyce in Nighttown* need to be reexamined with a closer understanding of the mythic and archetypal elements of Joyce's Irish cultural heritage. Insofar as Joyce's presentation of womanhood or manhood is "ambiguous," he is squarely within Irish mythological tradition. "Ambiguity" in the sexual roles of Joyce's characters need not be read as personal ambivalence; in Joyce's tradition it may be archetypal. At the same time, in delineating his characters' gender, Joyce is not necessarily attempting to present a "womanly man" or a "manly woman" in

37. See, for example, Bettelheim 277–310. This cycle of tales occurs with male metamorphosis in Modern Irish folklore as well.
38. Motif number H312.5 in Cross's *Motif-Index*; see also Tymoczko, "Animal Imagery" 146–49.

the contemporary sense of androgyny. His use of the Sovereignty pattern underlies much of the skewing of gender roles in *Ulysses* and delimits the areas of deviation from cultural norms. As a result, within a naturalistic framework Molly remains stereotypically female in her thought (Unkeless, "Conventional Molly Bloom" 157), however unusual she may be in other respects. Joyce does not reclaim gender stereotypes: it is only in virtue of her mythic and symbolic nature that Molly achieves a transcendent identity (Unkeless, "Conventional Molly Bloom" 164).

iv. Conclusion

The dyad of the unfaithful woman and the cuckolded husband is given heroic and mythic scaffolding in *Ulysses*: all the Irish goddesses and Sovereignty figures stand behind Molly, and their consorts second Bloom. These mythic structures from Irish literature support the meanings inherent in Joyce's treatment of Molly Bloom. Two representations of the Sovereignty emerge in *Ulysses*: the poor old milkwoman and Molly in her mythic aspects. The first manifestation Joyce rejects and undercuts; the second he elaborates and fleshes out in a contemporary guise. However, the two manifestations are not unrelated; it is no accident that Joyce has treated the Sovereignty theme twice in his book and that he has positioned the two treatments as he has. To see the import of these treatments of the Sovereignty, the way they structure *Ulysses*, and the significance of Molly's sexuality, we must look at the movement of the entire book. We must return to the image of the poor old woman at the opening of *Ulysses*.

Joyce begins with the thin, wasted body of the old milkwoman in the first episode of *Ulysses*, and ends the book with Molly's youthful sexual vigor, her round fully ripe body. The old woman is connected with nourishment, but she is a "witch on her toadstool" with "old shrunken paps" and "wrinkled fingers" (1.398–402). Molly contrasts with the poor old woman as soon as she is introduced, and her full breasts are specially noted (4.304–05). Joyce begins with a woman who, like Cathleen Ni Houlihan, is a wanderer, milking her cows in the field, peddling her wares on the road, never shown at rest or at home, and ends with Molly at home in comfort, well bedded.

Joyce begins with images of the land, but they are desolate images. The opening landscape is the barren shingle bordering a sullen "snotgreen sea" (1.78). Images of death dominate: the drowned man, and the dog carcass, and his mother's body are in Stephen's thoughts as he walks by the sea. The land has apparently lost its fertility; images of the land, the lack of abundance, harmonize with the image of the poor old woman. Molly, like the old woman, is also associated with images of the land, but the landscapes she evokes are lush and rich. Fertility, which is a problem at the beginning of the book, is a leitmotif of the end: Molly dwells on images of abundance, and her soliloquy is laced with images of flowers, fruits, and vegetables.

The weather, too, is awry at the opening of the book. The land is in a "drouth" (4.44). The lack of rain has caused animals and plants alike to suffer. Bloom thinks of eggs for breakfast at the opening of his day and rejects them (4.43–44); since eggs are symbols of fertility, their failure here is significant. The end of the book brings rain, and the weather is restored to its proper patterns. The drought ends with thunder and a downpour, and the rain brings with it revival of the land. Fertility is restored, and Molly will be able to serve eggs for breakfast on the next day.

The mythic elements here are patent, but Joyce's images of barrenness in *Ulysses* do not depend solely on Irish tradition. They also relate to the wasteland imagery of the Grail legends, which were celebrated in Jessie Weston's stimulating book, *From Ritual to Romance*, published in 1920. Weston's influence on Eliot is well known, and he makes his debt to her explicit in his notes to *The Waste Land*, which, like the final episode of *Ulysses*, was written in 1921. In Ireland, where it rains almost daily during most seasons, four or five days of consecutive sunshine can be spoken of as "a drought"; in Ireland it is not therefore dry weather but overly wet weather that is the principal threat to fertility. Accordingly, in Modern Irish the expression meaning "to hay," *an féar a shábháil*, is literally 'to save the hay', a usage that carries over into Anglo-Irish; in most areas of Ireland the climate is so marginal for cereals that the harvesting of grain always has something of the nature of a rescue operation. For these reasons, in early Irish literature infertility of the land is associated primarily with wet, windy, and stormy weather—appropriately enough for a damp island where the annual rainfall ranges between thirty and eighty inches. This is the sort of weather associated with the failure of the sacral king and the wasteland motif in early Irish literature.

The drought and the rain that end it in *Ulysses* appear as an innocuous touch of realism, and in fact in June 1904 there was a dry spell. But these elements, associated as they are with the dual images of the Sovereignty figures at the beginning and end of the book, seem to be connected with the motif of the rightful king; rather than use the Irish iconography of stormy weather or rain for the motif, Joyce chooses a more international manifestation of the mythic pattern, the iconography of which is apparently indebted to sources other than those in early Irish literature. A plausible influence on his treatment of the wasteland motif, leaving aside Eliot and Weston, is James Frazer's *The Golden Bough*, where the motif of the monarch's responsibility for rain and drought is discussed several times in the two volumes of *Adonis, Attis, Osiris* (see 1: 183, 1: 225–26, 2: 201–202), volumes that Joyce appears to have used in *Finnegans Wake* as well.[39]

The movement of *Ulysses* is similar to the movement of Yeats's *Cathleen ni Houlihan*, and it is even closer to the movement of the earlier *Adventure of the Sons of Eochaid Muigmedon*: the old hag gives way to the young woman, asexuality to fecundity and union. The movement of *Ulysses* echoes the transformation of the Sovereignty goddess and is closer to early Irish stories of the Sovereignty than to Yeats's play because the Sovereignty figure in *Ulysses* does not remain chaste as she does in *Cathleen ni Houlihan*. The contrasting images of land and fertility in *Ulysses* are also related to Sovereignty themes of union with the rightful king: a fitting union secures the fruits of the earth and perfect weather; improper union results in the failure of animal and vegetable fertility, in bad weather and barrenness.

The two women, the two images of the Sovereignty of Ireland, the old milkwoman and Molly, bracket the action of the book. Representing morning and night, they sum up the progress of the day. Though the land and weather become transformed, Joyce cannot use the motif of the physical metamorphosis of the Sovereignty within his realistic framework. Rather than metamorphosis of the female figure, there is replacement of character, transformation of the text. The old woman gives way to the young, *the text turns* from the old woman to Molly. The Sovereignty fig-

___

39. These two volumes were also consulted by Eliot, and Atherton (193) finds traces of them in *Finnegans Wake*. Molly's heightened desire in spring ("it was May . . . Im always like that in the spring Id like a new fellow every year" [18.781–82]) may be intended to echo the motif of the annual slaughter of the ritual king that Frazer discusses. (Joyce's architectonics had been set and most of *Ulysses* written by the time Weston's *From Ritual to Romance* appeared.)

ure is a composite, the result of an iconographic palimpsest; and it is literary metamorphosis rather than physical shapeshifting that Joyce uses.

With respect to the relationship of *Ulysses* to Yeats's *Cathleen ni Houlihan*, it is significant that Molly's monologue is a kind of epilogue to *Ulysses*. The action of *Ulysses* properly ends in "Ithaca" (*Letters* 1: 172); yet as Joyce acknowledged to Budgen, Molly's episode is necessary and is the "clou" to the book (*Letters* 1: 170). Before Molly's interior monologue we hear about her from many sources but do not actually learn very much that can be held with certainty (cf. Hayman, "Empirical Molly" 103–11; D. O'Brien 140); it is only in the final episode that we see her ourselves, that Molly is revealed and the Sovereignty theme resolved. With regard to Molly and the Sovereignty mythos, *Ulysses* has the structure of an epiphany: the final chapter presents the reader with a sudden spiritual manifestation of Molly, in which her mythic nature is revealed. The narrative structure of *Ulysses* thus descends from Joyce's earliest experiments with literary prose and from his theory of epiphanies elaborated in *Stephen Hero* (210–13). But the trajectory of *Ulysses* should also be related to that of Yeats's *Cathleen ni Houlihan*, which concludes with an epiphany in which the transformation of the poor old woman happens offstage, outside the action of the play. In the same way the final revelation of Molly happens outside the action of Bloomsday per se.

Kenner argues that in Joyce's treatment of the Sovereignty theme there is no metamorphosis and that this absence constitutes Joyce's "profoundest critique of the mythology of the revival" ("Look of a Queen" 124). *Ulysses* does fit Kenner's observation concerning dyads of women in Joyce's writing, but as I have just argued, there *is* transformation in *Ulysses*. The transformation is a replacement or exchange of Sovereignty figures, textual metamorphosis rather than physical metamorphosis. We begin with an old crone and end with a young girl. And though she may not have "the walk of a queen," she is at least a rosy "flower of the mountain" (18.1602). It should come as no surprise that Joyce can be seen remolding the mythos of *Cathleen ni Houlihan* in *Ulysses*, since Yeats's play was one of the most important pieces of the Irish literary revival, a piece that seized the imagination of a generation and that inspired the Easter Rising.

The Sovereignty myth is at the foundation of Joyce's conception of *Ulysses*, a sign of which is that Joyce had sketched out "Penelope" as early as 1916 (*Letters* 3: 31; cf. Groden 77), conceptualizing the end of the work even as he worked on the initial episodes. The modulation of this controlling myth can also be traced in Joyce's revisions, for in the earliest draft of the first episode Joyce has Stephen (in an echo of Yeats's finale) recognize the old milkwoman as a "wandering queen," only later changing the phrase to "wandering crone" (1.404), thus muting the Sovereignty imagery just as he muted the Homeric parallels by removing the titles of the episodes. The initial version of Joyce's poor old milkwoman was less negative, bearing some of the grandeur of the *puella senilis*; and by changing "queen" to "crone" Joyce emphasizes both the aura of defeat that the old woman emanates as well as her pathos in the final text.[40] Joyce's views of the mythic complex are reflected as well in Stephen's musings about Yeats's *Cathleen*: "Gaptoothed Kathleen, her four beautiful green fields, the stranger in her house" (9.36–37). Stephen quotes lines from Yeats's text even as he embroiders with the adjective "gaptoothed," indicating an awareness of a sexualized version of the Sovereignty myth, which Yeats has bowdlerized.

Not only is the transformation of the Sovereignty suggested by the contrast between the old milkwoman and Molly, but it is also operative within the framework of Molly's monologue itself. The monologue is marked by a regression in time: Molly enters her memories and is transformed from a middle-aged housewife into a young girl. Critics have interpreted this development in a variety of ways—for instance, as indicating Molly's confused mentality or her unhappiness. But Molly's thought in the episode is as easily seen as a progression rather than regression: it is a reflex of the Sovereignty as *puella senilis* on the level of stream of consciousness. The dialectic of transformation is explicit as she worries, "its a wonder Im not an old shrivelled hag before my time living with him so cold never embracing me except sometimes when hes asleep the wrong end of me" (18.1399–1401), and reflects, "a woman wants to be embraced 20 times a day almost to make her look young" (18.1407–8). And it is the memory of the embrace on Howth Head that causes Molly to be regenerated at the end of the chapter in thought, if not in body.

The dual nature of the Irish Sovereignty—hag/girl, war goddess/fertility figure—may explain the devouring aspects that Kenner observes in

---

40. The change occurs in the first page proofs. Note that he first tries "woman" and then settles on "crone," which associates the milkwoman with the Shan Van Vocht. Joyce may also have felt that "queen" was too opaque for his international audience.

Joyce's women. Because Irish mythic females link fertility and dissolu-
tion, they tend to be ambivalent figures; they represent the earth as source
of life and final repository of the dead (Tymoczko, "Unity and Duality").
A writer who uses a mythic method and who refracts Irish Sovereignty
myths will mirror these dualities in his own female characterizations. In
Ulysses, however, Molly's "devouring" aspects are clearly secondary to
her fertility associations. She and the book end with the affirmation of
flowers, nourishment, revitalization: *Yes.*

Joyce does not avoid the physical shapeshifting of the old woman simply for the sake of realism or through a horror of romanticism, as Kenner
would have it. He is juxtaposing the two female figures—as signaled by
his placement of them at beginning and end—and implicitly posing a political question: which is the more appropriate and pleasing form for the
Sovereignty of Ireland? He does not attempt to revitalize the old crone/
queen who represents peasant Gaelic Ireland; her day is done and her de-
crepit condition signals the death for Joyce of Gaelic Ireland, including
its language and its rural, peasant life.

Kenner has shown that *Ulysses* begins with the "two peoples" theme
of captivity and bondage at six removes, as Mulligan parodies the opening of the mass and the raising of the chalice (*"Ulysses"* 35–36). This imagery is biblical and Judeo-Christian, but it is associated with *The Book
of Invasions* as well. By following this invocation with the appearance of
the Poor Old Woman, from the perspective of Irish literary tradition Joyce
fuses the bondage theme of the Milesians with the bondage themes in the
aisling and Sovereignty traditions. Joyce is raising the problem of Irish
nationalism covertly at the outset of his book in terms of the dual patterns
from Irish mythology that he uses to structure all of *Ulysses*: *The Book
of Invasions* and the Sovereignty myth. The ending of the book can be
seen as an attempt to resolve these issues, raised at the outset in symbolic
terms, a resolution that involves metempsychosis rather than transfiguration.

Joyce's treatment of the Sovereignty fits with his view of Irish politics:
he did not accept the hypothesis that Gaelic peasant Ireland should be
renewed so as to become the cornerstone of the new Ireland. Accordingly,
in *Ulysses* he does not rejuvenate the old woman with all her associations—Catholic piety, chastity, insularity, limited vision. In a sense Joyce
portrays the old woman as the wrong bride for the king; she is no longer

to be the object of union; she comes with images of the death of landscape, animals, and people.

Like early Irish literature, *Ulysses* poses ideological questions and sets answers in terms of mythic structures and literary formalism. Like early Irish literature also, *Ulysses* expresses these mythic and political elements humorously and lightheartedly, playfully and even ironically. Joyce's treatment of the Sovereignty material is never sanctimonious, and it may ultimately be the tonal differences between the Sovereignty pattern in *Ulysses* and its appearance in other writings of the Irish literary revival that have kept these elements of *Ulysses* from being recognized. It has been claimed that *Finnegans Wake* demonstrates that "for Joyce myth was not a way of mythologizing a nation; it was a way of demythologizing it" and that in *Finnegans Wake* Joyce was attempting to "demythologize the stock mythology of the new nationalist cult" (Hederman and Kearney, "Editorial").[41] In Joyce's choice of a sexualized version of the Sovereignty pattern for *Ulysses*, in his inversion of the nationalist values associated with the Sovereignty in Anglo-Irish literature, and in the humor associated with the mythic patterns, it is evident that long before *Finnegans Wake* Joyce was using Irish mythology in these ways. At the same time, in his use of Irish mythos and his encoding of ideological points in mythic and formal codes, Joyce acts like an Irish traditionalist.

The Sovereignty myth is also manipulated by Joyce in a visionary way. The development of *Ulysses* can be seen as a turning from the consecration of the blood of the chalice to the consecration of the blood of the chamberpot (Ellmann, *Ulysses on the Liffey* 171). That chamberpot blood is a symbolic node referring to native Irish mythology; thus, the consecration of the Christian chalice is replaced by the consecration of the blood of the Sovereignty, the blood of Ireland as woman. In weaving together realistic elements, Christian imagery, and Irish myth, Joyce stresses the potential of the emergent English-speaking urban Ireland for restoring and reviving the nation. He manifests this new Ireland in a woman with a new morality, with a naturalism of religion, and an international outlook. In Joyce's version of the renewal of the Sovereignty, chaste, religious woman-as-Ireland with her loss of Gaelic and her bank-

---

41. The editorial continues, "Whereas Yeats's use of the myth was idolatrous, Joyce's was at all times iconoclastic."

rupt tradition gives way to modern, English-speaking, urban woman-as-Ireland with the richness of an expanding international outlook, contemporary morality, acceptance of the body, and a new religious freedom. Molly is a woman who, in Joyce's terms, is both spiritually and physically liberated, and in the context of Irish myth she represents a resolution of the dual theme of bondage that opens the book.[42] By using a sexualized form of the Sovereignty myth rather than the asexual version promulgated by the other authors of the revival, Joyce also links his view of national liberation more closely to the native heritage of Ireland.

In a sense *Ulysses*, first published in February 1922, can be seen as a birthday gift for the new Irish nation emerging in that year. Richard Ellmann has suggested that Joyce was offering in *Ulysses* a model of "new Irishmen to live in Arthur Griffith's new state" (*Consciousness of Joyce* 89). Joyce's political themes here move, however, on a mythic level as well as a naturalistic one. As he does with the mythic structures from *The Book of Invasions*, Joyce is creating the new free Irishman for the new Free State by actually returning to Ireland its ancient heritage, which predates the English conquest; in this case he restores the heritage of the Sovereignty myth, returning it in a form less mutilated than the one used by Yeats and the other Anglo-Irish writers, who were bound by an Anglophile morality and aesthetic. *Ulysses*, like *Finnegans Wake* later, shows that Joyce shared the revivalists' "preoccupation with the mythic figures and motifs of ancient Ireland," but "rather than sanctify modern Irish consciousness, [Joyce uses myth] to challenge its complacency and open up alternatives" (Hederman and Kearney, "Editorial" 156). With the Sovereignty patterns in *Ulysses* Joyce offers Ireland new physical, mental, and spiritual alternatives, which he paradoxically presents as Ireland's legitimate heritage since they stem from native mythos, native symbolism, and native archetypes. Joyce's thematic use of the Sovereignty myth again coincides with his thematic treatment of *The Book of Invasions* in this respect.[43]

---

42. In feminist terms, of course, she is far from "liberated"; see Unkeless, "Conventional Molly Bloom" 150–68.

43. Joyce saw *Dubliners* as "the first step towards the spiritual liberation of [his] country" (*Letters* 1: 62–63), and *Ulysses* may be taken as a major advance. From our vantage point we may question whether sexual liberation is so significant, but for Joyce sexual repression and sexual hypocrisy were a cultural function of church and state. Thus, sexual liberation was a first step toward spiritual liberation. On these points, see Manganiello 37–42; Shechner 105, 149, 176. On the rather late entry of sexual puritanism into Irish culture, see Lee.

The spiritual and political renewal of Ireland associated with the scaffolding from *The Book of Invasions* in *Ulysses* is reified in the Sovereignty symbolism of the book. Far from being simply ironic or even affirmative in merely a realistic way, Molly's sexuality is also sacramental. Joyce points the way to a new order: an Ireland for a free people as a free race; an Ireland free of the repressive yoke of England, Catholicism, and small minds; an Ireland able to affirm life spiritually and physically; an Ireland ready to reassume its own proper character after years of denial by political and spiritual oppressors. Though the change is formal, and hence subliminal for many readers, the overall movement of *Ulysses* brings transformation and renewal in images connected with the figure of the Sovereignty and the oldest strata of Irish literature.

Chapter 5

Genre Echoes from Early Irish Literature

CECILY: (*to Gwendolen*) That certainly seems a
satisfactory explanation, does it not?

GWENDOLEN: Yes, dear, if you can believe him.

CECILY: I don't. But that does not affect the wonderful
beauty of his answer.

GWENDOLEN: True. In matters of grave importance,
style, not sincerity, is the vital thing.

Oscar Wilde, *The Importance of Being Earnest*

Although the mythic method that Joyce pioneered has been productive for
the modern novel, his stylistic and formal innovations, particularly those
of *Ulysses*, are primarily responsible for securing his place as a major
writer. Joyce himself felt that the formal innovations were the most significant achievement of *Ulysses*; after *Ulysses* was published, he said, "The
value of the book is its new style" (quoted in *JJ2* 557). The ways in which
Ulysses is indebted to the mythos of the native literature of Ireland for its
architectonics and to Irish literature for the basic framework of its epic
mode suggest that other innovative formal characteristics of *Ulysses*, including its stylistics in the broadest sense, must be reappraised in terms of
Irish literature. Stuart Gilbert, presumably at Joyce's suggestion, proposes
that the detail of Joyce's narrative ties his work to that of the fili (71–72),
but other features of the narrative of *Ulysses* indicate this relationship as
well; such considerations lie at the heart of the investigations in this chapter.

An epic cast in the mold of Irish heroic narrative, *Ulysses* is at the same

time a copious compendium of virtually the full range of early Irish literary prose genres, a range that can be understood only in light of the
nature and function of the early Irish professional classes. After the ad-
vent of Christianity to Ireland, the early Irish *fili* (pl. *filid*), 'poet', inherited the varied functions of all the learned classes of the early Celts. At
once seer, magician, jurist, historian, storyteller, praise poet, and satirist,
the fili at the earliest period was sacred guardian of the traditions of the
people. The fili was the source of knowledge of the future through his skill
at divination; the repository of knowledge of the past as historian, storyteller, and genealogist; and the guardian of the norms of the present as
praise poet, satirist, and keeper of law, precept, and proverb.[1]

The etymological meaning of the early Irish words for 'poet', *fili* and
éices, is in each case 'seer', the former cognate with Old Irish *fil* ('there is',
originally 'behold') and the latter cognate with Old Irish *do-éccai* ('sees').
In early Irish culture the fili was the visionary of the tribe, and that role
affected all his other functions and his entire literary output. The early Irish
poet was a seer and a shaper, able to frame in suitable words his natural
vision; as Ifor Williams asserts regarding the Irish poet's Welsh counterpart, the poet had "a good eye": "The poet was the man who saw. Over
and over again in our early poetry the bard sings *'gwelais'*—'I have seen.'
. . . The poet is a seer, and has a good eye; he has the gift of vision: when
he looks at a warrior in splendid armour, or gazes upon a landscape, or the
life of society, he can frame or shape his vision in fitting words, in metre
and assonance, measure and adornment" (7–10). But the poet also had second sight—not only his natural eye, his *súil*, but his inner eye, his *rosc*—
which permitted his vision to extend through time and space. Many early
Irish stories concern poets who are able to recover information about the
past (often by summoning a dead witness);[2] others relate the poet's ability
to discern the truth of a situation despite distance or deceptive illusion
(e.g., *AIT* 360ff., 370ff.; Meyer, *Fianaigecht* 38–39). The ability to see
afar structures even such seemingly simple genres as nature poetry (Tymoczko, "'Cétamon'"; cf. Tymoczko, "Knowledge and Vision"). Stories
also show poets as able to foretell the future (e.g., *AIT* 240–41, 131–33),

---

1. For a more comprehensive view of the role of the early Irish poet, see Knott
and Murphy 1–93; Flower; Dillon and Chadwick chs. 1, 9; Watkins 213–17; I.
Williams ch. 1; Robinson; Carney; J. Williams and Ford 21–49; as well as references cited in these sources.
2. See, for example, Kinsella, *Táin* 1–2.

and some textual information has survived about the poet's incantations and rituals used to achieve these visions.³ As a visionary, therefore, the poet could establish the truth of the past, the existential or normative truth of the present, and the truth to be revealed in future events.

Many, though not all, of these varied functions passed to the *senchaid* (pl. *senchaide*), 'storyteller', of later Irish folk tradition.⁴ Thus, Irish literature has wider boundaries than those of modern English literature, because Irish literature includes in its domain various types of *senchas* ('ancient or traditional lore'), such as history and magical charms, as well as imaginative prose and poetry and other literary genres. It follows that the genres of Irish literature have a different mapping from those included in the dominant center of the English literary system and, further, that a writer importing genres from Irish literature into English will be perceived as innovative or erratic when judged by the standards of English literature. These wider boundaries for literature are in fact archaic; Terry Eagleton, for example, has observed that the restriction of literature to imaginative writing is a relatively recent phenomenon even in English literature, dating only to the Romantics (17–22).

Once we permit ourselves to consider *Ulysses* as reflecting in part the *system* of Irish literature as well as that of English literature, it is immediately apparent that many of the textual types represented in *Ulysses*, textual types that disrupt the form of the novel, take their place easily within the field of Irish literature. In this chapter I sample Joyce's use of Irish genres and Ireland's formal repertory. The chapter is not meant to be exhaustive; rather, it indicates lines of future inquiry. Here we will consider Joyce as keeper of lore (*senchas*), as historian, and as visionary able to mediate perception of the otherworld.

i. Joyce as Irish *senchaid*: Nonhierarchical narrative, "catechism," and lists in *Ulysses*

Many critics have commented on the encyclopedic character of *Ulysses*; for example, Karen Lawrence, in *The Odyssey of Style in "Ulysses"* (83),

---

3. Watkins 216 and T. O'Rahilly 317–40, as well as sources cited by these authors, examine the evidence for the poets' incantations.

4. For an introduction to the modern oral storyteller, see Delargy. Mac Cana, *Learned Tales* 3–18, discusses the debt of the Modern Irish storyteller to "his medieval forebears."

has characterized the narrative in "Wandering Rocks" as spewing forth a stream of facts. Streets are named, the characters' courses charted. Throughout the book we get facts about natural science and geography, about history and politics, about literature and language, with the lore transmitted being naturalized to the stream of consciousness; while the inquiring mind of Bloom recollects certain types of facts, Stephen and Molly hold quite different repertories of lore in their minds. As is clear from the etymological connection between *senchas*, 'lore' (*DIL*, 'old tales, ancient history, tradition; genealogy; traditional law'), and *senchaid*—in Old Irish 'a reciter of lore, a historian' and later 'storyteller'—Irish storytellers were responsible both for providing entertainment and for safeguarding the knowledge of the tribe. Literary practitioners in Irish tradition, the senchaide and the filid before them, were not simply storytellers but keepers of traditional lore of all sorts, including at the earliest period history, genealogy, kinglists, law, precepts, proverbs, and natural science; and their tales are filled with all sorts of information of this kind, which sometimes dominates the narrative to a degree frustrating to the modern reader (C. Bowen, "Historical Inventory of the *Dindshenchas*" 115). Even the fragmentary anecdotes remaining about John Stanislaus Joyce indicate that Joyce's father was a storyteller in this tradition; his stories melded placelore, history, and family traditions. Joyce himself assumes the role of senchaid as he stuffs *Ulysses* with all sorts of information, set partly in the voices of his characters and partly in the voice of the narrator or arranger; and this feature of Joyce's narrative increases geometrically, even if in a fractured manner, in *Finnegans Wake*.

Since Gilbert's early and ground-breaking study of *Ulysses*, the detail of Joyce's narrative has been compared to the "detailed and elaborate" prose narratives of the professional Irish poets, and the relation of that detailed narrative tradition to Joyce's blurred margin has already been explored. It is not merely the quantity of detail that forms the link between *Ulysses* and early Irish narrative, however; the nature of the materials detailed and the narrative techniques of representing the lore in *Ulysses* are of central importance in establishing the intertextual connections. Joyce emerges most clearly as senchaid in two specific episodes of *Ulysses*, "Wandering Rocks" and "Ithaca." In these episodes Joyce's senchas becomes the center of the narrative, molding the narrative texture in formal and generic ways as well as informing the content. An investigation of these two episodes illustrates the intertextuality between *Ulysses* and the lore-bearing texts of early Irish literature.

In episode ten, "Wandering Rocks," Joyce presents nineteen short episodes about the doings of a great number of characters.[5] Their stories are presented, as Lawrence has observed (83), with lateral logic: the "paratactic imagination . . . catalogues facts without synthesizing them. It documents the events that occur but fails to give the causal, logical, or even temporal connections between them." This treatment of characters, she continues, violates the standards of novel writing and confounds our expectations of plot because "the kind of conceptualization and logical subordination of events that one would expect in narrative discourse is . . . strangely absent" (84–85); moreover, repetitions impart "a curiously mechanical quality to the narrative" (85). She goes on to say: "The limitations imposed upon novel writing by the exigencies of plot making are ignored, and the reader's expectation of the functional relevance of narrative details is undermined. . . . Plot is the novelistic counterpart of history; especially in 'Aeolus,' 'Wandering Rocks,' and 'Ithaca,' Joyce investigates the possibilities that are ousted by conventional novelistic plot" (88).

In assessing Joyce's means of exploring alternate narrative modes, it is important to note that collections of stories such as exist in "Wandering Rocks" are common in many types of early Irish senchas: the episode is similar to the historical anecdotes grouped in the medieval manuscripts, to genealogical information and anecdotes, to certain collections of onomastic lore, and to collections of placelore. The form of these grouped snippets of narrative is related to their function. These collections of tribal lore were preserved in the manuscripts for professional purposes; the preservation per se of senchas was paramount, resulting at times in a kind of paratactic or nonhierarchical arrangement including the recording of alternate or even contradictory variants and the cataloguing of facts without synthesis or subordination. Though causal or temporal connections might at times be recorded, it was sufficient for the senchaid to record the raw data in a "mechanical" or "scholarly" manner, leaving the tasks of logical arrangement, causal or temporal connection, and synthesis for the ex tempore demands of oral presentation.

5. Frequently the episode is described as composed of eighteen scenes and a coda and is considered a "small-scale model of *Ulysses* as a whole" (Gilbert 227).

Though Joyce uses the narrative technique of cataloguing materials and events for his own purposes in shaping and redefining the modern novel, he is one with the Irish *senchaid* in acting in "Wandering Rocks" as a repository for all these stories, presenting each on a par, rather than acting as the narrator of a novel who narrows his interests, selecting, organizing, and establishing an order of hierarchical importance. Although it can be argued that to some extent such lateral and paratactic narrative is typical of medieval literature as a whole and that Joyce's use of these narrative strategies is therefore consonant with his medievalism in general, his reversion to this narrative mode and to the persona of *senchaid* at precisely episode ten in *Ulysses* signals his definitive break with the initial, signature, or establishing style of *Ulysses*; the break comes at the beginning of the second half of the book, a point taken up below.

Many collections of early Irish lore seem to be presented in serial fashion with few ordering principles in the body of the collection, but a rough order or organization is frequently suggested by the beginning and ending of the collection, which act as a sort of frame to the material. The collections of placelore, for example, are organized clockwise around Ireland, with Tara as the initial reference point (C. Bowen, "Historical Inventory of the *Dindshenchas*" 124–25). In "Wandering Rocks" an analogous principle of organization is suggested by the opening itinerary of Father Conmee, who traverses Dublin in one way, and the closing itinerary of the Viceroy, who traverses Dublin in another way. These two individuals represent the two dominant forces of Irish life under English rule: they are the two masters whom ordinary Dubliners like Stephen Dedalus serve.

—I am a servant of two masters, Stephen said, an English and an Italian.
—Italian? Haines said.
A crazy queen, old and jealous. Kneel down before me.
—And a third, Stephen said, there is who wants me for odd jobs.
—Italian? Haines said again. What do you mean?
—The imperial British state, Stephen answered, his colour rising, and the holy Roman catholic and apostolic church. (1.638–44)

The Dubliners whose paths are followed in the center sections of the episode are servants of these two masters, with Haines's puzzlement about "Italian" a reminder that not all of the representatives of the Roman church need be foreign. By framing the series of paratactic stories within these confines, Joyce links this central episode of *Ulysses* to the ideology informing both *Dubliners* and *A Portrait of the Artist*, the theme of hemiplegia that ramifies through the short stories and is the dominant factor causing the young artist to go into exile.

Joyce presents lore in an even balder form in "Ithaca," the episode he considered both his "ugly ducking" and his favorite (Budgen, *Making of "Ulysses"* 258). In most critical studies the style of this episode has been called "catechistic," following Joyce's own description of it as a "mathematical catechism" (*Letters* 1: 159); however, the model for the episode is far from certain, and the question has engendered lively debate about whether "Ithaca" represents secular or religious catechism. The episode is at once an encyclopedia of knowledge about the fictive world and a parody of the arrangement of knowledge, as Lawrence observes:

Critics have had difficulty in agreeing on the particular system parodied in "Ithaca" (for example, the Christian catechism, nineteenth-century books of knowledge, or nineteenth-century science) because it is the *idea* of a taxonomic system itself, not any particular system, that is parodied. Science, logic, mathematics, theology, and literary criticism are all implicated in the parody, for they are all systems of ordering and containing knowledge. (195)

One is tempted to deconstruct Joyce's own description of the episode and note that Hans Christian Andersen's Ugly Duckling is ugly only because it is a foster child and does not fit the expectations of its foster family: in the same way, Joyce's form in the seventeenth episode of *Ulysses* can be seen as a fosterling in English, imported from an Irish literary context and awkward primarily because of its new narrative context. But the argument need not rely solely on the deconstruction of Joyce's own statements; it can be conducted on an evidential basis.

Joyce's many non-Irish sources for his form in this episode converge with Irish models, since senchas and collections of stories of all sorts in the medieval Irish manuscripts regularly begin with a question to which the manuscript record or the story provides the answer. Thus, for example, the tale *Aided Con Roi* (*The Death of Cu Roi*) begins, "Why did the men of Ulster slay Cu Roi mac Dairi? Easy to say. Because of Blathnat who was carried off from the siege of the Fir Falgae, because of the three cows of Iuchna and the 'three men of Ochain,' that is, the little birds that used to be on the ears of Iuchna's cows" (*AIT* 328). Thereafter the narrative is given. The same structure is found in the genre of *tecosca*, 'instructions', where the following examples from *Tecosca Chormaic* (*The Instructions of Cormac*) are typical:

"O grandson of Conn, O Cormac," said Carbre, "what is best for a king?"
"Not hard to tell," said Cormac. "Best for him

Firmness without anger,
Patience without strife,
Affability without haughtiness,
Taking care of ancient lore
Giving truth for truth . . ."

"O grandson of Conn, O Cormac," said Carbre, "what are the dues of a chief and of an ale-house?"
"Not hard to tell," said Cormac.

"Good behaviour around a good chief,
Lights to lamps,
Exerting oneself for the company,
Settling seats,
Liberality of dispensers,
A nimble hand at distributing,
Attentive service,
To love one's lord,
Music in moderation,
Short story-telling
A joyous countenance,
Welcome to companies,
Silence during a recital . . .
Harmonious choruses—

those are the dues of a chief and of an ale-house," said Cormac to Carbre. (Meyer, *Instructions* 3, 11–13)

Similar patterns are found in early Irish onomastic lore and placelore, as well as in some genealogical and legal materials; this question-and-answer format became a major formal principle of organization and coherence in certain collections of lore (see, for example, C. Bowen, "Historical Inventory of the *Dindshenchas*" 123). Celtic literature is full of compendia that lack the hierarchical structure, taxonomic arrangements, or abstract conceptual schemata of the types that structure most dominant European forms of knowledge; this is one reason that the Celts have been accused of lacking a scientific mentality. Joyce's catalogue in "Ithaca" reads exactly this way; it represents, in fact, an archaic way of preserving knowledge and for this reason can be read as a parody of all modern systems of ordering. We should observe here again the double consciousness of these early Irish materials, a quality illustrated in the quote from *The Instructions of Cormac*; though the answer does set out excellent conditions for drinking and is thus instructive, it is clearly also intended to be witty and entertaining, even to some extent overstated and tongue-in-cheek. In much the same manner Joyce's answers in "Ithaca" provide a good deal of instructive material—mined regularly by critics to explicate the earlier narrative of *Ulysses*—yet the episode is still lighthearted and even parodic.

Lawrence has called the questions in "Ithaca" "expansible"—that is, they subdivide knowledge into finer and finer gradations: "It is the breakdown of the plot into discrete questions and answers that is the primary model of the infinite divisibility of experience and the expansibility of writing. Ironically, no answer is definitive because it has the potential to generate another, more specific question, which leads to another answer, and so on" (190). Similar structures of query and probing are also common in Irish senchas. The opening paragraph of *Cóir Anmann* (*The Fitness of Names*) offers a convenient example:

Mumu 'Munster,' whence was it named? Not hard (to say); a nomine alicuius regis, that is from the name of a king who ruled it, to wit, Eochaid *Mumo*, son of Nia Febis was he.

Eochaid Mumo, whence is it? Not hard (to say). Eochaid *mómó* 'greater-greater'; for greater were his strength and might than the strength and might of every one in Erin who lived at the same time as he. From him *Mumu* 'Munster' is named. (Stokes, *Cóir Anmann* 289)

This passage moves from the general to the particular (and back again), ranging through the levels of knowledge that a poet should master, for it was part of a poet's honor to be able to answer whatever question a patron might ask in whatever detail demanded.[6]

The Irish senchas considered here can be viewed as expanded or explicated lists, annotated with anecdote or narrative as the case may be. But listing per se is also a feature of early Irish narrative as a whole, a feature eminently consistent with narrative as a form of learning and lore.

---

6. Cf. *AIT* 548–50; Connellan 90ff.

Examples can be multiplied from virtually any Irish story, but a few cases will suffice. The text of *Táin Bó Cúailnge* includes a list of the members of Conchobor's men when he orders them to be summoned (C. O'Rahilly ll. 4053–4100), and a tract in the Book of Leinster lists the names of the shields of Conchobor's host:

> Ochain was there, Conchobor's shield, the Ear of Beauty—it had four gold borders around it;
> Cúchulainn's black shield Dubán;
> Lámthapad—the swift to hand—belonging to Conall Cernach;
> Ochnech belonging to Flidais;
> Furbaide's red-gold Orderg;
> Cúscraid's triumphant sword Coscrach. . . .
>
> (Kinsella, *Táin* 5)[7]

A list of CuChulainn's gifts is included in *Tochmarc Emire* (*The Wooing of Emer*): "Many were his gifts. First, his gift of prudence until his warrior's flame appeared, the gift of feats, the gift of *buanfach* (a game like draughts), the gift of chess-playing, the gift of calculating, the gift of sooth-saying, the gift of discernment, the gift of beauty" (*AIT* 154). *The Story of Mac Datho's Pig* has a list of the banquet halls of Ireland and their appurtenances (*AIT* 199), and an itinerary of the route taken by Medb's forces to Ulster is found in *Táin Bó Cúailnge* (C. O'Rahilly ll. 280–96). A list of lists in early Irish literature could be extended at some length.

Joyce's fondness for lists and catalogues is therefore another feature linking *Ulysses* and the Irish narrative tradition.[8] Although both "Wandering Rocks" and "Ithaca" can be considered as expanded or annotated lists, the catalogue or list per se in its simplest form is found frequently. Perhaps the most striking example is the list of motifs opening episode eleven:

> Bronze by gold heard the hoofirons, steelyringing.
> Imperthnthn thnthnthn.

---

7. For the translation Joyce might have known, see Stokes, "Tidings of Conchobor Mac Nessa" 28–29.

8. Umberto Eco discusses the broader medieval context of this encyclopedic approach to reality reflected in Joyce's work; he considers such features as inventories, lists, catalogues, and *enumeratio* and notes that coherent wholes are built through bricolage (8–11).

Chips, picking chips off rocky thumbnail, chips.
Horrid! And gold flushed more.
A husky fifenote blew.
Blew. Blue bloom is on the.
Goldpinnacled hair.
A jumping rose on satiny breast of satin, rose of Castile.
Trilling, trilling: Idolores.
Peep! Who's in the . . . peepofgold?   (11.1–10)

The list continues for another fifty-three lines; though it serves primarily to enumerate the themes of the episode and is analogous to the listing of musical motifs in a fugue or other musical piece, it is an extended example of a feature that is characteristic of the narrative of *Ulysses* as a whole and that recapitulates the lists featured in early Irish narrative.

A more modest list or catalogue in *Ulysses* is the enumeration of the statues at the National Museum in "Circe":

The keeper of the Kildare street museum appears, dragging a lorry on which are the shaking statues of several naked goddesses, Venus Callipyge, Venus Pandemos, Venus Metempsychosis, and plaster figures, also naked, representing the new nine muses, Commerce, Operatic Music, Amor, Publicity, Manufacture, Liberty of Speech, Plural Voting, Gastronomy, Private Hygiene, Seaside Concert Entertainments, Painless Obstetrics and Astronomy for the People. (15.1703–10)

There is a delicious incongruity between the anticipated number of statues ("the new nine muses") and the actual number in the list (twelve); this touch mirrors another feature of some of the lists in the early texts, where there is frequently a discrepancy between the definition of a list as it is introduced and the actual list itself. In *The Destruction of Da Derga's Hostel*, for example, the list of the seven sons of Ailill and Medb contains eight names: "There was . . . a troop of still haughtier heroes, namely, the seven sons of Ailill and Medb of Connacht, each of whom was called 'Mane.' And each Mane had a nickname, to wit, Mane Fatherlike and Mane Motherlike, and Mane Gentle-pious, Mane Very-pious, Mane Unslow, and Mane Honeywords, Mane Grasp-them-all, and Mane the Talkative" (*AIT* 103). The incongruities in passages such as these prompted medieval parody of the listing form as early as the twelfth century, as *Aislinge Meic Conglinne* (*The Vision of Mac Conglinne*) illustrates: "And they entreated him by each of the seven universal things,—sun and moon, dew and sea, heaven and earth, day and night" (*AIT* 552).[9] Medievals no less than twentieth-century readers could appreciate the wit in an author's deliberate inconsistency.

In *Ulysses* "Ithaca" is a list of lists, so to speak, but even Molly's soliloquy often moves into catalogue mode: "I was thinking of so many things he didnt know of Mulvey and Mr Stanhope and Hester and father and old captain Groves and the sailors playing all birds fly" (18.1582–84). The hyperbolic sections of "Cyclops" carry the listing tendency to extremes:

From his girdle hung a row of seastones which jangled at every movement of his portentous frame and on these were graven with rude yet striking art the tribal images of many Irish heroes and heroines of antiquity, Cuchulin, Conn of hundred battles, Niall of nine hostages, Brian of Kincora, the ardri Malachi, Art MacMurragh, Shane O'Neill, Father John Murphy, Owen Roe, Patrick Sarsfield, Red Hugh O'Donnell, Red Jim MacDermott, Soggarth Eoghan O'Growney, Michael Dwyer, Francy Higgins, Henry Joy McCracken, Goliath, Horace Wheatley. . . . (12.173–81)

This list continues with another sixty-nine names; it is obviously a parody of certain medieval Irish lists since it includes "unknown" heroes and also has, as it were, scribal interpolations of such figures as Benjamin Franklin, Cleopatra, Gautama Buddha, and Lady Godiva, alongside the more predictable S. Brendan and Theobald Wolfe Tone. Yet the parody itself here has antecedents in the early texts.[10]

Listing became a more prominent feature of Irish narrative after the twelfth century; this development coincides with the popularity of the later alliterative prose style, which is characterized by alliterative runs, including descriptions replete with lists of alliterative adjectives. The alliterative style is a stylistic correlate to the lists per se in the early texts and translates the function of narrative as *senchas* to the level of *lexis*.

9. Although most inconsistencies in the early Irish lists can be traced to scribal interpolations or textual corruption, the medieval parodies suggest that glossators had been busy enough and scribes assiduous enough at copying all marginalia that inconsistency had become a pervasive feature of the medieval manuscripts.

10. Robert Adams (151–58) analyzes a number of lists in *Ulysses*, including this list, showing how Joyce has crafted the burlesque in it; similar techniques are found in Irish lists including alliterating and rhyming names, names based on geographical features, and common nouns or adjectives used as personal names. See also Benstock and Benstock, appendix A.

An early example of the alliterative style is found in *In Carpat Serda* (*The Scythed Chariot*), a section of *Táin Bó Cúailnge*, translated by Thomas Kinsella to reflect some of the alliteration of the Irish text:

When that spasm had run through the high hero Cúchulainn he stepped into his sickle war-chariot that bristled with points of iron and narrow blades, with hooks and hard prongs and heroic frontal spikes, with ripping instruments and tearing nails on its shafts and straps and loops and cords. The body of the chariot was spare and slight and erect, fitted for the feats of a champion, with space for a lordly warrior's eight weapons, speedy as the wind or as a swallow or a deer darting over the level plain. The chariot was settled down on two fast steeds, wild and wicked, neat-headed and narrow-bodied, with slender quarters and roan breast, firm in hoof and harness—a notable sight in the trim chariot-shafts. One horse was lithe and swift-leaping, high-arched and powerful, long-bodied and with great hooves. The other flowing-maned and shining, slight and slender in hoof and heel. (Kinsella, *Táin* 153)

Joyce adapts and simultaneously parodies the lists of early Irish prose and the adjectival style in some of the hyperbolic sections of "Cyclops":

The figure seated on a large boulder at the foot of a round tower was that of a broadshouldered deepchested stronglimbed frankeyed redhaired freely-freckled shaggybearded widemouthed largenosed longheaded deepvoiced barekneed brawnyhanded hairylegged ruddyfaced sinewyarmed hero. From shoulder to shoulder he measured several ells and his rocklike mountainous knees were covered, as was likewise the rest of his body wherever visible, with a strong growth of tawny prickly hair in hue and toughness similar to the mountain gorse (*Ulex Europeus*). The widewinged nostrils, from which bristles of the same tawny hue projected, were of such capaciousness that within their cavernous obscurity the fieldlark might easily have lodged her nest. (12.151–61)

Here Joyce's text reflects the formal qualities of Irish prose quite well; at the same time Joyce's exuberance, generally read as parody, can be seen as transposing the fun-loving qualities of the Irish adjectival style.

Lists in the medieval Irish texts are often outrageous and absurd because of a tendency for Irish schemata to become symmetrical or artificial in other ways, even to the point of inconsistency. This tendency to schematize and to produce symmetrical patterns is characteristic of Ireland's ancient jurist-made law texts as well: "We also find [in early Irish law texts] that unreal schematism and passion for classification which meet us in the Hindu law books. In other words the jurists, while their work undoubtedly rested on a basis of actual custom, tended to produce a symmetrical pattern, and in the interests of symmetry they sometimes generalized rules and institutions which in real life had a much more restricted ambit" (Binchy 214).

Inclusive schematization thus represents an ancient strand of Irish intellectual life, appearing in the traditional stories as overblown or inconsistent schemata and outrageous and hyperbolic lists that were probably taken as comic even by the original audiences.[11] Indeed, lore of various sorts is used at times for comic purposes in the early narratives and parodied as early as the twelfth-century *Vision of Mac Conglinne*, perhaps the best medieval parody in any language, where there is, for example, a parodic genealogy presented in foodstuffs:

> Bless us, O cleric, famous pillar of learning,
> Son of honey-bag, son of juice, son of lard,
>   Son of stirabout, son of pottage, son of fair speckled fruit-clusters,
> Son of smooth clustering cream, son of buttermilk, son of curds,
>   Son of beer (glory of liquors!), son of pleasant bragget,
> Son of twisted leek, son of bacon, son of butter,
>   Son of full-fat sausage, son of pure new milk,
> Son of nut-fruit, son of tree-fruit, son of gravy, son of drippings,
>   Son of fat, son of kidney, son of rib, son of shoulder. . . .
>
>   (*AIT* 561)

The same text also parodies the alliterative style: "Then putting a linen apron about him below, and placing a flat linen cap on the crown of his head, he lighted a fair four-ridged, four-apertured, four-cleft fire of ash-wood, without smoke, without fume, without sparks" (*AIT* 571). In *Ulysses*, when listing and lore become absurd or outrageous and when catalogues are amusing for their symmetry or inconsistency, Joyce merely continues a feature implicit and explicit in the medieval texts of Ireland as well as in later Irish literature, a feature that may be another reflex of the mixed tone or double consciousness in Irish tradition that

---

11. The heptad of Fergus discussed above is an example. The combination of humor, oversystematization, inclusion of mutually contradictory materials, and manuscript errors results also in many of the catalogue materials in the early texts being fantastic or contrary to fact; thus, they have analogues to some of the unreliable and counterfactual features of "Ithaca" deriving from logic, mathematics, and deliberate factual error, as discussed by McCarthy.

has already been discussed at several points. This double consciousness is nicely captured in *Ulysses* in the final rhymed list of "Ithaca," which is linguistically systematic within the boundaries of the English phonemic system, hence in the realm of the Word cosmogonic and all-encompassing, mesmerizing with its rhythms, and at the same time amusing and parodic:

He rests. He has travelled.
With?
Sinbad the Sailor and Tinbad the Tailor and Jinbad the Jailer and Whinbad the Whaler and Ninbad the Nailer and Finbad the Failer and Binbad the Bailer and Pinbad the Pailer and Minbad the Mailer and Hinbad the Hailer and Rinbad the Railer and Dinbad the Kailer and Vinbad the Quailer and Linbad the Yailer and Xinbad the Phthailer. (17.2320–26)

An exhaustive study of Joyce's use of senchas and his management of lists and catalogues in relation to Irish tradition is needed; it is evident, however, that in general lore functions much the same way in *Ulysses* as it does in early Irish literature. Lore, or senchas, grounds the narrative in time and space; it historicizes the narrative—a function particularly of genealogical, historical, natural, and geographical lore—thus contributing to the sense of verisimilitude. Lore in the form of catalogues and lists contributes as well to the illusion of density: to the illusion that the incidents foregrounded are part of a dense, though distanced and perhaps blurred, texture of human event and context. Lore, even when it may be absurd or artificial in its particulars, suggests solidity through the concatenation of the individual data, each of which is presented as self-contained, impenetrable, opaque—as a given of the situation. When those data are coterminous with the data of the experiential world, as they are to a large extent both in *Ulysses* and early Irish literature, lore projects an illusion of reality. These features are notable in *Ulysses*, and they distinguish early Irish literature as well.[12]

The sources of Joyce's knowledge of this feature of early Irish literature are difficult to establish, in part because it is such a pervasive feature of the literature and in part because Joyce is borrowing the *concept* of lore, catalogues, and listings rather than any particular instance of these early Irish elements. By the time Joyce was writing *Ulysses*, virtually every ma-

---

12. Garvin (77) traces Joyce's use of lists as early as "The Dead" and sees listing as dominating the structure of his major works.

jor collection of early Irish lore had been published or discussed in the critical literature: *The Fitness of Names*, a repository of onomastic lore; collections of placelore and other topographical materials; the ancient laws of Ireland; annals and pseudohistory; collections of sententious materials, including proverbs and the triads of Ireland.[13] Though Joyce would not have known all these materials firsthand, he would have been made aware of this facet of Irish tradition by the popular press as well as by its presence in texts he was familiar with.

Michael Groden has demonstrated that Joyce's "goal of encyclopedism" determined many of Joyce's late revisions to the manuscript of *Ulysses*, including the lengthening of many of the lists:

In these elaborate lists (which have been seen as part of the Homeric parallel), Joyce worked toward encyclopedism by taking a specific incident and cataloguing its observers or participants. In most cases his techniques of revision caused him to extend the lists to such comical lengths that they eventually assumed a logic of their own beyond any logic in the events that originally inspired them. . . . By sheer persistence such repeated accumulations ultimately achieved the effect of all-inclusiveness Joyce desired. (195–96)[14]

Groden's characterization of Joyce's method here indicates its kinship to the methods of the early Irish jurists. Although the encyclopedism of the lists may be read as part of the epic (hence, Homeric) shell of *Ulysses*, it is equally if not more relevant that this final shaping of the book brought it closer to an Irish poetics. Joyce was pointing up elements in his text that fit *Ulysses* into the Irish tradition of senchas.

ii. *Immaginable itinerary through the particular universal*: *Ulysses* and the *dindsenchas* tradition

Celebrated in the annual pilgrimage of Joyceans to Dublin on 16 June, a characteristic of *Ulysses* affording much delight to Joyce specialists is the meticulous attention given to place in the book. The topographical precision is essential to the texture of realism in *Ulysses*, and it is well known

13. For bibliography of the materials published by 1912, see Best, *Bibliography* (1913) 117–22, 249–66.
14. Cf. also the principal argument in Litz, *Art of James Joyce*.

that Joyce exploited the 1904 volume of *Thom's Official Directory of the United Kingdom of Great Britain and Ireland* so as to be scrupulously precise in *Ulysses* about the Dublin landscape—even to the fact that 7 Eccles Street was vacant in 1904 and hence available for the Bloom occupation (Kain, *Fabulous Voyager* 121–23, appendix C; cf. R. Adams 172–73; Hart and Knuth 14). He was fanatic as well about verifying certain geographical minutiae, writing to his Aunt Josephine, for example, to inquire whether "an ordinary person" might climb over the area railing at 7 Eccles Street and safely lower himself down in order to gain entry through the lower level of the house (*Letters* 1: 175). Though Joyce might manipulate Dublin geography for the sake of artistic order, moving away from strict historicism as he does in "The Dead" when he shifts the Morkan house from Ellis's Quay to Usher's Island (Kelleher, "Irish History" 429–30), the narrative in *Ulysses* has an overall geographical accuracy that has seldom been paralleled in literature.[15]

James Joyce may have inherited his interest in Dublin's topography in part from his father and, by extension, from Irish tradition: John Joyce used to enjoy taking his sons for walks, pointing out the places of Dublin and telling stories of Dublin's public and private life. As discussed above, John Joyce also took delight in the fact that he often knew more of the local history and topography than did native Dubliners, despite the fact that he himself was a Cork man. Thus, surviving evidence suggests that placelore is one of the aspects of Irish senchas that John Joyce was most interested in and knew best. In working out his own interest in placelore in *Ulysses*, however, James Joyce did not rely solely on the knowledge that came to him from his own experience or his father's tales or the traditional oral forms of Irish placelore stories: he supplemented these traditional dispositions with bookish research.

It is essential to a consideration of topography in *Ulysses* that virtually all Irish literature has a fascination with place. The sense of place dominates contemporary poetry from Kavanagh to Kinsella, Montague to Heaney; and it is preceded by an interest in place among the writers of the Irish literary revival. Yeats's poetry has memorialized for his readers a number of sites—his tower, Coole Park, Innisfree, and, above all, Ben Bulben:

---

15. See the studies by Hart and Knuth, *Topographical Guide*, and Seidel, *Epic Geography*, for two rather different approaches to the geography of *Ulysses*.

Under bare Ben Bulben's head
In Drumcliff churchyard Yeats is laid,
An ancestor was rector there
Long years ago; a church stands near,
By the road an ancient Cross.
                    (*Poems* 327–28)

It has been argued that preservation of topography and toponymy and the nationalistic implications of the material gathered by the Ordnance Survey are at the cornerstone of the Irish literary revival (W. Thompson 11–13), and place is a central focus of early Irish literature as well. The interest in place in Irish literature may have to do with the mentality of the insular Celts, who, as my teacher Máire Mac Neill put it, have been "so long dwelling in one place." It may also be related to the inalienability of land in the Irish legal system or to the association of the land with the earth goddesses of native myth, many of whom continued to play an important role in the culture to the present century in the form of the fairy queens of folklore. The importance of place and placelore is, in short, a central feature of the Irish literary tradition at every period; in putting placelore and geographical structures at the heart of all his narratives, Joyce shows himself to be paradigmatically an Irish writer.

Early Irish stories are frequently mappable and show a persistent interest in place names; the conclusion of *The Story of Mac Datho's Pig* serves as a convenient example of these traits:

Then Mac Datho came out with the hound in his hand, and let him in amongst them to see which side he would choose; and the hound chose Ulster and set to tearing the men of Connacht greatly. Ailill and Medb went into their chariot, and their charioteer with them, and Mac Datho let the hound after them, and they say it was in the Plain of Ailbe that the hound seized the pole of the chariot that was under Ailill and Medb. Then the charioteer of Ailill and Medb dealt the hound a blow so that he sent its body aside and that the head of the hound remained on the pole of the chariot at Ibar Cinn Chon (the Yew-tree of the Hound's Head), whence Connacht takes its name. And they also say that from that hound Mag Ailbe (the Plain of Ailbe) is called, for Ailbe was the name of the hound.

This now is the road which the men of Connacht went southward, to wit, over Belach Mugna, past Roiriu, past Ath Midbine in Maistiu, past Kildare, past Raith Imgan into Feeguile, to Ath Mic Lugna, past Druim Da Maige over Drochat Cairpri. There at Ath Cinn Chon (Hound's Head Ford) in Fir Bili the head of the hound fell from the chariot. (*AIT* 207)

The places mentioned in the itinerary are actual places, still of significance today in some cases; thus, the course of this section of the story can
be charted. The passage also exemplifies the common conceit that the
events of the heroic narrative have actually left their impress on the landscape, giving names to the places noted. *Mac Datho's Pig* is entirely typical in these respects, and the affinity of such a narrative to aspects of
Finnegans Wake should be obvious.

The most improbable stories in early Irish literature have topographical precision. Voyages to or adventures in the otherworld typically begin
at actual locations specified in the medieval texts; the otherworld is therefore tied to the known landscape and is considered to be geographically
accessible. Despite its seeming improbabilities, *The Book of Invasions* is
also mappable after its fashion, for the geographical peculiarities in the
story (the idea, for example, that Ireland can be seen from a high tower
in Spain) are naturalistic within the confines of the medieval circular map
of the world in which Spain and Ireland are adjacent (Kelleher, "Humor
in the Ulster Saga" 36). Placelore is the structural principle of several major early Irish stories, including *Táin Bó Cúailnge*, in which the characters proceed along a definite route, summarized at points by itineraries.[16]

Placelore was so central to early Irish literature that a separate genre
was devoted to it, the category called *dindšenchas*, literally 'placelore'.[17]
There are several extant collections of dindšenchas, and the genre is found
in prose and poetic forms as well as in forms mixing poetry and prose.
Most of those collections of dindšenchas had been published by the time
Joyce began studying Irish.[18] Joyce would have known some of these collections, if only at second hand, particularly since the metrical dindšenchas was being published by Edward Gwynn during the period 1900–
1906, a period when Joyce was actively interested in Irish literature.[19]
Joyce would also have known toponymic episodes from many of the early

---

16. See Kinsella, *Táin* xiii–xxiii; and Haley.
17. Tarzia discusses the functional aspect of placelore in Irish culture.
18. C. Bowen, "Historical Inventory of the *Dindshenchas*," gives a good overview of the dindšenchas tradition. See Best, *Bibliography* (1913) 80–82, 262–63,
for the publication history of these materials.
19. Gwynn published *Poems from the Dindshenchas* in 1900, a preliminary
selection of the metrical dindšenchas. His systematic series published under the
title *The Metrical Dindshenchas* was published by the Todd Lecture Series in five
volumes in 1903, 1906, 1913, 1924, and 1935. The first two volumes would have
been most likely to attract Joyce's attention.

tales that he read either in summary or in extenso, and he would have found itineraries widespread also.[20]

The Irish oral tradition of placelore had also attracted scholarly and critical interest in the nineteenth and early twentieth centuries, notably in the work of the Ordnance Survey as well as the later publications of such scholars as Eugene O'Curry and John O'Donovan. It was acknowledged that Irish place names frequently had semantic meaning, often referring to historical events, and the significance of Irish toponymy was, accordingly, discussed widely. One of the most important contemporary secondary sources on Irish placelore was the work of P. W. Joyce, particularly his *Origin and History of Irish Names of Places*, a volume that was widely recognized in Ireland at the time, discussed in the popular press, and known to James Joyce himself. Joyce's attention would also have been drawn to topography and toponymy by discussions in the popular press; in the *United Irishman*, for example, placelore and toponymy are taken up time and again, and the importance of preserving the knowledge of Irish topography, local legend, and local history are stressed.[21] The concern for localism in the Irish popular press is of such importance that the topic will be considered at greater length in chapter 7.

Because Joyce writes about urban Ireland rather than the rural Ireland to which most of the early Irish placelore refers, identifying specific sources for Joyce's knowledge of early Irish placelore is less critical than establishing his knowledge of the genre of dindšenchas, his understanding of the cultural significance of placelore, and his exposure to the role of placelore in early Irish narrative tradition.[22] Joyce is not merely a raconteur of events and anecdotes about Dublin, following his father's interests and storytelling proclivities; his attention to the topography and traditions of Dublin is an extension of the nationalist validation of local tradition, history, and geography in Ireland at the turn of the century, even if the immediate sources of the particulars are nontraditional materials such as *Thom's Directory*. Though Joyce rarely has Irish nomenclature

20. Kelleher ("Irish History," 420–30) has argued that Joyce makes use of the itinerary of *The Destruction of Da Derga's Hostel* in "The Dead."

21. For example, articles on this topic are found in the issues of 9 Dec. 1899, 24 Nov. 1900, and 16 Feb. 1905.

22. Joyce does, however, use early legends that have topographical connections with the geography of Dublin, including *The Destruction of Da Derga's Hostel*, the story of Isolde, and various legends about Finn. Cf. Nilsen 24–32.

to preserve in his geographical purview, his precise research into the topography of Dublin and his interest in Dublin stories and legends are undertaken with the zeal worthy of the Ordnance Survey in the days of O'Donovan and Petrie. Moreover, despite the fact that Irish nomenclature and etymology per se are not central to Joyce's topography of Dublin, the dindšenchas tradition in Irish narrative illuminates the singularity of Joyce's topographical interests—the fact that "it is not by way of description that Dublin is created in *Ulysses*," but by way of naming: "Streets are named but never described. . . . Bridges over the Liffey are crossed and recrossed, named and that is all" (Budgen, *Making of "Ulysses"* 68).[23] Joyce's interest in topographical names links his work to the narratives of the early Irish literary classes, and his practice of naming without describing in *Ulysses*, while fitting with a stream-of-consciousness technique, also has a mantic quality about it.

In 1905 Joyce wrote about *Dubliners*, "When you remember that Dublin has been a capital for thousands of years, that it is the 'second' city of the British Empire, that it is nearly three times as big as Venice it seems strange that no artist has given it to the world" (*Letters* 2: 111; cf. 2: 122). It is clear that he aspired to the task both in *Dubliners* and in *A Portrait*, that *Ulysses* is the keystone of the project, and that *Finnegans Wake* translates the enterprise to a mythic and surrealistic mode. Joyce was explicit about the centrality of place in *Ulysses*; speaking of his intentions in *Ulysses*, Joyce said, "I want . . . to give a picture of Dublin so complete that if the city one day suddenly disappeared from the earth it could be reconstructed out of my book" (Budgen, *Making of "Ulysses"* 67–68). It is thus difficult to overstate the importance of placelore in *Ulysses*; in one sense *Ulysses* is an extended piece of dindšenchas.

In this aspiration Joyce acts like a senchaid of Irish tradition: he states directly that he wishes to preserve geographical knowledge and local history from extinction, and in this desire he is acting on behalf of the tribe. It is thus ironic that much of the Dublin Joyce preserves in his narrative did indeed disappear in the troubles from 1916 to 1923 (Kenner, "*Ulysses*" 93–96, 139). His writing answers the call in the popular nationalist press for the preservation of topography; at the same time, by celebrating urban, English-speaking Ireland, Joyce curiously twists that same pro-

23. Cf. Kain, *Fabulous Voyager* 20; Hart and Knuth 19.

gram away from a backward-looking celebration of the countryside and the Gaeltacht. It is typical of Joyce that the Dublin he celebrates is not primarily the Dublin defined by the memorable sites of the Protestant Ascendancy, including Trinity College and the Georgian townhouses; the Dublin of Joyce's narratives is the Dublin of the common people afoot, Catholic as well as Protestant. As it were, Joyce retakes Dublin from the Irish Ascendancy, giving us a memorable Everyman's Dublin, an English-speaking Dublin upon which to build a free state. This attention to Dublin topography is an ironic expression of Joyce's nationalism, an expression not likely to be appreciated by the nativist nationalists who were interested in promoting and preserving a rural Irish Ireland.

iii. *Back in the presurnames*: Onomastics in *Ulysses*

In Joyce's works naming frequently has special import, and Joyce uses names deliberately, often with a discernible subtext. Joyce uses a carefully chosen network of names in *Dubliners* "to strengthen his theme that the Dubliners of his day were wallowing about in a black pool from which they could not escape" (Nilsen 33). The name "Stephen Dedalus" is "the wedge by which symbolism enters" *A Portrait of the Artist* (Levin, *James Joyce* 46), signifying the metamorphic relationship between protagonist and the Greek mythic hero(es) of the Daedalus myth and between protagonist and the first Christian martyr. His special name is also an aspect of the Sovereignty theme as it is developed in *A Portrait of the Artist*: here 'crown', the Greek meaning of *Stephen*, is significant (cf. Kain, "Motif as Meaning" 64). In *Ulysses* Stephen's name cues the reader to the Greek affiliations of the Irish and the Greek element in the mythic substructure from *The Book of Invasions* as well as continuing the symbolic functions from *A Portrait of the Artist*. The significance of names in *Finnegans Wake* was such that Joyce was reluctant to reveal the title of the book, calling it instead "Work in Progress" from 1924 to 1939, revealing the title only when the book was published (*JJ*2 563; cf. 543, 597, 708); the magic of naming in the title invokes and reifies the multileveled meanings coded throughout the text. As for *Ulysses* the title itself—a name—remains as the single exiguous sign of the classical counterpart of the narrative and a sign of Joyce's mythic method itself. Within the text names also present themselves as meaningful, and naming has several levels of significance, with names forming a web of meaning that shapes the text and helps to integrate the disparate parts.[24]

Joyce's lifelong interest in naming and his pervasive manipulation of naming in his writing is another part of his heritage, for onomastics plays an essential role in early Irish literature and Gaelic culture. The naming of characters, like the naming of places, is frequently a result of a significant event in the early tales, as the naming of CuChulainn or the boasts in *The Story of Mac Datho's Pig* illustrate (C. O'Rahilly 161–63; *AIT* 203–5). Names of characters, like place names, frequently have a semantic meaning, and names bestowed on characters become emblems of the characters' true natures. A name frequently indicates the essence of the one named; it is thus not surprising that misnaming is a significant act and that in medieval Ireland it was a legal offense to confer a derisive "nickname" that stuck to a person (Robinson 105–6). The number of heroes in the tales with amusing names suggests that receiving a nickname was a real peril, even as it indicates the ironic treatment of heroes in the tradition as a whole. As in many cultures worldwide, names in Irish tradition are numinous, hence the widespread use of propitiary names for deities and for the fairies as well. The importance of personal names is seen also in the early collections of names that have survived in the manuscripts, including extensive genealogies and genealogical poetry.[25] It is possible that merely to recite the names of a chief's ancestors, to rehearse a litany of names, was a significant and evocative act.[26]

Doris Edel sets this interest in names in a broader epistemological context when she stresses the importance of etymological speculation in the methods of the native Celtic intellectuals:

The so-called *bélre n-etarscartha* or 'language of separation' had been elevated into a science, to use D. A. Binchy's words. The jurists were among its leading exponents, but it also contributed extensively to other fields of learning, e.g. place-lore. To resolve a word into its 'original' elements, each of them

24. For a thorough inventory of the names in *Ulysses*, as well as an analysis of the patterns of naming in the book, see Benstock and Benstock.

25. M. A. O'Brien's 764-page edition of the medieval Irish genealogies indicates the volume of the surviving materials. The medieval interest in names is also indicated by the etymological tract *Cóir Anmann (The Fitness of Names)*, which has been edited by Stokes.

26. Still today in India, to quote the genealogy of a deity is an act of worship.

a separate word—even monosyllables were not safe from this approach—a superficial similarity in sound or meaning was sometimes enough. This method of interpretation seems to have had its roots in the pre-Christian tradition, although in later times it must have gained addition prestige from the *Etymologies* of Isidore of Seville, which had a great impact on insular thought. What we are dealing with here is basically a primitive sort of learning which survived outside the Roman *imperium* and was dominated by magical beliefs. Within this intellectual horizon, correspondences between words pointed to correspondences between the objects they named, and so language itself was seen as a source of knowledge. For the initiated, this juggling with synonyms and homonyms (or near-synonyms and near-homonyms), punning, even a slip of the tongue, represented indispensable instruments of inspiration. (256–57)[27]

It is not too much to say that one of the chief ways by which the fili determined knowledge was through sound and the magic of language, so that the cultivation of language per se and names in particular was a central feature of the maintenance of senchas. The magic of names and naming permeates early Celtic literature: not only are names etymologized, but they also occur in lists of all sorts, including genealogies; they are preserved as mnemonics, and they are used metonymically to evoke particular stories or even a sense of the whole tradition.[28] The interest in etymology is typical of much medieval thought, but no other medieval vernacular tradition attends to names and naming so minutely as does that of Ireland.

Though Joyce's naming remains principally within the realm of English phonology and English nominal practice, his manipulation of names has affinities to the linguistic realism and verbal magic permeating early Irish narrative. The importance of the word per se in Joyce's writing is captured by Frank O'Connor: "Style ceases to be a relationship between author and reader and becomes a relationship of a magical kind between author and object. Here *le mot juste* is no longer *juste* for the reader, but for the object" (304). O'Connor observed the same quality in Joyce's relationship to the world, a quality illuminated for O'Connor by Joyce's framing a picture of Cork in cork. He concluded that Joyce was suffering

27. Binchy (210–12) also has an interesting discussion of the *bélre n-etarscartha* and the etymological impulse of the early period.
28. Names are etymologized in *The Fitness of Names*, for example, and a collection of names preserved as mnemonics is found in the Welsh triads (Bromwich).

from "associative mania" (301), an apt description by a scientific man of one whose relationship to language—like that of the fili—was governed by an older habit of thought in which language is a source of knowledge and in which a primitive magical relationship obtains between word and object.[29]

Thus, names are more than arbitrary signs in the world of *Ulysses*: they can signify the reality. Molly thinks of her mysterious mother and observes, "my mother whoever she was might have given me a nicer name the Lord knows after the lovely one she had Lunita Laredo" (18.846–48). In the narrative Molly's mother's name *is* her mother, and critics have turned to this name, parsing its meaning to unravel the secrets of her being.[30] Joyce also mirrors the semantic significance of Irish naming. Within the text both Bloom and Molly see names as important, and Bloom's name in particular is portentous for both of them. Molly muses in her soliloquy both on Bloom's name and on the other names she might have had:

I never thought that would be my name Bloom when I used to write it in print to see how it looked on a visiting card or practising for the butcher and oblige M Bloom youre looking blooming Josie used to say after I married him well its better than Breen or Briggs does brig or those awful names with bottom in them Mrs Ramsbottom or some other kind of a bottom Mulvey I wouldnt go mad about either or suppose I divorced him Mrs Boylan (18.840–46)

But it is not merely that the name has semantic value. Names are of the essence here, and when Bloom picks a name for a secret correspondence, it is no accident that he chooses the name *Flower*. *Virag*, 'flower' in Hungarian, becomes *Bloom* becomes *Flower*. The arbitrariness of phonology

29. In this regard Joyce's double is Bloom with his characteristic mental form, the "bloomism" that Ellmann has defined as "an uneasy but scrupulous recollection of a factual near-miss," involving "similar sounds as well as similar facts," and thus has the whole of *Finnegans Wake* implicit in it (*Ulysses* 36). Cf. Eco 80. Joyce's use of Skeat's *Etymological Dictionary* is well known (cf. *SH* 26). As a youth Joyce also showed a penchant for etymologizing the names of places where he lived, a practice that makes his choice of all the Irish personal and place names in *Finnegans Wake* potentially significant (see O Hehir vii–viii).

30. See, for example, Herring, "Toward an Historical Molly Bloom" 507–16; B. Scott 179.

By virtue of her name, Molly's mother is a Sephardic Jew, and her daughter Molly is at once Spanish, Jewish, and Moorish. The mother's name thus gives Molly yet another position in the substructure from *The Book of Invasions*.

gives way to semantic stability, pointing to Leopold's essence; the metamorphosis of names mirrors the metempsychosis of characters in the text. It is almost as if Bloom's name/essence brings with it the flowers dominating Molly's memories, and her love of blossoms folds into her love of her husband: "I love flowers Id love to have the whole place swimming in roses God of heaven theres nothing like nature . . . that would do your heart good to see rivers and lakes and flowers all sorts of shapes and smells and colours springing up even out of the ditches primroses and violets nature it is" (18.1558–63). The likeness of Molly's essence to the name/essence of her suitor in a sense destines them to be mates as discussed in the last chapter.

Names also engender things in the world of *Ulysses*; the case of the unknown mourner, the man in the brown macintosh who *becomes* M'Intosh, is the prime example (6.805ff., 6.891ff., 15.1558ff., 16.1261).[31] But Molly also wonders whether "bloomers" have been named for her husband: "that old Bishop that spoke off the altar his long preach about womans higher functions about girls now riding the bicycle and wearing peak caps and the new woman bloomers God send him sense and me more money I suppose theyre called after him" (18.837–40).[32] This possibility seems likely to her given her husband's obsession with women's undergarments:

of course hes mad on the subject of drawers thats plain to be seen always skeezing at those brazenfaced things on the bicycles with their skirts blowing up to their navels even when Milly and I were out with him at the open air fete that one in the cream muslin standing right against the sun so he could see every atom she had on when he saw me from behind following in the rain I saw him before he saw me however standing at the corner of the Harolds cross road with a new raincoat on him with the muffler in the Zingari colours to show off his complexion and the brown hat looking slyboots as usual what was he doing there where hed no business they can go and get whatever they like from anything at all with a skirt on it and were not to ask any questions but they want to know where were you where are you going I could feel him coming along skulking after me his eyes on my neck he had been keeping away from the house he felt it was getting too warm for him so I halfturned

---

31. Nilsen (26–27) discusses the possibility that this figure, through verbal realism, should be identified with the Irish god of the dead.

32. The garment is in fact named after Amelia Bloomer, an American reformer who worked for women's rights.

and stopped then he pestered me to say yes till I took off my glove slowly
watching him he said my openwork sleeves were too cold for the rain anything for an excuse to put his hand anear me drawers drawers the whole
blessed time till I promised to give him the pair off my doll to carry about in
his waistcoat pocket (18.289–306)

It is no wonder that Bloom is nettled about the mistake regarding his
name in Dignam's obituary:

*The obsequies, at which many friends of the deceased were present, were car-
ried out by . . . Messrs H. J. O'Neill and Son. . . . The mourners included:
Patk. Dignam (son), Bernard Corrigan (brother-in-law), Jno. Henry Menton,
solr, Martin Cunningham, John Power . . . Thomas Kernan, Simon Dedalus,
Stephen Dedalus B.A., Edw. J. Lambert, Cornelius T. Kelleher, Joseph M'C
Hynes, L. Boom, C P M'Coy,—M'Intosh and several others.* (16.1253–61)

It is perfectly consistent with the power of names in the text and in Irish
culture that the newspaper error should itself engender a new identity for
the hero in the narrative: "Nettled not a little by L. Boom (as it incorrectly
stated) . . . but tickled to death simultaneously by C. P. M'Coy and Stephen Dedalus B.A. who were conspicuous, needless to say, by their total
absence (to say nothing of M'Intosh) L. Boom pointed it out to his companion B.A. engaged in stifling another yawn" (16.1262–66). Still another level of the onomastics of *Ulysses* is indicated by Joyce's choice of
names for some of his characters with referents and connotations or associations outside the fictive world. This practice can be traced earlier in
his work, as well; thus, in *A Portrait of the Artist* Joyce named the character based on his friend Cosgrave after Lynch, the mayor of Galway who
had hanged his own son, because of Cosgrave's "betrayal" of Joyce with
respect to Nora, the significance of which was well observed by Joyce's
contemporaries (*JJ*2 160, 205, 286). In the tradition of the Irish satirists,
Joyce has "put a name" on an enemy, indicating the essence of the person.
Similarly, Joyce chose to name the child of Molly and Leopold *Milly* not
merely for the euphony with her mother's name but also for the connection with the "Clan Milly" of *The Book of Invasions*.

Bloom's name is the most significant of these instances in *Ulysses*. As
mentioned above, Joyce chooses *Bloom* as the name for his protagonist
because it too has an exiguous significance as the English eponym of the
mountain in Ireland called *Slieve Bloom*, in Irish *Sliab Bladma*, a mountain that was the residence of the consort of Eriu, the territorial goddess

of Ireland itself.[33] Thus, the name *Bloom* is an appropriate assimilative name for Rudolph Virag to have picked as a translation of *Virag*, but it also suggests that the character Bloom is *the man* of Ireland. Joyce uses names for their symbolic signification as ways of binding his narrative to the major Irish mythic schemata on which *Ulysses* is based. Here Joyce depends precisely on the magic of language to make things alike—as Edel says, "correspondences between words point to correspondences between the objects they name"—for the naming is made potent not merely by referential correspondence, the result of the metempsychosis that resonates through the book, but also by the manner in which the fortuitous similarity of sounds in English links these characters to their Irish counterparts. The magic of nominal translation makes Bloom the equivalent of Eriu's mate. Thus, the name *Bloom* is an onomastic node: it is naturalistic, representing a common "Jewish" name; it has semantic significance in reference to flowers (and bloomers); it embodies Leopold's essence, metamorphosing with his changes; and it has a symbolic and mythological reference as well. Joyce's interest in and exploration of these various onomastic levels in *Ulysses* are part of his heritage from Irish tradition, and they become central features of the verbal play in *Finnegans Wake*.

Early Irish narrative is notable for its high density of personal names; unlike European folktales, for example, which use descriptors (e.g., "the wicked stepmother") for many characters, early Irish tales have few unnamed characters. Early Irish narrative is also characterized by the frequent use of patronymics and other genealogical specifications for characters (features that increase the density of personal names in the narrative) and by a low rate of nominal redundancy (that is, few characters bear the same name). For these reasons, the repertory of personal names in early Irish tales is complex and highly specific. Not only do the characters have personal names, but they are also usually associated with a location or a tribe and hence with place names.[34] These features of naming in the early tales give the narratives an illusion of historicity; the naming sets up a social, temporal, and spatial texture that distinguishes early Irish hero tales from folktale, for example, or from most medieval nar-

---

33. See the full discussion in chapter 4, above.
34. These points are treated at greater length in Tymoczko, "Personal Names."

rative, particularly medieval romance. Though specificity of name and historicism of this type is more typical of epic in general than, say, romance, Irish hero tale is even more historicized with respect to names than are most heroic literatures, including English or French epic. The same tendency to use particularized names characterizes later Irish tradition, even permeating Irish wondertales.[35] In regard to naming, the narrative technique of early Irish literature coincides to a large extent with the aesthetic of the nineteenth-century novel and realistic narrative. To generalize broadly, early Irish stories are much more like Russian novels than European folktales with respect to the number of names and the individuation of characters by naming. Joyce's narrative is dense in names, including genealogical and kinship specifiers, in much the same way that his antecedent Irish literary tradition is, and he inherits the technique from a variety of sources, including early Irish literature and the oral tradition in Ireland. As with early Irish literature, Joyce's use of names contributes to the historicity and specificity of his fictive world.

In *Ulysses* Joyce has created a narrative world in which there is verbal realism, and the operation of language in the text is doubled by evidence from the events of Joyce's own life that reveal a belief in the magic of language. We see these beliefs in Joyce's suggestion that James Stephens finish *Finnegans Wake* in case of Joyce's early death—a belief based largely on their commonality of first name and their supposed identity of birthdate (see *JJ2* 591–93). Similar inclinations are revealed by his acceptance of "found language" in the writing of his texts—for example, the incorporation of "come in" into the text of *Finnegans Wake* as he was dictating to Samuel Beckett, or the changes he tolerated in the meaning of his texts in typesetting or translation (e.g., *JJ2* 649, 700).[36] Thus, the nominal realism in *Ulysses*, which ties Joyce to his own cultural tradition, opens up a whole strand in Joyce's thought and life that could profitably be explored at greater length.[37]

35. Ó Súilleabháin, *Handbook of Irish Folklore* 607–11, discusses the broad range of names and the high rate of personal names found in Irish folktales; this is notable in comparison with European folk tradition as a whole, particularly in comparison with English folktales.

36. The use of found elements is, of course, also characteristic of contemporary movements in the visual arts and not unrelated to Dada.

37. Related issues to those discussed here are taken up by Senn, " 'He Was Too Scrupulous Always' " 67–69, and Palencia-Roth 162ff.

iv. History and pseudohistory in *Ulysses*

A principal job of the Irish fili was to be historian and guardian of the knowledge of the past, knowledge that took various traditional forms. Genealogy was primary, and volumes of medieval Irish genealogies are preserved in the manuscripts, often organized for mnemonic purposes as rhymed, stanzaic verses.[38] Genealogy was a guide to dynasty and dynastic succession, and for questions of succession, kinglists also represented essential knowledge of the past to be preserved by the fili.[39]

Although maintaining genealogies and kinglists was an essential aspect of the job of poet, history primarily took the form of tale and anecdote. The ancestors celebrated in genealogy were also remembered for their words and their deeds; and their deeds, particularly their interactions with the otherworld, might be a sign of their descendants' right to rule. As a consequence a variety of tale types was the province of the poets: birth and death tales, hero tales, king tales, tales about succession, tales about battles and heroic deeds, tales about adventures to the otherworld, tales about tribal migrations, and so forth.[40] Like other types of heroic narratives, such tales were comparatively short, and they were in prose with varying amounts of fixed verse insets. Locked into the matrix of ge-

---

38. The standard modern edition of the early genealogies is M. A. O'Brien's *Corpus Genealogiarum Hiberniae*. Many of the early genealogical tracts had been published by the time Joyce was writing *Ulysses* (see, for example, Best, *Bibliography* [1913] 261–62, for the publications through 1912), but written sources for this feature of Irish culture are superfluous. The interest in genealogy continues to be notable in Irish oral culture to the present. For the genealogy of Leopold and Molly Bloom embedded in *Ulysses*, see Raleigh 12.

39. Perhaps the most famous kinglist is that appended to *The Book of Invasions* (Macalister 5: 152–581).

Because succession was based on descent within four generations of a king rather than on primogeniture, kinglists are generally associated with genealogies; and genealogies with lateral branches rather than simple pedigrees were requisite historical information for both family and tribe in medieval Ireland. Genealogies were also used at the early period to reify political alliance, with tribes electing a common ancient ancestor as a sign of political union; the filid were therefore often required to maintain very long lineages for political purposes as well for the purposes of succession.

40. Dillon, *Cycles of the Kings*, contains a good overview of the tales pertaining to Ireland's traditional kings; Mac Cana, *Learned Tales of Medieval Ireland*, discusses the early Irish genres or categories of tales, as well as the surviving lists of medieval narratives.

nealogy and located by tribal affiliation, tales were established in a spatiotemporal grid that helped to keep them stable in content as well as
memorable. Annal keeping was an outgrowth of all this historical impulse in medieval Ireland, and it may come as no surprise that the early
Irish annals are marked by some of the same features that characterize
oral history, rather than being a spare and objective recording of events
as they occurred. Like oral history, the annals were not exempt from
being reshaped when political changes occurred and new interpretations
of the past were necessary.[41]

Pseudohistory is another type of Irish historical literature, a genre
going back to the seventh and early eighth century, when the Irish learned
classes attempted to reconcile the relatively short time line of traditional
oral history with the long time line contained in Christian and classical
history. The most important piece of Irish pseudohistory is, of course,
The Book of Invasions, which has a significant position in European literary history and historiography. On the model of Irish pseudohistory
Welsh pseudohistory was constructed, and Welsh pseudohistory in turn
underlies Geoffrey of Monmouth's *Historia Regum Britanniae*, the principal European source of the history of Arthur and other productive
stories, including the story of Lear. As I have noted already, *The Book of
Invasions* is the centerpiece of Irish literature, and some version of it
opens most of the later popular general histories of Ireland.

Because maintaining history was a primary duty of the Irish learned
classes, virtually all of the extant early Irish literature and much of later
Irish literature has a historical cast. This coloring is also partly a result
of the fact that *The Book of Invasions* acted as a magnet for Irish tradition; the mass of floating mythological and historical senchas came to
be organized around the pseudohistorical time line of *The Book of Invasions*. Later, during the period of the penal laws when the native ar-
istocracy was suppressed, when the Irish learned classes were dispossessed of their social position and social function, and when it was illegal
to print books in the Irish language, the Irish poets turned to folk audi-

41. Kelleher, "Táin and the Annals," has an interesting discussion of aspects
of the political manipulation of the Irish annals. Most of the Irish annals were
edited and translated at an early date and would have been known, at least by
repute, at the turn of the century in Ireland. See Best, *Bibliography* (1913) 249–
56, for early publications of the Irish annals that were available to Joyce and his
contemporaries.

ences for support; the result was that folk storytellers became the bearers of Irish traditional history, a fact that has permanently colored the character of Modern Irish oral tradition. Even wondertales in Irish folklore are historicized, commonly opening with the line, "There was a king in Ireland."[42]

Ulysses can be situated within this tradition of historicized narrative. The geographical precision and the ample placelore set a historically accurate spatial stage for the events of *Ulysses*, and at the same time Joyce provides temporal historicity as well. The book is filled with allusions to antecedent historical events, particularly allusions to Ireland's political and cultural history, that give the narrative temporal depth. Joyce also obsessively outfits his work with topical allusions and historically accurate details regarding the physical and social world of 16 June 1904. It has taken critics decades to plumb the topical historicity of the book, and the process continues.[43] Even the mythic framework of *Ulysses* is carefully euhemerized and naturalized; thus, for example, in order to represent Molly as a Spanish woman for the architectonic framework of *The Book of Invasions*, Joyce makes her a daughter of an Irish officer in the British garrison at Gibraltar. These are some of the levels on which the narrative of *Ulysses* is given a historical spatiotemporal context and a historicized content.

Although *Ulysses* can be read as historicized narrative (history, as it were), it can also be read as an example of the genre of pseudohistory. Joyce builds up a dense texture of allusions to events and deeds that antedate the action in the book, thereby creating a *fictitious* history not merely for the main characters of the book but for scores of minor characters as well. Indeed, it is possible to construct from this set of allusions a detailed pseudohistory of Molly and Leopold Bloom, a task undertaken by John Henry Raleigh in *A Chronicle of Leopold and Molly Bloom*, a chronicle beginning in the eighteenth century. The pseudohistorical apparatus of *Ulysses* is facilitated by intertextual allusions to characters

---

42. Dillon, *There Was a King in Ireland*, gives examples; some stories also use a variant of the more common atemporal European formulas (e.g., the English "once upon a time"), and some tellers combine the two (Dillon, *There Was a King* 19, 39, 55).

43. A ground-breaking study in this regard is Robert Adams, *Surface and Symbol*, in which the author attempts to sort out surface realism and symbolic structure.

who appear in *Dubliners* and *A Portrait of the Artist as a Young Man*. These allusions reveal a deliberateness on the part of the author, as Kelleher has remarked in his discussion of "The Dead":

It must be noted that in *Ulysses* Joyce goes to some trouble to indicate that the Conroys are still, in 1904, a well-known jog-trot married couple. Molly Bloom asks what Gretta Conroy had on, and Bloom remembers that Father Conroy, the curate at Star of the Sea Church, Sandymount, is Gabriel's brother. References to the last illness and death of Julia Morkan, Gabriel's aunt and Stephen Dedalus's grandaunt, show that the Christmas party in "The Dead" must be dated to the early 1890's, from which it would seem plain that Gabriel and Gretta have survived the dozen or more years intervening without noticeable catastrophe. At least, I can see no other purpose to this series of references. They are certainly deliberate on Joyce's part. ("Irish History" 417)

Moreover, with respect to the central action of the day, Joyce provides us enough information so that we can write the pseudohistory of Bloomsday, hour by hour, for several literary characters, thereby enabling us to fill the narrative "gaps."

Joyce has also riveted the pseudohistory of *Ulysses* into the actual events of Ireland's patriotic history, thus writing in *Ulysses* a pseudohistory for Ireland as well as for the characters.[44] Joyce presents Bloom as an actor, albeit a shadowy one, on the wider stage of Irish politics, crediting him with providing Griffith the ideas for Sinn Féin: "It was Bloom gave the ideas for Sinn Fein to Griffith to put in his paper all kinds of jerrymandering, packed juries and swindling the taxes off of the government and appointing consuls all over the world to walk about selling Irish industries" (12.1574–77). Bloom is also represented as responsible for the ideas underlying Sinn Féin's revolutionáry mode of passive resistance, a technique actually taken from Hungarian politics; in *Ulysses* the ideas are ascribed to Bloom because of his Hungarian ancestry: "He's a perverted jew, says Martin, from a place in Hungary and it was he drew up all the plans according to the Hungarian system" (12.1635–36). The parallels to Griffith's ideas exemplified in Hungarian politics were presented in issue after issue of the *United Irishman* in the series "The Resurrection of Hungary" (which ran from 2 January 1904 to 2 July 1904) and were therefore of topical interest on Bloomsday and part of the current dis-

44. I am indebted to Dominic Manganiello for suggesting that I discuss this aspect of *Ulysses*.

course of nationalist Dubliners.⁴⁵ Historically, Griffith's tactics came to fruition in the later events of the Irish nationalist struggle.

Joyce gives Bloom an even earlier pseudohistorical interface with the giants of Irish politics, making him the shadowy figure who returns the headgear to the hatless Parnell:⁴⁶ "He saw him once on the auspicious occasion when they broke up the type in the *Insuppressible* or was it *United Ireland*, a privilege he keenly appreciated, and, in point of fact, handed him his silk hat when it was knocked off and he said *Thank you*, excited as he undoubtedly was under his frigid exterior notwithstanding" (16.1333–37). Joyce expands on the circumstantial details of the incident at length later in the text (16.1495–1523), ironically underscoring the claim to historicity in his pseudohistorical fabrication: "His hat (Parnell's) a silk one was inadvertently knocked off and, *as a matter of strict history*, Bloom was the man who picked it up in the crush after witnessing the occurrence meaning to return it to him (and return it to him he did with the utmost celerity)" (16.1513–17; my italics).

In these varied ways, then, Joyce fulfills the function of Irish senchaid as historian, writing the history of his city and his nation, creating a pseudohistory where it is needed, writing in a form that integrates the historical and the fictitious.

v. Conclusion

In this chapter I have given a brief overview of the genres from early Irish literature echoed in *Ulysses*; each argument has been schematic, and it is clear that the material could be expanded and detailed and that examples could be multiplied. Rather than belabor the point, I prefer to turn from specific correspondences to the larger question of Joyce's use of early Irish literature to challenge and redirect epic and novel, the privileged genres of English and European literature. Joyce's construction of a national epic follows the lines of Irish hero tale with its variation in style, its mixed tone, its episodic structure, its gaps, and its blurred margin. In a similar

45. The series was later published as an independent pamphlet, which by 1908 had sold thirty thousand copies (Younger 22–27). On this aspect of the pseudohistory in *Ulysses*, see also R. Adams 99–106 and Manganiello 119–37, 171.
46. Cf. Kenner, *"Ulysses"* 131–33, who discusses these political pseudohistorical incidents in a somewhat different vein.

fashion, *Ulysses* violates dominant expectations of the novel through its variation in style and mode, including the field of literary types included in the text. Joyce himself saw the style as the most significant aspect of the book, and it was this aspect of writing *Ulysses* that was most taxing to him.

Lawrence, in her treatment of the form of *Ulysses*, observes that the changing styles are the key to the violation of the reader's expectations of the genre of the novel:

The segmented quality of *Ulysses*—the discontinuity of the narrative as it dons various stylistic "masks"—can be treated as successive breaks in "narrative contracts" and successive rhetorical experiments rather than segments in a spatial whole. The reader of *Ulysses* comes to each chapter with expectations that are contingent upon what he has experienced not only in other novels but also in the preceding chapters of this one. These expectations are frustrated and altered as the book progresses. The narrative contract we form at the beginning of the book—the implicit agreement between the writer and the reader about the way the book is to be read—is broken. (6)

Lawrence continues, "The book becomes an encyclopedia of possibilities of plot as well as style, deliberately breaking the conventions of selectivity and relevance upon which most novels are based" (10).[47] At the same time, as she argues in the second chapter of her book, before Joyce can set up this dynamic with the reader, it is essential that he establish a set of narrative expectations through the "initial style" of the first six chapters, the style Lawrence calls Joyce's "signature style."[48]

Lawrence suggests that a way of characterizing Joyce's innovations in *Ulysses* is to see in them the injection of subliterary genres into the framework of the novel—genres such as catechism, journalism, magazine fiction, and so forth (10–11). This insertion of subliterary genres, she contends, is a major way in which Joyce breaks the conventions of the novel; the opening up of the novel results in a greater sense of possibilities, for it sensitizes the reader to the range of experience that overflows the conventional boundaries of the structured and causally linked rational novel (201–2). Lawrence's analysis is acute, but in light of what has been presented in the argument at hand, it may be more to the point to speak of

---

47. Cf. French, esp. 54.
48. Lawrence ch. 2. Joyce uses the phrase "initial style" in a letter to Harriet Weaver in 1919 (*Letters* 1: 129).

generic convention rather than style as the prime mover of the variation in *Ulysses*. Stylistic variation is a function of genre in the cases considered in this chapter; thus, generic multiplicity is a factor that drives much, though not all, of the stylistic change in *Ulysses*. As is consonant with Joyce's techniques and methods in general, Irish literature is only partially responsible for Joyce's stylistic and generic variation in *Ulysses*, and the Irish models converge with those from other sources. The styles in "Oxen" are clearly and ostensibly parodies of English prose styles; contemporary culture provided the journalistic signals of "Aeolus" and the prose of "Nausicaa." The form of "Nighttown" is that of drama—a genre not part of the Irish repertory at all. Nonetheless, it seems that Joyce's *idea* of using multiple styles, genres, forms, and modes in *Ulysses* can be traced to the Irish literary tradition.

A key point to consider is Joyce's complaint to Harriet Weaver: "The task I set myself technically in writing a book from eighteen different points of view and in as many styles, all apparently unknown or undiscovered by my fellow tradesmen, that and the nature of the legend chosen would be enough to upset anyone's mental balance" (*Letters* 1: 167). Joyce's statement that his "styles" were "unknown or undiscovered by [his] fellow tradesmen" is noteworthy. The implication is clear that Joyce's "styles" were not invented or created by him but rather *known* and *discovered* by him: *known* because of his familiarity with the Irish literary tradition that was at the root of his own popular culture but was marginalized elsewhere in the English-speaking world and in Europe; *discovered* because it was Joyce who found ways to use these "styles" effectively in modern narrative. Joyce emphasizes this implication by speaking of himself not as an artist but a "tradesman"—one who retails wares purchased elsewhere. Irish literature was not only instrumental but essential in Joyce's discovery of stylistic and generic variation and in his strategy for the reformulation of the novel.

Early Irish tales are characterized by a great deal of variation, as suggested briefly in chapter 3. There is formal variation: not only are the stories generally composed of a combination of poetry and prose, but there are two types of poetry and at least three types of prose. There is in addition an extraordinary variation in language variety and register; in any piece of early Irish literature there may be archaic language, technical language, informal or affective language, crude language or slang, and formal or ritual language, besides the unmarked narrative prose. The tex-

ture of the stories is also uneven, with, for example, radical variations in
the amount of dialogue: at times narratives will suddenly open up into
extended passages of dialogue, whereas elsewhere the narrative voice may
predominate. Although the passages of extensive dialogue are not drama
per se, they border on script and probably reflect the performance ca-
pabilities of what is basically an oral literature. Joyce exploits all these
types of variation in his own narratives of *Ulysses* and *Finnegans Wake*.

In addition, a major characteristic of Irish tradition is that it includes
genres that the modern definition of English literature considers "subliterary"—genres such as catalogues, placelore, genealogy, rhymed historical
and genealogical verse, onomastics, precepts, history, and pseudohistory.
Such genres are part of the field of early Irish literature and are integrated
into much of Irish narrative per se, and Irish "subliterary" genres impinge
on *Ulysses* over and over again as well. Thus, Joyce's narrative field in
Ulysses can be seen as a modern analogue in English to the field of what
is accepted as literature in Irish tradition, and this aspect of Joyce's restructuring of the novel, like the treatment of epic material considered earlier,
fits comfortably in Irish tradition. Joyce's challenges to the novel in fact
recapitulate many of the principles of Irish literature: he includes many
styles; he embraces a wide scope of genres, narrative types, and formal
structures; he has a double consciousness in his tone; and so on.

Joyce is best known for his stylistic and formal innovations; his formalism is rich and complex, and he himself was the first to acknowledge
that "with me the thought is always simple" (*JJ*2 476). The material presented here demonstrates that the ways in which Joyce experiments with
style, genre, and form in *Ulysses* cannot be divorced from Irish literary
tradition. It is ironic that Joyce should have challenged the privileged center of narrative—the genres of both novel and epic—in English poetics
and in the dominant Western poetics using the rhetorical resources of
Irish tradition, because behind his seemingly radical innovations we can
see his atavistic use of an archaic literature. The placement of these stylistic innovations is significant. Though the headlines in "Aeolus" (which
Joyce added late in the manuscript history) violate our stylistic expectations for the novel, the most radical departures begin with "Wandering
Rocks" and the episodes that follow.[49] "Wandering Rocks," the tenth ep-

---

49. Groden (105) notes that the headlines in "Aeolus" were added in August
1921, when the book was in press. Cf. Kenner, *"Ulysses"* 71 n. 1.

isode of eighteen, marks the beginning of what Joyce identified as the second half of the book (*Letters* 1: 145, 1: 149). It is thus in the second half of the book that Joyce's formal debt to Irish literature becomes apparent, and it seems more than accidental and more than the result of Joyce's development as an artist that the book falls into two halves. Indeed, Joyce was playing with the idea of demarcating the two halves rather radically as he was finishing *Ulysses*, thinking of adding an "*Entr'acte*" (*Letters* 1: 149). The first half of the book fits adequately into English formal structures and with minor dislocations confirms most generic expectations of English literature; the second half incarnates the generic range and many of the narrative structures of Irish poetics. In a sense, these two halves stand for the divided literary tradition of Ireland since the Tudor conquest, as well as the divided literary tradition of an Irish author writing in English after the nationalist revival had sharpened the awareness of the importance of Irish culture in distinguishing the Irish from West Britons.[50]

Joyce both exemplifies and reconciles his divided literary tradition in *Ulysses*, merging the two and in the process transcending both. Joyce's fierce attachment to English as a language as well as his disdain for certain features of the Irish literary revival are well known. But it is part of Joyce's genius to have recognized the potential of Irish form and Irish rhetoric for enriching modern narrative; to have seen the twentieth-century possibilities inherent in the genres of Irish literature, the multiplicity of styles, the comic-heroic mix, the gaps in narrative structure of the episodic heroic cycles; and to have transposed these features into English and the English literary tradition. These formal aspects of *Ulysses*, which have at times been read (incorrectly) as Joyce's aestheticism, also have political and nationalist dimensions: in choosing to renew Irish narrative form and myth in *Ulysses*, Joyce both asserts his Irishness and rejects the formal participation in English poetics chosen by most members of the Irish literary revival writing in English.

Ezra Pound proposes that technique is a test of a writer's sincerity ("Ulysses" 9). Though the writers of the Anglo-Irish literary revival use Irish content as Yeats and Synge do, or mirror Irish speech as Synge and

---

50. In the Linati scheme, the division between episodes 9 and 10 is marked "Punto Centrale—Ombelico" (cf. Ellmann, *Ulysses on the Liffey* 88, appendix). The suggestion is perhaps that the two traditions descend equally from the primordial Word: "The cords of all link back, strandentwining cable of all flesh" (3.37).

Gregory do, they are as a group committed to English poetics and English rhetorical resources. They employ English genres, English prosody, and English standards of narrative. While committed to the use of the resources of English as a language, Joyce breaks with English poetics in *Ulysses*, particularly in the second half, and thus with the poetics of his Anglo-Irish counterparts. If technique is a test of sincerity, then Joyce shows his loyalties. He writes with Irish techniques, refusing to rest content to be a West Briton in his poetics.

The Irish experience has been a colonial experience, and the colonizers of Ireland treated Irish national traditions and culture with as little regard as those of any other English colony; it has been claimed that Ireland is the only "Third World" nation of Europe. Whatever stand one takes on these questions, identification of the Irish formal and mythic elements in *Ulysses* suggests comparison of Joyce with twentieth-century postcolonial writers. Joyce, like such writers, was able to transform the language and poetics of English literature in part through the use of rhetorical resources, genres, formal structures, and the very conception of the role of literary practitioners derived from a literary tradition that came under the political and cultural domination of England but that continued to maintain its integrity and vitality to the twentieth century. Like many another postcolonial author, Joyce's importations from the colonized literary system are frequently misread primarily as personal invention rather than as a brilliant synthesis of two literary realms.

Chapter 6

Ulysses and the
Irish Otherworld

FATHER HART: What are you reading?

MARY: How a Princess Edain,
A daughter of a King of Ireland, heard
A voice singing on a May Eve like this,
And followed, half awake and half asleep,
Until she came into the Land of Faery,
Where nobody gets old and godly and grave . . .

MAURTEEN: Persuade the colleen to put down the book . . .
W. B. Yeats, *The Land of Heart's Desire*

FIGURE OF CUCHULAIN: You have but to pay the price and
he is free.

EMER: Do the Sidhe bargain?

FIGURE OF CUCHULAIN: When they would free a captive
They take in ransom a less valued thing.
W. B. Yeats, *The Only Jealousy of Emer*

The principal argument of this book is that to be well understood, *Ulysses* must be considered in an intertextual grid that includes both halves of Ireland's divided literary tradition. Cruxes in the text of *Ulysses* have here been illuminated by looking to features of Irish myth and literature for Joyce's resonance and embedded significance and by setting the Irish testimony beside material offered by English and Continental literature.

Another such crux is Joyce's portrait of Gibraltar in Molly's interior monologue. Phillip Herring and other scholars including James Card ("Gibraltar Sourcebook") and Robert Adams (233) have demonstrated the limitations of Joyce's historicity in the representation of Gibraltar in Molly's soliloquy. The flaws in the historical surface Herring attributes to the artistic problems Joyce faced in creating a setting beyond that of his own experience. Never before, Herring suggests, had Joyce to depend so heavily on a semblance of truth resting on so thin a veneer of substance ("Toward an Historical Molly Bloom" 501, 518).[1] Herring sees Gibraltar as "a dash of local color in the drab landscape of Dublin that was never meant to be examined closely"; Molly, Herring concludes, is "unconvincing" as a historical woman from Gibraltar ("Toward an Historical Molly Bloom" 516).

A central aspect of the tension between the social reality of Gibraltar and Molly's portrayal of Gibraltar results from a third structural element in *Ulysses* taken from Irish myth: the morphology of the Celtic happy otherworld. If indeed Joyce chose to present a "Spanish" Molly in part to fit the architectonic structure from *The Book of Invasions* and if, in addition, Molly's character owes much to the typologies of Irish earth goddess and Sovereignty goddess, then we should not be surprised to find mythic imperatives determining the delineation of Gibraltar itself in *Ulysses*. Thus, the artistic task Joyce undertook in Molly's episode was somewhat different from the one that Herring and others have defined: Joyce was not simply creating a realistic setting removed from those he knew firsthand. This chapter explores aspects of Gibraltar that have Irish mythic resonance; as with Joyce's other mythic structures in *Ulysses*, the Irish dimensions of Gibraltar complement but do not supplant the significance of Gibraltar that has previously been identified in the critical literature.[2]

The episode in Nighttown presents a set of related problems: while the form, a surrealist play, most disrupts the reader's generic expectations of

1. Herring's arguments about Molly considered in this chapter can also be found in *Joyce's Uncertainty Principle* 117–40.

2. Thus, Gibraltar provides a "Mediterranean axis" to the story, and it offers a link with Dante's Ulysses. At the same time Gibraltar gives biographical resonance to Nora, whom Joyce thought of as "Spanish." See, for example, Herring, "Toward an Historical Molly Bloom" 518, and the references he cites there.

the novel, the events themselves, specifically Bloom's trials and transformations, require critical exegesis in an assessment of Bloom's character. As in Molly's monologue, the departures from realism in this episode can be contextualized by Irish otherworld literature: some of the more sinister aspects of the Irish otherworld provide an Irish subtext for the episode, even as the configuration of Celtic otherworld belief provides a mythic imperative for Joyce's formal structuring of the text and for his manipulation of Bloom's character in the episode. When the Nighttown episode as a whole is seen in the context of Irish otherworld literature, a coherent pattern emerges linking the disparate elements.

i. *We've lived in two worlds*: The otherworld literature of Ireland

At the start of the last chapter, I briefly considered the importance of sight to the professional duties of the Irish poet. The concept of the poet as seer, particularly as possessor of second sight, is related to and reinforced by the early Irish belief in the otherworld, as Thomas O'Rahilly indicates: "In Celtic belief the Otherworld was the source of all wisdom and especially of that occult wisdom to which humanity could not (except in a very limited degree) attain" (318). The wisdom of the otherworld was attainable through contact with various otherworld entities and locations, including the Salmon of Knowledge and the otherworld well associated with the drink that the Sovereignty offers to the sacral king. O'Rahilly continues: "While the boundless knowledge which was a prerogative of the Otherworld was in general hidden from mortals, it was yet not wholly inaccessible to them. A class of men known as 'seers,' *filid* . . . claimed to be able, by practising certain rites, to acquire as much of this supernatural knowledge as was required for a particular purpose" (323).[3] Doc-

---

3. The otherworld as source of the poet's knowledge is epitomized in the story of Finn, who acquires his second sight by tasting the Salmon of Knowledge, to which Joyce alludes in *Finnegans Wake*:

> Finn [also called Demne as a boy] bade farewell to Crimall, and went to learn poetry from Finneces, who was on the Boyne. . . . Seven years Finneces had been on the Boyne, watching the salmon of Fec's Pool; for it had been prophesied of him that he would eat the salmon of Fec, after which nothing would remain unknown to him. The salmon was found, and Demne was then ordered to cook it; and the poet told him not to eat any-

umented for two millennia, the belief in the otherworld is one of the most important and most persistent aspects of Celtic thought, and it is therefore, not surprisingly, a dominant theme of the literature of every Celtic country. Otherworld elements are found in Irish literature from the earliest time to the modern period, in both written and oral texts, in folk and aristocratic strata, in both halves of the divided Irish literary tradition. Although the full range of ideas about the otherworld is complex, the otherworld can be characterized as another space-time continuum, separate from and parallel to that of mortals, with its own rules and properties.[4]

The Irish otherworld is known by a variety of names, including *Tír na nÓg* and *Tír inna mBan*, 'the land of youth' and 'the land of women'. Though these names are most common, there are other names such as *Tír inna mBéo*, 'the land of the living', *Mag Mell*, 'the plain of delight', and *Magh da Chéo*, 'the plain of the two mists', all relevant to aspects of the Irish otherworld discussed below. The otherworld in Irish tradition is located in a variety of places: in islands to the west of Ireland; under deep lakes; in "fairy mounds" (such as the Neolithic burial mounds that are plentiful in Ireland, including the great mounds of Newgrange, Knowth, and Dowth); in the hollow hills of Ireland and in caves; and in various other locations. Needless to say, the mode of getting to the otherworld varies in Irish tradition depending on the location in question: in some tales a boat is necessary, but for locations in Ireland itself, such as caves and mounds, one can penetrate by foot. At times the otherworld is conceptualized as coterminous with the world of experience, as existing parallel to the Ireland known to mortals, but in another plane; the two

---

thing of the salmon. The youth brought him the salmon after cooking it. "Hast thou eaten any of the salmon, my lad?" said the poet.

"No," said the youth, "but I burned my thumb, and put it into my mouth afterwards."

"What is thy name, my lad?" said he.

"Demne," said the youth. "Finn is thy name, my lad," said he; "and to thee was the salmon given to be eaten, and indeed thou art the Finn." Thereupon the youth ate the salmon. It is that which gave the knowledge to Finn, so that, whenever he put his thumb into his mouth and sang through *teinm laida* [an incantation], then whatever he had been ignorant of would be revealed to him. (*AIT* 365)

4. For a fuller discussion of the Irish otherworld, see Patch ch. 2; Nutt, "Happy Otherworld"; Mac Cana, "Sinless Otherworld"; Mac Cana, *Celtic Mythology* 123–29; and sources cited by these authors.

worlds are permeable at special locations and special times. Although the concept of the otherworld is found in many cultures, the mappable quality of the Irish otherworld, the specificity of its locations, and its accessibility are notable.

The otherworld and the mortal world are, as noted, permeable at special times, particularly at the great Celtic feasts of Samain (November 1) and Beltaine (May 1), which divide the yearly cycle into two halves, winter and summer respectively; Samain marks the beginning of the new year. The temporal relations between the two worlds are, however, highly unpredictable: a mortal may enter the otherworld and pass a considerable time there, only to return to the human world at exactly the same time he or she entered (see *AIT* 251); conversely, mortals may seek to return to their world after an apparently short lapse of time only to discover that hundreds of years have passed in human time (cf. *AIT* 454, 595).

The happy otherworld of the Celts is best known in critical literature, but the otherworld is also conceptualized at times as an ominous, hostile, entrapping, or dangerous place. In some tales inhabitants of the otherworld make war on human beings,[5] and people who find their way into the otherworld may find it difficult to leave (*AIT* 248–53).[6] The women of the otherworld are attractive and usually welcoming, but such women may also entrap men despite their will (cf. *AIT* 595). The otherworld inhabitants at times also take revenge on mortals (*AIT* 92, 215). In both its beauty and its danger the otherworld is perilous. Thus, the early Irish (and Celtic) conception of the otherworld is clearly multifaceted, and Proinsias Mac Cana has commented on the seeming inconsistencies:

Being, as it is ultimately, an imaginative reflex of human attitudes and aspirations, this other kingdom assumes different forms according to the occasion and circumstance, but these forms are not sharply or consistently distin-

---

5. Note also the hostility of the otherworld to Conaire Mor in *The Destruction of Da Derga's Hostel* (AIT 93–126), as well as the colophon to one version of *Tochmarc Étaíne (The Wooing of Etain)*, to the effect that Conaire was destroyed as revenge of the otherworld people (*AIT* 92).

6. In *The Adventures of Nera*, Nera is given the job of hauling wood, very low-status work requiring daily reporting and hence daily surveillance, in part so that he will have difficulty leaving. In the voyage tales some of the companions of the main character are almost invariably lost, and Etain is reclaimed by her husband from the otherworld only with great difficulty. See *AIT* 248–53, 588–95, and 82–92.

guished. When a mortal visits the otherworld by invitation, it is usually pictured as a land of contentment and joy. But when it is invaded by human heroes—a favourite theme in storytelling and one which is related to Cú Chulainn, Fionn and Arthur among others—then it wears a very different image. It may still be a country of riches and of wonders—and frequently the declared object of such heroic expeditions is to seize its treasures and its magic talismans—but inevitably its status relative to mankind has been transformed: its rulers and its welcoming hosts are now formidable and even monstrous enemies, fit to test the mettle of the greatest hero. (*Celtic Mythology* 126)[7]

Modern Irish folk traditions about the fairy world and folk tales about Finn's encounters with the otherworld portray it in much the same way. A principal theme of fairy lore is the fairy taking and the changeling motif: the fairies abduct a child or young adult, substituting a log or other entity that appears to be the body of the abducted person; occasionally such a person can be rescued but only with difficulty, and should the person have eaten in the otherworld it is virtually impossible to return him or her to the human world. Even a person who has been brought to the fairy world to render a service, such as a midwife, may find that the fairies become dangerous or hostile. In otherworld tales about Finn, both in the earlier texts and in modern oral tradition, entrapment takes still other forms: the Fianna are frequently bound or rendered incapable of movement in a variety of ways and must be rescued by a comrade.[8]

Illusion and transformation are themes found in the otherworld literature of Ireland from the earliest period to the twentieth century. Otherworld figures have the power to transform themselves: for example, the war goddesses can assume the form of crows (e.g., *AIT* 213), and other figures also assume animal forms at will (*AIT* 54). Otherworld figures may also have the power to cause others to transform, as the early story of *The Wooing of Etain* illustrates (Bergin and Best 152–57). In the early tales and particularly in modern fairy lore, the otherworld is at times not all that it seems to be: its splendor, for example, may turn out to be il-

---

7. Cf. Sjoestedt 64–65.
8. For collections of Irish folktales about the otherworld illustrating these aspects and these motifs, see Ó Súilleabháin, *Folktales of Ireland* 21–37, 169–220; Ó Súilleabháin, *Folklore of Ireland* 35–53, 94–125; Ó hEochaidh, Mac Neill, and Ó Catháin, *Síscéalta ó Thír Chonaill*; Yeats, *Fairy and Folk Tales*. See also the stories about Finn and the perils of the otherworld included in P. W. Joyce, *Old Celtic Romances*, a source Joyce probably knew.

lusory, with the fine hall revealed to be a dank cave, the food shown to be unappetizing, or the fine steed proved to be an illusion. Themes of transformation are one aspect of the general fluidity and ambivalence of this metamorphic realm.

Perhaps by virtue of its association with the timeless order of the gods, the otherworld was the repository of various types of specific knowledge—knowledge of the future or the past, including historical or literary knowledge, as well as knowledge of practical aspects of life or the appropriate social order. In some tales the otherworld is linked to the existential assertion of an absolute hierarchy of values, the delineation of which is revealed by otherworld agency and the observance of which in turn is guaranteed by otherworld powers (see, for example, AIT 98ff.). Contact with the otherworld can result in the possession or retrieval of important truths or knowledge. The motif of gaining information, even abstract allegorical information, is found in modern folklore pertaining to the otherworld as well.[9] The early tales also contain episodes in which the otherworld reveals future succession in a kingship (AIT 97, 184) or validates a royal line; the otherworld was thus, in some conceptualizations, both kingmaker and kingbreaker. As a result, the otherworld has a special relation to kings as well as to poets, and it is therefore perhaps not surprising that the truthfulness of the king was an essential aspect of his sacred role.[10]

Early Irish literature about the relations of this world and the otherworld forms a substantial portion of the extant narratives. Several of the early genres are specifically about encounters with the otherworld, of which three shed light on episodes in Ulysses: the *imram*, the *echtra*, and the *bruiden* tale. These genres are not perfectly demarcated, but in general the *imram* (literally 'a rowing about, a voyage', in particular 'a voyage to the otherworld') is a tale about a voyage over the sea to otherworld

---

9. For examples in the early literature of knowledge originating in the otherworld, see AIT 503–7, 548–50; Kinsella, *Táin* 1–2. Ó Súilleabháin, *Folklore of Ireland* 43–46, is an analogue in folk tradition involving allegorical knowledge.

10. The idea of the otherworld as kingmaker and kingbreaker is central to the plot of *The Destruction of Da Derga's Hostel*, which Joyce used in "The Dead." Otherworld connections appear as an alternative to the Sovereignty theme as a mode of designating a sacral king in the early tales, including the tales of Mongan and tales about a number of the Ui Neill kings; examples are found in AIT 491–517. On *fír flathemon*, or the truthfulness of the king, see Kelly, introduction.

islands; several faces of the otherworld are discovered, each conceptualized as a single island. The genre was Christianized at an early period and was used as a vehicle for the exposition of Christian concepts of heaven and hell. The *echtra*, 'an adventure, an expedition,' is a more generalized form of encounter with the otherworld; the otherworld may be found underwater or in a mound, or it may be entered in a less precise way, as through a magic mist. Such adventures to the otherworld generally involve an encounter that has some perilous aspect, but if successfully completed, the expedition garners for the adventurer or his people an important boon: knowledge, an otherworld gift, or some other element won from the otherworld (see *AIT* 503–7, for example). By contrast, the *bruiden* ('hostel, large banqueting hall, house') tale is specifically an adventure to a fairy mound where the inhabitants are generally hostile to the human invaders; the humans, however, may wrest from these encounters important powers, knowledge, or other good.[11]

Because of its connection with knowledge, the otherworld is a factor in the literature of inspiration in the early texts; thus, we find a series of medieval Irish genres in which characters have visions, go into trances, prophesy, and so on.[12] This is the branch of otherworld literature that survives in the early modern aisling tradition discussed in chapter 4, in which the poet has a vision of an otherworldly woman to be identified as the emblem of Ireland, a Sovereignty figure. Clearly, literary genres such as these are closely related to the tradition of the poet as visionary; they reinforce the view that the poet's second sight, including his ability to see into

11. On the tale types of the echtra and the imram, see Mac Cana, *Learned Tales* 75–77, who suggests that the imram is later than the echtra as a genre. The bruiden tale is later still, not appearing as a category in the medieval Irish tale lists.

Examples of the motif of the magic mist are found in Kinsella, *Táin* 1–2, and *AIT* 504.

The otherworld impinges on early Irish literature in many other ways than in these specific genres about incursions to the otherworld. Early Irish literature is noted, in fact, for the role of the gods in the stories; in Irish hero tales, as in the Homeric epics, the gods play an active role, and this is one of the ways in which early Irish literature is much closer to classical tradition than to its medieval counterparts in other European vernaculars. Otherworld figures meddle in human wars, beget offspring, seek human lovers, ask for human assistance, and so forth. See, for example, *AIT* 134–36, 176–98, 229, 439–56, 488–90, 546–50. The deities of the early Irish otherworld literature in some cases have lingered on as fairy kings or queens in the living oral tradition. For examples, see Mac Cana, *Celtic Mythology* 85–86.

12. Mac Cana, *Learned Tales* 75–76, discusses the genres *baile/buile* and *fís*.

the future and his clear vision of the norms by which humans live, is related to the poet's role as mediator between the human world and the
otherworld.[13]

Joyce's familiarity with the features of the Irish otherworld can be am-
ply demonstrated; indeed, this is perhaps the aspect of Irish mythos that
is most overdetermined in the sources Joyce had to hand. The literature
of the Anglo-Irish literary revival is full of material about the Irish otherworld, as the epigraphs from Yeats illustrate, and must be counted
among Joyce's sources for the mythic patterns related to the otherworld
in Joyce's work. Yeats's early narrative poem "The Wanderings of Oisin"
(1889) serves as a passable introduction to the concept of the Irish otherworld, including as it does many of the features of the otherworld discussed in this chapter, and Yeats returns to the various faces of the otherworld in work after work; in addition, his folklore collections, on
which he collaborated with Augusta Gregory, are filled with fairy lore.[14]
Yeats also uses the concept of the otherworld in his plays, and Joyce
owned *The Land of Heart's Desire* in 1920 (Ellmann, *Consciousness of
Joyce* 134; Gillespie #559). The Irish otherworld is present not only in
Yeats's work but in Augusta Gregory's adaptations and translations of
early Irish literature; and it is also used thematically by authors such as
A. E. and Synge.[15]

A specific connection between *Ulysses* and early Irish literature about
the otherworld is provided by a series of essays in the *United Irishman,*
"The Old Irish Bardic Tales." In the course of this series, between 18 October and 8 November 1902, R. I. Best discusses *Imram Curaig Máele
Dúin (The Voyage of Mael Duin), Imram Snedgusa ocus Maic Ríagla
(The Voyage of Snedgus and Mac Riagla), The Voyage of Bran,* and *Imram Curaig hua Corra (The Voyage of the Ui Corra),* summarizing the
stories in such detail that the features of the early Irish otherworld are
readily apparent to readers; he also offers extensive bibliographical information for further reading. Following these summaries, which provide

13. Some of the various types of early Irish texts related to the otherworld are
summarized and discussed briefly in Dillon, *Early Irish Literature* 101–48.
14. See Yeats, *Celtic Twilight* and *Fairy and Folk Tales.*
15. For examples of Synge's otherworld imagery, see Roche, "Two Worlds";
A. E.'s *Deirdre,* which uses otherworld themes extensively, illustrates A. E.'s interest in and promulgation of this facet of the Irish literary tradition. Roche,
"'Strange Light,'" indicates that Joyce's otherworld imagery in *A Portrait of the
Artist* echoes that of both Yeats and Synge.

an excellent introduction to the genre of the imram, Best turns to two tales that also have important treatments of the Irish otherworld, *The Adventures of Nera* (an echtra) and *Aided Fergusa maic Léiti* (*The Death of Fergus mac Leiti*), each of which illustrates some of the more sinister and entrapping features of the Irish otherworld. As a regular reader of this periodical, Joyce would have known these articles, and Joyce had earlier found substantial material on the Celtic otherworld in Best's translation of Henri d'Arbois de Jubainville's *Irish Mythological Cycle*, which had been serialized in the *United Irishman*.

Another probable source of Joyce's knowledge of Irish otherworld literature is P. W. Joyce's *Old Celtic Romances*, a book widely discussed in the popular literature and specifically recommended by Yeats (Sultan 43). James Joyce was familiar with other works of this author and respected his work, and there is reason to believe that he knew this volume in particular (Sultan 43–48). In *Old Celtic Romances* P. W. Joyce presents a collection of translations of early Irish stories, most of which have otherworld themes; the book includes a number of Fenian bruiden tales; the late "sorrowful" tales *Aided Chlainne Lir* (*The Fate of the Children of Lir*) and *Aided Chlainne Tuirenn* (*The Fate of the Children of Tuirenn*), which involve transformations and metamorphoses; the story of Oisin in the Land of Youth; the echtra entitled *Echtra Conlai* (*The Adventure of Connla*); as well as an imram, *The Voyage of Mael Duin*.[16]

Internal evidence in *Ulysses* suggests that Joyce had also read Kuno Meyer's edition of *The Voyage of Bran*, along with the accompanying important essays by Alfred Nutt on the Irish otherworld and Irish ideas of rebirth. This volume, which was celebrated at the time, would have been the most substantial contemporary source for knowledge of and ideas about certain features of early Irish myth, including the early Irish otherworld and Irish conceptions of metempsychosis. Nutt provides a thorough discussion of the Irish otherworld, synopsizes all the relevant primary texts, and marshals comparative material showing the relationship of the Irish otherworld to similar materials in other Indo-European traditions. Nutt concludes that the Irish representations of the happy otherworld are closest to those of the Greeks, thus representing another

16. The second enlarged edition includes *The Voyage of the Ui Corra* as well. P. W. Joyce's translation of *Mael Duin* is the source of Tennyson's "Voyage of Maeldune."

point de départ for Joyce's coordination of Irish and Greek mythic elements in *Ulysses*. Nutt's essays on Celtic mythological literature not only show detailed correspondences to various mythological elements in *Ulysses*, including the presentation of the otherworld, but are also antecedents to Joyce's later program of mythic syncretism in *Finnegans Wake*.

Joyce's familiarity with the concept of the poet's second sight and the Irish otherworld is patent, and these elements play a significant role in his writings. The theme of sight is a leitmotif of *Finnegans Wake*, not surprisingly since in Irish literature Finn is a poet and visionary.[17] In *Finnegans Wake* there is a reference to the episode in which Finn eats the Salmon of Knowledge caught by Finneces ('Finn the poet'), thereby gaining his second sight: "The finnecies of poetry wed music" (377.16–17). But there are numerous more general references to second sight as well, including vision of the otherworld: "he skuld never ask to see sight or light of this world or the other world or any either world, of Tyre-nan-Og" (91.24–26).[18] Although Joyce's familiarity with the concept of the poet's second sight can be traced explicitly only in his later work, the Irish conception of the poet as seer, hence as mediator between this world and the otherworld, is related to the notion of poet as priest found in *A Portrait of the Artist*. There the Irish and Christian meanings fuse in the pervasive imagery of poet as priest, a coalescence that probably has implications for how Joyce saw himself in life as well.[19]

Joyce had used otherworld themes before *Ulysses*. "The Dead" is a sort of ghost story (cf. Stanislaus Joyce, *Recollections of James Joyce* 20); based in part on *The Destruction of Da Derga's Hostel* (Kelleher "Irish History"), it contains some of the same somber and sinister otherworldly atmosphere of Joyce's mythic source.[20] The otherworld imagery is even more explicit in *A Portrait of the Artist*, where the theme of "islanding"

17. For a discussion of Finn as seer, see T. O'Rahilly 318–40; R. Scott, esp. chs. 1, 2, 7; Tymoczko, "'Cétamon'"; Nagy, esp. ch. 1, 129–30, ch. 6; as well as references cited in these sources.

18. On second sight, see, for example, *FW* 75.13, 143.26, 157.21, 269.2, 303.10, 364.18.

19. It is telling that Joyce believed his books were "acts of prophecy" (*JJ*2 550).

These Irish traditions coalesce in Joyce with the romantic and symbolist traditions of the poet as seer; on the latter, see Herring, *Joyce's Uncertainty Principle* 140–60.

20. Cf. also Nilsen, who traces references to the Irish god of the dead throughout *Dubliners*.

(173) and the mystical music and voice calling Stephen from "beyond the world" (167) suggest that he undertakes a symbolic imram to the otherworld (Roche, " 'Strange Light' "). Here Joyce uses otherworld imagery to symbolize the poet's acquisition of vision in "the strange light of some new world" (172); like Finn's otherworldly Salmon of Knowledge, the bird-girl in Stephen's otherworld vision makes it possible for him to assume the vocation of poet and acts in this regard as his muse.

In *A Portrait of the Artist* the girl of the otherworld vision is set implicitly against the girls of Stephen's dissolute sexual experiences, and it is no accident that Joyce signals Stephen's entry into the brothel area of Dublin by using language suggesting a transition to the otherworld:

Women and girls dressed in long vivid gowns traversed the street from house to house. They were leisurely and perfumed. A trembling seized him and his eyes grew dim. The yellow gasflames arose before his troubled vision against the vapoury sky, burning as if before an altar. Before the doors and in the lighted halls groups were gathered arrayed as for some rite. He was in another world: he had awakened from a slumber of centuries. (*PA* 100)

The language evokes a number of motifs associated with the Irish otherworld: the "yellow gasflames" and "vapoury sky" suggest the mist that in some early stories permits the transition between worlds; at the same time the women dressed in bright colors, wandering at their leisure, suggests the otherworld as the land of women. There is a suggestion of ritual, and the motif of temporal disjunction is suggested by the last phrase of the quotation—a temporal disjunction not unlike that at the end of *The Voyage of Bran*. Joyce's phrase "he was in another world" gathers and makes explicit all the otherworld imagery and contrasts with the "strange light of some new world" associated with the later vision of the bird-girl. In *A Portrait of the Artist* there is in fact a quaternary representation of the otherworld, for these two versions of the early Irish otherworld are in turn contrasted with the two otherworlds of Christian belief: the vision of hell at the centerpiece of the retreat sermon (107ff.) and the vision of heaven held out to the Stephen as a possible reward. The complex interplay of these otherworlds provides the field against which Stephen chooses his vocation as poet.

In *Ulysses* Joyce returns to otherworld themes, manipulating the material in multiple ways. The imram is reflected in *Ulysses* as a whole, since the motif of the voyage from wonder to wonder can be seen as doubling the voyage of Ulysses as well as the voyage of the Milesians in *The Book of Invasions*.[21] In Molly's Gibraltar, Joyce recycles the same material, recreating the typical configuration of the happy otherworld of Irish literature and at the same time suggesting with the otherworld themes a vision of Ireland's future after independence. On behalf of the community, Joyce acts as poetic visionary, and he presents his vision in Molly's flowing, continuous, lyrical prose, the closest Joyce gets in *Ulysses* to the alliterative, cadenced visionary poetry, the *roscada*, of the early Irish seer-poets. Yet prior to the vision of the happy otherworld in *Ulysses*, Joyce gives a permutation of the more sinister incursions of Irish heroes into the otherworld found in such genres as the echtra and the bruiden tale. Naturalized as the brothel district of Dublin, in "Circe" the threatening and ominous side of the Irish otherworld becomes a vehicle for representing the workings of the psyche. Though used for rather different purposes, the elements of Irish otherworld imagery that contrast embryonically in *A Portrait of the Artist* are explored and developed at length in *Ulysses*.[22]

ii. *Adiaptotously farseeing* the otherworld: Echtra in Nighttown

A key to seeing the connection between Joyce's "Circe" episode and Irish tale types about incursions to the otherworld is the recognition that, although the adventure in Nighttown has a dreamlike quality to it and although the organizing principles of the narrative are those of the unconscious, the episode takes place in a space-time framework that is physically accessible and yet distinct from that of the ordinary world: the characters in *Ulysses* geographically enter into and then leave the location in which strange manifestations occur, just as in Irish folklore or early

21. As early as 1892 d'Arbois de Jubainville had noted that both the *Odyssey* and the story of the Argonauts could be seen as imrama (*L'épopée celtique* 449). Stanley Sultan, following this train of thought, has argued that Joyce was influenced in particular by *The Voyage of Mael Duin*, citing details within *Ulysses* and references to Mael Duin in *Finnegans Wake* to bolster his argument, noting in particular the commonality of lack of revenge at the end of both *Ulysses* and *The Voyage of Mael Duin*.

22. There are also scattered references to the otherworld: see, e.g., 9.413; cf. 8.902–03.

Irish otherworld texts characters enter into or depart from the fairy world or the otherworld at specific geographical points in Ireland.[23] So Bran returns to Ireland from the otherworld at Srub Brain (*AIT* 595), and Eochaid Airem goes to the mound at Bri Leith when he wishes to reclaim his wife from the otherworld (*AIT* 92); both Srub Brain and Bri Leith are actual and identifiable places. Similarly, Bloom enters Nighttown at Mabbot Street, and he and Stephen depart from Nighttown at Butt Bridge; their path is mappable and concrete, however distorted and supernatural their experiences in Nighttown may be. The characters in *Ulysses* are able to return to the normal world after their adventures by leaving the otherworld *geographically*, as do so many characters in early Irish stories about the otherworld.

In early Irish tales the hero frequently enters the otherworld unintentionally or by accident, sometimes by following another character. An example is found in *The Adventures of Nera*, where Nera is outdoors on Samain, the Celtic new year festival, when the passage between this world and the other lies open. After seeing a supernatural vision of the otherworld host destroying Cruachan, Nera follows that host, not precisely understanding what he has seen or whom he is following and thereby accidentally entering the otherworld through the cave of Cruachan:[24]

Thereupon Nera . . . returned to Cruachan. Then he saw something. The stronghold of Cruachan seemed to be burnt before him, and he beheld a heap of heads of his people cut off by the warriors of the fairy-mound. He went after the fairy host into the cave of Cruachan. "There is a man on our track here!" said the last man to Nera. "The heavier is the track," said his comrade to him, and each man said that word to his mate from the last man to the first man. Thereupon they reached the fairy-mound of Cruachan and went into it. (*AIT* 249)[25]

---

23. As in earlier chapters, the discussion here is intended to supplement earlier critical studies of "Circe." For other parallels to the contents and technique of the episode, see Ellmann, *Ulysses on the Liffey* 141; Kenner, *"Ulysses"* 119; Kain, *Fabulous Voyager* 31; Hayman, "Forms of Folly in Joyce" 277–78; Herr 96–221; and Seidel 214.

24. This is an actual location that can be visited today in Connacht, though the way to the otherworld does not presently lie open for everyone.

25. Similar cases of accidental entry to the otherworld are found in Fenian *bruiden* tales. See, for example, some of the Fenian tales translated by P. W. Joyce in *Celtic Romances*.

Leopold Bloom, like the hero of an echtra or bruiden tale, enters Nighttown as it were by accident, following Stephen and the medicals.

A common location for the otherworld in Irish tradition is under the ground in mounds or in a realm under deep water, and Joyce naturalizes this feature of the Irish otherworld by locating the surrealistic adventures in Dublin's brothel district. In his venue Joyce is playing on language, for he is assimilating the Irish otherworld located under earth or water to the *underworld* of Victorian society, the areas of Victorian cities populated by the poor, the beggars, the thieves, and the whores, those outside the economic and moral structures of bourgeois society. The term *underworld* was commonly used to denote such segments of society as well as the urban areas inhabited by such people, the brothel districts in particular, during the nineteenth century. The underworld had been brought to the consciousness of polite society though a series of articles written by Henry Mayhew on these segments of London's culture; the series began in 1849 and was later published in book form in 1861–62 as *London Labour and the London Poor.*[26] This play on the word *underworld*, used literally in the case of the Irish otherworld and figuratively for the brothel district, is signaled explicitly in *Ulysses* when Stephen uses the term *underworld* in thinking of his attraction to "the sin of Paris" (2.70–73). This is another example of Joyce's use of verbal magic to establish connection or identity, an instance of verbal realism linking Joyce's work to earlier Irish tradition.

Though accessible geographically, the Irish otherworld represents a different order of existence: it has different rules, different properties, and residents with different habits, capacities, and moral strictures.[27] Like the early Irish otherworld, Nighttown is also a world geographically proximate but morally apart. Gilbert discusses the paradox of a brothel district's being tolerated in Dublin, "the great Catholic city of northern Europe":

The Catholic religion, upholding the inviolable sanctity of marriage, accepts no compromise, and condemns the ostrich morality of those hybrid creeds which, burying their heads in the sands of seemliness, refuse recognition of

26. Mayhew's discussion of prostitutes is found in 4.35–272. On changes in the patterns of prostitution in the nineteenth century, see Walkowitz.

27. Mac Cana, "Sinless Otherworld," discusses some of the moral freedoms and inversions of the otherworld.

the weakness of the flesh. . . . The man who, passing under the red beacon of ill fame, visits a "regulated" brothel cannot but know that he is committing deadly sin; no compromise with conscience is possible. . . . The Catholic religion, relentlessly logical, sets in sharp contrast virtue on the one side, vice on the other; white light of heaven, red of hell; the Holy Eucharist and the Black Mass. (316)

Not only different moral standing but different mores and even different laws: the night watch in Nighttown condones and even to some extent facilitates the operations of the brothels. Behaviors, modes of dress, and social interactions that would be unthinkable elsewhere in Dublin are the norm in Nighttown. The Dublin red-light district is a world of its own, distorting everyone who enters, presenting everyone and everything in a new light. This separate order of existence attributed to Nighttown is in part an element of naturalism; it was precisely the different order of existence of the Victorian underworld that touched and startled the readers of Mayhew's work. At the same time the difference mirrors a distinction between the world of mortals and the otherworld in Celtic thought.[28]

While the action is surrealistic and supernatural—note the semantic links between the words—the events in the Nighttown episode of *Ulysses* are very different from those of a dream. In a dream, whatever the logic of the events, the action is internal to the dreamer; nothing actually happens in the external world. In Nighttown, by contrast, events happen in the physical world itself, and in the episode the narrative line proceeds and develops; although some of the events are internalized to the characters, this is not the sole level of the activity. This tension between, on the one hand, startlingly defamiliarized object and event and, on the other, forward narrative movement is characteristic of stories of the Irish otherworld at every period. Both the early Irish otherworld and the otherworld of Irish fairy lore have manifestations that remind us of those in Joyce's Nighttown episode—absurdities, terror-inspiring visions, metamorphoses, wish fulfillment—ultimately because the Celtic otherworld, like most conceptions of the otherworld worldwide, is a reflection of the human unconscious (cf. Mac Cana, *Celtic Mythology* 126), much as the

---

28. In the early Irish otherworld time is also inverted: winter in the mortal realm is summer in the otherworld (e.g., *AIT* 251). In Nighttown, too, time is inverted: the underworld is active at night rather than during the day as the respectable world is.

visions in Joyce's Nighttown are manifestations of the characters' psyches. With his fine psychological sense Joyce perceived the psychic basis of otherworld literature and chose Nighttown as the place for otherworld manifestations because the red-light district was a location adapted to his naturalistic framework in which the same sorts of fantasies were expressed: the loosening of sexual proprieties, the indulgence in sexual fantasy and taboo, and the acting out of guilt, fear, and illicit desire. In early Irish literature, dream logic structures some of the adventures to the otherworld as it does Joyce's episode; however, because the otherworld was part of the Irish belief system, events there become structural features of the plot. Events in the Nighttown episode of *Ulysses* are likewise part of the action of the plot: Leopold searches for Stephen in the brothel district, finds him, has a confrontation with Bella, and rescues Stephen from the soldiers; money is spent, a lamp is broken; and each character has a vision of central importance to him. As for the weird events, Joyce offers rationalization for the reader in need by presenting his characters as under the influence of alcohol, fatigue, and stress: drunken or exhausted, none is fully rational.[29]

A feature stressed in some early Irish texts about the otherworld is the inconsistency of the perspectives of ordinary humans and the residents of the otherworld. In early Irish stories about the otherworld over the sea, otherworldly horsemen can ride over the waves to actual destinations; the leaping salmon observed by the mortals are to the residents of the otherworld calves and lambs; the dead can move and speak; the bounds of time are broken. Manannan mac Lir speaks of some of these points to Bran in *Imram Brain* (*The Voyage of Bran*):

> Bran deems it a marvellous beauty
> In his coracle across the clear sea:
> While to me in my chariot from afar
> It is a flowery plain on which he rows about.
>
> That which is a clear sea
> For the prowed skiff in which Bran is,
> That is a happy plain with profusion of flowers
> To me from the chariot of two wheels.

29. However, these factors do not explain all the distortions of Nighttown, which begin before either protagonist appears on the scene; see Kimpel 299–300 and French 186–87.

Bran sees
The number of waves beating across the clear sea:
I myself see in Mag Mon
Rosy-colored flowers without fault. . . .

Speckled salmon leap from the womb
Of the white sea, on which thou lookest:
They are calves, they are colored lambs
With friendliness, without mutual slaughter.

Though but one chariot-rider is seen
In Mag Mell of many flowers,
There are many steeds on its surface,
Though them thou seest not. . . .

Along the top of a wood has swum
Thy coracle across ridges,
There is a wood of beautiful fruit
Under the prow of thy little boat.

A wood with blossom and fruit,
On which is the vine's veritable fragrance,
A wood without decay, without defect,
On which are leaves of golden hue.   (*AIT* 592)

The "some see it, some don't" quality of Joyce's episode in Nighttown is in this mold. Bloom's fantasy of his rise and fall as Lord-mayor-of-Dublin-Leopold-the-First-and-great-reformer occurs between two of Zoe's sentences as he speaks a few words (15.1353–1958), and she notices nothing. While Stephen sees the vision of his dead mother, the whores remark only that he is white (15.4155ff.). Joyce inverts the capacity of special vision, stripping it from the inhabitants of his underworld and ironically reserving it for his protagonists, who are visitors; this inversion is a function of the psychological focus of the narrative.[30]

As mentioned in the last section, in many early Celtic stories the otherworld is hostile or forbidding to humans, particularly if they come as invaders, and it may be in part a function of Bloom's "invasion" of Nighttown that he runs into trouble. The hostility of the otherworld is usually associated with the early Irish genres of echtra and bruiden rather than

---

30. The special vision is not unlike the vision in early Irish stories of chosen ones to whom members of the otherworld appear; those around the favored mortals may see nothing. See, for example, *AIT* 488.

the imram tales, and there are specific motifs in the Nighttown episode linking it with the echtra and the bruiden tales in which the protagonist enters the otherworld accidentally or as a result of following others. The hostility of Joyce's underworld is embodied in the hugeness, the "mag-magnificence" of Bella/Bello (15.2846ff.). As her sadism increases, it brings the threat of destruction and consumption:

BELLO: (*savagely*) The nosering, the pliers, the bastinado, the hanging hook, the knout I'll make you kiss while the flutes play like the Nubian slave of old. You're in for it this time! I'll make you remember me for the balance of your natural life. (*his forehead veins swollen, his face congested*) I shall sit on your ottoman saddleback every morning after my thumping good break-fast of Matterson's fat hamrashers and a bottle of Guinness's porter. (*he belches*) And suck my thumping good Stock Exchange cigar while I read the *Licensed Victualler's Gazette*. Very possibly I shall have you slaughtered and skewered in my stables and enjoy a slice of you with crisp crackling from the baking tin basted and baked like suckling pig with rice and lemon or currant sauce. It will hurt you. (*He twists her arm. Bloom squeals, turning turtle.*)

(15.2890–2901)

The suggestion of being eaten by the residents of the otherworld is, of course, a motif that goes well beyond Irish literature: it is the oldest threat of wondertales.

One of the early names for the otherworld is *Tír inna mBan*, 'the land of women', which could be a delicious interlingual description for the brothel district of Dublin and thus suggests another piece of Joyce's verbal realism. In the early Irish tales the women are generally receptive, wel-coming, sensual; and such a land—like actual brothel districts—is ob-viously a manifestation of patriarchal culture serving the wish fulfillment of male desire. Yet the idea of a land of women may also involve projec-tion of other male feelings as well, including male fears of women and male desires to be dominated. Even in the early Irish tales where the oth-erworld is benevolent to its human visitors, the women are sometimes seen as seductive, entrapping, and hence frightening, as noted earlier.[31] It is not surprising, therefore, that in some of the bruiden tales the heroes are threatened or held hostage by otherworldly women who at times also have metamorphic powers; the hero escapes with difficulty, and the es-cape can take the form of breaking some type of enchantment.

31. See, for example, the actions of the otherworld women in *AIT* 179, 595.

The term *bruiden* ('hostel, banqueting hall', later also 'a fairy palace') might be a witticism applied to Mrs Cohen's house, reinforcing the notion that this land of women is an otherworld. If Bella Cohen, doubling as Circe, is keeper of a hostel, then she maintains a hostile hostel; the paronymy here, sound echoing rather than homophony in Irish dialects of English, is another element of the verbal magic underlying the frightening and grotesque aspects of the episode. Bella's bruiden is an abode of women and a guest house providing entertainment, but the environment is sinister. Like Da Derga's bruiden, the site of the demise of Conaire in the early Irish tale which Joyce uses as a subtext in "The Dead," Bella's hostel is also a perilous place: it endangers and entraps the men who visit it and even, through the possibility of a dose of clap, threatens their lives.

One of the most important Irish texts in which the otherworld is a perilous land of women is Brian Merriman's eighteenth-century poem *The Midnight Court*; Merriman was a contemporary of Jonathan Swift, and much in the work of the two links them, including their use of satire and humor for social commentary. This 1100-line poem, an outgrowth of the aisling tradition, includes a dream vision of the otherworld in which the poet is summoned to the court of Aoibheall, a fairy queen of Munster, by a gigantic, intimidating woman. *The Midnight Court* is perhaps the best-known work of Modern Irish literature; its satirical tone and lively content make it a perennial favorite, and it would have been known to Joyce, if in no other way, from his period of study of Modern Irish in the years before leaving Ireland. Moreover, the 1905 publication of Merriman's text in *Zeitschrift für celtische Philologie* was announced in *Dana* (February 1905) and the text summarized in some detail. This issue of the journal was owned by Joyce in 1920 (Ellmann, *Consciousness of James Joyce* 105).

Several features of *The Midnight Court* suggest that Joyce is incorporating a refraction of Merriman's poem as one element of his Nighttown episode. The central element of *The Midnight Court* is the complaint of Munster's women against men: the women languish for lack of sexual fulfillment; the men fail in their duty to marry; and the old men who do marry are inadequate to the needs and vigor of the young women. The queen, Aiobheall, finds for the women and, noticing the poet, is about to have him bound and flayed for his own offenses when the dream ends. The women's accusations in the poem are overtly sexual, and the tone of the poem is typical of the sexual content of Irish literature as a whole before the famine.[32] The poem clearly provides a literary paradigm for the trial scene of Nighttown, in which the women of Bloom's sexual fantasies and misdeeds step forward to accuse him and to bear witness against him (15.774ff.), though their complaints are not those leveled against men at Aoibheall's court. Less obviously perhaps, *The Midnight Court* is a subtext for Bella/Bello's humiliating accusations of Bloom and the suggestions that Bloom is sexually inadequate:

BELLO: What else are you good for, an impotent thing like you? *(he stoops and, peering, pokes with his fan rudely under the fat suet folds of Bloom's haunches)* Up! Up! Manx cat! What have we here? Where's your curly teapot gone to or who docked it on you, cockyolly? Sing, birdy, sing. It's as limp as a boy of six's doing his pooly behind a cart. Buy a bucket or sell your pump. *(loudly)* Can you do a man's job?

(15.3126–32)

Later she taunts Bloom again:

BELLA: *(contemptuously)* You're not game, in fact. *(her sowcunt barks)* Fbhracht!

(15.3488–90)

The Merriman poem, like all Joyce's mythic parallels, is freely manipulated here; marriage is certainly not the central issue of the accusations at the trial of Bloom, yet Joyce's work resonates with the tone and the content of the earlier work. In light of the affinities with the situation of the Merriman poem, it is perhaps significant that the Nighttown episode is positioned at twelve o'clock midnight, a correspondence that involved the deliberate omission of an hour in the progress of the day as well as other temporal disruptions.[33] Midnight strikes just before Bloom enters Bella Cohen's house (15.1362), and though midnight is the traditional "witching hour," the time Joyce sets is also a link to the title of Merriman's poem. The trial scene in the Nighttown episode and Bella's challenge of Bloom are each literally "a midnight court." This "coincidence" is a sign, a portal of discovery, that links Joyce's work with Merriman's important text. Thus, the sexual content of the Nighttown episode and of *Ulysses* as a whole have important anteced-

---

32. Lee (40) discusses the change in morality and the move toward greater prudery in Irish culture after the great famine.

33. See Joyce's schemata in Ellmann, *Ulysses on the Liffey* appendix; cf. Gilbert 30. Gifford (2–3) discusses the dislocations of time in *Ulysses*, particularly after midnight.

ents in Irish literature. It is typical that Joyce should have incorporated *The Midnight Court* in his mythic parallels, a work that his contemporaries in the Irish literary revival found difficult to use because of the conflict it presented with Victorian prudery and Catholic morality.

In a plot sequence that is similar to many stories from fairy lore, as well as to some versions of the early Irish echtra and bruiden tales, Bloom manages to rescue Stephen from "entrapment" and mistreatment in the underworld environment.[34] Entrapment in *Ulysses* takes the form of unsavory sexual relations and monetary bilking, as well as more generalized mockery, but these are to be read as the modern expressions of the timeless dangers run by mortals in the underworld. The motif of entrapment in the otherworld can be traced in Irish literature for more than a millennium, and it is connected with the most widespread motifs of fairy lore: the fairy taking and the changeling motifs.[35] In Nighttown-as-otherworld it is therefore no surprise that the dead appear—from Rudolph Virag and Ellen Bloom to Stephen's mother and Paddy Dignam, who explains that the situation is possible "By metempsychosis. Spooks" (15.1226). The episode is in some ways a ghost story, not entirely divorced from "The Dead," but the otherworldly and fairy aspect has come to the fore, as Joyce clearly indicates in the final scene:

(*Against the dark wall a figure appears slowly, a fairy body of eleven, a changeling, kidnapped, dressed in an Eton suit with glass shoes and a little bronze helmet, holding a book in his hand. He reads from right to left inaudibly, smiling, kissing the page.*)

BLOOM: (*wonderstruck, calls inaudibly*) Rudy!

(15.4956–62)

The changeling motif is accompanied here by the clear suggestion that Rudy is not dead: he has continued to grow and develop and is now eleven, the age he would be had he survived.

A common motif of fairy lore is the rescue from the fairy world of a

34. For example, in *Echtra Chormaic i Tír Tairngiri* (*The Adventures of Cormac in the Land of Promise*) (*AIT* 503–7), Cormac rescues his daughter, son, and wife from the otherworld.

35. In Irish folklore untimely death, particularly that of a child or a blooming young adult, is frequently attributed to a fairy taking, in which the dead human is replaced with a wooden branch or other artifact metamorphosed to the human shape; alternatively the human (particularly a baby) is replaced with a fairy, often a wizened, old fairy disguised to appear like the missing human.

person thought to be dead, or at the least conversation with such a person. Though Bloom sees Rudy, he cannot recapture his own child from the otherworld; at the same time, by rescuing Stephen from Nighttown, he is in a sense rescuing a son from the otherworld. In *Ulysses* no less than in *Dubliners* and *A Portrait of the Artist*, the repetition of key words sets up chains of meaning essential to the significance and metaphorical structure of the book.[36] Here the identification of Rudy and Stephen is facilitated by a node of meaning represented by Rudy's Eton suit in his apparition in Nighttown: for if Bloom sees Rudy in an Eton suit in his mind's eye (cf. 6.76), it is Stephen that Bloom has seen with his corporeal eye actually dressed this way (17.467–76, 18.1311–13, 14.1371–78), setting a model for his desired and ideal son. Indeed, it is the sight of the grown Stephen and the memory of the young Stephen throughout Bloomsday that have triggered Bloom's nostalgia for the lost Rudy (e.g., 6.74–84). The conflation of the two is established as well by the word *changeling*, for Stephen no less than Rudy has been presented to the reader in this role (3.308). Stephen thus doubles for Rudy in the plot sequence of one of the tale types that Joyce uses as backdrop for this episode—the rescue of one taken to the fairy world. It is partly in virtue of this doubling that Joyce is able to establish the father-son linkage between the two characters, at the same time maintaining Stephen's disinclination to be anyone's son. This is an example of the way that Joyce uses the fabula of a traditional tale as his subtext, raising expectations and at the same time undercutting those expectations by his manipulations and countermanipulations of the skeletal outline of the substructures.

In fairy lore in Ireland rescue from the otherworld may become impossible if the person taken has eaten while in the otherworld; the motif is well known from the Greek story of Persephone.[37] Rudy has grown, and we may thus infer that he has eaten. The question of eating in the otherworld is raised obliquely elsewhere in the Nighttown episode:

(*The cigarette slips from Stephen's fingers. Bloom picks it up and throws it in the grate.*)

36. See O'Connor for the full argument; cf. Kain's concept of integrating themes, *Fabulous Voyager*, esp. 48–71, appendix D.
37. This is motif C211, which is widespread both worldwide and in Irish literature of all periods; for examples, see S. Thompson, *Motif-Index of Folk-Literature*, and Cross, *Motif-Index*.

BLOOM: Don't smoke. You ought to eat. Cursed dog I met. (*to Zoe*) You have nothing?

ZOE: Is he hungry?

(15.3641–3647)

It is perhaps fortunate that Stephen never eats, and it is reasonable to suppose that had Joyce allowed Stephen to eat in the brothel, the subsequent plotting would have been substantially altered: rescue from the otherworld would have become compromised.

Rescue, however, is not the only, or perhaps even the primary, retrieval possible in the otherworld; the otherworld is also the source of truth, revelation, and information, including special poetic knowledge and knowledge of regnal succession. The motif of the otherworld as maker and unmaker of kings resonates behind the amusing sequence of Bloom's ascendancy as Lord Mayor of Dublin and Leopold the First, as well as his summary carbonization (15.1362–1956). Joyce had used this facet of the Irish otherworld before *Ulysses*, since the otherworld is responsible for making Conaire Mor king of Ireland and for bringing about his downfall in *The Destruction of Da Derga's Hostel*, the early Irish tale that Joyce uses obliquely in the plotting of "The Dead" and in his characterization of Gabriel Conroy.

Within *Ulysses* the episode in Nighttown reveals more truth than Bloom's sacral status. Truth is revealed on several levels, including Stephen's realization that his comrades have little concern for him and that even Lynch is a Judas in his life (15.4723–30). The primary gain from the adventures in Nighttown is the retrieval of psychic truth on the part of both protagonists. For Stephen, the adventure brings a crisis: his vision of his mother as the devouring maw of death ("All must go through it, Stephen. . . . You too. Time will come." 15.4182–84), the corpsechewer (15.4214) who calls him to repentance and the bonds of religious duty (15.4212–40), coalesces with the vision of Ireland as Gummy Granny, the devouring incubus who promises heaven for self-sacrifice in nationalist terrorism ("Remove him, acushla. At 8:35 a.m. you will be in heaven and Ireland will be free" [15.4737–38]). Mothers, grandmothers, religion, patriotism—for Stephen, in Ireland, they all mean death; they are all manifestations of Banba, an ancient name for Ireland, homophonous with *banb*, 'young pig'. Abandoned by his comrades, faced only with varied manifestations of "the old sow that eats her farrow" (15.4582–83; cf. *PA*

203), Stephen finds that his course is clear: he must leave Ireland. Stephen's vision at the climax of *Ulysses* leads to the same conclusion as his realizations at the ending of *A Portrait of the Artist*, but the motivation is less intellectual, less cerebral: his departure and exile are essential for his survival.

Bloom also comes away from his Nighttown adventure having met with his own psychic truths. He has encountered his sexual guilt and his desires, his fears of inadequacy, his sexual ambivalences, his shame about cuckoldry, his longing to be dominated. His megalomania has been played out, as have his desire to be a reformer and his fears of betrayal and rejection. He has met with the shades of parents and child and experienced once more the loss of his son. He has survived it all and returns to the normal world in fuller possession of himself: more individuated, more integrated. He is able to command eggs for breakfast in bed, and a drink from the Sovereignty as well ("tea in the moustachecup" [18.1505]). The "Circe" episode was conflated by some early critics with "Hades" (cf. Gilbert 320), in part no doubt because it *is* a ghost story. This identification, though wrong structurally with respect to the Homeric parallels, is not altogether off the mark, for the hero's mythic descent to the otherworld is usually a rite of passage: the hero returns to the mortal world having lived through a crisis, having integrated and transcended human development in ways that will enable him to go beyond the common limitations of humanity.[38] Bloom does not have this experience in the "Hades" episode of *Ulysses*; the dead he encounters in the graveyard are as much the hemiplegiacs of Dublin—Simon Dedalus, and John Power, and Martin Cunningham, and all the rest, the dead of *Dubliners* and *A Portrait of the Artist*[39]—as they are Paddy Dignam, "poor mamma" (6.683), and the notables of Glasnevin. There is no heroic crisis for Bloom in "Hades"; he escapes "back to the world again" (6.995), but he returns relatively unchanged. The personal crisis and integration characteristic of the hero's incursion to the otherworld are reserved for the adventure in Nighttown.

Joyce has bifurcated the hero's descent to the otherworld, representing the primary encounter with the dead in "Hades" and reserving the testing and spiritual crisis of the hero for "Circe." There are some realistic rea-

---

38. See, for example, the argument developed in Campbell 90ff., 217ff.
39. Cf. *Letters* 1: 55; *PA* 248; Scholes and Kain 68.

sons for this bifurcation: Joyce used the motif of the ordinary funeral to a variety of good ends, and funerals in Ireland are held in the morning. The hero's crisis and hence the climax of the book could not be placed this early in the course of the day if the unity of time was to be observed. Moreover, in *Ulysses* the Homeric enchantments of Circe are assimilated to intrapsychic experience: in a post-Freudian world it is the natural conjurings of the psyche, not the enchantments of a sorceress, that make men pigs, just as it is the encounter with the psyche that must occur for a man to emerge a hero—even such a hero as Bloom is. By integrating Celtic otherworld themes with his classical framework in the "Circe" episode, Joyce welds together the heroic encounter with the otherworld and the heroic encounter with the psyche. This is the heart of the test that changes the hero(es) in *Ulysses*, and it is the Irish mythic underlay that provides the structural justification for their heroic transcendence in the episode that is properly speaking the climax of the story.

iii. The *intertemporal eye*: Molly's Gibraltar and the morphology of the Irish happy otherworld

The Celtic otherworld is bivalent: it can be welcoming to mortals if they are invited, but hostile if it is invaded or if mortals come unbidden. Joyce has represented both faces of the otherworld in *Ulysses*: the hostile and frightening elements in the adventure in Nighttown and the delightful aspects in Molly's interior monologue. Together these episodes represent the unconscious desires as well as the unconscious fears and guilts that underlie the human construction of any system of otherworld beliefs. Joyce mediates these representations and at the same time disambiguates the bivalent values of the Irish otherworld in adapting the motifs for a modern English-speaking audience.[40] This disambiguation and the consequent doubling of otherworld genres in *Ulysses* have been among the factors that obscured Joyce's use of motifs and genres from early Irish literature.

Several early Irish primary sources delineate the characteristics of the

---

40. Teasing apart the ambivalence of Irish mythological motifs as Joyce does in *Ulysses* has been a long-standing process; it is a way of assimilating Celtic modalities to the dominant norms of Western culture and can be traced in the history of the assimilation of Celtic myth to Christian-Latin norms. See Tymoczko, "Unity and Duality," for more extensive discussion of the issues involved.

Celtic happy otherworld; most important are the early Irish voyage tales including *The Voyage of Bran*, but there are also other narratives such as *The Sickbed of CuChulainn*. The early texts portray the Irish happy otherworld as a land of youth in which people neither die nor wither. There is no sickness. The otherworld is a land of warmth and light where there are exotic colors and plants; blossoms coexist with fruit. It is a place of beauty, abounding in poetry and music. There is no work; it is a land of feasting and play. There is a limitless supply of food and drink; the otherworld has its caldron of plenty, *bithlán*, 'ever full'. There can be fighting in the otherworld, but the otherworld is characterized primarily by peace and lack of conflict. The otherworld is a sensual land, where sexuality is sinless and innocent. It is a land of women, and the women are generally sensual and friendly. Though the otherworld may be located in a mound or under a lake or entered through a magical mist, the happy otherworld is most frequently located on islands in the western sea; one form such islands assume is that of a land mounted on an inaccessible pillar. Thus, the otherworld is frequently reached by a sea voyage. Once left behind, it is difficult to regain.

These are some of the features that impinge on the configuration of Molly's Gibraltar, causing perturbations in the historicity that Herring and others have observed. Joyce highlights the natural aspects of Gibraltar—the botany and climate—in ways that emphasize its likeness to the Irish happy otherworld. Gibraltar is a land of warmth; Molly remembers the heat, particularly at night, and the heat is sensual, causing her clothing to stick and cling: "I used to be weltering then in the heat my shift drenched with the sweat stuck in the cheeks of my bottom on the chair when I stood up" (18.662–63). Gibraltar is bright and light: the sun beats down and shimmers, causing mortal clothes to fade: "red sentries here and there the poplars and they all whitehot and the smell of the rainwater in those tanks watching the sun all the time weltering down on you faded all that lovely frock fathers friend Mrs Stanhope sent me from the B Marche paris what a shame" (18.610–13). Molly remembers the beauty and color of Gibraltar, in particular the fruit and flowers, including exotic plants: "O and the sea the sea crimson sometimes like fire and the glorious sunsets and the figtrees in the Alameda gardens yes and all the queer little streets and the pink and blue and yellow houses and the rosegardens and the jessamine and geraniums and cactuses" (18.1598–1601).

All the names of the Irish otherworld—from the most common *Tír na nÓg* and *Tír inna mBan,* 'the land of youth' and 'the land of women', to the less common *Tír inna mBéo,* 'the land of the living', *Mag Mell,* 'the plain of delight', and *Magh da Chéo,* 'the plain of the two mists'—are relevant to aspects of the Irish happy otherworld reflected by Joyce in Molly's monologue. Molly's memories of Gibraltar center on young people—her young man Mulvey is central, and she remembers Mulvey's boyishness: "he was the first man kissed me under the Moorish wall my sweetheart when a boy it never entered my head what kissing meant till he put his tongue in my mouth his mouth was sweetlike young" (18.769–71). Even her Mrs Stanhope is youthful: "she didn't look a bit married just like a girl" (18.623–24). The older generation—including her duenna, Mrs Rubio—is active and vigorous. Gibraltar is also "the land of youth," the land of Molly's youth, the land whose very memories make her feel rejuvenated: "Lord its just like yesterday to me" (18.821); "well small blame to me if I am a harumscarum I know I am a bit I declare to God I dont feel a day older than then" (18.1469–71). We should note, too, that though in fact the society of Gibraltar was predominantly male, Molly's memories of Gibraltar give women a dominant place. We see this also in her frequent references to the Spanish or Andalusian girls and women (18.440, 18.632–33, 18.778, 18.1586).

Molly has no memory of death in Gibraltar. Though Captain Rubio is dead (18.858), and Molly has seen an officer's funeral (18.1262), and the consul is in mourning for his son (18.684), none of these deaths is said explicitly to have occurred in Gibraltar. It seems that in Molly's Gibraltar people do not die: as with the Celtic otherworld, they die only when they leave. In 1904 the Stanhopes are lost and presumed dead—"I suppose theyre dead long ago the 2 of them" (18.636)—and Major Tweedy has died in Ireland, but Molly has no memory of death associated with Gibraltar itself. Like Bran's company in *The Voyage of Bran,* the mortals who come to Molly's Gibraltar become dust only when they land on other shores.[41]

As with the Celtic otherworld, the passage to Gibraltar is not simple. In Molly's memories the men come and go as a result of sea voyages, connecting the passage to Gibraltar with the Irish genre of the *imram,* literally 'rowing' or 'voyage': "he went to India he was to write the voyages

---

41. Note that Molly wonders whether Mulvey is still alive (18.823) and considers that he may have been drowned or killed on his trip to India (18.855).

those men have to make to the ends of the world and back its the least they might get a squeeze or two at a woman while they can going out to be drowned or blown up somewhere" (18.853–56). As with the early Irish otherworld, it is difficult if not impossible to return to Gibraltar once one goes away, as the previous passage suggests. Moreover, a decision to leave is decisive: "of course they never came back . . . people were always going away and we never" (18.666–68). After people leave Gibraltar, contact with the inhabitants of Gibraltar fails, and neither Mulvey (18.853) nor the Stanhopes (18.667) maintain a correspondence with Molly once they have left: "not a letter from a living soul" (18.698). Molly wonders whether she herself will ever return (18.1338), and at times she seems cut off even from her memories of Gibraltar: "its like all through a mist makes you feel so old" (18.636–37). Joyce's use of the figure of the mist here connects the passage with the motif of the magic mist as an entryway to the Irish otherworld as well as with one of the names for the Irish otherworld, *Magh da Chéo*, 'the plain of the two mists'.

Herring notes that Molly is portrayed as "growing to maturity in a carefree atmosphere of warm nights, lazy summer days, free of worries or obligations" ("Toward an Historical Molly Bloom" 513). Such an atmosphere is, of course, an otherworldly one, and the activities that Molly associates with Gibraltar underscore its likeness to the Celtic otherworld with its pleasant sounds and music. Molly's Gibraltar is a land of music and poetry: "where softly sighs of love the light guitar where poetry is in the air the blue sea and the moon shining so beautifully coming back on the nightboat from Tarifa the lighthouse at Europa point the guitar that fellow played was so expressive" (18.1335–38; see also 18.441, 18.644, 18.700, 18.1596).[42]

Molly's memories stress eating and drinking (18.692–98; cf. 18.749, 18.831, 18.973–74, 18.1593–94). Indeed, when the Stanhopes leave Gibraltar, it is the teas that they remember: "will always think of the lovely teas we had together scrumptious currant scones and raspberry wafers I adore" (18.620–21). It is noteworthy that Molly has little memory of work in Gibraltar and only once mentions her father's military duties as he oversees and instructs at drill (18.766–67), remembered because the

---

42. Note that in Irish *láid* is both 'song' and 'poem'. By association Molly seems to credit her own sensitivity to these arts to her place of origin.

occasion may have given her the freedom to contact Mulvey. Her memories of her father's activities center on his relaxation with his friend over drinks (18.690–98), and she remembers other types of amusements, including parades, visits of dignitaries, band concerts, shopping, strolling, bullfights, picnics, and excursions (18.610–885). All these are otherworld themes; in fact, the abundance of food and drink, the absence of work, and the atmosphere of leisure and pleasure are typical paradisiacal motifs worldwide (cf. Patch).

Finally, Joyce's choice of Gibraltar for the location of his happy otherworld is piquant. The very geography of the place is an amusingly realistic correlate to the Celtic otherworld island located on a pillar. Here the unscalable fortress of the Rock of Gibraltar is a correlate to the crystal or metal pillar of the medieval texts.[43] In *Ulysses* there is a doubling of the motif of the pillar: Joyce calls our attention both to the unscalable fortress of the Rock and to O'Hara's Tower located on the rock, near which Molly and Mulvey have their sexual encounter. O'Hara's Tower— itself built for the fantastic purpose of spying on far-distant Cadiz (Herring, *Joyce's Uncertainty Principle* 124)—functions also as the tower from which the Milesians sight Ireland in *The Book of Invasions*; in *Ulysses* the "sighting of Ireland" gets conflated with a glimpse of "natural" sexual relations between Molly and her young man. There is both a doubling of the tower and a doubling of perspective: the tower is at once the object of vision and the location of mythic otherworldly vision.

Several nonhistorical aspects of Molly's Gibraltar have been stressed by Herring, and Irish literary and mythic correlates are relevant to these critical problems. Herring claims that Joyce gives us "a tourist-eye view" of Gibraltar, devoid of information about the misery or daily lives of Gibraltarians, a view largely conditioned by Joyce's sources for Gibraltar ("Toward an Historical Molly Bloom" 505). He notes that in fact military prerogatives predominated in Gibraltar; over a third of its eighteeen thousand inhabitants were in the garrison. Uniforms were everywhere, and he speaks of "six thousand bored soldiers, plus visiting sailors" ("Toward an Historical Molly Bloom" 502, 504). Despite the strong military presence in the English colony of Gibraltar, it is only the ceremonial and curiously peaceful aspects of Gibraltar's military that find a place in Molly's mem-

---

43. The motif of the island on a pillar is old and is found in both branches of Celtic literature, as Jarman (14) shows.

ories—the parades, the young men in their uniforms, the visits of royalty. She remembers "the same old bugles for reveille in the morning and drums rolling and the unfortunate poor devils of soldiers walking about with messtins smelling the place more than the old longbearded jews in their jellibees and levites assembly and sound clear and gunfire for the men to cross the lines and the warden marching with his keys to lock the gates and the bagpipes" (18.685–89). The "damn guns bursting and booming all over the shop" signal only ceremonial occasions, "especially the Queens birthday . . . [and] general Ulysses Grant whoever he was or did supposed to be some great fellow landed off the ship" (18.679–83). The transmutation of the military cast of Gibraltar to the peaceful ambience of Molly's memories may reflect Joyce's sources for his information about Gibraltar, as Herring suggests, but the peaceful and ceremonial atmosphere also echoes the Irish happy otherworld, in which there are warriors but seldom war. Indeed, the very name for the otherworld, *síd*, signifies 'peace' (Ó Cathasaigh).

The historical anomaly of Molly's unchaperoned freedom and hence her sexual encounters have also been noted: a freedom from "parental guidance or social censure" that places demands on our "credulity" (Herring, "Toward an Historical Molly Bloom" 513). Again, Joyce's presentation of Gibraltar is illuminated by noting that, like many other conceptions of paradise worldwide, the Irish happy otherworld is sensual. The Celtic otherworld is an erotic place with a great deal of sexual license; similarly, in Gibraltar there are graffiti of naked women (18.325–26), men and women expose themselves (18.544ff., 18.919ff.), and the women wear scant clothing ("I dont know what kind of drawers he likes none at all I think didnt he say yes and half the girls in Gibraltar never wore them either naked as God made them that Andalusian singing her Manola she didn't make much secret of what she hadnt" [18.439–42]). As in other delineations of paradise, the Celtic otherworld is also sinless: "Sin has not come to us" (*AIT* 593). Even sexuality in the otherworld is innocent: "Men and gentle women under a bush, / Without sin, without crime" (*AIT* 592).

These mythic elements are determinants of Molly's open-air lovemaking with Mulvey near O'Hara's Tower, an episode where the surface of Victorian naturalism cracks as Mulvey and Molly dally "under a bush": "she little knows what I did with her beloved husband before he ever dreamt of her in broad daylight too in the sight of the whole world you might say" (18.827–29). The mythic substratum explains why in the Gibraltar of *Ulysses*, though not in the historical Gibraltar, Molly could have had such physical and moral freedom. At the same time we can note that Molly's sensuality does include a typical Victorian episode of female-female sensuality, a memory of her having slept with Mrs Stanhope on the slim pretext of a thunderstorm: "I slept in her bed she had her arms round me" (18.641–42). All these sexual activities in Molly's Gibraltar are conducted without conflict about morality, sin, or guilt; they reflect a moral freedom that is typical not only of the Irish otherworld but of conceptions of paradise and holy places worldwide (Mac Cana, "Sinless Otherworld"). In a psychoanalytic analysis of Molly's monologue, Mark Shechner notes that she betrays little evidence of anxiety or guilt but that "her liberated condition is not particularly admirable, for it has not been won. Molly has overcome no psychic or social barriers to gain her freedom. . . . And insofar as she exists in a realm beyond conflict, she is unreal" (205). He therefore concludes that the psychology of the episode is superficial. It is perhaps more to the point to note that Molly's psychology is the morality of the inhabitants of paradise: as such it is a birthright and does not need to be won.

Herring also rightly questions the realism of Molly's ethnic identity, suggesting that the child of a local Jew and a British major would have had no social context in which she could have been accepted: "Molly could well have been rejected by all but the most tolerant in Gibraltar: by Jews as an outcast (though legally Jewish) like her mother; by local society as a daughter of the regiment . . . ; by the garrison as the product of a scandalous union" ("Toward an Historical Molly Bloom" 514). The paradox is resolved if Molly's mixed identity—Jewish, Moorish, Irish, Spanish—is related to the *Book of Invasions* theme: her heritage in *Ulysses* is less realistic than emblematic of the pseudohistorical background of the Milesians that Joyce invokes. At the same time the absence of sectarian and racial conflict in her idealized Gibraltar mirrors the peacefulness of the Irish otherworld, where there is no conflict and strife, rather than a temporal and geographical reality.

It has often been observed that there are problems with time in Molly's monologue and that there is no chronological orderliness. Just as all the men of her life become the indeterminate, archetypal *he* in her thoughts (Kenner, *"Ulysses"* 147–49; Shechner 199; Ellmann, *Ulysses on the Liffey* 166; cf. Benstock and Benstock 229–33), so all her life experiences run together and merge without regard for chronology. Hayman observes that she has "a mind which makes no real distinction between past and present" and that for her "time is one continuous erotic present" ("Empirical Molly" 124, 127). Indeed, Molly has been criticized for being psychologically immature and regressive because of these characteristics of her thought, but the temporal anomalies of Molly's thought, like many of the other critical puzzles about Molly, are illuminated by a mythic perspective. We must begin by recognizing that in his scheme for the book Joyce assigns an hour for every episode but the last, which he marks "∞." That sign for infinity indicates that Molly's episode is to include all time and to be no time, to be both eternal and beyond time. As Richard Ellmann has put it, "The ruins of time and space and the mansions of eternity here coexist" (*Ulysses on the Liffey* 163). This timelessness of Molly's thought is the time of the gods and constitutes a reversion to primordial time, where past, present, and future are all equally accessible. Such a temporal context—all time, bounded by no time—is appropriate for a deity and is to be expected in the supernatural realm of the gods; thus the movement of time in this episode fits Molly's status as a Sovereignty figure and an earth goddess. It is no wonder that, as Molly herself observes, she has a problem with mortal time: "I never know the time even that watch he gave me never seems to go properly Id want to get it looked after" (18.344–46).[44] The temporal framework of the otherworld—as well as the closed form created by the dúnad to the episode—enabled Joyce to assert that "*Penelope* has no beginning, middle or end" (*Letters* 1: 172).

This infinity of time also mirrors specific temporal characteristics of the Celtic otherworld. The Irish otherworld has a timelessness in the sense that things neither wither nor decay nor die, aspects reflected in Molly's Gibraltar.[45] But the flow of time in the otherworld is also disengaged from that of the mortal world: one can be in the otherworld for a short time only to discover that centuries have passed in the world of men, or one can spend a long time in the otherworld only to return to one's own world at the moment one left (*AIT* 250–51, 595). The shifting perspective on time associated with the Irish otherworld explains some

44. Bloom also has a problem with his watch in the narrative; cf. 13.983–89.
45. Though inhabitants of the otherworld do not die, in some tales they can be killed (e.g., *AIT* 191).

of Molly's temporal dislocation. She has the sense of immense gulfs of time ("how long ago it seems centuries" [18.666]), and the sense that time does double duty ("the days like years" [18.698]), as well as the sense that no time has elapsed at all ("I dont feel a day older than then" [18.1471–72]; cf. 18.821: "its just like yesterday").

Some of the otherworldly aspects of Molly's episode have been recognized before. Ellmann, for example, concludes that Molly's monologue "bursts through . . . to 'that other world,'" a world that is "a paradise lost" (172). What has not been recognized is the specifically Irish quality of this paradise lost. The appendix to this chapter summarizes some of the correspondences between Molly's Gibraltar and the presentation of the Irish otherworld in *The Voyage of Bran*, perhaps the most famous of the Irish otherworld texts.⁴⁶ It can be seen that some of the correspondences are ironically delicious and amusing: "the best of wine" becomes "Bushmills whisky" in Gibraltar, "strange raiment" becomes lack of drawers. Joyce treats the Irish myth of the happy otherworld with the same comic freedom that he does Greek myth; and while using Irish myth to give structural form to his work, he never solemnizes or sentimentalizes the material, as did most other Anglo-Irish writers of the period. Joyce's playful and humorous tone does more justice to Irish tradition, gives a more adequate reading of the early material, and represents a more seamless continuation of the tradition than did the treatment of such materials by any of the members of the Irish revival, including Yeats.

After identifying breaks in the historical surface of Molly's Gibraltar, breaks that to Herring seem infelicitous but that are meaningful in the context of Irish myth, Herring concludes that Joyce also actively and consciously undermines the social reality of Gibraltar to imbue Molly's past with a mysterious dimension ("Toward an Historical Molly Bloom" 513). Herring notes in particular that Molly's parents seem to have been designed to challenge our credulity (515). Herring's reading is essentially correct: the structures from Irish myth reflected in *Ulysses* indicate that Joyce has deliberately broken the surface historicization of Molly and that this presentation is part of Joyce's mythic method. Molly's mysterious origin is related to her status as a Sovereignty figure: she has the uncertain parentage characteristic of many mythological figures. Thus, the

46. Citations to *The Voyage of Bran* are taken from *AIT*, where Meyer's text is reprinted.

breaks in the historical surface of Gibraltar reinforce Molly's mythic stature at the same time that they coincide with the morphology of the Irish otherworld. Indeed, the structures from *The Book of Invasions*, the delineation of Molly as Irish Sovereignty goddess, and the presentation of Gibraltar as Irish otherworld together make a mythic pattern of great intricacy and texture; the mythic elements from Irish literature complement and amplify each other, even as they shatter the realistic surface.

Without knowing the Irish dimensions of the material, Shechner has concluded that the end of *Ulysses*, "this most psychological of modern novels," derives from folklore and myth; Shechner sees this ending as a failure on Joyce's part, a retreat (206). A comparative perspective including Irish literature indicates to the contrary that Joyce's methods in Molly's monologue are an epitome and summation of the mythic elements from Irish literature that provide one axis of the framework of *Ulysses* and that structure the book from its beginning. Rather than beating a narratological retreat from realism, Joyce uses a technique in the final episode of *Ulysses* that anticipates the postmodernism of *Finnegans Wake*. The shearing of the historical surface of Gibraltar is deliberate on Joyce's part; instead of caviling at the ahistoricity of Molly's memories or Molly's speech (Herring, "Toward an Historical Molly Bloom" 516), critics should consider the implications of Joyce's craft here: the "errors" are a portal of discovery. It seems clear that the breaks in the historical surface of Gibraltar are neither simply an absurdist abandonment of the "sudden reality which smashes romanticism into a pulp" (Herring, "Toward an Historical Molly Bloom" 501, 518–19) nor an indication of Molly's nostalgic and inadequate psyche. Instead, they are indications that Molly's Gibraltar is less a geographical location than a mythic and a symbolic one. Joyce's purposes for the symbolism must be considered.[47]

47. The mythic determinants of Molly's Gibraltar are largely Irish, as I have shown, but as with much of Joyce's mythic material they coincide also with prototypes from classical literature and from Joyce's other sources. Joyce's otherworldly imagery is implicit also in Field's description of sunset at Gibraltar, in which "the straits shine as if they were the very gates of gold that open into a fairer world than ours" (quoted in Card 167); Field was one of Joyce's sources for Gibraltar. That this passage made an impact on Joyce we can see from an allusion to it set in Molly's voice in her interior monologue: "the straits shining I could see over to Morocco almost the bay of Tangier white and the Atlas mountain with snow on it and the straits like a river so clear" (18.859–61). Joyce truncates the passage and makes the otherworldly associations implicit rather than explicit, letting them pervade his whole treatment of Gibraltar. But Joyce's Gi-

iv. Joyce's sovereign vision of
an Irish other world

To have an autonomous mythos and an autonomous symbology is to have an autonomous worldview. This has been true to a large extent of Irish and Celtic cultures, which have preserved ancient—archaic—ways of thinking and being into the modern world. This may be true of other marginalized cultures as well, as the powerful mythic material mobilized by Isaac Bashevis Singer or Toni Morrison illustrates. In these respects Irish culture is again paradoxically like the remaining well-organized cultures of the Third World that also have brought living mythic systems into the modern world. Though such cultures are at risk when they engage with dominant Western cultures, at risk of crumbling under contact (Chinua Achebe's *Things Fall Apart* inevitably comes to mind), the interface can also be dynamic, potent, explosive. Writers who are members of such cultures, steeped in their living traditions as Joyce was steeped in his but writing in the dominant languages of the West, may gain power from the interface, mobilizing the resources of both literary systems in their work. They can use the old autonomous symbols, myths, and poetics to make meaning—new meaning—in the new cultural context. It is in this sense that the identification of Irish elements in *Ulysses* and elsewhere in Joyce's oeuvre suggests the comparison of Joyce with twentieth-century postcolonial writers. A major aspect of Joyce's status as an innovator in English narrative and, indeed, as one of the founders of modernism resides precisely in his importation of mythic elements, mythic imagery, linguistic richness, and formal resources from Irish tradition. The otherworld subtexts of "Circe" and the happy otherworld morphology of Molly's Gibraltar are but two examples of this process.

In this regard one may ask why Joyce chooses a dramatic form for "Circe," particularly in view of the fact that drama is not a native Irish literary form at all and in view of the fact that dramatic form violates reader expectations in a narrative text purporting to be either (or both)

---

braltar also suggests the happy otherworlds of classical tradition, particularly the Hesperides, both by its location and the universal aspects of his paradisiacal imagery. Thus, Molly's Gibraltar is at once the otherworld of Field's imagination, the happy otherworld of the Greeks, and the otherworldly western isles of the Celts; Joyce's syncretism here, as noted above, follows Nutt's placement of the Irish otherworld in a comparative mythological context.

novel or epic. To be sure, an Irish writer of the generation that saw the birth and flowering of the Irish dramatic movement would have been hard pressed to resist dramatic form, and the theater is the most powerful illusionary art of the twentieth century.[48] But an equally compelling reason for the form lies in Joyce's incorporation of elements from Irish otherworld narratives into this episode of *Ulysses*. In Irish culture, belief in the otherworld has been part of the worldview since time immemorial, and this belief has lingered on in folk culture and popular culture to the present day; otherworld narratives, however strange, have therefore been part of the repertory of belief tales in Ireland rather than the repertory of fantasy tales. In adapting Irish tale types and motifs having to do with the otherworld, Joyce was therefore faced with the problem of representing Irish belief in the otherworld. This belief, like many beliefs in Third World cultures, is part of an alternate worldview in the twentieth century, a view at odds with the dominant worldview of Western culture. In certain respects, therefore, traditional Irish culture—no less than, for example, Latin American culture—is at odds with the dominant Western belief system and Western rationality. Like Gabriel García Márquez, Joyce faced the problem of how to represent the interface of two conceptions of reality; and the nature of magic realism, "characterized by the presentation of two different world views,"[49] illuminates Joyce's methods, particularly in the episodes where the Irish otherworld plays a significant role.

For a writer emerging from a marginalized culture with an autonomous worldview at odds with dominant Western scientific culture, there is an affiliative dilemma: does the writer stand with the tradition or against the tradition? Does the writer assert the tradition or undercut it, trivialize it, ironize it? The affiliative problem, which is essentially an ideological problem, brings with it artistic problems, not the least of which is how to secure a readership in the dominant culture. Like García Márquez working within Latin American worldviews, to be true to his

48. Just as the fugal form of episode 11 is an objective correlative of the song of the Sirens, the dramatic form of episode 15 may be viewed as the objective correlative of the enchantments cast by Circe.

49. See Chanady (18–20) and the sources she cites. Some authors take the view that magic realism is a uniquely Latin American phenomenon, but with Amaryll Chanady, I would see the mode as emerging from a more generalized conflict of worldviews that can theoretically occur at any cultural interface.

Irish tradition Joyce could not suggest that the otherworld was false, but to assert belief in the otherworld to his international audience was to court ridicule and critical rejection. In using otherworld imagery and narrative types, Joyce was presented with an artistic dilemma with ideological implications for himself as an Irish writer: a knife edge of choice, but Joyce of course wants it all—to affiliate with and assert the tradition, but also to ironize it, laugh at it, undercut it.

It is no coincidence that the two episodes in which the otherworld mythos is predominant are the two episodes most structurally different in their techniques from the rest of the narrative of *Ulysses*; indeed, properly speaking neither the Nighttown episode nor Molly's epilogue is narrative at all. Joyce chose a dramatic form for the echtra in Nighttown and a dramatic monologue for the final episode as answers to the artistic and ideological problems posed by using otherworld beliefs and narrative structures from Irish tradition. A standard narrative form involves a point of view, a narrative *voice*, which would have required Joyce to leave the knife edge of ambiguity. A dramatic form, by contrast, allows Joyce to present the materials without comment: a drama is "a direct presentation." The theater is mimetic; it is an art form that presents material *as if*, and characters act out "an imitation" of life. Dramatic form was the perfect way out of Joyce's problem of how to present the otherworld beliefs of Irish culture, for while narrative is a story told by a storyteller, drama is experience objectified, "a story without a story teller."[50] Oscar Wilde had called drama "the most objective form known to art" (*Letters of Oscar Wilde* 466). No storyteller, no narrative point of view, no voice. The dramatic form allowed Joyce to present the otherworld elements— used in part as correlatives of the psychic manifestations of his protagonists—as unproblematic, unmediated, objectified phenomena, as "real" "events"; and at the same time it obviated any necessity for comment on those phenomena.

Through the dramatic forms in "Circe" and "Penelope," Joyce gains the advantages of the narrative stance of writers of magic realism: the quality that Amaryll Beatrice Chanady has called "authorial reticence," in which unusual and supernatural events or beliefs are presented without comment. The mode of magic realism sensitizes the reader to additional dimensions of reality "in order to create a more complete picture of the

---

50. See Scholes and Kellogg (4) for some of these distinctions.

world"; it destroys a conventional view of reality, transforms reality. But in order to accomplish this task, the writer must present the unusual events as "objectively real"; the narrator must suspend judgment, neither censure nor even show surprise (Chanady 27–30). It is a stance that fits Joyce's view of the dramatic in Stephen's theory of literary forms:

The personality of the artist, at first a cry or a cadence or a mood [in lyric] and then a fluid and lambent narrative, finally refines itself out of existence, impersonalises itself, so to speak. . . . The mystery of esthetic like that of material creation is accomplished. The artist, like the God of the creation, remains within or behind or beyond or above his handiwork, invisible, refined out of existence, indifferent, paring his fingernails. (*PA* 215)

This is the reason that all the events in Nighttown are presented on a par, the reason that nothing distinguishes hallucinations from "real" events (Kenner, *"Ulysses"* 123; Ferrer 132ff.). Like García Márquez working with the form of magic realism, Joyce shows authorial reticence and retains his ideological loyalty without appearing parochial by choosing a dramatic form in "Circe" and "Penelope."

But "Circe" is not solely drama; it is *published* drama. As in any dramatic piece intended to be read, "Circe" must include "stage directions," which for the *readers* of drama carry the information that enactment on the stage carries for a live audience, particularly when drama moves away from a rhetorical tradition. Joyce exploits the stage directions and uses them to carry much of the information that a narrator would present: it is not at all incidental that a very large percentage of the Nighttown episode paradoxically takes the form of stage directions. As a consequence, Joyce both does and does not have a "narrator" in the episode. Joyce's dramatic form in the episode is an interesting one: it is in the tradition of Shaw and Yeats, who were among the innovators in the field of dramatic *literature*, insisting that anything worth staging was also worthy of being published as written literature and initiating the tradition of extensive stage directions in reading texts in order to enable the reader to visualize the drama in a sort of mental enactment.[51]

---

51. Ferrer makes the important observation that the stage directions are objective; they are neither interpretive nor descriptive but prescriptive (132, 140). A way of unpacking this idea is to say that narration and stage direction are two different speech acts: the former does give a point of view, that of the storyteller, as the story is told; the latter, like the cosmological Word of the deity, brings into being, and the attitude toward that creation is a separate matter. See also Herr 98–99.

In the final episode of *Ulysses* Joyce chose a different solution to the problem of authorial reticence, the interior monologue, still another dramatic form. Here too there is no narration per se, not even first-person narration; there is only direct presentation. By casting the entire episode as a monologue, Joyce could avoid authorial commentary altogether on the material presented: even the elusive Arranger or Stage Director fades away, and Joyce can remain hidden behind Molly's mask.[52] It is no accident that this formal structure is used for the second otherworld episode of the book. It is interesting that Molly has absorbed a great deal of negative criticism, and we can speculate that the critics are irritated in part by her aberrant worldview: the folding over of time and space, the cyclical nature of life, the metamorphic quality of persons in her thought, all of which are features of Irish otherworld beliefs. Those who hold such beliefs are not popular with the devotees of Western rationalism, and I am tempted to suggest that the critics have been trying to "persuade the colleen to put down the book"—to put down the book of the otherworld that structures Molly's thought. Joyce has cleverly deflected such criticism from himself onto his character by his formal strategy. He has, as it were, bargained, paid the price, given in ransom "some less valued thing" than himself: he has given Molly.

For Joyce, working with many of the same problems of cultural interface that later postcolonial writers have confronted, formal innovation was a necessity. He invented as he could, choosing to insert into his narrative two dramatic forms, conditioned and encouraged no doubt by the vitality of the theater in his day, and following in the steps of his older Anglo-Irish contemporaries, Shaw and Wilde, Yeats and Synge. Because drama is a form that presents material *as if* it were the case, it is useful for the presentation of fantasy, interior states, different levels of reality, and also different worldviews. In taking up drama, Joyce was also returning to the form he was first interested in: the form of Ibsen and Strindberg, with their great innovations on the stage, but also the form par excellence of the Irish nationalist literary movement.

It remained for others such as Jorge Luis Borges, Julio Cortázar, and Gabriel García Márquez to find *narrative* solutions to the problem of cultural interface, to find narrative voices and narrative strategies that would be compatible with authorial reticence. Magic realism as a *narrative* so-

---

52. This is in fact the episode of *Ulysses* that is most frequently performed.

lution involves finding a voice; García Márquez is in fact explicit about this aspect of his development as a writer, attributing his tone to his grandmother, who used to tell all manner of amazing stories with a straight face (Bell-Villada 43), and to his aunt, who had a knack for convincing others of the truthfulness of her ridiculous explanations, a naturalness "in which the most frightful, the most unusual things are told with [a] deadpan expression" (quoted in R. Williams 78). García Márquez also achieves his effects through the technique of fictionalizing two readers in the text, one a simple and innocent reader, an open-mouthed ingenue who will be impressed by the extraordinary tale to be unfolded, and the second a critical reader able to demythify the text and receive folk legend critically, who will reject a literal reading of the tale.[53] But these solutions evolved after 1922; they rely on whole literary movements, like theater of the absurd, which postdate *Ulysses*, and depend on Joyce's own experiments with narrative possibilities in the twentieth century. Still there is a commonality: the search for form in all these cases is not arbitrary: it is necessitated by the dilemma of an author between two cultures and two worldviews. When formal innovation emerges from such cultural depths as Joyce's does, it has an authenticity, a power, an imperative that grips even those outside the author's tradition, outside the dilemma.

53. See R. Williams (45–46) and the sources he cites. Obviously, the ironic gap opened between these fictionalized readers is related to the humor in the work of García Márquez and suggests a comparison with the means by which Joyce achieves a double consciousness in his own work.

Appendix

The Voyage of Bran	*Ulysses*
1. There is a distant isle . . . Four pillars uphold it. (589)	1. and the glare of the rock standing up in it like a big giant (18.608–9)
2. Whose view is a fair country, Incomparable is its haze. (589)	2. it was lovely after looking across the bay from Algeciras all the lights of the rock like fireflies (18.399–400)
3. The sea washes the wave against the land. (589)	3. I remember that day with the waves (18.668–69)
4. A host will come across the clear sea, To the land they show their rowing. (590) . . . the prowed skiff in which Bran is . . . (592)	4. and the boats with their high heads rocking and the smell of ship (18.669–70)
5. A delight of the eyes . . . Is the plain on which the hosts hold games. (589)	5. I love to see a regiment pass in review the first time I saw the Spanish cavalry at La Roque it was lovely . . . or those sham battles on the 15 acres the Black Watch with their kilts in time at the march past the 10th hussars the prince of Wales own or the lancers O the lancers theyre grand or the Dublins that won Tugela (18.397–403)
6. Lovely land throughout the world's age, On which the many blossoms drop. (589) That is a happy plain with profusion of flowers. . . . I myself see in Mag Mon Rosy-colored flowers without fault. (592)	6. and the rose gardens and the jessamine and geraniums and cactuses (18.1600–1601)

7. There is a wood of beautiful
   fruit . . .
   A wood with blossom and fruit,
   On which is the vine's veritable
   fragrance,
   A wood without decay, without
   defect,
   On which are leaves of golden
   hue. (592–93)

7. and the figtrees in the Alameda
   gardens (18.1599)

   I was jumping up at the pepper
   trees and the white poplars pull-
   ing the leaves off and throwing
   them at him (18.851–53)

8. Splendors of every color glisten.
   (589)

8. and the pink and blue and yellow houses (18.1600)

9. It is a day of lasting weather
   That showers silver on the
   lands,
   A pure-white cliff on the range
   of the sea,
   Which from the sun receives its
   heat. (590)

9. watching the sun all the time
   weltering down on you (18.611–
   12)

   I used to be weltering then in
   the heat my shift drenched with
   the sweat (18.662–63)

10. There is nothing rough or harsh,
    But sweet music striking on the
    ear. (589)

    Listening to sweet music . . .
    (589)

10. the band on the Alameda espla-
    nade (18.643–44)

    that Andalusian singing her
    Manola (18.441)

    and the bagpipes (18.689)

    listening to that old Arab with
    the one eye and his heass of an
    instrument singing his heah heah
    aheah (18.700–701)

    and the castanets (18.1596)

11. Listening to music at night . . .
    (591)

11. and the moon shining so beauti-
    fully coming back on the night-
    boat from Tarifa the lighthouse
    at Europa point the guitar that
    fellow played was so expressive
    (18.1336–38)

12. Drinking the best of wine. (589)

12. the Bushmills whisky (18.696)

    the wineshops half open at night
    (18.1596)

13. The food that was put on every
    dish vanished not from
    them. . . . No savor was
    wanting to them. (595)

13. will always think of the lovely
    teas we had together scrump-
    tious currant scones and rasp-
    berry wafers I adore (18.620–
    21)

    the recipe I had for pisto madri-
    leno (18.719–20)

14. In which are many thousands of
    variegated women . . . (590)

14. the Spanish girls (18.776–77)

    when I put the rose in my hair
    like the Andalusian girls used
    (18.1602–3)

15. They saw a woman in strange
    raiment. (588)

15. half the girls in Gibraltar never
    wore [drawers] either (18.440)

    the women . . . in their nice
    white mantillas (18.632–33)

16. There will come happiness with
    health
    To the land against which
    laughter peals. (590)

16. and the Spanish girls laughing in
    their shawls and their tall combs
    (18.1586–87)

17. Without grief, without sorrow,
    without death,
    Without any sickness, without
    debility . . . (589)

    They look for neither decay nor
    death. (590)

17. she didnt look a bit married just
    like a girl (18.623–24)

    his mouth was sweetlike young
    (18.771)

18. Sin has not come to us. (593)

18. naked as God made them
    (18.440–41)

19. Men and gentle women under a
    bush,
    Without sin, without crime.
    (592)

19. we lay over the firtree cove a
    wild place (18.789–90)

    she little knows what I did with
    her beloved husband before he
    ever dreamt of her in broad day-
    light too in the sight of the
    whole world you might say
    (18.827–29)

Chapter 7

"The Broken Lights of Irish Myth"

Early Irish Literature in Irish Popular Culture

VLADIMIR: And yet . . . (*pause*) . . . how is it—this is
not boring you I hope—how is it that of the four Evangelists only one speaks of a thief being saved. The four of
them were there—or thereabouts—and only one speaks of
a thief being saved. . . . One out of four. Of the other
three two don't mention any thieves at all and the third
says that both of them abused him. . . .

ESTRAGON: Well? They don't agree and that's all there is
to it.

VLADIMIR: But all four were there. And only one speaks
of a thief being saved. Why believe him rather than the
others?

ESTRAGON: Who believes him?

VLADIMIR: Everybody. It's the only version they know.

ESTRAGON: People are bloody ignorant apes.
Samuel Beckett, Waiting for Godot

In the last five chapters I have explored ways in which Irish mythos and
Irish poetics contributed to *Ulysses*; though this study has by no means
been exhaustive, it is time to turn to the question of Joyce's familiarity

with Irish tradition and to the sources he might have had for elements
from Irish literature that he reused in his early work and in *Ulysses*. I have
already noted that Joyce's knowledge of early Irish literature and culture
is overdetermined: the problem is not lack of plausible sources but an
appropriate delimiting of the materials to be considered. School histories,
Anglo-Irish literary refractions, and oral circulation of material over-
lapped in conveying to the Irish population at the turn of the century a
sense of their literary and historical heritage; in turn these sources of information were reinforced by periodical literature, scholarly publications,
and the activities of both scholarly groups and nationalist societies. As
the argument for Joyce's use of Irish literature in *Ulysses* has unfolded in
the earlier chapters, specific sources for Joyce's Irish materials have been
discussed. In this chapter and the next I survey briefly all the types of
sources that Joyce drew upon, less with a view to determining specific
texts that he used than to suggesting the range and depth of Joyce's
knowledge of early Irish literature.

Here the focus will be on the information related to early Irish literature and society available in popular Irish culture and in the writings of
the Anglo-Irish literary revival. Joyce naturally would have become acquainted with most of these materials before he left Ireland permanently
in 1904, though his later visits to Ireland in 1909 and 1912, his correspondence with relatives and friends, his personal contact with and visits
from people resident in Ireland, and his reading of Irish periodicals maintained his contact with Irish popular culture throughout the period he
was writing *Ulysses*. The materials surveyed in this chapter are principally refractions of Irish literature: summaries, retellings, contemporary
literary versions, critical discussions, and the like. Most of these refractions were produced at the turn of the century in the highly charged political climate of Ireland, when the movement of cultural nationalism was
preparing the political and military movements that resulted ultimately in
Irish independence and the creation of the Irish Free State. The seemingly
innocuous act of summarizing early Irish stories in a periodical was an
act of cultural nationalism and thus had political and ideological overtones, for the very existence of early Irish literature confirmed "the hypothesis that there was a civilization in Ireland long before the English
could boast of one"; translations, lectures to literary societies, language
study programs and other seemingly scholarly activities were similarly

politicized and charged with "nationalistic power" (W. Thompson 13).[1] Joyce resisted the use of literature for propaganda and the prostitution of Irish culture to politics, but his familiarity with Irish popular culture at the turn of the century meant that he was nonetheless acquainted with a surprisingly large and full matrix of politically charged materials related to early Irish literature.

In this chapter I examine the early Irish materials presented in popular culture and conclude with a sampling of issues and positions regarding Irish tradition that were discussed and promulgated in the popular press at the turn of the century in Dublin, issues that are reflected in and have informed *Ulysses*. In the following chapter I consider Joyce's use of more scholarly studies, scholarly translations, and other monographs.

i. Early Irish history and literature in the school curriculum

Although Irish speakers would have known about many aspects of early Irish literature and history as their birthright, in the middle of the nineteenth century it was possible for English speakers to be educated in Ireland and yet know nothing of early Irish history and literature. Standish O'Grady has left a vivid description of his own Ascendancy education, which left him ignorant of Irish history and literature:

At school and in Trinity College I was an industrious lad and worked through curriculums with abundant energy and some success; yet in the curriculums never read one word about Irish history and legend, nor even heard one word about these things from my pastors and masters. When I was twenty-three years of age, had anyone told me—as later on a professor of Dublin University actually did—that Brian Boromh was a mythical character, I would have believed him. I knew absolutely nothing about our past, not through my own fault, for I was willing enough to learn anything set before me, but owing to the stupid educational system of the country. (Quoted in W. Thompson 20)

Often called the father of the Anglo-Irish literary revival and responsible to a large degree for the popular dissemination of Irish tales, O'Grady contributed to a change in the educational program. By the end of the

---

1. Lefevere, "Literary Theory and Translated Literature," discusses the functions of refractions in literary systems.

century, when Joyce was being schooled, things were different, particularly for the Catholic population being educated in English; a number of
school histories summarized features of early Irish history, literature, and
culture for young readers. Such books include *A Concise History of Ireland from the Earliest Times* and *A Child's History of Ireland*, both by
P. W. Joyce, as well as William Francis Collier's *History of Ireland for
Schools* (1884). In 1920 Collier's book was included in Joyce's library,
and in 1939 Joyce owned *An Illustrated History of Ireland*, a successor
to P. W. Joyce's *Child's History*. It is likely that Joyce owned these books
precisely because he had used them earlier in his life.[2]

The Collier book is an example of the sort of thing learned by school
children about early Irish tales and legends in Joyce's youth. Only the first
fifty-four pages of this very small book (5" × 7") are devoted to the period
before the Norman invasion, but in these pages are found a brief survey
of *The Book of Invasions*, including an account of the invasion of the
"Clan Milly from Spain," "descendants of Millya . . . or Milesius, King
of Spain, who . . . had married Scotta . . . the daughter of Pharaoh, King
of Egypt" (Collier 10–11); an account of Phoenician sailors visiting Ireland; references to the Ulstermen; and a short history of the pre-Christian
kings, including Conaire Mor. There are notes on the pre-Christian culture of Ireland, including material on the mounds and tombs of Ireland
and a brief account of the druids. A short chapter covers the early saints
of Ireland, and there is an account of early Irish social life giving among
other things a brief introduction to features of the Brehon laws. A chapter
devoted to the Viking period refers to Turgesius, Brian Boru, and the Battle of Clontarf. Both the ubiquity of Collier's history and the nature of his
treatment of early Irish tradition are indicated by a comment included in
a discussion of Irish mythology in the 26 August 1899 issue of the *United
Irishman*: "Those who have been unfortunate enough to have had Col-

---

2. Kelleher, "Identifying the Irish Printed Sources" 164, suggests that P. W.
Joyce's *A Child's History of Ireland* was "inescapable" in James Joyce's youth.
P. W. Joyce was the author of a number of short histories of Ireland, all covering
essentially the same materials and sharing the same language, of which the *Concise History* and the *Child's History* are two examples; the text of *A Child's History* was the basis of *An Illustrated History of Ireland*. The first edition of *A Concise History*, which appeared in 1893, took the history to 1837, but the text was
gradually updated so that the twenty-fourth edition, published in 1920, takes
Irish history to 1908.

lier's 'History of Ireland' shoved down their throats at school, may possibly recollect the first chapter, where mythology and matter-of-fact are mixed up in a delightful fashion."

Although it cannot be supposed that an introduction like Collier's supplied Joyce with all the information necessary for the Irish substructure of his major works, the material in the book suggests that Joyce was introduced early to the Irish subtexts he manipulates in his mature literary production. The simplified presentation of the Irish stories and historical materials in school texts is also consistent with the gestalt of Irish materials in *Ulysses*. Joyce's ability to use Irish tradition in the architectonic mode rests on his familiarity with the tradition from boyhood onward.

ii. The circus animals all on show: Early Irish literature and the Anglo-Irish literary revival

It may seem anomalous to survey the works of the Anglo-Irish literary revival as part of Joyce's background in Irish popular culture since in our literary curriculum and from our historical vantage the movement is generally considered part of high culture and its works are canonical. But in Joyce's youth canonized "modern literature" stopped with the Romantics, and the Anglo-Irish literary revival was in its infancy. Moreover, the particular affiliations of the Anglo-Irish writers during the early years of the century suggest that at this period their work was embedded in the matrix of popular culture. In fact in 1901 in "The Day of the Rabblement" Joyce had taken the members of the literary revival to task precisely for their involvement in politics and their currying of popular favor; Joyce's assessment of the politicization and popularization of the literary movement was confirmed by what he considered the "political and dramatic claptrap" (*MBK* 187) in Yeats's *Cathleen ni Houlihan*, a play first staged in the spring of 1902 by Maud Gonne's nationalist group, Inghinidhe na hÉireann 'the daughters of Ireland'. Only gradually did the literary revival distinguish itself from the broader Irish cultural revival and the movement of cultural nationalism, a distinction that began notably with the 1903 break of the Art for Art's Sake group from the Art for Propaganda crowd over J. M. Synge's *Shadow of the Glen* (cf. MacBride 332) and was probably not decisive before the riots over *The Playboy of the Western World* in 1907.[3]

Moreover, as a source of knowledge for early Irish literature per se, the literary works of the Anglo-Irish writers can only be counted as popular since they represent imaginative refractions of the texts rather than scholarly translations or other sorts of presentations oriented to the source texts themselves. A writer coming to his craft in the period Joyce did would have been exposed by the writings of his older contemporaries to the rudiments of fairy belief, to refractions of early Irish classics such as the Deirdre story and *Táin Bó Cúailnge*, to much of the CuChulainn and Finn cycles, to stories about the chief gods of the Tuatha De Danann, to a conception of the Irish otherworld, to tales about the kings of Ireland, and more. Though few Joyce scholars would dispute Joyce's familiarity with Yeats's work, they might be less willing to acknowledge that in virtue of that familiarity, Joyce had a substantial introduction to the main lines of Irish literary tradition.

A full survey of Yeats's use of Irish materials is hardly appropriate in this context, but it is clear that Yeats's work is densely textured with references to Irish literary themes.[4] Yeats uses Irish mythos in a comprehensive and detailed fashion; to understand his work fully, a knowledge of Irish tradition is necessary, and, conversely, his work would have inculcated an appreciation of Irish tradition in a reader such as Joyce. Among Yeats's early works that Joyce would have known there are references to and refractions of Ulster Cycle tales including *The Death of Aife's Only Son* (in *On Baile's Strand*), *The Feast of Bricriu* (in *The Green Helmet*), *The Wooing of Emer* (in *The Only Jealousy of Emer*), and *The Exile of the Sons of Uisliu* (in *Deirdre*), as well as various references to the stories of Fergus and Conchobor. Yeats offers as well treatments of the Finn

3. For a more detailed treatment of the popular culture matrix from which the Anglo-Irish literary revival emerged, see Tymoczko, "Amateur Political Theatricals."

The independence of the literary movement was still later fostered by Annie Horniman's gift of a theater to W. B. Yeats, in which she stipulated that no sixpenny seats be made available in the house, thus severing the dramatic movement from its dependence on a genuinely popular audience and making the movement much more an avant-garde affair. Frazier (171–72ff.) and Hunt (59–70) contain information about the seating restrictions, but the issue is also discussed widely in the *United Irishman* in 1904 and thereafter. The restrictions were later lifted.

4. See, for example, Richard Finneran's explanatory notes to his edition of Yeats's poems.

Cycle, including a retelling of *Laoidh Oisín ar Thír na nÓg* (*Oisin in the Land of Youth*) by Micheál Coimín (Michael Comyn) in *The Wanderings of Oisin* and the story of Diarmait and Grainne in the play entitled *Diarmuid and Grania*, which he wrote with George Moore for the 1901 season of the Irish Literary Theatre.[5] Fairy lore, including various conceptions of the Irish otherworld, is widespread in Yeats's work (see, for example, *The Celtic Twilight*, *Fairy and Folk Tales*, *The Wanderings of Oisin*, and *The Land of Heart's Desire*). Joyce knew this material since in 1903 he called *The Celtic Twilight* Yeats's "happiest book" (CW 104). Yeats's work is also full of traditional Irish imagery, such as that of the rose and the poor old woman.

We can also document Joyce's knowledge of other works of the Anglo-Irish literary revival. Augusta Gregory's retellings of the Ulster Cycle in *Cuchulain of Muirthemne* (1902) and her treatment of the Mythological Cycle and the Finn Cycle in *Gods and Fighting Men* (1904) give a comprehensive overview of the early literature in Ireland, albeit a view that is manipulated in various ways by her literary agenda to make the materials palatable to a popular audience. Although Joyce had scant respect for some of Lady Gregory's work, as his uncomplimentary review of her *Poets and Dreamers* for the *Daily Express* indicates (CW 102–5; cf. *JJ*2 121), his use of her refractions of the early tales should not be ruled out. Joyce had probably read *Cuchulain of Muirthemne*, for he has Buck Mulligan, in reproaching Stephen Dedalus for his treatment of Augusta Gregory, paraphrase a line of Yeats's preface to the book in the library scene of *Ulysses*:

O you inquisitional drunken jewjesuit! She gets you a job on the paper and then you go and slate her drivel to Jaysus. Couldn't you do the Yeats touch?
He went on and down, mopping, chanting with waving graceful arms:
—The most beautiful book that has come out of our country in my time. One thinks of Homer. (9.1159–65)[6]

Gregory often bowdlerizes the early texts, leaving out, for example, the sinless sexuality of the otherworld in her version of *The Voyage of Bran* (*Gods and Fighting Men* 103–6), and she does so unapologetically, stat-

---

5. *AIT* (439–56) includes a translation of Coimín's poem.
6. Cf. Yeats's opening sentences to his preface: "I think this book is the best that has come out of Ireland in my time. Perhaps I should say that it is the best book that has ever come out of Ireland" (Gregory, *Cuchulain of Muirthemne* 11). Mulligan's admonition of Dedalus with the quote of Yeats's praise may have been intended as a sort of reparation to Gregory.

ing in her dedication to the first volume, "I left out a good deal I thought
you would not care about for one reason or another" (*Cuchulain of Muirthemne* 5). Nonetheless, Gregory's treatments of the early literature are
not only comprehensive but at times surprisingly detailed. For many
stories, including *The Destruction of Da Derga's Hostel*, all the elements
of the tale are given in such detail that a reading of Gregory's adaptations
would have sufficed for the schematic use Joyce makes of Irish mythos in
Ulysses and his early works. Occasionally she even includes the sort of
telling detail that Joyce seems to have made use of, though because of the
overdetermined nature of Joyce's sources the detail cannot be traced specifically to Gregory's version. For example, though the sexual content of
the early tales is diminished throughout the two volumes, Gregory retains
the exchange between Ailill and Medb that may inform the relations between Leopold and Molly Bloom:

"For it is not a common marriage portion would have satisfied me, the same
as is asked by the other women of Ireland," [Maeve] said; "but it is what I
asked as a marriage portion, a man without stinginess, without jealousy,
without fear. For it would not be fitting for me to be with a man that would
be close-handed, for my own hand is open in wage-paying and in free-giving;
and it would be a reproach on my husband, I to be a better wage-payer than
himself. And it would not be fitting for me to be with a man that would be
cowardly, for I myself go into struggles and fights and battles and gain the
victory; and it would be a reproach to my husband, his wife to be braver than
himself. And it would not be fitting for me to be with a husband that would
be jealous, for I was never without one man being with me in the shadow of
another." (*Cuchulain of Muirthemne* 141–42)

The early productions of the Irish dramatic movement that Joyce fol-
lowed closely would also have contributed to his familiarity with early
Irish history and literature. In the years before 1904, for example, the
Irish Literary Theatre and its successor staged versions of Finn tales including Alice Milligan's *Last Feast of the Fianna* in February 1900 and
Yeats's collaboration with George Moore, *Diarmuid and Grania*, in October 1901. In April 1902 A. E.'s *Deirdre* played with Yeats's *Cathleen ni
Houlihan*, and in October 1903 *The King's Threshold* by Yeats was
staged. Meanwhile Inghinidhe na hÉireann was producing *tableaux vivants* dramatizing the early history and literature of Ireland,[7] and the Fays'

7. See the review in the *United Irishman* 13 Apr. 1901.

acting company was staging still other historical plays, including Alice Milligan's *Red Hugh*.[8] In part the early dramatic movement was intended to have an educative function and to expose the audiences to an Irish patriotic history and literature; as a follower of this movement, Joyce, like the rest of the audience, would have learned elements of Irish tradition.

Other authors of the Anglo-Irish literary revival also cannot be ruled out as sources of Joyce's familiarity with early Irish literature. It is hardly conceivable that Joyce could have spent his boyhood in Ireland without having read some of Standish O'Grady; strange as those presentations are of the Ulster Cycle and other tales, they do familiarize the readers with the major plot lines and major characters.[9] A. E. likewise may have contributed to Joyce's knowledge of the early literature, though possibly in his case more through conversation than through his writings. Joyce certainly knew A. E.'s *Deirdre* since he had seen one of its initial performances when it was staged with *Cathleen ni Houlihan*, and a line from the play is quoted in *Ulysses* (9.190–91).

iii. The *United Irishman*

Periodicals at the turn of the century were a major vehicle for the popular dissemination of Irish culture. In the period 1895–1905 a number of journals provided Irish readers with information about early Irish literature and, in addition, furnished material that was discussed and circulated orally. Besides such scholarly journals as *Revue celtique* and *Zeitschrift für celtische Philologie*, there were more popular cultural and artistic periodicals such as *Samhain* (the review Yeats wrote for the Irish dramatic movement), broad-gauge political periodicals such as the *United Irishman*, periodicals of specific political groups such as the *Irish Homestead* (the organ of the Irish Agricultural Association Society), periodicals devoted to cultural nationalism such as Standish O'Grady's *All Ireland Review*, and Gaelic periodicals including *Irisleabhar na Gaedhilge*. Because journals often reviewed the new numbers of other periodicals, much of the material published in this form passed into general knowledge, at least in a distilled form; the readers of one journal were thus likely to

---

8. For a chronology of the early performances, see Ellis-Fermor, appendix 1.
9. Marcus (86) traces Joyce's description of the Citizen to O'Grady's *Finn and His Companions*.

know the major issues covered in many. These periodicals were an important source of knowledge about traditional Irish life, including popular manifestations such as music or folk calendar customs as well as patriotic history and early Irish literature.

In the face of the variety of potential sources for Joyce's knowledge of Irish literature and culture, the overdetermination of sources, and the difficulty of documenting Joyce's knowledge of Irish material, it is welcome to be able to identify the *United Irishman* as a significant and documentable source that offers a preliminary index of the range and depth of Joyce's knowledge of early Irish literature and history obtained from popular sources.[10] It is well known that Joyce read the *United Irishman* every week, having it sent to him on the Continent after he left Ireland (*Letters* 2.149–50). Joyce considered it the best newspaper in Ireland, as Stanislaus Joyce reports in *My Brother's Keeper*:

> He said that the *United Irishman* was the only paper in Dublin worth reading, and in fact, he used to read it every week. . . . In spite of its perfervid nationalism, the paper had found very little favour with the students of University College or with their masters. Its tone was too independent, its line too unusual; it was suspected of lukewarm Catholicism, of disrespect for priests (Griffith had been a Parnellite); and it did not seem to be hostile to intellectual movements in Ireland and on the continent. Yeats and AE, and others who contributed to it gratuitously, were of Protestant stock and on the Catholic blacklist. (173–74)

Joyce himself, in a letter to Stanislaus dated 6 September 1906, characteristically put the matter in somewhat more restrained terms: "In my opinion [the *United Irishman*] is the only newspaper of any pretensions in Ireland. I believe that its policy would benefit Ireland very much. Of course so far as any intellectual interest is concerned it is hopelessly deaf. But even that deafness is preferable to the alertness of *Dialogues of the Day*" (*Letters* 2: 157–58).[11]

The *United Irishman* would have attracted Joyce's attention and allegiance for many reasons. The journal gave extensive coverage to artistic questions; meetings of literary societies were reported; publications, per-

---

10. A more detailed version of this subject is found in Tymoczko, "'Broken Lights of Irish Myth.'"
11. *Dialogues of the Day* was a weekly commentary put out by Francis Sheehy-Skeffington, Joyce's old school friend.

formances, and exhibits were reviewed; poems and stories were published in virtually every issue.[12] A great part of the debate about the role of the theater in Ireland and the role of literature in building a nationalist consciousness was carried out in the pages of the *United Irishman*; both Frank Fay and W. B. Yeats contributed to the periodical frequently. The appeal of the *United Irishman* to Joyce was no doubt enhanced by the fact that it had taken notice of his "Day of the Rabblement" on 2 November 1901.[13]

The journal was edited by Arthur Griffith and was a vehicle for Griffith's early views, which emerged in 1905 as the policies of Sinn Féin; at the time the *United Irishman* was being published, those policies were mildly socialist and separatist yet constitutional (Henry 57–78). The newspaper was neither Republican nor militaristic, though Griffith included some articles that tended to those views, seeing the *United Irishman* as a forum for bringing together in one nationalistic movement the varied patriotic and political factions (*United Irishman* 4 Mar. 1899; Younger 15ff.; Henry 61–63). The journal respected the memory of Joyce's hero Parnell. Moreover, though the *United Irishman* supported the Irish language movement, it did not reject the use of English for a nationalist literary movement, particularly early in its publication history. Stanislaus Joyce summarizes his brother's early political views as follows:

> My brother did not belong to the Sinn Fein movement, though he afterwards wrote about it in Trieste, but he favoured it rather than the "ineffectual parliamentary struggle" in which I believed. His political leanings were towards socialism, and he had frequented meetings of socialist groups in back rooms in the manner ascribed to Mr. Duffy in "A Painful Case." . . . My brother thought that fanned nationalisms, which he loathed, were to blame for wars and world troubles. Mr. Duffy's disillusionment with socialism, however, does not reflect my brother's ideas but mine. At Trieste he still called

---

12. Generally the poetry is doggerel, in part because the editors of the *United Irishman* took the view that literature should be subordinated to political purposes, but occasionally there are pieces of literary merit. Much of the poetry in the early years of the *United Irishman* was by William Rooney; Joyce's views on this poetry can be seen in his scathing review of Rooney's collected poetry, published in 1902 as "An Irish Poet" (*CW* 84–87).

13. Stanislaus Joyce notes that "[my brother] and I distributed it to the newspapers and people in Dublin that my brother wished to see it" (*MBK* 152). The fact that Joyce would have taken his broadside to the *United Irishman* is another indication that Joyce valued the journal.

himself a socialist. This political attitude of his I considered inconsequent in an artist. . . . Nor did I follow him in his approval of Sinn Fein. (*MBK* 174)[14]

The *United Irishman* had a relatively short life span, appearing weekly from 4 March 1899 to 24 June 1899 in a four-page format, and from 1 July 1899 to 14 April 1906 in an eight-page format. It was succeeded by *Sinn Féin*, which was published from May 1906 until December 1914, when it and other publications were suppressed under the security regulations of wartime.[15] Despite the short period of publication, the *United Irishman* had a significant impact on Joyce in part because it came at a formative period of his life and in part because it was one of his lifelines to Ireland after he emigrated. As Dominic Manganiello has shown (see esp. 123ff., 140ff., 171ff.), the *United Irishman* and its successor *Sinn Féin* were influential on Joyce's political thought, and articles in these papers are reflected in Joyce's literary work, including *Ulysses*; the *United Irishman* is thus likely to have affected Joyce's work in broader ways as well.

The journal had an overt educative function as an element of its program. In addition to many series of political articles intended to radicalize its readers, the *United Irishman* carried regular features meant to inculcate in its readers an Irish patriotic history, to expose them to pre-Christian Irish myth, and to acquaint them with some principal texts of early Irish literature; the journal also attempted to familiarize its readers with contemporary nationalist Anglo-Irish literature through its reviews and notices. The educative purpose waxed and waned during the periodical's years of publication, with the varying amount of space dedicated to cultural materials determined in part by current events. During periods of intense political activity current events dominated the newspaper and provided enough grist for the nationalist mill; during quieter political periods there was more cultural material in the periodical. Through the greater part of the journal's lifetime, page two was dedicated to back-

14. For a comprehensive discussion of Joyce's political views, see Manganiello; Manganiello's characterization of the political position of the *United Irishman* is found on 26–30.

15. *Sinn Féin* appeared weekly except for a brief period (24 Aug. 1909–22 Jan. 1910) during which it was a daily (Younger 35–37, 49; Henry 89–90). At times Joyce referred to *Sinn Féin* as "the U. I." in 1906 after the *United Irishman* ceased publishing; see *Letters* 2: 149–50, 157–58, 164, 195.

ground articles on a variety of Irish cultural topics, often organized as extensive series about a particular subject. As a long-term reader of the *United Irishman*, Joyce was thus presented with a great deal of material related to early Irish history, literature, poetics, and art.

Three of the series represent significant funds of information about early Irish literature, and they are complementary in their coverage. Richard Irvine Best's translation of *The Irish Mythological Cycle* by Henri d'Arbois de Jubainville appeared in weekly installments between 9 November 1901 and 19 July 1902. Best is memorialized for us in the library episode of *Ulysses*, where he is represented, significantly, as showing d'Arbois de Jubainville's book to Haines (9.93).[16] This series would have furnished Joyce with summaries and analyses of the major texts of the Mythological Cycle: a detailed consideration of *The Book of Invasions*; more summary treatment of *The Second Battle of Mag Tuired*, the legends of Tuan mac Cairill and Fintan, *The Taking of the Sid*, *The Dream of Oengus*, and *The Wooing of Etain*; and stories of Mongan, Crimthann Nia Nair, and other heroes. Moreover, d'Arbois de Jubainville discusses some basic elements of Irish myth, presenting the repertory of the principal deities and canvassing such features as the configuration of the otherworld and Celtic attitudes toward the realm of the dead. The value of this material lies primarily in the systematic coverage of the mythic and religious substratum of early Irish literature, and aspects of Joyce's use of this series have been discussed above.

Shortly after *The Irish Mythological Cycle* was complete, R. I. Best wrote a series entitled "The Old Irish Bardic Tales," which ran weekly from 11 October 1902 to 25 April 1903. In this series Best gave detailed summaries of and provided bibliographical information about a number of central early Irish stories. This series is doubly important because it indicates not only that Joyce had been exposed to the main lines of a great deal of early Irish literature, the heroic literature in particular, but also that he had specific bibliographical guidance for further work on these tales coming from the competent hand of the man who was to become the standard bibliographer of early Irish literature (see Best, *Bibliography*

16. By 1904 Best's translation had been published in monograph form; Joyce met Best when he returned to Ireland in 1902 for his Christmas visit (*JJ*2 118). Schutte (36–39) gives a good summary of Best's career as well as Joyce's treatment of him as a character in *Ulysses*.

of Irish Philology and of Printed Irish Literature [1913] and *Bibliography of Irish Philology and Manuscript Literature* [1942]).[17]

The series begins with synopses of and bibliographical background for four *imrama*, 'voyage tales': *The Voyage of Mael Duin*, *The Voyage of Snegdus and MacRiagla*, *The Voyage of Bran*, and *The Voyage of the Ui Corra*. These tales provide a touchstone for Joyce's presentation of Gibraltar as the Irish happy otherworld and the otherworld motifs in "Circe," as well as Joyce's use of the imram framework throughout (cf. Sultan 42–48). The series continues with summaries and bibliographical information about a number of Ulster Cycle tales: *The Adventures of Nera*, *The Death of Fergus mac Leiti*, *The Destruction of Dind Rig*, *The Story of Mac Datho's Pig*, *The Feast of Bricriu*, *The Sickbed of Cu-Chulainn*, *The Exile of the Sons of Doel Dermait*, *The Destruction of Da Choca's Hostel*, *The Destruction of Da Derga's Hostel*, *The Cattle Raid of Fraech*, *The Deaths of Garb and Goll*, *The Intoxication of the Ulstermen*, *The Story of the Two Swineherds*, *The Wooing of Emer*, *The Battle of Ros na Rig*, *The Death of CuChulainn*, and *The Death of Conchobor*. There are also articles on *The Second Battle of Mag Tuired*, *The Adventures of Cormac in the Land of Promise*, and *The Adventures of Tadg mac Cein*. The presence of this series in the *United Irishman* indicates that Joyce had been introduced to a substantial part of the early Irish narrative repertory in rather scholarly summaries.[18] Best's articles in the *United Irishman* provide an adequate base for the pervasive but relatively schematic use Joyce makes of these early Irish heroic tales.[19]

The third series that is significant for our assessment of Joyce's knowledge of early Irish material is "A Ballad History of Ireland"; it began in the first issue of 1904 and continued until 2 December 1905. The earlier numbers of the series deal with Irish pseudohistory and early medieval

17. The bibliographical components of these essays by Best could provide directions for further research on particular early Irish literary texts known to Joyce. For other bibliographical information provided by the *United Irishman*, see Tymoczko, "'Broken Lights of Irish Myth'" 769–70.

18. Some bowdlerization occurs, but the summaries are representative of the texts in most respects.

19. It is of particular interest to find *The Destruction of Da Derga's Hostel* included in Best's series, for John Kelleher ("Irish History") has argued that *Da Derga's Hostel* informs "The Dead." Best's summary of *Da Derga's Hostel* appeared in the *United Irishman* 24–31 Jan. 1903. It is a very full summary, at times a paraphrase of the original text, and it omits none of the episodes; thus, it provides an ample base for the parallels Kelleher has proposed.

history. In these columns Joyce again found summaries of *The Book of Invasions* and *The Destruction of Da Derga's Hostel* as well as accounts of texts of the Ulster Cycle, including the story of Conchobor's success in replacing Fergus as king of Ulster, *Táin Bó Cúailnge*, and *The Exile of the Sons of Uisliu*. There are also accounts of various traditional kings, including Conn Cetcathach and Brian Boru; accounts of Finn and the Fenians, the early Christian saints, and the Vikings; summaries of battles such as Mag Rath and Clontarf; and material on the Norman conquest of Ireland. Much of this material has parallels in Joyce's speeches and essays and is found as well in *Finnegans Wake*, particularly the material on Clontarf and the Norman conquest. The series is important for the raw material it provided Joyce, but it is also significant because the historical essays are accompanied by poetry and ballads on the same subjects. Though in some cases the poetic material takes the form of translations of early Irish poetry related to the historical subject, in most cases the poetry is part of Anglo-Irish literature or the Anglo-Irish ballad tradition. Thus, Joyce found in the *United Irishman* a comprehensive survey of the poetic uses to which his Anglo-Irish literary predecessors had put early Irish history and literature.

These three series are not the only sources of information about early Irish literature in the *United Irishman*. Specific stories are alluded to in isolated articles throughout the run of the journal. There are summaries of or references to the story of Lug and Tailltiu, the story of Donn Bo, the story of Aine, the story of the Children of Lir, the tale of Cliodna, the story of Baile and Ailinn, *The Dream of Oengus*, CuChulainn at the ford, and the Deirdre tale.[20] Other stories are discussed or mentioned in passing in the course of articles, reviews, poems, and so forth. Even this partial listing of tales indicates that Joyce had been introduced to some of the minor or arcane stories of early Irish literature. Thus, even if Joyce's sources for Irish literature were restricted to popular materials, one could not use the major stories found in Gregory's translations and adaptations, for example, as an index of his knowledge.

The *United Irishman* also reported on speeches about Irish literature and culture, often quoting them in extenso, thus providing readers like Joyce with knowledge of the contemporary discourse about Irish culture.

20. For specific dates here and below, see Tymoczko, "'Broken Lights of Irish Myth.'"

In this way Joyce would have been aware of a number of lectures about Modern Irish literature. There are also transcripts of lectures about early Irish topics, such as the lecture on Brigit, the goddess and saint, carried on 3 November 1900; Maud Gonne's lecture on Medb on 5 October 1901;[21] and a lecture on the seventeenth-century Irish historian Geoffrey Keating on 9 November 1901. The *United Irishman* also provided general knowledge about Irish culture. The saints of Ireland are discussed in several articles in the journal, and Mangan is the topic of other articles. These articles contributed background for Joyce's Trieste lectures. The Celtic festivals, including Samain and Beltaine, are discussed or alluded to in significant ways. Irish music was a perennial topic of interest and formed the subject of two series in the *United Irishman*. Finally, there is abundant information about Irish folk life, folk belief, and folklore, including Irish folktales in translation.

Joyce would also have become acquainted with some Irish literary forms, genres, and typologies, which were discussed or instantiated in the *United Irishman*. There are, for example, extensive discussions of placelore, the most significant of which is the series "The Woods of Ireland," which ran for sixty-eight times listing the locations and names of vanished Irish woods (29 Oct. 1904–14 Apr. 1906). This was one of the less scintillating series published in Griffith's journal, but it served to make the political point that Ireland had been deforested under English rule.[22] Other discussions of placelore and dindśenchas occur in various issues. Anglo-Irish versions of the Irish genre of the aisling are found several times. There is a discussion of Irish *cáoine*, 'keening', and Irish poetics, Irish rhyme, and related topics are mentioned frequently.

Not the least of the contributions of the *United Irishman* to the nationalist literary repertory is the mythopoeic imagery perpetuated in its pages. The image of the rose, in particular the little dark rose, is found frequently. We find also the image of Cathleen Ni Houlihan, the Shan Van Vocht, and the poor old wandering woman, as well as the image of Ireland as mother or queen. There are poems about fairy raths, Tír na nÓg,

---

21. In this lecture Gonne notes that Medb always had one man in the shadow of another.

22. There is an elaborate parody of this discourse in "Cyclops," 12.1239–95, which not only takes up deforestation and reforestation but also parodies more broadly the nationalist rhetoric about English imperialism and exploitation.

Hy Breasail, and magic hazels. Such imagery is the stock in trade of Irish cultural nationalism; when we find these elements in Joyce's works, we must be aware that he knew the resonances he was evoking. No reader of the *United Irishman* could be innocent of them.

Even a brief inventory such as I have given here of the coverage in the *United Irishman* of early Irish literature and literary form, early Irish history, and early Irish culture reveals an immense wealth of resources for a regular, albeit critical reader of the journal like James Joyce. Most of Joyce's use of Irish plots, motifs, myths, and genres identified in previous chapters have sources in articles Joyce found in the *United Irishman*, even in the absence of his familiarity with other texts, readings, or oral exposure.

iv. The popular press and Joyce's knowledge of early Irish literature

Material about early Irish and Modern Irish literature, Irish history, and the Irish language, as well as coverage of the Anglo-Irish literary revival, is widespread in most periodical literature published in Ireland at the turn of the century, and the general pattern that emerges regarding Joyce's knowledge of Irish literature and history from the detailed analysis of articles in the *United Irishman* is confirmed by a survey of Irish periodicals as a whole. Irish cultural topics were discussed in most periodicals—the daily newspapers, the general weeklies, and the weeklies on special topics. A study of such periodicals demonstrates that the cultural ambience of the period provided both a working knowledge of the main narratives of early Irish literature and a skeletal patriotic history, illustrating that at the time one did not need to resort to scholarly journals or publications in the Irish language for such knowledge. Thus, the broad lines of the argument sketched above regarding the *United Irishman* are substantiated by a wider study of the periodical literature in Ireland in Joyce's youth. Of all the popular periodicals current, however, the coverage of Irish history and literature is most systematic and most extensive in the *United Irishman*, a point with implications for an assessment of how Joyce was positioned with respect to Irish citizens in general regarding knowledge about early Irish literature.

In the following discussion of Irish periodical literature I consider three categories of periodicals: daily papers and their weekly counterparts, general reviews, and publications with a narrow topical focus.[23] The format of daily newspapers at the turn of the century sets bounds on their treatment of Irish culture. Because the dailies were small (between four and eight pages) yet charged with providing all the news in an era when there were no other media such as radio and television to carry the burden, type is small and dense, and articles are typically short. There are few feature articles or surveys of general cultural and political topics. Such studies are reserved instead for the weeklies. Moreover, the treatment of Irish culture in the dailies is determined by political orientation; the Irish periodicals of this period held marked political positions that determined what they deemed newsworthy. The strong ideological bias of Irish journalism at the time, as with most European papers still today, means that events that are major news in one daily may receive scant if any coverage in another.

As a result there is very little news about Irish literature, history, language, or culture in the Ascendancy and Unionist dailies, for the coverage of these topics had political implications, as already mentioned. The Unionist papers differ among themselves in focus and in the breadth of their general coverage. The *Irish Times* of the period, for example, is oriented to sports, finance, and London news, while the *Dublin Evening Mail* has less sporting news and more general features, including a daily story, theater news, and sensational news. The *Daily Express*—for which

---

23. I surveyed major Irish periodicals for the period 1900–1904, with a particular systematic focus on the reporting of Irish cultural news in the period between January and May 1902, using the treatment of two major Irish cultural events as an index: the events of the week 16–22 March, which was designated Irish Language Week by the leaders of the language movement and which included a large parade in Dublin on Sunday, 16 March; and the staging of Yeats's *Cathleen ni Houlihan* and A. E.'s *Deirdre* in April 1902 by the combined forces of the dramatic movement including the Fays' acting company, Inghinidhe na hÉireann, and two of the founders of the Irish Literary Theatre (Yeats and Augusta Gregory), a production that inaugurated the Irish National Theatre Society. Where this preliminary sampling indicated substantial coverage of Irish cultural material, I surveyed the periodical in question at greater length; in the case of some short-lived journals, I covered the entire run. I chose spring 1902 as the focus of research in part because the two important cultural events could be used as an index of comparison but also because Joyce was in Dublin and actively involved in Irish culture during this period. Thus, it was a time of his life in which Irish periodical literature would have affected him.

For a general survey of the press in Ireland, see Brown. Rose and O'Hanlon (xxii–xxiv) discuss Joyce's use of specific dailies in the construction of *Ulysses*.

Joyce wrote in 1902 and 1903 (*JJ*2 108, 112, 138–39; cf. *CW* 84–140) and for which Gabriel Conroy writes in "The Dead" and is still writing in 1904 when the action of *Ulysses* takes place (7.307), despite all of Miss Ivors's criticism and his own resolution to journey "westward"—carries reports about all manner of Ascendancy societies as well as detailed news about the Protestant churches. Despite their shades of difference, these papers are united in the treatment of the Irish language movement and the Irish literary movement; on the whole where this movement is not consigned to silence, it is reported with contempt.[24] Thus, for example, in the *Evening Mail* the 16 March 1902 demonstration of the Irish language movement is passed off with a scant, hostile paragraph:

That the Irish language movement is growing in strength and stature we are not concerned to deny. We can see, indeed, that under certain circumstances it might be made a movement with which every Irishman could sympathise. But unfortunately, under present conditions, we fear the Irish language campaign is only another side of the eternal political agitation with which this land is cursed. We are afraid it is impossible to deny that its yearning for the de-Anglicization of Ireland is not confined to the literary side of life, but that the political hostility to England which is the pulse of Nationalism is also the pulse of the language movement. It is Nationalist, not national, and we are inclined to regret the fact. If we could believe that yesterday's procession was not, after all, a political demonstration and that "God Save Ireland" was a pious aspiration rather than a fierce battle-shout, we would be heartily glad; but it would be unwise, we think, to accept the demonstration in this light. (17 Mar. 1902)

The *Irish Times* was most infamous among contemporaries for its treatment of Irish cultural subjects: not only did it suppress Irish topics in general, but when it spoke, it was hostile. In spring 1902, for example, the *Times* carried a series of letters criticizing the Irish language movement and the movement to teach Irish in the National Schools. This hostility was relieved only by letters from authors such as Douglas Hyde and T. W. Rolleston defending the language movement; even these rejoinders were carefully controlled, and the *Times* refused on at least one occasion to publish a letter by Hyde on the subject, a refusal that itself made news

24. In this regard it is telling that in *Ulysses* George Russell will be able to arrange a puff in the *Express* for his projected volume of work by younger poets (9.302).

in the nationalist dailies of the period.[25] The *Times* thus provided readers with no information about Irish literature and history per se and was even marginal in its coverage of such cultural events as Irish Language Week in March 1902 and the monster demonstration in Dublin on 16 March. Only half of a column was devoted to the topic in the Monday issue following the parade.

The nationalist dailies, by contrast, all treat the Irish language movement and the Irish literary revival as part of the ongoing news, yet they often do it in such ways that the movement is contained or even patronized. In Home Rule and Republican dailies and weeklies of the period, the coverage of Irish literary and linguistic questions is fairly broad but very shallow. The *Freeman's Journal* and the *Weekly Freeman*, of interest to Joyce scholars because Leopold Bloom is employed by the *Freeman*, are both Home Rule in their orientation and are typical of the daily newspapers and popular weeklies that were sympathetic to the language movement for political reasons. The *Freeman's Journal*, a large-format, eight-page daily varying in width between seven and nine columns, notes most of the significant aspects of the revival. The Gaelic League and other revival groups are covered systematically, if briefly, and the Gaelic Athletic Association finds a place in the paper's news as well, though in a less systematic fashion. Lectures on Irish literary and historical topics are reported, often in some detail. There are reviews of Irish plays and of plays produced by Anglo-Irish dramatic organizations, including the 1902 performances of the A. E.'s *Deirdre* and Yeats's *Cathleen ni Houlihan.* Such reviews can be quite enthusiastic. The events of Irish Language Week are covered well, including a full report of the extensive parade and rally of 16 March 1902. There is also a daily article entitled "Le h-aghaidh na nGaedhilgeoiridhe," 'For the Irish Enthusiasts', a feature that published a variety of types of texts in Irish, from wondertales to opinion columns, thus meeting one of the Irish language movement's goals to have some Irish published in every issue of a periodical; in the *Freeman* the Irish text is occasionally accompanied by an English translation.

Much the same pattern is found in the *Weekly Freeman*, a large-format, sixteen-page, seven-column weekly in two sections. As regular

25. See, for example, the *Irish Daily Independent* of 12 February 1902, p. 2, col. 7. Hyde's letter was ultimately published in the February 1902 issue of *An Claidheamh Soluis.*

weekly features the *Weekly Freeman* has material about the Gaelic League and an article in Irish. There are serialized features as well. Thus, for example, throughout most of 1902 the *Weekly Freeman* printed installments of Douglas Hyde's edition of Raftery's poems, accompanied by an English translation of the material; this series was followed in 1903, the centenary of Emmet's execution, by a serialized biography of Robert Emmet. In addition there is topical news about the Irish revival as well as the occasional background article about issues pertaining to Irish history, literature, biography, and culture. We find, for example, a three-column article on the schools of ancient Ireland in the 1903 Saint Patrick's Day issue of the *Weekly Freeman*.

Nonetheless, in both the daily and weekly *Freeman* the reporting of Irish cultural materials is dwarfed by the presentation of the general news of the country and the world: Irish history and literature stand side by side with notices of suicides, murders, accidents; economic and trade information command more space; international news, such as coverage of the Boer War, takes precedence; political reporting of Parliament is emphasized; and greater attention is paid to such local news as Queen Victoria's daily activities during her 1900 visit to Ireland. Moreover, in the *Weekly Freeman* most Irish features are carried in the second section of the paper—the culture section containing articles aimed at women and children as well as the general readership. They are thus marked clearly as secondary in importance to the major political and commercial news in section one. The placement of these Irish literary and cultural materials defines them as out of the scope of politics; it is, of course, ironic to a modern reader to find this arrangement, knowing as we do that Irish cultural nationalism was the cornerstone of future Irish politics and that Standish O'Grady's 1899 prophecy was to come true: "We have now a literary movement, it is not very important; it will be followed by a political movement, that will not be very important; then must come a military movement, that will be important indeed" (quoted in Yeats, *Autobiography* 257).

Even when priority is given to Irish cultural issues, as it ostensibly is in the Saint Patrick's Day issues of the weekly, a similar analysis obtains. The Saint Patrick's Day issue is almost entirely given up to Irish cultural topics, and the cultural features precede the political and economic news. Nevertheless, by being segregated in a special holiday issue, an issue printed on green paper, Irish cultural topics are defined as outside the main concerns of life; they are relegated to the status of a leisure activity. Much of the potential political effect of an article such as "The Makers of Fenianism," found in the 1902 Saint Patrick's Day issue of the *Weekly Freeman*, is muted and defused by the position of the article in the overall format of the periodical.

Thus, the *Freeman*, in its daily and weekly format, can be said to trivialize the Irish revival by placement, proportion, and juxtaposition of the materials pertaining to literary and cultural issues; the same is true of policies having to do with an Irish Ireland or Sinn Féin. Indeed, the *Freeman* was criticized by other periodicals at the time for precisely these tactics. The 12 April 1902 issue of the *Leader* charges, "The *Freeman* is an expert clipper from British papers, but it is very weak on the side of Irish news." The criticism of the *Leader* on 1 March 1902 is more specific: "The *Freeman* of Monday gives over a column report to the meeting of the Delegates of the St. Patrick's Eve Demonstration. Nearly the whole of the next column on the right is headed, 'Fashions of the Week,' and comprises a clipping from a British fashion paper. Oh, what a Press." Similar amusing juxtapositions can be noted from the *Weekly Freeman*. On 2 August 1902 the Irish cultural news shares an opening with "Horse-breeding in Ulster" and "Watering Flowering Plants in Pots," and on 6 September of the same year "The Orthography of the Irish Language" is adjacent to a column entitled "Certain Manures"; on 7 February 1903 the Gaelic League news is next to an article entitled "Swine Fever." It is hard to make much of a cultural revival that must compete for space in the second section of this paper with weekly articles on poultry and beekeeping, as well as the practical "Veterinary Answers," important as those topics were to the agrarian interests of the readers.

In addition, a restricted range of Irish literature is covered in the *Freeman's Journal* and the *Weekly Freeman*, and there is no systematic educative program related to Irish culture similar to that of the *United Irishman*. Though the weekly does carry Hyde's edition of Raftery in 1902, the references to Irish literature are generally to stories that have already become canonized in the contemporary cultural milieu—for example, the narratives about Deirdre or Diarmait and Grainne. There is little program of literary exposure and expansion; rather the *Freeman* reports on or alludes to Irish literature that has already become popularized in some way. In addition, reviews of Irish publications are limited, for such publications must compete with the entire range of publications in English letters; as a result the space dedicated to Irish books and drama is dwarfed by the space allocated to mainstream theater and mainstream English literature. Authors such as Arthur Conan Doyle and English dramatic productions at the commercial theaters get the lion's share of attention in a publication like the *Freeman's Journal*. An ironic example of this pattern can be seen in the 2 April 1904 issue of the *Weekly Freeman*, which devotes almost a column on page one to the National Theatre Society's London performances of five plays by Yeats, Synge, and Colum: the society received scant coverage for its Irish performances of the same plays. It is the larger world of England that determines the hierarchy of values in the *Freeman*. In such ways, then, the *Freeman's Journal* and the *Weekly Freeman* define Irish literature as marginal while still reporting about it and presupposing it to a surprising extent; Irish literature is presented when it is in the news, but it is not valorized per se.

The patterns revealed by the coverage of Irish material in the *Freeman* are similar to those of the other nationalist dailies and weeklies. Like the *Freeman*, the *Irish Daily Independent and Daily Nation*, an eight-page, nine-column daily, covers most events having to do with the Irish revival and the language movement: lectures on such topics as Irish architecture of the early Christian period are summarized; there are announcements of the activities and meetings of groups such as the Feis Ceoil Association and the Gaelic League; public events, including the 16 March 1902 demonstration, are reported; a series contrasts the national movements in Ireland and other countries; and so forth.[26] The *Independent* also meets the Gaelic League's ideal of publishing some text in Irish—if not daily, then several times a week—often reprinting articles from *An Claidheamh Soluis*, the weekly penny newspaper of the Gaelic League. Moreover, the *Independent* shows its sympathy to the language movement by publishing a weekly article entitled "The Irish Language Movement (From Information Supplied by the Gaelic League)," which surveys the most significant events of the week related to the language movement and includes commentary as well. The weekly published by the same press, the *Illustrated Irish Weekly Independent and Nation*, is similar, reprinting the column entitled "The Irish Language Movement" from the daily,

26. The *Independent* was founded by Parnell after the *Freeman's Journal* withdrew its support from him following his marriage to Kitty O'Shea (Thornton, *Allusions in "Ulysses"* 266), though it rather quickly became associated with an anti-Parnellite position (Gifford 134, 327).

carrying news of the Gaelic Athletic Association and other organizations related to the Irish revival, and running background articles on Irish topics such as Saint Brendan. Yet we see the same pattern of trivialization of the Irish news by its positioning. In the *Weekly Independent*, for example, the Irish news may at times be found just before features entitled "The Farm" and "Veterinary Replies," suggesting that its interest is nonpolitical and rural. Paradoxically, also, by having the Gaelic League write the column entitled "The Irish Language Movement," the editorial policy reveals a program of delegation and containment: Irish news is primarily contained in a single weekly article, the writing of which is delegated elsewhere rather than becoming a task to which reportorial staff must be committed.[27]

In summary, then, the nationalist dailies kept their readers informed of the Irish language movement and the Irish revival as a whole, and frequently they published articles in the Irish language. The allusions to Irish literary topics in the daily press presuppose widespread knowledge of Irish literature and Irish myth among the readers, but the dailies restrict consideration of Irish literature to established or canonized material. The format of these journals does not provide for a systematic educative function about Irish literature, nor do they cover marginal literary subject matter, thereby serving as primary source material for knowledge of literary topics.

The independent weeklies—that is, those unconnected with dailies— are more various in their treatment of the Irish revival and Irish literature and are more situated by their format and function in the culture to have an educative component and thus more apt to have served as sources of literary knowledge for James Joyce and others. These periodicals are generally small in format, rarely larger than 10″ × 18″. They range from periodicals with specific subject content, such as cycling or gardening, to

27. The *Evening Telegraph*, a Home Rule daily also published by the *Freeman's Journal*, is a large-format paper, between eight and ten columns, four pages on weekdays and eight on Saturday. Like the *Freeman* and the *Independent*, it too carries news of the Gaelic League, the Gaelic Athletic Association, and similar groups, and it gives a prominent place to news about Irish language events such as Irish Language Week in March 1902. The *Telegraph* also carries the daily article entitled "Le h-aghaidh na nGaedhilgeoiridhe." But this Irish news is swallowed up in the general coverage, and there is virtually no cultural news or literary news in the smaller weekday issues of the *Telegraph* at all.

more general publications, which might or might not have a particular political thrust.

The *Leader* stands as an example of a small-format weekly with a particular political perspective, addressing itself to a broad range of political and cultural concerns. The *Leader*, a nationalist publication founded by D. P. Moran, was begun in 1900; its sixteen small-format (8.5″ × 13″), pages of articles are encased in an advertising supplement of eight additional pages. The periodical's issues are divided roughly in two, with an extensive commentary on current events by the editor preceding a series of signed articles on particular topics. The *Leader* is more radical in its politics than are most of the weeklies, and it approaches the *United Irishman* in its political orientation, though a greater moral conservatism is plain throughout; it was very influential among the undergraduates of University College, with Joyce one of the few to resist its influence.[28] The publication promotes an "Irish Ireland" program and actively supports the language movement, though it lacks the coherent political program of Arthur Griffith's publication. Essentially political commentary, often of a polemical sort, with highly charged rhetoric in the editor's commentary, the magazine focused on politics; Manganiello has characterized its policies as "almost entirely negative" (25). The editor enjoyed controversy, as indicated, for example, by the publication on 2 May 1904 of Osborn Bergin's acidic review of Douglas Hyde's prize essay published by the Society for the Preservation of the Irish Language; Bergin intimated that Hyde's command of Irish was less than adequate, and the review occasioned a defense of Hyde by Eleanor Hull on 23 May and an another acerbic response by Bergin, then a relatively young man, on 6 June. It was Moran who led the sloganeering against "West Britons" and "shoneens" in Ireland. Although Joyce disagreed with many of its positions, he read the *Leader* and used its materials: disagreement did not deter him from using the publication as a source for his work.[29]

The subtitle of the *Leader* is "A Review of Current Affairs, Politics, Literature, Art and Industry," but the space devoted to literary questions is restricted, and the periodical is primarily political in its orientation. An

28. Manganiello (24–25, 116–18, 124) discusses the political views of the *Leader*.

29. Manganiello (117–18) gives an example of how material from the *Leader* lies behind the interchange between Bloom and the Citizen.

article in Irish on a topic of current interest is a weekly feature. There are reviews of Irish theater and regular announcements of the publication of new books on Irish literature and language, but there are few sustained articles on Irish literary topics and there is no attempt at a systematic educative program like that of the *United Irishman*. Nonetheless, some material about Irish culture is included; in 1902, for example, the *Leader* provided its readers with, among other things, a series of articles about traditional Irish singing, a review of a lecture on Celtic ornament (15 Mar.), articles debating the direction of modern drama in Irish and English, articles on the Feis Ceoil, an article on Eoghan Ruadh O'Sullivan (10 May), articles on Irish poetic composition (31 May, 7 June, 28 June, 12 July), a series of articles on Irish prose composition, a concerted campaign against the Stage Irishman, and an overview of Irish literature in 1902 (6 Dec.).

Of the small-format periodicals, Standish O'Grady's *All Ireland Review* comes the closest to the *United Irishman* in the volume of its coverage of early Irish literature. The publication began on 6 January 1900 as an eight-page, two-column magazine; its paper covers were filled with advertisements. It was considered by many the organ of the Irish literary revival and is much more a literary and cultural journal than a political one, though many issues with broad political implications are discussed. There are regular reviews of Irish books and the theatrical productions of the Irish dramatic movement; Irish musical events are publicized and reviewed; and contributors to the periodical include Yeats, Gregory, A. E., and other members of the literary revival. A weekly article gives simple instruction in the Irish language.

O'Grady published weekly features pertaining to early Irish literature and history as well. Initially O'Grady serialized his own retelling of *Táin Bó Cúailnge*, which appeared under the title "In the Gates of the North," but he provided more substantive material also, such as his serialization of the initial segments of the Annals of the Four Masters to A.D. 432 accompanied by topographical notes, which began on 2 March 1901 and continued to the middle of 1902. In spring 1900, under the heading "Recent Translations from Gaelic," T. W. Rolleston discussed early Irish stories in Standish Hayes O'Grady's *Silva Gadelica*, Kuno Meyer's *Voyage of Bran*, Eleanor Hull's *Cuchullin Saga*, and the Irish Texts Society's publication of *The Feast of Bricriu*; Rolleston also included in his survey folklore materials by Jeremiah Curtin and William Larminie, George Sigerson's *Bards of the Gael and Gall*, and Douglas Hyde's translations of "The Adventures of the Lad of the Ferule" and "The Adventures of the Sons of the King of Norway," both published by the Irish Texts Society. Other summaries of early Irish stories are found scattered throughout the run, such as the summaries of *The Wooing of Etain* and *Cophur in dá Muccida* (*The Story of the Two Swineherds*) (6 Oct. 1900), the stories of Cliodna and Rudraige (6 Apr. 1901), *The Adventures of Cormac in the Land of Promise* (6 Apr. 1901), and tales of lake eruptions (25 May 1901). In the first issue of 1902 O'Grady began the serialization of Whitley Stokes's translation of *The Destruction of Da Derga's Hostel*, reprinting it from *Revue celtique* but with the "nude-antique" elements expunged (cf. 8 Feb. 1902, 433); this series continued until 19 July 1902. Windisch's translation of *The Story of Mac Datho's Pig* was reprinted from *Irische Texte* in the issue of 20 December 1902. Beginning 8 November 1902, a sustained series on the gods of Ireland discusses material in *The Book of Invasions*, as well as specific figures including the Dagda, MacCecht, Anu, the sons of Tuirenn, Oengus, Bodb Derg, Lug, Midir, the Morrigan, Macha, Manannan, Fintan, Diancecht, and others. There is also other material about mythic figures, including Cesair (30 Mar. 1901), the Dagda (27 Apr. 1901), MacColl, MacCecht, and MacGreine (7 Sept. 1901), and the mythical invaders of Ireland (18 and 25 May 1901). The Irish festivals are discussed with articles on Beltaine (4 Jan. 1902) and Lugnasad (14 Sept. 1901). In addition O'Grady provides various critical discussions of early Irish literature, stressing the interlacing of history and myth in Irish literature (18 Aug. 1900, 2 Mar. 1901, 16 Mar. 1901, 4 May 1901) and comparing Irish tradition to the Greek in this regard. An extract from D'Alton's *History of Ireland* was published on 29 November 1902. The periodical carries the text of a lecture by Sigerson entitled "The Basis of Irish Myths" (25 May 1901), underscoring the mythopoeic imagination of the Irish, as well as a lecture on Irish poetry in the same issue that contains important early Irish poems. O'Grady's weekly also provides material about Irish prosody (e.g., 9 Aug. 1902).

In addition to discussions and summaries of early Irish literature, Modern Irish folklore, particularly fairy lore, is discussed or summarized frequently. Other cultural material is provided as well, including material about Irish costume (18 Aug. 1900). Irish history has a regular place in O'Grady's periodical. Under the title "The Spaniards in Ireland" a systematic account of seventeenth-century Irish history is given beginning in

August 1900 and continuing piecemeal for most of a year. We find material about Irish saints (14 Dec. 1901), and a series questioning the traditions about Saint Patrick is reprinted from Heinrich Zimmer's *Celtic
Church in Great Britain and Ireland* (beginning 15 Nov. 1902). Particulars of the Irish language are discussed including the Irish dual (14 Dec.
1901), and one series discusses cognates to Irish words in other Indo-
European languages (beginning 16 Mar. 1901).

The range and volume of materials presented by O'Grady are impres-
sive, but the coverage of such topics in the *All Ireland Review* is more
dilute and less systematic than is the presentation of corresponding material in the *United Irishman*. This difference is apparent in O'Grady's
tendency to print fictionalized retellings such as "In the Gates of the
North" rather than more straightforward presentations such as Best's extensive summaries with bibliographical apparatus in the *United Irishman*. Moreover, when O'Grady does set out to summarize or publish
scholarly material, the treatment is less thorough. The format of the *All
Ireland Review* is partly responsible for the restrictions in its literary materials, for the small format of the periodical (eight pages of 10"×14.75"),
the large print (two columns of nine words per line), and the wide leading
between lines (eighty-six lines per page) mean that the contents of any
one issue are quite limited. It follows that there is a corresponding limitation on the total output of the paper with respect to any one topic such
as early Irish literature. Thus, even in the case of a scholarly publication,
such as the reprinting of Stokes's translation of *The Destruction of Da
Derga's Hostel*, publication must be protracted over a period of seven
months in order to fit the text within the scope of interests represented
in the periodical as a whole. This compares with the 6600-word detailed
summary of the same tale published in three weeks in the *United Irishman* in Best's "Bardic Tales" series, made possible by the dense format
and larger size of that publication. The systematic educative purpose of
O'Grady's periodical likewise suffers in comparison to that of the *United
Irishman*; again the publication of *Da Derga's Hostel* is instructive, for
in the same time that O'Grady devotes to this important story, the
United Irishman was able to survey and summarize almost two dozen
central stories of early Irish literature, thus giving its readers a much
broader and more systematic exposure to the range of early Irish literature.

The political tenor of O'Grady's weekly is also much more conservative than is that of the *United Irishman*. O'Grady appeals to the Ascendancy in various ways. In a series called "Mr. Goodenough," he focuses on the land question, expressing confidence in the landed gentry to see the light and reform their practice voluntarily; he satirizes rather than execrates the position of the landlords. O'Grady also stays strictly loyalist, in 1900 signing an open letter to Queen Victoria on the occasion of her visit to Ireland "your loving subject"—this at a time when the *United Irishman* was supporting a boycott of the Queen's visit. Though the journal presented interesting materials pertaining to early Irish history and literature—materials that Joyce might have used, such as the articles on the Spaniards in Ireland—the overall appeal of O'Grady's periodical to Joyce would have been limited.

Another periodical not unlike O'Grady's is *Dana*, a small (5.25″ × 8.25″), thirty-two-page monthly begun in May 1904 by W. K. Magee (John Eglinton) and Frederick Ryan that ran until April 1905. Magee figures in the library episode of *Ulysses*, where there is ironic byplay about his having taken the "poetic" pseudonym of John Eglinton; in the discussion about *Hamlet*, prefiguring the techniques of the Nighttown episode, the text reads: "MAGEEGLINJOHN: Names! What's in a name?" (9.900–901). The episode also refers overtly to the goddess Danu (Dana) (9.376) and to the periodical itself (9.322, 9.1081), which was named after the goddess. The majority of the young men conversing in the library episode are associated with *Dana*, either as editor or as contributors; the latter include Magee himself, T. W. Lyster, and A. E., as well as Oliver St. John Gogarty (as Mulligan) and Joyce (as Stephen). Thus, the company gathered is part of a certain intellectual niche in contemporary Dublin associated with the program and views of *Dana*.

The particular interest of this periodical is literature, as its inaugural statement makes clear: "Of the various forms which patriotic ambition takes in the minds of Irishmen at the present time, perhaps the most generally favoured and the least impracticable, is a zeal for the promotion of a national literature" (May 1904). Though Joyce left Ireland soon after the publication was begun, he continued to be interested (however ironically that interest is expressed) in it and its editors once he was abroad, as his correspondence indicates (e.g., *Letters* 2: 208–9), in part because *Dana* published his poem "My love is in a light attire" in August 1904.

In 1920 *Dana* was part of Joyce's library left behind in Trieste when he moved to Paris (Ellmann, *Consciousness of Joyce* 105);[30] articles in *Dana* therefore contributed to Joyce's thinking about various topics. In the January 1905 issue an article by John Eglinton, "The Island of Saints," may have provided source material for Joyce's Trieste lectures in 1907, and the February 1905 issue has an article on Merriman that appeared as *The Midnight Court* was being concurrently published by *Zeitschrift für celtische Philologie*. *The Midnight Court* is summarized carefully and described as "the most tasteful composition in modern Irish," lacking "pessimistic alienation from the joy of life"; the form is identified as "the mediaeval *Aisling*" (Feb. 1905, 297–99). Had Joyce not known Merriman's text from other sources, the *Dana* article would have served his purposes in *Ulysses*.

There are also reviews of the first two volumes of *Ériu* as well as the supplementary volume containing the edition of the Yellow Book of Lecan text of *Táin Bó Cúailnge* edited by John Strachan and J. G. O'Keeffe (Sept. 1904 and Mar. 1905); *Ériu* is recommended as "interesting to anyone who without knowing the language wishes to know something of Celtic literature in its original shape and native garb" (Sept. 1904, 156). A reader of this issue would have here clear notice that the refractions of the Irish revival diverged from the medieval originals. The September 1904 issue of *Dana* also includes a review of Eleanor Knott's *Pagan Ireland*.

Most of the Irish weeklies are specialized in their content orientation and, because of their focus, carry little information about the Irish literary revival or Irish literature. The *Irish Field and Gentleman's Gazette*, for example, restricts its purview to such topics as horses and hounds, coursing, shooting, hunting, racing, rugby, and motoring, as well as ancillary news related to the audience—society news. Other specialty weeklies carry materials related to Irish literature and the Irish revival in a marginal capacity. Here we must place the *Irish Catholic*, a weekly with the format of a daily paper (20.5″ × 24″, eight pages, eight columns per page). Most of the news concerns Rome, Irish ecclesiastics, and world news with specific interest to Catholics. But Irish literary topics find a

---

30. Manganiello (38) discusses Joyce's views on *Dana* and its political positions.

place when they intersect with Catholic interests: thus, the lectures by the Rev. Edmund Hogan, S.J., on such topics as "The Story of Irish Speech" (15 Mar. 1902) and "Language and Nationality" (29 Mar. 1902) are reported in the periodical. In the same way, since Irish Language Week and the demonstration on 16 March 1902 were supported by various Catholic groups including the Christian Brothers, these events are included in the news of the weekly. Naturally, the *Irish Catholic* also includes articles about Saint Patrick and other medieval saints. This periodical is of interest less as a source for Joyce, who by temperament would scarcely have been a regular reader, than as an index of the extent to which a modicum of knowledge about Irish literature and history was widespread throughout the Catholic population of Ireland, even the most conservative.

The *Irish Homestead* serves as another example of a specialized weekly with a narrow content orientation that nonetheless disseminated material about the Irish revival. The *Homestead* was the organ of the Irish Agricultural Organization Society; as such, it is almost rigorously apolitical in the narrow sense of the word, and it has such regular features as "Seasonable Farm Notes," "Creamery Management," and "Poultry Notes." A. E. assumed the editorship of this periodical in 1906, but even before this period he and others of the literary revival were frequent contributors. The agricultural articles are placed first in the *Irish Homestead*, with the second half of the periodical having more general domestic appeal. It is here we find a weekly short story; the literary interests of the *Homestead* are banal, and the weekly story is of the most sentimental sort. In 1904 A. E. suggested that Joyce write a story for the *Homestead*, thus giving the idea for *Dubliners* to Joyce, but it is no wonder that Joyce was unable to place more than three of his short stories ("The Sisters," "Eveline," and "After the Race") with the publication; indeed, given the tone of most stories published by the *Homestead*, it is surprising that he should have been published at all in this forum.[31]

31. "The Sisters" appears in the 13 August 1904 issue, and Joyce signed it "Stephen Daedalus" because he was ashamed to publish in the journal. Joyce was asked not to submit other stories because readers had complained about his work. See *JJ*2 163–64 for these events. In *Ulysses* Stephen passes one copy of Deasy's letter to A. E. for publication in the *Homestead*, referring mentally to it as "the pigs' paper" (9.321); thus, Stephen's concern about becoming known as the "bullockbefriending" bard is related to Joyce's own embarrassment about publishing in this agricultural journal.

Yet even this publication tips its hat to the Irish language movement with a weekly literary piece in Irish that is accompanied by an English translation. Through this feature readers of the magazine would have been exposed to poems from Hyde's *Love Songs of Connacht*, poems from the dindšenchas, poems by Keating, and so forth; in some cases (e.g., 1 Feb. 1902) there are brief discussions of Irish metrics and other general cultural topics. The imagery of the Irish material is often typical of the tradition, including, for example, personifications of Ireland as woman, sacred well imagery, and the like. The Christmas supplement to the periodical also carries stories, poems, and drawings by members of the Anglo-Irish literary revival such as Augusta Gregory, W. B. Yeats, Douglas Hyde, and A. E. Overall the *Homestead* conveys an aura of timeless rural tranquility and well-being, assiduously avoiding politics and even simple cultural developments. Though the publication had only the scantest interest in the literary and cultural developments of the period—for example, not even mentioning the productions of the Irish National Theatre Society in 1902—it nevertheless offered its readers a minimal exposure to Irish literature and the Irish language, though the level on which these topics are incorporated would not suffice for any substantive knowledge.

Among the specialty periodicals of the time are also the publications of the Gaelic League: the weekly penny newspaper *Claidheamh Soluis* and the monthly *Irisleabhar na Gaedhilge, The Gaelic Journal*, a more "high-class" literary magazine (*United Irishman* 24 Nov. 1900). Paradoxically, these periodicals offer little more systematic education about Irish literature and history than do the periodicals already discussed, but for a different reason: the Gaelic League publications are too close to the topics to give a broad overview. In addition, it is language per se that engages the interest of the League rather than literature or history. These periodicals were widely read among nationalists, and notices of the issues appear regularly in the *United Irishman*.

The *Dublin Penny Journal*, subtitled "a Magazine of Art, Archaeology, Literature, and Science," is another specialty weekly in small format (9.5″ × 12″) that provided its readers with information about Irish culture; its articles contain a good deal of historical information, particularly about Dublin. It was short-lived, running from 5 April 1902 to 25 March 1905, but during this period it printed a number of interesting series, including the long-running (5 Apr.–20 Sept. 1902) series entitled "The History and Antiquities of Dublin," a reprinting of materials from Walter Harris's history of the same title. Series on Fenian lore and a reprinting of materials by John O'Donovan, "Origins and Meanings of Irish Family Names," in 1902 are also noteworthy. The antiquarian interest of the journal focuses primarily on the eighteenth and nineteenth centuries, but there are occasional pieces on medieval Ireland as well, including, for example, the 12 April 1902 article "Ancient Beverages of Ireland" or the 3 May 1902 article "Ancient Irish Society," which gives an adequate introduction to the familial, tribal, and hierarchical aspects of the culture. The journal contains a fair amount of information about placelore, particularly Dublin placelore; it is interesting to find that Chapelizod is discussed in particular (17 May and 31 May 1902). There are informative articles about Irish calendar customs, such as the article on May Day (Beltaine) on 31 May 1902, as well as articles about the Irish gods (31 May 1902) and numerous articles about the stories and placelore of the Finn Cycle (beginning June 1902). Robert Adams (141–42) has argued that Joyce used Harris rather than the annals in *Thom's Directory* for the reference to the beaching of turlehyde whales in Dublin harbor (*U* 3.303–6); inasmuch as the key words of Harris's text on which Adams's argument rests also appear in the *Dublin Penny Journal* reprinting, it is possible that Joyce is indebted to the periodical for his reading of Harris and, if so, that he would have known other articles as well.

This survey of the periodical literature of Ireland at the turn of the century indicates that there was a general awareness of Irish cultural nationalism among the population, particularly the Catholic nationalist population, and with it a relatively high level of knowledge about early Irish literature and history. Certain aspects of the literature had become canonical in Ireland. The main lines of a patriotic history and an Irish pseudohistory based on *The Book of Invasions* were also widely presumed. Moreover, the popular press extended the boundaries of that common knowledge with occasional features on Irish prosody and literary pieces that reinforced traditional Irish imagery, including rose imagery, otherworld imagery, and Sovereignty imagery. In short, the principal features of the Irish substructure of *Ulysses* were common knowledge in the Irish milieu that Joyce was part of at the beginning of the century, and most of the elements traced in this book would have been familiar to the public at large.[32] Yet even within a populace with a significant fund of common knowledge about Irish literary tradition, in choosing to be a regular reader of the *United Irishman,* Joyce would have been conspicuous among nonspecialists for his interest in and knowledge of Irish literature and history. No other periodical or popular source has a comparable range and depth of coverage of Irish cultural topics, nor does any have a similar educative program. Joyce preferred to read the Irish weekly most calculated to give him a broad, systematic, and sympathetic presentation of Irish history and literature. Thus, the view of Joyce as an author antipathetical to the Irish cultural revival and uninterested in Irish tradition or mythos must be reevaluated; Joyce situated himself in the cultural spectrum in such a way that he was among the best informed of those who used popular vehicles to instruct themselves about Irish literary and historical tradition.

v. Ideas in general circulation in popular Irish culture at the turn of the century

Beyond acting as indicators of Joyce's familiarity with Irish literature and history, the periodicals are also useful in illuminating Joyce's literary program in *Ulysses.* Even from a small sampling, what quickly emerges is that much of what is taken as original to Joyce's views and a Joycean aesthetic was widely discussed in the popular press in Ireland before Joyce's departure in 1904. The following discussion, which could be broadened considerably, is restricted to the way popular culture influenced Joyce's treatment of Irish mythos and literary tradition in *Ulysses.* More general values and positions affecting Joyce's role as an artist are deferred to another occasion, but the following sampling should indicate how promising an area of research this is for Joyce scholars.

32. The widespread knowledge of many stories is indicated in articles in the *United Irishman,* for example. On 3 March 1900, in a review of the Irish Literary Theatre, Frank Fay writes, "*Maeve* which would probably succeed in mystifying an English audience was listened to with rapt attention and with an instinctive understanding of its symbolism"; cf. Gregory, *Our Irish Theatre* 28–29. Again on 26 October 1901, in writing about *Diarmuid and Grania,* Fay indicates that the story was familiar to the audience and the public at large; Holloway (16–17) indicates that the symbolism of *Cathleen ni Houlihan* was likewise familiar to its initial audiences. Such examples of the observed familiarity of Irish audiences and the Irish readership with a "canon" of Irish stories and a repertory of Irish symbols is thus well documented.

The method here is to contextualize features of the contents and poetics of *Ulysses* by juxtaposing materials from contemporary sources with Joyce's views and his manipulation of Irish literature. Examination of related materials from the popular press makes it easier to apprehend the ways in which Joyce continued to be influenced by popular Irish culture, even after he had left Ireland. Working on the Continent, he nonetheless took partisan stands in the nationalist debates of Ireland; as Manganiello has put it, "Exile did not mean escape but a widening of political consciousness; it did not mean indifference but preserving his intimacy with his country by intensifying his quarrel with her. . . . In whatever part of Europe he resided, Joyce, like Dante, carried with him a consciousness of the political situation of his city and of his country" (41–43). An examination of the periodical literature that Joyce read in his formative years enables us to position his poetics in the spectrum of the discourse of Irish cultural nationalism and to understand his writings, particularly *Ulysses*, as a partial response to the issues raised in contemporary Ireland.

Discussions of racial identity: the everyday Celt

Joyce's interest in racial identity, discussed in chapter 2, is in part an outgrowth of a discourse about race and nationality that had been a leitmotif of Western thought for more than a century and that is in turn reflected in Irish journals at the turn of the century.[33] The connection between political autonomy and racial or cultural distinctiveness was an issue of paramount interest, and it partly underlies the emergence of the movement toward cultural autonomy in Sinn Féin. For example, in the *Illustrated Irish Weekly Independent and Nation* of 29 March 1902 an article entitled "Language and Nationality" argues against the thesis that Ireland has forfeited her right to autonomy because (unlike Hungary, Bohemia, Finland, and Norway) she has put aside her native language and adopted the dress, customs, speech, and literature of her conquerors. The writers of the Anglo-Irish literary revival all carry on a dialogue about Irish racial and cultural identity: such figures as A. E. and Yeats stress the mysticism of the Irish, thus following in Matthew Arnold's wake, while others such as Gregory focus more on the simplicity and integrity of the

33. See the discussion of these issues in Martin Bernal, *Black Athena*.

Irish countrypeople, and still others such as Synge subvert the views of fellow writers by writing of the earthy, sensual aspects of country life.

Joyce's concern about *race* must be understood in the context of this dialogue; he is interested in retaining English as a language in Ireland, and he is content with international urban dress, customs, and mores, but his search for an Irish identity, even as he rejects the notion of Irish racial purity, suggests the force of this dilemma for him. Although the surface of Joyce's narrative appears to be less involved in this question than are the overt treatments of it by his contemporaries, the racial parameter of the architectonics from *The Book of Invasions* in *Ulysses* also shows that these issues were important to Joyce. Joyce's architectonic structure permitted him to engage in a dialectic about Irishness and the characteristics of "the Irish race" in *Ulysses* while submerging the topic in the mythic structuring, thus giving him scope to comment on a central issue of his culture without being polemical or didactic. Such mythic discourse, whether implicit or sublimated, provided Joyce an opportunity to speak to the ideological concerns of his time while remaining within the bounds of art as he viewed it.

In *Ulysses* and *Finnegans Wake* Joyce has characters who are worlds apart from the mystical nature of many of Yeats's mythic Irish figures. This is one of the many polarities in the treatment of Ireland-as-literary-world by Yeats and Joyce; still another is the dichotomy of city and country. Joyce's stand on how to represent Ireland is related to views debated in the popular press. The *United Irishman*, for example, observes as early as 6 May 1899 that "there are other things in Ireland beside the rowan-crested rath, the dew upon the grass, or the reeds above the rivers." The debate can best be illustrated by an article in the *Leader* on 7 May 1904 entitled "The Different Kinds of Celt":

The new Celt is the Yeats type, to say which should be almost enough. The new Celt is a mixture of moonshine, and mist, and dreams; he wanders (both corporeally and mentally) in waste places, such as bogs, moors, mountain sides, woods, and so forth. He is haunted by the lapping of lakes . . . , by the murmur of druid forests. . . .

A striking peculiarity of the new Celt is that he does not eat or drink. How does he live, then? On dreams, thou fool, on dreams!—plus "visions," occasionally. He does not sully the soulfulness of his nature with sordid mundaneity; he lives as a spirit, and is consequently a cut or two above bread or bacon.

Now this sort of Celt, the "literary" Celt let us call him, had begun to gain a certain amount of acceptance in London—that is, in literary London. . . . However, a revulsion of feeling seems to have set in, and it appears to be dawning even on literary London that the new Celt does not quite square with facts. A writer in the *Spectator* . . . had been reading Dr. Joyce's *Social History of Ancient Ireland*, and it began to strike him that the Celt of mere history was not quite like the Celt of Mr. Yeats. . . . We are all with the writer when, after some bantering remarks he adds: "But seriously, it is time to turn from the mystic to the more human sides of the Gael: the men of the ancient epics could dream, but they could love and fight on occasion, and could look on Nature without an ever-boding sense of the presence of unseen powers."

Quite so. Now there is another, and altogether un-Yeats-like Celt—the Celt I want to see. I mean the everyday Celt. The Celt who doesn't live on visions or mists, but who eats rashers and eggs; who smokes a pipe and drinks a pint; who may be met with in the streets, on the country roads, in third-class carriages, and on the tops of trams; who reads the ha'penny evening papers, goes to "the bob place" in the theatre or music-hall now and then, and to a football match whenever he can; I want to see that Celt.

The article proceeds to call for the representation of the everyday Celt in the contemporary novel:

Do you know what Ireland badly wants? She wants a great novelist. Not simply a very high-class second-rank one, but a *great* one, and no mistake about his—or her—greatness. We want a novelist with as good a head, as much solid culture, as much genuine knowledge of the people as George Eliot possessed. . . . We want to have Irish life thrown into the alembic of genius and drawn off as literature; given back again to us in a sort of sublimated realism, delightful, yet recognisably true, and free from all the mud and vitriol of politics and polemics. We want to get rid of that tenuous exiguity, the "literary" Celt, no less than of that over-whiskified person, the Celt of the "rollicking" school of writers. We want the Irishman that we know; a man that we can mix with, and not feel revolted at; that we can laugh *with* rather oftener than *at*; a man that we are not ashamed of, because we see that he is not only quite human, but has no mean sordid faults, and no inherent coarseness of soul. In a word, we want justice done to the Irish character through the medium of prose literature—of the novel.

Leopold Bloom is cousin to this everyday Celt, and it is perhaps no accident that Joyce shows him eating and drinking repeatedly, leaving none of these repasts to the gaps between episodes. The note of "the everyday Celt" is sounded at the first appearance of Bloom: though Bloom rejects eggs because of the drouth and prefers animal organs to rashers, and though his trip to the jakes would no doubt have offended the sensibilities of the writer of this *Leader* article, Joyce makes clear from the outset that Bloom lives on more than dreams and visions. Bloom is met in the streets, in carriages, on trams; he reads ordinary papers and goes to common amusements. He loves and occasionally fights like the men of the ancient epics. It is only gradually in the course of *Ulysses* that the reader realizes that Bloom also has the decency and refinement of soul that the article calls for. As this article indicates, criticism of Yeats's mystic Celt was common in contemporary Irish culture; thus, Joyce's revisionism is inscribed in a wider cultural context.

Bloom and the characters of *Ulysses* are in part representative of the Irish in virtue of the subtext from *The Book of Invasions*, but in their realistic or everyday guise they are also continuous with the types to be found in Dublin. *Ulysses* fits the criterion set forth in the *Leader* article of having Irish life thrown into the alembic of genius and drawn off as literature—given back in realism sublimated by form, a form delightful, playful, yet recognizably true. For all the objectionable matter in the book,[34] in its own way *Ulysses* is free from "the mud and vitriol of politics and polemics," and it is written by an author with "solid culture" and "a genuine knowledge of the people."

Irish meet Greeks meet Jews meet Spaniards
meet Norse

In the popular press the Irish character is often defined through comparison and contrast with a wide variety of other "races" being used as a standard. The English naturally come in for a variety of invidious comments, but other groups are also discussed. There are, for example, discussions of the "racial" characteristics of the Jews; in the *Leader* of 4 June 1904, an article entitled "The Jew Question in Ireland" characterizes the Jews as possessing the virtues of sobriety, thrift, and providence. The Norse (e.g., *All Ireland Review* 12 May 1900) and the Spanish (discussed, for example, at length in the *All Ireland Review*, which carried a series in the spring of 1901 entitled "The Spaniards in Ireland") also come in

---

34. See, for example, Bernard Shaw's comments quoted in *JJ*2 506–7, 576–77.

for examination. These issues pervade *Ulysses* as, for example, in the leitmotif of discussions about the characteristics of the English (e.g. 2.243–54, 7.483–501). The question of Jews in Ireland was particularly topical before Bloomsday because of an episode of persecution of Jews in Limerick in spring 1904 (cf. *Leader* 7 May 1904);[35] the historical context may explain much of the sensitivity to the question of Bloom's "racial" background among the characters of *Ulysses* on Bloomsday. Joyce's interest in these questions is also pursued in *Ulysses* through the substructure from *The Book of Invasions*, by means of which Joyce represents the relations of the Irish to the Jews and the Spanish, just as in *Finnegans Wake* the affinities and contrasts between Gael and Gall, Irish and Norse, are embodied in HCE's mixed ancestry.

A frequent topic in the popular press is a comparison of Irish and Greek character and culture. O'Grady in the *All Ireland Review* compares the unity of thought and feeling in Ireland to that of Greece in the issue of 2 March 1901; two weeks later he compares Irish and Greek myth; and on 4 May of the same year he compares the interlacing of history and myth in both cultures. In a similar vein the *Illustrated Irish Weekly Independent and Nation* of 29 March 1902 carries a report about a lecture to the Irish Literary Society in which the speaker stresses that the Irish nation dates back to the time of Greece and Rome. At times the comparison could turn to the advantage of the Irish: thus, in an article entitled "Gael and Greek" of 10 May 1902, the *Leader* criticizes a lecture delivered by Dr. Barry to the National Literary Society and maintains that Greek ideals are not worthy of imitation.

Because of the prestige and status associated with Greek culture, either to equate or to prefer early Irish culture to Greek culture was a means of validating Irish literature and society. Such comparisons became *topoi* of Irish nationalism, and they were found in monographs as well as in the popular press. Obviously this discourse conditions *Ulysses* with its melding of Greek and Irish character, myth, and literature; rather than comment on or argue for the parity of Greek and Irish culture, however, Joyce presupposes this nationalist position in the conflation of the mythic systems, a mythic method that makes Bloom simultaneously a Greek hero and Irish Milesian. The mythic structuring presents the two traditions as

---

35. Manganiello (52) discusses this episode in relation to Joyce's views about anti-Semitism.

equivalent, thus asserting Joyce's estimation of the ranking of Irish culture while permitting him a certain ironic disengagement from both.

Localism

Joyce's detestation of "nationalisms" is well known,[36] and in a letter of 25 September 1906 to his brother Stanislaus he criticizes Arthur Griffith and the *United Irishman* in these terms: "What I object to most of all in his paper is that it is educating the people of Ireland on the old pap of racial hatred whereas anyone can see that if the Irish question exists, it exists for the Irish proletariat chiefly" (*Letters* 2: 167). Joyce's desire to be European and universal is generally stressed in critical works on his texts. Though Joyce objected to nationalism, at the same time he believed that artists had to be national. Let us return to the encounter between Joyce and Arthur Power in 1921. When Power objected that he was tired of nationality and wanted to be international like all the great writers, Joyce responded:

But they were national first . . . and it was the intensity of their own nationalism which made them international in the end, as in the case of Turgenieff. You remember his "Tales of the Sportsman," how local they were—and yet out of that germ he became a great international writer. For myself, I always write about Dublin, because if I can get to the heart of Dublin I can get to the heart of all the cities of the world. In the particular is contained the universal. (Quoted in Power, *From the Old Waterford House* 64–65)

The same quality that he praises here in Turgenev he found in Ibsen; in his January 1900 lecture entitled "Drama and Life" he contends, "Ghosts, the action of which passes in a common parlour, is of universal import" (*CW* 45). For Joyce the universal in literature is manifest in the local, and it is interesting to find that the views he expressed to Power were anticipated twenty years earlier by articles in the popular Irish press.

The polarities of localism and universality were debated in the pages of the *United Irishman*. A particularly telling article, "Localism in Poetry," appeared on 18 August 1900, signed "Hy Faely":

Now, no man ever was, or in this life, ever can be universal in the sense of knowing all things. But he who has studied his fellows around him, and

---

36. See, for example, *MBK* 174 and *JJ2* 66.

he who has studied himself, if he have the power of wielding a pen, can give you such a representation of the whole working of humanity from his knowledge of a few, that would almost make us think his mind was all-seeing and his knowledge unlimited. Nowhere, have we found more real philosophy compressed into a few words than in this line from an Irish poet "I sing of *what I know.*" He sang of the lives and pleasures of those he *knew*, "of the hills and the streams and glens that he knew and loved," and, unconsciously, perhaps, he was singing the great paean of humanity. The greatest minds that have ever illumined the world have gone no further than this. Take up the works of any great writer you will who has made a romance and a story of our follies and our passions and you will find him, while universal, yet local. . . .

. . . Localism in literature is a distinctive mark of genius! But I wish to be understood. When I say localism I mean the localism that will suggest to *any* man home-thoughts and feelings. William Allingham sang of the "Winding Banks of Erne," of the town of Ballyshannon, of the townspeople and the boatmen, of all he knew there. His poems must touch everyone, not because he writes of Ballyshannon, but because he sang a universal song, the love of home; but that it should touch the hearts of others the song required to come from his own heart. To me his poem brings up in visionary light another town upon the coast, another stream, another harbour, other ruins than those of Assaroe, and other people. Because he sang our song, because he felt our feelings, because he pictured what we all would picture, he is universal. Thus is localism universal.

But to be a distinctive mark of genius, this localism must represent universality. To make this localism universally felt the poet must possess genius. Without the localism the genius is wasted. No man can sing of what he knows not; both powers must go hand in hand. A poet may sing of nothing but home scenes, and yet because he lacks the power to make his picture representative he will fail to reach us; he may have genius, and yet, wanting the power of localising, he is lost. . . .

To our poets, I would say: speak from the heart; doing so you must speak of what you love; love will lend you power; and singing, as Allingham did, of what you know, if you are poets possessing the Promethean fire, you will sing the while the mighty song of humanity all the world over.

In a sense this view of localism informs the work of the entire Irish literary revival. It is the striving to write "what they knew"—what they knew that English writers did not—that forms the theoretical ground of the Irish literary movement. In the case of the principal writers localism takes a variety of forms. Thus, Augusta Gregory attempts to represent peasant life and peasant speech, particularly the Anglo-Irish dialect of Kiltartan. J. M. Synge turns his hand principally to life in the Gaeltacht and to the transposition of the Irish language into English. Yeats shows his localism chiefly in his use of Irish myth, hero tale, and legend—localism of the imagination rather than localism of geography or dialect. Localism of various sorts is the driving force behind the minor figures of the revival as well, and it has continued to dominate Irish literature throughout the twentieth century, from O'Casey and Austin Clarke to Kavanagh, Kinsella, and Heaney.

In the *United Irishman* time and again we also find the view that preservation of the knowledge of Irish geography, topography, local legend, and local history are of particular importance. These concerns are stressed in an article entitled "Irish Topography" by William Rooney on 24 November 1900:[37]

It does not need the present writer to point out how inseparably intertwined with each other are geography and topography. Both are fascinating studies, but the latter is possibly the more fascinating, because it is the local and the homely, it tells us of things about us, it brings us from the generalities of geography to the particularities of the places we have grown up in. It is the blending of tradition, history, and locality that makes the past live and keeps the memory of great things and abiding influence to inspire the present.

Rooney himself is particularly interested in preserving the Irish nomenclature, concerns echoed recently in Brian Friel's *Translations*. He continues:

We, by turning our backs on our language, have lost the power that these memories would give us. . . . We feel not the sympathy [in places] . . . which the knowledge of the story of their names would give us. . . . These old names carry us back even beyond historic days, recall names and deeds that loom on the border line of history, in those dim days where the mists of tradition bide and all the figures have a mighty majesty. They tell us of the origin of loughs and rivers, why this hollow is so called, and where is the cairn that has lived down time upon yon mountain top. They teach us of the work of the centuries, hold within them the secrets of the far off years. . . . The value

37. This article is signed "Shel Martin," one of Rooney's pseudonyms; for a list of the pseudonyms, see the obituary on Rooney in the *United Irishman*, 11 May 1901.

of such knowledge cannot be overestimated. It is a priceless heirloom, for the loss of which no amount of commercial success can compensate.

In the article Rooney recommends P. W. Joyce's *Irish Names of Places*; despite its defects he finds it "the only volume on the subject yet obtainable . . . an excellent book."

Knowledge of local sites and topography at the turn of the century was accordingly considered an index of nationalism in some quarters. On 18 February 1905 the *United Irishman* ran an article entitled "The Study of Local History," from which the following excerpts are taken:

> The attitude of immovable apathy and unconcern towards all things Irish which characterises so many of those whom, by courtesy, we call Irishmen, is nowhere more evident than in their ignorance of Local History, and of the traditions (veracious or legendary), of the fine old ruins that in bewildering profusion dot every parish of our country. . . .
>
> There are, for instance, Dubliners who would distinguish themselves in a discussion on the Legends of the Rhine, but are unaware of the existence of Kilgobbin Castle. . . .
>
> One reason why the study of local history would not be without profit to us is that it could hardly fail to develop a feeling of national self-respect, a virtue with which it will not be contended that we are unduly gifted at present. . . .
>
> . . . The writer who is sufficiently energetic to apply himself to such necessary and patriotic work will earn the gratitude, not only of his thoughtful contemporaries, but of generations of Irishmen yet unborn.

Though there is much in these articles that Joyce would have found objectionable, it is clear that the role of topography in Joyce's works is related to ideas concerning localism in literature and the importance of Irish topography that were widespread in Ireland at the turn of the century. Joyce begins with the impulse toward localism that is characteristic of the Irish literary revival as a whole; as Joyce himself noted to Arthur Power, his localism is seen in the fact that all his works are written about Ireland and about Dublin in particular. Like O'Casey, Joyce's localism is expressed in terms of Irish urban life rather than country life, but the scrupulous attention to the topography and traditions of Dublin found in Joyce's writings fit squarely in Rooney's program, even though Joyce rarely has Irish nomenclature to preserve in virtue of his geographical

purview. While Joyce preserves many of the features of the generic and
literary tradition of the medieval dindśenchas in his attention to geography and topography in *Ulysses*, thus acting as senchaid for his age, he
is at the same time responsive to the calls of the nationalists for localism
in literature.

The relationship of history and literature

In the article of 24 November 1900 quoted above, Rooney distinguishes
between geography and topography, noting the importance of local history to the latter. The interest in the role of history in literature is a topic
found elsewhere in the popular press. O'Grady's *All Ireland Review* has
some of the most illuminating material related to both *Ulysses* and *Finnegans Wake* on this subject, for in a series of articles in 1901 O'Grady
stresses the interrelation of history and myth. On 9 February 1901, in an
article that was part of a series entitled "Pre-Historic Ireland," O'Grady
makes a telling argument that one must understand myth in order to
comprehend the history and character of a people:

An escape from the actual is supplied to some more favoured or more gifted
nations in the possession of a great mythical age lying behind their progress
through time, imparting to their lives its own greatness and glory, inspiring
life and hope and a buoyancy which laughs at obstacles and will not recog-
nise defeat. . . .
    To the Greek bards who shaped the mythology of Hellas we must remotely
attribute all the enormous influence which Greece has exercised on the world.
But for them the Greece that we know would not have been; without them
the Iliad and Odyssey would never have arisen, nor the Athenian drama, nor
Greek art, nor architecture. All of these, as we find them, are concerned with
the gods and heroes who were the creation of pre-historic bards. . . .
    As compared with the history of Greece, that of our own land is, of course,
a small thing, its real greatness lying in the promise of the future, not in the
actualities of the past; of which future that far off mythic age is a prophecy.
But no more than Grecian is Irish History comprehensible without a knowledge of those Gods, giants, and heroes, with whose crowded cycles prehistoric pages are filled.

O'Grady's position is reminiscent of T. S. Eliot's view that Joyce's mythic
method gives structure and stature to modern life, and it is interesting
that O'Grady sees the Irish mythic age as prophetic of the future, a view

that is compatible with Joyce's use of material from *The Book of Invasions* on the eve of Irish statehood.

On 2 March 1901, in a later article in the same series, O'Grady goes on to discuss the merger of history and literature, views that are obviously related to Joyce's historical impetus in both *Ulysses* and *Finnegans Wake* as well as his mythic structuring of the two works:

I think Ireland alone among the nations of the world exhibits as to its history, the same progress from the mythological and heroic to the mundane, not even excepting that of Greece, which comes next. In the history of Greece, there occurs between the two regions an era of mere barren names which indicate that here is debateable and uncertain land. On one side is the purple light of imagination, amid which loom and glitter the heroes and the gods—a land illuminated by the mind of Hesiod and Homer and the great tragedians; on the other the clear dry light of history prevails. We see clearly that one is history and the other fiction. But in the progress of the Irish national record the purple light is never absent. The weird, the supernatural, the heroic, surround characters as certain as Brian Borom—events as trustworthy as the Norman Invasion. The bards never relinquished their right to view their history with the eyes of poets, to convert their kings into heroes and adorn battles and events with hues drawn from mythology.

O'Grady could here be describing the merger of the supernatural and the heroic with the mundane and the everyday that so characterizes Joyce's major works; and insofar as Joyce was conscious of writing in a tradition, he may have viewed himself as appropriating the prerogatives of the Irish poets that O'Grady describes. It is interesting that in a letter to the editor printed in the 16 March 1901 issue of the *All Ireland Review*, an unnamed correspondent writes: "I am very glad to see that notwithstanding many intimations which would discourage a less resolute man you are going to deal with the mythology no less than the written and actual history of our race. History itself is daily and hourly approaching the inevitable period when it too will be mythical." Such a Joycean statement from an anonymous correspondent suggests that widespread cultural sentiments underlie Joyce's integration of fiction, history, and mythology.

Clearly the blending of myth and history that O'Grady delineates is related to the strand of pseudohistory in Irish literature and also to the historicization of mythic figures. O'Grady's most apt statement about this quality of Irish literature is found in his essay "Introduction of the Bardic History of Ireland":

There is not perhaps in existence a product of the human mind so extraordinary as the Irish annals. From a time dating for more than three thousand years before the birth of Christ, the stream of Hibernian history flows down uninterrupted, copious and abounding, between accurately defined banks. . . . As the centuries wend their way, king succeeds king with a regularity most gratifying, and fights no battle, marries no wife, begets not children, does no doughty deed of which a contemporaneous note was not taken, and which has not been incorporated in the annals of his country. To think that this mighty fabric of recorded events, so stupendous in its dimensions, so clean and accurate in its details, so symmetrical and elegant, should be after all a mirage and delusion. . . .

Doubtless the legendary blends at some point with the historic narrative. The cloud and mist somewhere condense into the clear stream of indubitable fact. But how to discern under the rich and teeming mythus [sic] of the bards, the course of that slender and doubtful rivulet. . . . In this minute, circumstantial, and most imposing body of history, where the certain legend exhibits the form of plain and probable narrative, and the certain fact displays itself with a mythical flourish, how there to fix upon any one point and say here is the first truth. It is a task perilous and perplexing. (23–24)

The blending of history and myth, as well as the creation of a pseudohistory in *Ulysses*, recapitulates the narrative mode of early Irish literature and also fits in the context of the discourse of Joyce's contemporaries about the relations of history, literature, and myth.

The role of humor in an Irish literature

In the popular Irish press of Joyce's youth, the question of humor is sensitive: because of the stigmatization associated with the Stage Irishman,[38] there is widespread sensitivity in the periodicals about laughter at the expense of Irish subjects or subject matter, as well as frequent denunciations of portrayals of the Stage Irishman. This stereotyping of the Irish had contributed to the political and cultural oppression of the nation; thus, for the Republican movement and the movement of cultural nationalism the entire question of humor was a prickly issue. In some periodicals, notably the *United Irishman*, a counterreaction set in, and the overwhelming bur-

---

38. See Duggan, particularly 279–96; Hunt 3–5; Waters, esp. 1–57; Cave; and Kiberd, "Fall of the Stage Irishman."

den of the editorial policy was to demonstrate that the Irish were serious, heroic, and noble (e.g., *United Irishman* 4 Mar. 1899, 11 Mar. 1899, 18 Mar. 1899, 12 Apr. 1902; *Sinn Féin* 19 Jan. 1907, 4 May 1907). Such a viewpoint was in part fueled by Matthew Arnold's delineation of "Celtic melancholy" as an important "racial" trait.

At the same time other views were more receptive to humor. We have seen above that in 1904 the *Leader* called for a portrait of the Celt as a man "that we can laugh *with* rather oftener than *at.*" In an earlier article of 1 March 1902 entitled "The Comic Irishman," after deploring the image of the Irishman as fool and menial both at home and abroad, O'Grady's periodical continues:

The revolution in Irish thought caused by the Irish Revival has given the Irish mind an earnest and dignified tone, and has given the country a basis for the growth of a healthy and intellectual school of humour.

There is, perhaps, nothing that this country needs more than the free play of real humour. The "humour" that we have been accustomed to, labelled "Irish humour," was lacking in thought, the basis of all true humour.

Joyce's interest in humor thus has a broader cultural context. In his desire to revive Elizabethan gaiety (*JJ*2 150), in his own estimation of the importance of the humor of *Ulysses*, Joyce participated in a dialectic of Irish nationalism that was debated hotly in the press at the turn of the century. Joyce's choice of a nativist epic style that mixes the heroic and the humorous is thus a formal correlate to a position in an ideological debate that preoccupied Irish cultural nationalists year after year.

The question of a national literature

The main agenda of the Irish literary revival was the development of a national literature, but that said, there was a good deal less unanimity about what a national literature would consist of. The May 1904 issue of *Dana* summarizes some of the problems:

Of the various forms which patriotic ambition takes in the minds of Irishmen at the present time, perhaps the most generally favoured and the least impracticable, is a zeal for the promotion of a national literature. . . .

Since the days of the worthy Thomas Davis, who made a great, a noble, and an epoch-making effort to turn the national spirit in the direction of literature, Irish literary enterprise has concerned itself mainly with the aim of securing the nationality of Irish literature by the choice of Irish subjects, the revival of the Irish language, and so forth.

The essay continues that the movement has failed to secure "the elemental freedom of the human mind which is really the essential of all independent and therefore national literature"; this freedom has "hardly made its appearance in the Irish literary movement" because of a fashion of promoting an artificial and sentimental unity of Irish life by ignoring matters on which the Irish have held diverse opinions. The result, the article maintains, is a hollowness of Irish literature. The *Leader* (5 July 1902) had earlier criticized the Irish literary revival for, among other things, Augusta Gregory's sentimentalized view of CuChulainn and her use of a "half-way house English" reminiscent of the "broken English" of "Irish slavery" in *Cuchulain of Muirthemne*; Yeats is taken to task for his view that the volume was "the best book that has ever come out of Ireland." Such particular criticisms of individual figures are widespread.

In the 7 June 1902 issue of the *Leader*, Peter O'Leary had taken another tack, criticizing the use of English literary forms in an Irish literature. In "Irish Poetical Composition" he writes,

If you are a real poet, an Irish poet, born into the Irish language, there is one thing which you certainly will never do. You will never write in the shape of the English rhyming couplet, nor in the shape of English blank verse, nor in fact in any of the shapes in which English poetry is composed and written. . . .

. . . The very thing which the builders of an Irish literature have got to do at the very start is to put the English models completely out of sight. They must build their Irish literature as if there was no English literature in existence.

O'Leary here is primarily addressing the importation of English poetics into literature into Irish, but the points relate to the development of an Irish literature in English as well. For an advocate, like Joyce, of the use of English to create an Irish literature, the question of an Irish poetics would be raised by arguments such as those of O'Leary. I have taken the position that Joyce did in fact reject English models, building an innovative poetic in English that is based in part on Irish genres and literary conventions; the kinds of arguments regarding Irish poetics and an Irish literature found in the nationalist press at the turn of the century indicate that Joyce built his literary program as a concomitant of a nationalist position.

Summary

These are but a few issues discussed in the popular press that can be related to Joyce's poetics in his major writings. A great deal remains to be done in contextualizing Joyce's thought in terms of Irish discourse. In his treatment of history and myth, his use of Irish content and symbols, his realistic decor of time and place, and his manipulation of humor and heroism, Joyce shows himself to be working out in a literary forum some of the ideological questions that were at the heart of the nationalist debate in the three decades prior to the appearance of *Ulysses*.

vi. Conversation and oral transfer of information about early Irish literature

In all his narratives Joyce portrays the importance of conversation in Dublin, but he does so particularly in *A Portrait of the Artist as a Young Man* and *Ulysses*, illustrating how information and attitudes were circulated among the intellectuals of Ireland and among the ordinary people as well. Material about Ireland's history, literature, and language became current in this manner; and in *Ulysses* Joyce gives a specific example of this sort of transfer when Haines explains to Mulligan the early Irish idea of the otherworld (10.1076–84). The book is full of other conversations and anecdotes about historical figures and patriotic history, indicating that such exchange was a commonplace; Bloom's stories about Parnell shared with Stephen stand as a convenient example (16.1480ff.). The conversation in "Cyclops" gives an idea of how allusions to Irish tales infiltrated Irish nationalist conversation at the period; a youth like Joyce growing up in the culture at the time either would have had to learn the repertory of materials upon which such conversation was based or would have remained a kind of cultural illiterate, something certainly alien to Joyce's nature. Finally, the library episode in *Ulysses* illustrates that the sorts of predispositions toward Irish tradition represented in the popular press were also discussed widely.

Joyce was particularly apt to have been influenced by the oral transfer of material about Irish tradition, and the importance of oral culture, story-telling, and oral lore is signaled by the voice of the father as the primal memory of the boy-to-be-artist in *A Portrait of the Artist.* Joyce had a pro-digious memory; even material to which he was exposed briefly in a con-versational exchange could remain with him in a vivid manner. John Kel-leher notes that in 1906 Joyce complained that Dublin was already growing hazy in his memory, and observes: "I doubt it ever really grew hazy. I doubt that his memory, particular and capacious as a bard's, ever relinquished anything once learned from books, from observation, or from his father whose knowledge of Dublin was as intimate and curious as his own" ("Irish History" 431). Joyce's ability to remember material presented to him orally stood him well during the years when he was virtually blind and could not read; we are indebted for much of his later work to his ability to compose without pencil and paper and to absorb material spoken to him. Thus, oral sources for Joyce's knowledge of Irish tradition cannot be ignored; at the same time, in the absence of a recorder, conversation is ephemeral by its very nature. Though Joyce at times acts as his own re-corder and though we have accounts by others of conversations with Joyce, most of these transactions necessarily left no traces, and reconstruction of this level of Joyce's source material is inevitably conjectural.

The possibilities, moreover, are broad. In Joyce's childhood there were family members and friends, notably his father, who told him stories and instructed him in what it was to be Irish; but there were also school-masters and neighbors and priests speaking from the pulpit. In *A Portrait of the Artist* Stephen remembers being taken by his father to the ceremony in 1898 at which the cornerstone of a monument to Wolfe Tone was set by Maud Gonne and Yeats, among others; the speeches at this sort of public political event would also have been occasions on which the pa-triotic history of Ireland would have been transmitted orally to Joyce (*PA* 184; cf. MacBride 280–86). Later in his life, at University College, Joyce engaged in extensive conversational exchanges with his school friends, many of whom, like George Clancy, were involved in the activities spon-sored by the cultural nationalists, supported the Gaelic League, attended cultural events and classes of various types, and adopted the "party line" as required (*JJ2* 61ff.). And there was also Joyce's ubiquitous brother Stanislaus, himself devoted to conversation and argument and active in the same cultural milieu.

Joyce's teachers at University College must also be accounted as potential oral sources. Though a complete inventory of the faculty is not necessary in this context, specific teachers should be noted.[39] One of his English teachers at University College was Thomas Arnold, the brother of Matthew Arnold, whose essay "On the Study of Celtic Literature" was a milestone in the recognition of Celtic literature in the English-speaking world; and Édouard Cadic, his French professor, was a Breton. But more important members of the faculty were George Sigerson, who lectured and published materials on Irish poetry and poetics, and Edmund Hogan (editor of the placelore manual *Onomasticon Godelicum*), who held the chair of Irish language, history, and archaeology (Gorman 56). Patrick Dinneen, later the compiler of the standard Irish-English dictionary, was professor of Irish (*MBK* 153; O Hehir vii). Eoin Mac Neill (the foremost Irish historian of his generation), Patrick Henry Pearse, and Douglas Hyde had all lectured on Irish topics at University College during the period Joyce was a student (Gorman 56). Joyce, persuaded by his friend Clancy to take Irish for some time, was also instructed in Irish by Pearse, whose classes would have contained more than grammar and who would have provoked conversation of a cultural and nationalist sort among the students (cf. *JJ*2 61).[40]

Members of the Anglo-Irish literary movement must also be numbered among Joyce's oral sources for Irish history and literature. A. E., Gregory, Yeats all had conversations with Joyce; it is inconceivable that their conversation at no time turned to Irish literature. In *Ulysses* when Stephen mentally acknowledges "A. E. I. O. U." (9.213), is there nothing but money that he owes to A. E.? As a source of this type John Millington Synge is probably a key figure since Synge had read and studied early Irish material extensively, even attending d'Arbois de Jubainville's Celtic literature classes in Paris (Greene and Stephens 72; cf. 64–65). Synge may have passed on important material orally to Joyce in the brief but intense period they spent together in Paris in March 1903;[41] Joyce's acute mem-

---

39. For a more complete discussion of the faculty in fields not related to Irish culture, see Gorman 54–56; *JJ*2 58–60. Ellmann's omission of many of the faculty members in Irish history, language, and literature indicates the critical bias in Joyce studies.

40. Cf. Hughes in *Stephen Hero*.

41. I am grateful to Anthony Roche for the suggestion that Synge in particular may have been an important oral source for Joyce. Cf. Gorman (101), who says that Joyce and Synge met seven or eight times and that Synge's voluble talk was always of literature.

ory of Maurya's speeches in *Riders to the Sea*, which he gained from reading Synge's manuscript in March 1903 (*JJ2* 124), suggests that this period
was a particularly influential and stimulating one for him. Synge was
aware of the differences between the early Irish originals and the pro-
cessed versions promulgated by the Anglo-Irish revival, as his review of
Gregory's *Cuchulain of Muirthemne* makes clear:

For readers who take more than literary interest in these stories a word of
warning may be needed. Lady Gregory has omitted certain barbarous features, such as the descriptions of the fury of Cuchulain, and, in consequence,
some of her versions have a much less archaic aspect than the original texts.
Students of mythology will read this book with interest, yet for their severer
studies they must still turn to the works of German scholars, and others, who
translate without hesitation all that has come down to us in the MSS. (Synge,
"An Epic of Ulster" 370)

Possibly alerting Joyce to the way that the translators of the literary revival bowdlerized the medieval Irish texts, Synge may have been an influence on Joyce to read scholarly translations of the medieval texts or
other scholarly treatments of the material, rather than rely solely on popularizations, but Synge may also have told Joyce orally of various elements in the Irish texts not found in any source texts that Joyce himself
read. In conversations with Synge, Joyce may have received a fund of information about such elements as the humor and earthiness of Irish narrative, as well as its gappiness and inconsistencies. Synge was in a position to know and appreciate these things.

   Just as in contemporary culture not everyone who "knows about"
Freud's theory of the Oedipus complex has read Freud or even has read
a written summary of Freud—it is not necessary to read about Freud because his work is in the air, and the ignorant are informed orally, in conversation, in classes and lectures, in jokes and repartee—so in Joyce's
Dublin were Irish literature, history, and culture in the air. These topics
were in fact privileged cultural material at the time, in part because cultural nationalism was a vehicle for the coalescence of the nationalist
movement as a whole. Thus, the specific oral sources suggested here are
really just indicative of the various conversational environments that
Joyce was part of, environments that would have passed Irish cultural
materials to him, varying in their shades of significance and detail but
essentially converging on the main lines of Irish tradition.

vii. Conclusion

In certain respects recognition of the substratum from popular culture in Joyce's work has become one of the orthodoxies of Joyce criticism, and John Gross notes "Joyce's constant use of colloquial, mass-produced, and plebeian materials" (51).[42] The popular element is reflected in the spoken word recorded by Joyce, which includes slang, shoptalk, and all sorts of idiomatic and everyday speech; and it is evident in the musical elements—particularly in lines from the ballads of '98, the pantomimes, and the music-hall songs—that fill the text. Popular journalistic elements are accompaniments to Bloom's profession, and there are elements from jokes, riddles, romantic novelettes, pornography, and familiar quotations. All the "miscellaneous cultural bric-a-brac that clutters up the life of urban man" finds its place in *Ulysses*, and popular culture becomes "the element in which most of his characters live and the medium through which they express their feelings" (Gross 53, 55). Gross argues that "much of the vitality of *Ulysses* is borrowed from the popular material which it half mocks" (55–56) and that in fact Joyce's interest in popular culture can be traced through much of his life. In this context it is all the more important to consider the way in which popular culture influenced Joyce's thinking about Irish history and literature.

The brief survey in this chapter illustrates the ways in which Joyce's knowledge of the early Irish literature used in shaping *Ulysses* was omnipresent in Irish popular culture early in the twentieth century. Stories and myths that Joyce became acquainted with in his school days were recycled in the works of the Anglo-Irish literary revival, discussed in the daily and weekly periodicals, and circulated or augmented in oral culture. Dispositions about Irish literature and Irish culture were likewise transmitted in these several ways, such that it is to the generalized field of Irish popular culture that much of Joyce's knowledge of early Irish literature must be attributed.[43] *The Destruction of Da Derga's Hostel* is a convenient example of the futility of trying to determine a single specific source

42. See also, for example, Budgen, *Making of "Ulysses,"* esp. 132.
43. Kelleher, "Identifying the Irish Printed Sources," also has a useful discussion of the problems of tracking down Joyce's sources, and he touches on both the overdetermination of Joyce's sources and the importance of oral and popular culture.

for Joyce's knowledge of an Irish tale, a tale that in this case he used in the construction of "The Dead." Although Joyce may have read the edition and translation of the story that appeared in *Revue celtique*, he could as well have drawn his knowledge from Best's extensive summary in the *United Irishman*, from the retelling of the tale in Augusta Gregory's *Cuchulain of Muirthemne*, or from the reprint of the translation of the tale serialized in the *All Ireland Review*. But his knowledge of the tale also depended on information in the school curriculum, as well as secondary literature such as d'Arbois de Jubainville's *Irish Mythological Cycle*, which was serialized in the *United Irishman*. The simple fact is that in most cases Joyce had no single source for his knowledge of elements of early Irish history and literature; he had multiple and overlapping sources, and the topics were part of his general knowledge.

The survey here indicates that some arguments about Joyce's use of Irish texts need revision. Both John Kelleher in "Irish History and Mythology in James Joyce's 'The Dead'" and Stanley Sultan in *Eliot, Joyce, and Company* (42–48) take the view that Joyce had read translations of his early Irish sources in extenso. Though he may have done, it is probably more realistic, in the absence of textual evidence to the contrary, to consider the *United Irishman* or similar popular texts as the primary source of his knowledge of, say, *The Voyage of Mael Duin* or *The Destruction of Da Derga's Hostel* than to expect that he read full translations of the primary materials. At the same time the materials contained in the *United Irishman* and other popular periodicals indicate the surprising range of information about early Irish literature that was absorbed into the general and popular culture of English speakers in Ireland at the turn of the century and that provided mental furnishings at the time, at least for those like Joyce who took the trouble to read a nationalist periodical regularly. Minor and even arcane tales and traditions were circulated and discussed along with the major stories; the main lines of a patriotic history were defined and iterated; an aesthetics was defended; a cultural inheritance was acknowledged by Irish and English speakers alike. To have been party to these things, it was not necessary to have been a radical nationalist, to have taken an extremist view of Irish literature and culture, or to have enrolled in classes on the topic; one needed only to have read popular newspapers and periodicals, of which the *United Irishman* is but a single, though rich, example.

As noted early in this book, the structures from early Irish literature in Joyce's work are pervasive and fundamental, but they are not necessarily elaborated in a detailed way. The combination of the broad inclusion of Irish literature in popular culture and Joyce's relatively skeletal and allusive use of the same materials is suggestive. If we conclude that Joyce's sources were in the first instance popular ones, of which the *United Irishman* is a prototypical example for which we can document Joyce's knowledge, we better understand why Joyce's use of Irish materials shows a comprehensive but relatively schematic pattern rather than the more particularized but perhaps deeper use of texts that one might find if he had read the tales primarily in full translations. Although additional research in the topic is necessary, we may ultimately determine that in most cases such sources as the popular essays in the *United Irishman* and knowledge that was part of the cultural background of nationalists in Ireland provided sufficient imaginative stimulus for Joyce to have used early Irish literature and culture as he did in his work and that, in short, there is no necessity to determine specific source texts for most of the Irish literary elements in Joyce's works. For Joyce to have known of these materials and to have incorporated them in his mythic method, it sufficed for him to have been raised and educated in Ireland, to have been immersed in Irish popular culture, to have been aware of contemporary Irish speeches and intellectual life, to have participated in Irish discourse, to have read the Irish papers. At the same time, while Joyce may often have relied on popular journalism and general cultural background for his Irish literary materials, we cannot therefore dismiss his acquaintance with Irish culture as insignificant or trivial, something to be ignored in our consideration of his works. The example of Joyce's relation to Irish popular culture serves as a reminder of the necessity of establishing the popular cultural background of writers who emerge from marginalized cultures, including cultures resulting from the assimilation of another linguistic tradition or marginalized colonial and postcolonial cultures like that of Ireland. The use of the *United Irishman* as an index to Joyce's popular cultural background offers a methodological model for such investigations.

Joyce's interest in Irish literature and Irish culture is manifest not only in the mythic contents of his works but in the manipulation of those contents, in his narrative mode, and in his poetics; these various features of his work can be related to aspects of the discourse about Irish cultural nationalism in the periodical literature and in general intellectual life in

Ireland at the turn of the century. Joyce was neither a Hyde, able to write a literary history of Ireland, nor a Lady Gregory, able to collect folklore in Irish or translate and systematically retell much of the early Irish literary corpus; nevertheless, far from being lukewarm to Irish literature and the Irish renaissance, Joyce found congenial the journal most sympathetic to the Irish cultural revival in both its artistic and political reflexes. By his choice of the *United Irishman* as regular reading and his estimation of it as the best of the lot Ireland had to offer, Joyce was among the most concerned and best educated on the topic of early Irish history and literature among his contemporaries, leaving aside those who were specialists. Accordingly, he must be repositioned with respect to the other writers of the Anglo-Irish literary revival; his criticisms of the authors of that movement emerge from a context of his own interest in, knowledge of, and commitment to Irish literary, historical, and political questions, from an informed position that went beyond the common knowledge of his time.

Chapter 8

Monographs and Scholarly Sources

BOYLE: "Mr. Nugent," says I, "Father Farrell is a man o' the people, an', as far as I know the History o' me country, the priests was always in the van of the fight for Irelan's freedom." . . . "Who are you tellin'?" says he. "Didn't they let down the Fenians, an' didn't they do in Parnell? An' now . . ." "You ought to be ashamed o' yourself," says I, interruptin' him, "not to know the History o' your country." An' I left him gawkin' where he was.

JOXER: Where ignorance's bliss 'tis folly to be wise; I wondher did he ever read the Story o' Irelan'.

BOYLE: Be J. L. Sullivan? Don't you know he didn't.

JOXER: Ah, it's a darlin' buk, a daarlin' buk!

Sean O'Casey, *Juno and the Paycock*

From popular sources and oral culture Joyce had obtained a general fund of knowledge about early Irish literature. At several periods of his life he apparently added to this fund by reading monographs and more scholarly sources related to Irish literature, particularly when he studied the Irish language in 1901–2 and again, it would seem, when he was writing both *Ulysses* and *Finnegans Wake*. Such specific readings are often the most difficult of Joyce's sources to determine, as John Kelleher has illustrated with respect to *Finnegans Wake*:

In the best of circumstances it is difficult to prove that Joyce used a particular book for a particular word or passage in *Finnegans Wake* or, if obviously it was the source, that he knew it at first-hand and did not merely hear of it from some informant or temporary assistant. With most Irish allusions the difficulty is compounded by the fact that Joyce was born, raised and schooled in Ireland and that his fantastic memory was stored with all kinds of Irish lore, literary and popular. How then are we to say of any apparent reference to an Irish book that Joyce actually looked at the book while working on the *Wake*, or that he remembered having read it when he was young or that he just knew of it in the way that each of us knows the title or general substance of many books he has not read? ("Identifying the Irish Printed Sources" 161)[1]

We may see prima facie evidence of familiarity with a book or a story, but in the absence of a request to Aunt Josephine, or a notesheet with quotes, we cannot be certain whether Joyce actually read any particular monograph or whether he might have known of the material at second hand from the type of source considered in the preceding chapter. In this chapter I consider monographs and scholarly sources for the Irish literary and historical material in *Ulysses* that we have evidence Joyce knew.

i. Joyce's knowledge of Modern Irish

It is well known that Joyce, like many people in Ireland at the turn of the century, spent time learning Modern Irish. The pressure to learn Irish is thematized in *A Portrait of the Artist* in Davin's conversation with Stephen Dedalus: "Then be one with us, said Davin. Why don't you learn Irish? Why did you drop out of the league class after the first lesson?" (202). In the last decade of the nineteenth century the Gaelic League had made learning Irish a nationalist act—an act that distinguished the "Irish" from "West Britons." This is the point behind the conversation between Miss Ivors and Gabriel Conroy in "The Dead" when she reproaches him for his reviews in the *Daily Express* and criticizes his vacation plans and his language learning as well:

---

1. It is well to remember Clive Hart's warning that Joyce was not often a great reader, particularly later in his life, and that it is wise to be guarded in one's assumptions about the depth of his literary background (Power, *Conversations with James Joyce*, foreword 5). Garvin (227) notes as well that Joyce got people to summarize or mark books for him.

— And why do you go to France and Belgium, said Miss Ivors, instead of visiting your own land?

— Well, said Gabriel, it's partly to keep in touch with the languages and partly for a change.

— And haven't you your own language to keep in touch with—Irish? asked Miss Ivors. (*D* 189)

The language movement was a central feature of Irish cultural nationalism, and study of Irish became a test of an individual's nationalism, as Joyce indicates in these passages.

Not a great deal is known about Joyce's engagement with Modern Irish. In *My Brother's Keeper* Stanislaus Joyce says: "First among [Joyce's friendships] was George Clancy ('Davin'), who became a teacher of Irish. . . . As a student, Clancy was an Irish language enthusiast. . . . It was under his influence that my brother studied Irish for a year or two" (175). Joyce's instructor was Patrick Pearse, the Irish nationalist and future martyr of the 1916 Easter Rising, so it is reasonable to suppose that Joyce got a good deal of politics along with his language tuition, much of it nauseating to Joyce, as the portrait of Hughes in *Stephen Hero* indicates. Joyce engaged in these Irish lessons at the time when he was busy acquiring a number of modern European languages, including French, Italian, German, and Dano-Norwegian (cf. *JJ2* 59–61, 75–76); his interest in Irish can thus be related as much to his major area of university studies as to an interest in cultural nationalism. Indeed, it would have been strange had a student of modern languages totally ignored the Irish language movement burgeoning around him in view of the intrinsic linguistic interest of Celtic languages in general and Irish in particular. It is probably not irrelevant that in *Stephen Hero* Daedalus, lured to Irish classes by his attraction to Emma Clery, gives as his acknowledged reason for learning Irish, "I would like to learn it—as a language" (55).

Joyce gives a rather dismal picture of Gaelic League Irish classes in *Stephen Hero* (59ff.), and the portrait of the teacher Hughes—bad poet, monomaniacal hibernophile, and artistic philistine—is not an attractive view of Pearse (59–63, 82–83, 103–4). Joyce later told Budgen he stopped attending classes because Pearse insisted on denigrating English in favor of Irish (Budgen, *Further Recollections of James Joyce* 323), and the picture of Hughes as Pearse offers sufficient reason to quit the classes. But Joyce also notes in *Stephen Hero* that the books used were those of

Father O'Growney, the standard Gaelic League grammars; these are very simple chapbooks whose tuition hardly goes beyond the simple declarative sentence.[2] Moreover, although most students learned quickly and worked very hard, the progress of the class "was retarded by the stupidity of two of the young men" (*SH* 60). An able language learner like Joyce would have found such a learning environment stultifying at best and more like maddening. What Joyce's real mastery of the language came to be remains difficult to assess, but it must be remembered that he was gifted at languages: he graduated from University College in modern languages and worked professionally as a language teacher. He lived and worked comfortably in foreign-language environments, switching from English to Italian, German, and French with ease. He taught himself Norwegian so that he could read Ibsen in the original. With this sort of orientation, it would have been extraordinary had Joyce *not* learned a credible amount of Modern Irish in "a year or two," especially considering the political import of the language movement, even given the obstacles of the depressing classes Joyce portrays.[3]

Joyce's accomplishments in Modern Irish can be judged by a number of indices largely related to the Irish that he incorporates in *Finnegans Wake*. Not only is there a large Irish lexical repertory in the *Wake*, but it is clear from the puns on other Irish words, and also interlingual puns, that Joyce had Irish "in his ears": he had more than a bookish knowledge of the language. His usage of phonetic spellings (O Hehir xi) fits with this hypothesis. There are grammatical constructions in the Irish in *Finnegans Wake* (including errors that may have been intentional, as similar errors in English are; cf. O Hehir ix) and some idioms as well, indicating that Joyce knew more than just Irish words: he had some facility with the morphology and syntax of the language, including an understanding of the initial mutations.

Many of the Irish expressions in *Finnegans Wake* are proper names, including place names, tribal names, and personal names. Joyce and his brother had the practice of etymologizing names during their walks in Dublin (O Hehir viii), and that interest in names is reflected in Joyce's naming in his literary work as a whole, his verbal realism in *Ulysses* and

---

2. A line from O'Growney is quoted in *Ulysses* 9.366; cf. Schutte 38–39.
3. Cf. O Hehir (vii), who comes to a similar conclusion.

elsewhere, and the punning on Irish names in *Finnegans Wake*. There are other stray indications of Joyce's facility in Irish in his other works, including the punning on *Banba* discussed in chapter 4 and, curiously, the triad of things that, Stephen remembers, an Irishman ought to avoid: "Horn of a bull, hoof of a horse, smile of a Saxon" (1.732). Although Joyce may have known an English version from oral sources, the Irish source may be the Irish column in the *Freeman's Journal* entitled "Le h'aghaidh na nGaedhilgeoiridhe," which appeared during the period Joyce was working on his Irish; on 3 March 1902 the column gives an English translation accompanying the Irish text, and the translation reads, "Shun the smile of the Saxon, the bull's forehead, the snarling of a dog, and the hind-part of a stallion," and goes on to comment, "The Irish cannot avoid the deceitful smile of the Saxon."⁴ Joyce knows enough about Irish senchas to pare the saying down to the traditional form of a triad and to translate it in a way that captures the pithy quality of the original. His translation also introduces alliteration, which is common in many Irish precepts. In *Ulysses* Stephen is presented as one who knows Irish expressions, who can understand simple Irish when it is spoken, and who has Irish words and phrases come to mind in appropriate circumstances.

Citing the growing number of Irish words in Joyce's texts between *Dubliners* and *Finnegans Wake*, Kenneth Nilsen observes, "It might seem reasonable to assume that Joyce's knowledge of Irish was at its high point in the early years of this century but a look at his writings seems to indicate exactly the opposite" (24). After writing *Ulysses* Joyce continued his interest in Irish, and in 1939 he retained in his possession two dictionaries of Irish, including an abridgment of Patrick Dinneen's standard dictionary of Irish, entitled *A Smaller Irish-English Dictionary for the Use of Schools* (1923; Connolly #58 and #271; cf. O Hehir vii–viii).⁵ Though the possession of these works indicates a significant interest in

4. The Irish text reads, "Seachain gáire sacsanach, éadan tairbh, dranntadh madaidh, agus deireadh staile"; cf. O Hehir (337), who also gives the Irish of this tetrad. Cf. Thornton (*Allusions in "Ulysses"* 26) and Gifford (27) for additional English sources for the expression.

5. In July 1924 Joyce also wrote to Larbaud some simple observations regarding features of Irish orthography and phonology and indicating that the borrowings from Latin and Norman French are relatively restricted. The content of the letter does not say much for Joyce's Irish, but his willingness to speak with some authority does. See *Letters* 1: 217–18.

the language, the fact that he added the Irish to *Finnegans Wake* after the first draft suggests that Irish was not natural to him (O Hehir ix). O Hehir concludes that he had "elementary and common Irish," though the fact that it is the second of the languages listed as contributing to the *Wake* indicates its importance to Joyce in that work.

Although Modern Irish is very different in its morphology from Old and Middle Irish, the syntax of the three states of the language has much that is continuous; moreover, the lexis of the three periods of Irish overlaps to a great extent. Thus, even the sort of facility in Modern Irish that Joyce seems to have acquired serves to make some elements of an early Irish text accessible to an attentive reader of a facing translation. The accessibility of the early texts was still greater when Joyce was learning Irish than it is today since the spelling reforms had not yet been instituted; thus, the spellings Joyce learned were those inherited from the medieval orthographical conventions, making the early texts more approachable from a lexical point of view than they are to those who currently learn Modern Irish. It follows, therefore, that any scholarly editions of medieval Irish texts that Joyce would have used for their translations would have offered partially transparent texts to him as well. If it is correct, as some scholars have suggested (Kelleher, "Irish History" 419), that Joyce read scholarly editions and facing translations of some early Irish stories at the time he was studying Irish or later in his life, thereby familiarizing himself with certain texts that he later used in the mythic structuring of his own works, he may have been able to make determinations on his own about certain of the more obvious features of the style of early Irish narrative. The argument that he knew the content or poetics of much of the early literature does not turn on this possibility, however. In any case the inclusion of a considerable Gaelic lexicon in *Finnegans Wake* indicates that Joyce did not forget his Irish once he went to the Continent: to the contrary, he seems to have augmented his knowledge. And where original Irish texts or scholarly sources are indicated for his architectonic structuring, it is not necessary to restrict Joyce's reading of these materials to the time before his departure from Ireland nor to restrict his knowledge of the texts purely to translations. Joyce seems to have renewed his interest in Irish materials whenever he had need of them for his own writing and whenever he had access to suitable collections of books, as he did both in Zurich and Paris.

ii. Monographs

It is quite possible to know the contents of a book sufficiently well to use the material in conversation or in artistic creation without having read the volume: this fact is obvious in daily life, but it is often forgotten in criticism. Reviews, conversation, lectures, classroom instruction—all summarize books in ways that make the contents utilizable to the audience. There are many monographs related to early Irish literature and culture that Joyce could have read either casually in his youth or more deliberately later in his life; the possibilities, indeed, are so large that the task of determining his possible reading almost defies definition. In picking out some few monographs for the following discussion I have focused on specific books as likely to have informed Joyce's thinking for one of the following reasons: the book was part of Joyce's library, particularly at the period when he was writing *Ulysses*; the book or author is mentioned by Joyce, either in one of his literary texts or in his letters or other papers; internal evidence in *Ulysses* suggests that the book underlies *Ulysses*; or the book was widely discussed in popular periodicals, so its contents had passed into the general discourse of Irish culture. Several foci of discussion emerge, not all of which result in commensurate categories. They are bound together by being likely materials known to Joyce, though his depth of knowledge may have been quite shallow in some cases. As with the knowledge gleaned from popular sources discussed in the previous chapter, Joyce's use of early Irish materials from book-length studies is usually general rather than specific, architectonic rather than detailed. Thus, a cursory reading, a conversation about the salient points of a monograph, or even a detailed summary in a review may have sufficed to fire his imagination in the directions we can trace.

Histories

Joyce pays tribute to Irish historians in a passage in *Finnegans Wake* in which various historical writers are cited as authorities (572.19–573.32).[6]

---

6. In *The Books at the Wake* James S. Atherton has identified these authors as well as other Irish historians mentioned throughout the text of *Finnegans Wake*; they include James Ware, Edward Alfred D'Alton, Charles Haliday, John T. Gilbert, Giraldus Cambrensis, Luke Wadding, D. A. Chart, J. M. Flood, John

Although James Atherton believes that in *Finnegans Wake* Joyce depended largely on the annals appended to *Thom's Directory*, he concludes that Joyce "probably . . . made use of all the Irish histories that he could find to write his own version of the History of Ireland" (93; cf. 90–93). In *Finnegans Wake* there are many references to modern historians, but Joyce's most extensive tribute is to Michael O'Clery, Conary O'Clery, Cucogry O'Clery, and Fearfesa O'Mulconry, who, better known as the "Four Masters," merge with the Four Evangelists and are essential elements in the mythic fabric of *Finnegans Wake*. The Four Masters are at the foundation of written Irish history, for it is their annals, compiled from much older books even as native Irish culture was crumbling in the seventeenth century, that constitute the main extant source for early Irish history. The standard edition of the Four Masters had been published with notes and translation in seven quarto volumes by John O'Donovan between 1848 and 1851, a work justly celebrated by Irish cultural nationalists. Discussions of the Four Masters are found in the periodical literature of the time—for example, in the *United Irishman* of 18 November 1899—and O'Grady had summarized the account of Irish prehistory to A.D. 432 from the Annals of the Four Masters in his *All Ireland Review*, as mentioned in chapter 7; there are also references to the Four Masters in the general histories and in school histories. Although, as Atherton believes (89), the Four Masters may not have been cited directly by Joyce in *Finnegans Wake*, he would have been aware from his youth that the Annals of the Four Masters were the fountainhead of Irish history, and this general knowledge suffices for the iconographic role of the Four Masters in his last work.

Lannigan, W. E. H. Lecky, Thomas Leland, Thomas D'Arcy McGee, P. S. O'Hegarty (whose work appeared after *Ulysses* was published), and Walter Harris. To this list should be added John D'Alton and Eoin Mac Neill as well (Kelleher, "Identifying the Irish Printed Sources" 166–67).

Atherton and Kelleher ("Identifying the Irish Printed Sources") have shown that Joyce used various passages from the historians he cites in *Finnegans Wake*, and Joyce probably did additional reading in the Irish histories after he wrote *Ulysses*. Although specific instances of textual borrowings may be discovered, it is very unlikely that Joyce had read all of the historians he cites. To have done so would have been tedium in the extreme as the material becomes exceedingly repetitious from volume to volume. The general contours of Irish history can be gleaned from a single study, and its outline would have in any case been familiar to Joyce from his schoolboy studies, as Kelleher indicates ("Identifying the Irish Printed Sources" 164–65).

If *Finnegans Wake* is Joyce's history of Ireland, *Ulysses* is his pseudohistory of Ireland; and because the majority of Irish general histories begin with a brief account of Irish pseudohistory, the historical sources that Joyce invokes in *Finnegans Wake* overlap to a considerable extent with sources for Irish pseudohistory that Joyce may have used earlier when he was working on *Ulysses*. The pseudohistory in the general histories is based on three major sources: *The Book of Invasions* and its attendant kinglist; the pseudohistorical entries in the Annals of the Four Masters, which are themselves dependent in part on *The Book of Invasions*; and the general history of Geoffrey Keating entitled *Foras Feasa ar Éirinn* (*The History of Ireland*). Keating, like the Four Masters, was a seventeenth-century historian composing from earlier sources; he includes summaries of *The Book of Invasions*, the major narratives of the Ulster Cycle, and other literary sources; and his work has served as the single major source of Irish tradition since his time.[7] In *Ulysses* I have found no specific use of editions of Keating, but it would be surprising if a close scrutiny of the Irish elements in *Finnegans Wake* failed to turn up significant allusions to Keating.

Certain textual allusions to traditional Irish pseudohistory in *Ulysses* do suggest that Joyce used some written sources for his pseudohistorical framework from *The Book of Invasions*. These references—like the title of the book itself, which signals the relationship to Greek myth—are also overt indicators of the mythic structure of the book. The first allusion refers to the intersection of Hebrew and Irish in Irish pseudohistory, an intersection that in turn leads outward to Vallancey's theories of the Phoenician origin of the Irish and to Bérard's theories of the Phoenician origin of the *Odyssey*:

What points of contact existed between these languages and between the peoples who spoke them?

The presence of guttural sounds, diacritic aspirations, epenthetic and servile letters in both languages: their antiquity, both having been taught on the plain of Shinar 242 years after the deluge in the seminary instituted by Fenius

---

7. Several early editions of Keating had appeared before *Ulysses* was published (see Best, *Bibliography* [1913] 255), but the standard edition by Patrick Dinneen was published in four volumes by the Irish Texts Society between 1902 and 1914, a period during which Joyce was particularly interested in Irish culture. As mentioned above, Dinneen was one of the professors at University College, and later in life Joyce owned his shorter Irish dictionary.

Farsaigh, descendant of Noah, progenitor of Israel, and ascendant of Heber and Heremon, progenitors of Ireland. (17.745–51)[8]

It is difficult to establish Joyce's particular written source for this passage, as I have been unable to find any edition of either *The Book of Invasions* or Keating that includes these spellings of the name *Fenius Farsaigh* and of the location *Shinar*; the latter has apparently been normalized by Joyce to the standard spelling in English Bibles, while the former is widespread enough to be indeterminate. Like traditional Irish historians before him Joyce here relies on a genealogy to encapsulate the broader affinities he is working with in *Ulysses*.

Joyce makes another oblique reference to traditional Irish pseudohistory in *Ulysses* by giving Bloom an Irish genealogy in episode 12: "Who comes through Michan's land, bedight in sable armour? O'Bloom, the son of Rory: it is he. Impervious to fear is Rory's son: he of the prudent soul" (12.215–17). Originally a Hungarian genealogy, "O'Bloom, the son of Rudolph the son of Leopold Peter, son of Peter Rudolph," Joyce changed it to a traditional Irish one (Groden 141), emphasizing *Rory* by the chiastic order and repetition. Although *Rory*, Old Irish *Rudraige*, occurs frequently in the Middle Irish and early Modern Irish period, the name is most famous as the traditional ancestor of the Ulster Cycle heroes in the genealogical tract entitled *Senchas Síl Ír*. Rudraige, in turn, is traced genealogically to the Milesian invaders of Ireland.[9] Thus, Joyce styles Bloom both as an Ulster hero and as a Milesian in the episode, humorously evoking the heroic and pseudohistorical literature of Ireland by a typical Irish genealogical connection.

Though *Ulysses* is primarily a refraction of Irish pseudohistory rather than Irish history, there is internal evidence that Joyce had been dipping

---

8. The passage goes on to suggest the "two peoples theme" in invoking "their dispersal, persecution, survival and revival." It is also interesting that Joyce notes the presence of gutturals in both Irish and Hebrew, since in *Stephen Hero* he writes about the Irish classes, "Stephen found it very troublesome to pronounce the gutturals but he did the best he could" (60).

9. The traditional genealogies are found in M. O'Brien (270–86), but Rudraige's name and genealogical indicators occur frequently in the Ulster Cycle tales, including *Táin Bó Cúailnge*, as well as in historical materials including Keating and the Four Masters.

Thornton (*Allusions in "Ulysses"* 266) identifies Rory in the genealogy with the last high king of Ireland; given Joyce's way of conflating mythic figures, he probably has both figures in mind, with the latter pointing to the Sovereignty themes in *Ulysses*.

into the Irish histories before 1921, when he was writing "Ithaca," for in that episode there is a synchronism of the ages of Leopold and Stephen that forms a nice parody of the type of synchronism found in some early modern histories of Ireland. The parody begins:

What relation existed between their ages?
16 years before in 1888 when Bloom was of Stephen's present age Stephen was 6. 16 years after in 1920 when Stephen would be of Bloom's present age Bloom would be 54. In 1936 when Bloom would be 70 and Stephen 54 their ages initially in the ration of 16 to 0 would be as 17½ to 13½, the proportion increasing and the disparity diminishing according as arbitrary future years were added, for if the proportion existing in 1883 had continued immutable, conceiving that to be possible, till then 1904 when Stephen was 22 Bloom would be 374 and in 1920 when Stephen would be 38, as Bloom then was, Bloom would be 646 while in 1952 when Stephen would have attained the maximum postdiluvian age of 70 Bloom, being 1190 years alive having been born in the year 714, would have surpassed by 221 years the maximum antediluvian age, that of Methusalah, 969 years, while, if Stephen would continue to live until he would attain that age in the year 3072 A.D., Bloom would have been obliged to have been alive 83,300 years, having been obliged to have been born in the year 81,396 B.C. (17.446–61)

This amusing passage plays on the relation of the ages of Stephen and Bloom, Joyce's two masks in this book, picking out key dates in Joyce's own life (since his chronology coincides with that of Stephen). At the same time, by projecting an immense life span for his two characters, Joyce takes them out of the time frame of realistic fiction and places them in the mythic framework of time-before-our-time, the time scale of biblical history and *The Book of Invasions*.[10]

We may compare this passage with part of a synchronism from Roderic O'Flaherty's *Ogygia, or a Chronological Account of Irish Events*, published in Latin in 1685 and translated by James Hely into English in 1793:

From the birth of Phaleg, to the eightieth year of Moses, the space of 695 years has elapsed; of which let us grant that Nuil was 60 years later, or even as they say a hundred and seven; but 588 years, which remain will be made up by multiplying 42, the age of Nuil, a generation, by 14, so many generations as were between them, and each of the four generations, which they only allow, required 147 years for a generation.

10. For an interesting discussion of the passage and its errors, see McCarthy 608–9.

But let us suppose Nuilus, according to the ideas of these ideots [*sic*] who give the longevity of our ancestors, as a pretext to unravel all these difficult and irreconcilable matters, was 500 years old, when sent for by Pharaoh, to the marriage of his daughter, and that he propagated an offspring to the fourth generation in 81 years. Abraham indeed was four hundred years prior to this Mosaic period, and even then, instances of people at an advanced age, having issue, began to be less frequent. (102)

O'Flaherty's text, like Joyce's, seems to be a parody of itself, not only because history is not done this way any more but because belief in biblical chronology has diminished considerably: the Bible has been demythologized. But traditional Irish pseudohistory upon which Joyce relies in *Ulysses* requires a suspension of positivist belief, a resumption of a mythologized perspective on both time and space. Such a perspective is assumed in many of the general histories of Ireland including some, such as *The Story of the Irish Race* (1921) by Seumas MacManus, written well into the twentieth century; in this regard the historiography of both *Ulysses* and *Finnegans Wake* is typical of Irish historiography as a whole.

For a convenient example of the persistence of a mythological perspective on space in the early histories, we may again turn to O'Flaherty. In discussing the names given to Ireland in antiquity, he makes the following argument about the island:

Whether this be Plutarch's *Ogygia*, which he places to the west of Britain, in his book of the Moon's appearance in her course, as some assert; or whether it be the contrary, as others think, is all the same to me. For I have intitled my book *Ogygia*, for the following reason given by Camden: "Ireland is justly called Ogygia, i.e. *very antient*, according to Plutarch, for the Irish date their history from the first aeras of the world; so that in comparison with them, the antiquity of all other countries is modern, and almost in its infancy!" The poets, as Rhodogonus says, call any thing *Ogygium*, as if you should say, very old, from *Ogyges*, the most antient. Likewise it appears, that Egypt was called Ogygia for this reason: for the Egyptians are said to be the most antient people in the world; and they have discovered and invented many useful arts and sciences which the Greeks borrowed and introduced into their own country; whererefore [*sic*] Egypt has been stiled the *parent* of the *universe*, and the *mistress* of *arts* and *sciences*. (34)

Throughout the nineteenth century the identification of Ireland with Ogygia is taken up by historians and lay writers alike, and it is obvious that this aspect of pseudohistory would have been attractive to Joyce in his own enterprise of coordinating Greek and Irish mythos in *Ulysses*. When, therefore, Joyce opens the second part of *Ulysses* with the episode of Calypso, identifying 7 Eccles Street as Ogygia, he is paradoxically opening the book in Ireland. There is a dubletting not only of Molly's role (Calypso/Penelope) but of space (Calypso's island/Ireland); at the same time the home (7 Eccles Street/Ireland) also stands for Ithaca. Thus, the geographical presuppositions of episode 18, where Gibraltar-as-otherworld folds over onto Ireland, are anticipated in episode 4, with its pseudohistorical underpinning in Irish tradition.[11]

The way in which history per se, including materials from the annals appended to *Thom's Directory*, impinges upon the contents of *Ulysses* has been adequately discussed in the critical literature and is beyond the scope of concern here. In general the Irish histories that have left the most significant traces in *Ulysses* include books, such as O'Flaherty's *Ogygia* and Vallancey's theories, which have a pseudohistorical quality to them. Despite the realistic surface to the narrative, the logos in *Ulysses* is mythical and pseudohistorical; history per se in the book has a relatively short temporal span and is relatively local in its focus. Only in *Finnegans Wake* does Joyce begin to integrate history in a more universal sense. Joyce's mixture of history, pseudohistory, and myth in both books, however, is typically Irish and should be attributed in part to his reading of Irish history, for the way in which history and pseudohistory blend even in the modern histories and annals of Ireland—or, as we might put it, the way in which history and literature blend—exemplifies the archaism of Irish tradition right up to the twentieth century. Elsewhere in Europe this blend is characteristic of medieval thought rather than later historiography, and it is one aspect of Joyce's thought that gives his writing a medieval temper.[12]

Studies by P. W. Joyce

In 1909 in answer to an inquiry by G. Molyneux Palmer, who was setting some of Joyce's poems to music, James Joyce wrote: "I have never seen *Billy Byrne* printed: but I am sure my namesake, Dr P. W. Joyce, will be

11. But Calypso's island could also be identified with Gibraltar (cf. Seidel, esp. 27–28), so the folding over of locations is even more complex.

12. Thus, Joyce would have become familiar with many of the medieval Irish sagas and stories through his study of history as well as through reading literature.

able to tell you where it has been printed. If not you could ask Mr Best of the *Feis Ceoil*" (*Letters* 1: 66). Patrick Weston Joyce is here credited as an authority on Irish music, seconded only by R. I. Best of the National Library, a figure discussed in the last chapter. In 1935, when Joyce was advising his son, Giorgio, about Irish songs that the latter might sing, he wrote that he intended to send a collection by P. W. Joyce that was in his possession: "I have an enormous collection of Irish folk music collected by Petrie and another lot by Joyce (P. W.) I shall send this out soon." This collection is evidently *Irish Peasant Songs in the English Language*, the publication that seemingly led Joyce to recommend his "namesake" to Palmer in 1909; in a postscript to the letter Joyce tells his son that apparently the composer Antheil had made off with Joyce's copy of the book (*Letters* 3: 343–44).

P. W. Joyce, LL.D., was one of the foremost authorities on Irish history, culture, topography, literature, and music of his day. One of the Commissioners for the Publication of the Ancient Laws of Ireland and president of the Royal Society of Antiquaries, P. W. Joyce was the author of many publications that still read today, even to a Celticist, as essentially sound, albeit early, investigations of the varied subject matter they cover.[13] In addition to his publications on music, P. W. Joyce is known for geographical and topographical works, most notably *Irish Local Names Explained* (1870) and *The Origin and History of Irish Names of Places* (3 vols.; 1869, 1870, 1913), as well as *The Geography of the Counties of Ireland with a General Description of the Country* (1883) and *The Wonders of Ireland* (1911). He was the author of books on the Irish and English languages, including *English as We Speak It in Ireland* (1910), *A Grammar of the Irish Language* (1878), and a student's edition of the initial sections of Keating's history (*Forus Feasa air Eirinn: Keating's History of Ireland*, 1886). His literary adaptations and translations in *Old Celtic Romances* (1879; rev. ed. 1894) were widely read. P. W. Joyce's major works include his social histories of Ireland, particularly *A Social History of Ancient Ireland* (2 vols., 1903), *A Smaller Social History of Ancient Ireland* (1906), and *The Story of Ancient Irish Civilisation* (1907), the latter two of which represent a condensation and a popularization respectively of the larger work. He was perhaps best known for a series

13. It should go without saying that much in P. W. Joyce's work has been superseded by the scholarship of this century.

of histories of Ireland, primarily *A Short History of Ireland from the Earliest Times to 1608* (1893, 565 pp.), as well as various condensations and adaptations of the longer work, including *A Concise History of Ireland from the Earliest Times to 1837* (1893; the twenty-fourth edition appeared in 1920), and *A Child's History of Ireland* (1897), which was later reissued as *An Illustrated History of Ireland* (1919).

P. W. Joyce was widely cited in the popular press; as mentioned in the last chapter, for example, his *Social History of Ancient Ireland* was discussed and implicitly recommended to readers by the author of the article on "The Everyday Celt" in the *Leader*, and in one of his discussions of localism cited above, William Rooney had recommended to readers of the *United Irishman* P. W. Joyce's *Irish Names of Places*. James Joyce apparently knew the latter well enough to refer appropriately to the book in his satire "Gas from a Burner," attributing to George Roberts of Maunsel and Company, who reneged on publishing *Dubliners* when it was already in sheets (*JJ*2 334ff.), the following words supposedly likening *Dubliners* to P. W. Joyce's work:

> Shite and onions! Do you think I'll print
> The name of the Wellington Monument,
> Sydney Parade and Sandymount tram,
> Downes's cakeshop and Williams's jam?
> I'm damned if I do—I'm damned to blazes!
> Talk about *Irish Names of Places*!
> It's a wonder to me, upon my soul,
> He forgot to mention Curly's Hole.
>
> (*CW* 244)

In 1939 a 1921 edition of the third volume of *Irish Names of Places* was part of Joyce's working library (Connolly #164). P. W. Joyce's work is a likely source for some of James Joyce's knowledge of the Irish tradition of dindšenchas. That James Joyce characterizes *Dubliners* as a kind of modern urban analogue to P. W. Joyce's *Irish Names of Places*, particularly as the role of topography and localism in *Ulysses* is even more marked, suggests he was aware of the ways in which his own work fit into this aspect of Irish literary tradition.[14] The comparison reinforces

---

14. Joyce's statement also supports Nilsen's argument about the Irish etymological significance of proper names in *Dubliners* since P. W. Joyce emphasizes etymological meanings in much of his work.

Joyce's reference to P. W. Joyce as his "namesake" and suggests that James Joyce felt an identification and affinity with this scholar of early Irish material, not unlike the sort of affinity he felt for James Stephens because of the sharing of a name and a birth year. These factors, as well as his ownership of a 1921 edition of P. W. Joyce's *Illustrated History* in 1939 (Connolly #163), indicate that all of P. W. Joyce's works should be considered as possible sources for James Joyce's conceptualization of Irish history and culture.[15]

Some of P. W. Joyce's works are most relevant as sources for material in *Finnegans Wake*; in particular, his history texts are handy compendia of the many periods of Irish history incorporated into James Joyce's later work. It is important to note that certain works of P. W. Joyce, particularly his *Social History of Ancient Ireland* in two volumes, appeared during the period before Joyce left Ireland but after he had studied Irish and done some initial study of Irish traditions; even if James Joyce did not read the text of P. W. Joyce's *Social History*, he would have absorbed some of the content since the materials in these volumes were discussed in popular sources and to some extent circulated orally. The *Social History* and its condensations contain significant discussions of the role of the Irish poet as well as important materials on Irish prosody. In these books P. W. Joyce also discusses such questions as the importance of music to the Irish, the preservation of Irish genealogies, and the workings of dindsenchas as a combination of legendary history and the etymology of names. He does not try to whitewash the moral tone of early Irish legends, noting, "As to the general moral tone of the ancient Irish tales, it is to be observed that in all early literatures, Irish among the rest, there is much plain speaking of a character that would now be considered coarse" (*Smaller Social History* 237).

Old Celtic Romances, which Stanley Sultan has suggested is the source of James Joyce's knowledge of *The Voyage of Mael Duin*, has in its preface a clear, if brief, statement about the mixture of history and fiction in Irish tales, a discussion of the mixture of poetry and prose in early texts, and comments about the tone of early Irish literature; P. W. Joyce notes also that his translations are not literal but instead attempt to capture the simple style and spirit of the original texts. The collection includes intro-

15. It is probably significant also that P. W. Joyce takes up Vallancey's theory of the Phoenician origin of the Irish in his *Irish Names of Places* (1: 81).

ductions to both the voyage tales and the bruiden tales, stressing the entrapment of the heroes by enchanters in the latter until "they are released by the bravery or mother-wit of some of their companions" (rev. ed., xiv); as a whole the stories in the volume would have provided James Joyce sufficient models for the motifs from early Irish adventures to the otherworld used in the Nighttown episode, while P. W. Joyce's commentary and introductory matter would have alerted James Joyce to the stylistic qualities of early Irish narratives.

In recommending P. W. Joyce and R. I. Best to Palmer, and in owning the music collections of Petrie and P. W. Joyce, James Joyce shows discrimination in his assessment of scholarly authorities on Irish tradition, for P. W. Joyce, Petrie, and Best were indeed among the most reputable writers on Irish topics. Joyce's discernment in this regard is consistent with the earlier observation that as a regular reader of the *United Irishman* he was among the more knowledgeable of the general public with respect to early Irish subject matters. Joyce's apparent interest in P. W. Joyce is particularly important, for P. W. Joyce is an author who balances scholarly sobriety with readability; his translations are literary rather than philological, and his works show a concern to communicate serious material about Irish literature and culture to a broad audience. Thus, his "namesake" sets a context for James Joyce's treatments of the same domain.

Henri d'Arbois de Jubainville

Joyce's exposure to *Le cycle mythologique irlandais et la mythologie celtique* (1884) by Henri d'Arbois de Jubainville (translated by R. I. Best as *The Irish Mythological Cycle*) has been documented. Among monographs that may have served to introduce Joyce to early Irish literature and history, other works by d'Arbois de Jubainville are excellent possibilities. D'Arbois de Jubainville was professor at the Sorbonne, lecturing on Celtic literature for many years, including the period that Joyce was in Paris in 1902–3. Although his list of publications is extensive, he was perhaps best known for the twelve-volume set published under his general editorship as *Cours de littérature celtique*, of which *Le cycle mythologique irlandais* was volume 2. The other titles in the series include *Introduction à l'étude de la littérature celtique* (vol. 1, 1883), a French translation of the *Mabinogi* (by J. Loth, vols. 3–4, 1889), *L'épopée cel-*

tique en Irlande (vol. 5, 1892), *La civilisation des Celtes et celle de l'épo-pée homérique* (vol. 6, 1899), *Études sur le droit celtique* (vols. 7–8, 1895), *La métrique galloise* (by J. Loth, vols. 9–11, 1900–1902), and *Principaux auteurs de l'antiquité à consulter sur l'histoire des celtes* (vol. 12, 1902). Although d'Arbois de Jubainville was not responsible for all the work in the series (as indicated above, J. Loth prepared the Welsh material in vols. 3–4 and 9–11, and other scholars contributed to vol. 5), his contribution to the series was substantial.

In the first volume of the series, *Introduction à l'étude de la littérature celtique,* Joyce would have found a rather full discussion of the Irish learned classes, including the druids and the poets; thirty-two chapters are devoted to these topics, and the discussion includes comments on the poets' satire as well as their second sight. An introduction to early Irish literature includes information on the genres of tales as well as material about the tale lists of medieval Ireland. In short, this volume contains everything that Joyce would have needed to know about the role of the early Irish *fili* as well as the poet's narrative output, material that may have influenced the poetics of *Ulysses.* The fifth volume of the series, *L'épopée celtique en Irlande,* is also important, since it contains rather close yet accessible translations of many of the most important early Irish tales; these translations are more representative of some of the narrative features of the tradition (such as the inconsistencies, the formal alterna-tion between poetry and prose, and the humor) than are the translations produced in English under the constraints of Irish cultural nationalism. The book contains the major tales of the Ulster Cycle as well as signifi-cant stories from the Finn Cycle; in it is also to be found a version of *The Voyage of Mael Duin.* Brief but useful guides to the tales include impor-tant introductory information—for example, the observation that in Irish stories as in Greek tales, love between a mortal and an immortal is not rare (170). Moreover, an introduction to the imrama includes the follow-ing: "Les Irlandais ont plusieurs voyages fantastiques sur mer, *imm-ram,* au pluriel *imm-rama.* Cette littérature ne leur est pas spéciale. Le voyage des Argonautes, dont l'auteur de l'*Odyssée* connaissait déjà une rédac-tion, a été un des plus anciens monuments de ce genre de composition; l'*Odyssée* en est un second" (449). The importance of *La civilisation des Celtes et celle de l'épopée homérique,* sixth in the series, is self-evident; it includes a comparison of early Irish hero tale with Greek epic, appro-

priately enough since Irish hero tale is in many ways closer to Greek heroic stories than to other medieval epics.

The Irish Mythological Cycle, however, remains the most important
book of the series for Joyce's purposes in Ulysses. Its thrust—like the
mythological structuring of Ulysses—is to equate Greek and Irish mythos
by comparing or juxtaposing the two. D'Arbois de Jubainville's presentations of The Book of Invasions (on which the book is based; see p. xv)
and of Balor, Tailltiu, and metempsychosis have already been discussed.
In light of the Sovereignty imagery in Ulysses it is significant that d'Arbois
de Jubainville states that the "Celtic race . . . worshipped at one time a
female divinity whose name in Great Britain at the time of the Roman
domination was Brigantia . . . while in mediaeval Ireland she was called
Brigit"; he derives the names from the root brig, 'superiority, power, authority' (82–83). The book presents the victory of the Milesians over the
Tuatha De as a parallel to the story of Prometheus (132–35), suggesting
a reading of Ulysses in which the haughty Stephen with his Olympian
ideals cedes to the all-too-human Bloom; it suggests the irony, as well,
behind Joyce's comment that Bloomsday was the day that made him a
man (JJ2 156). In chapter 10 d'Arbois de Jubainville discusses the Spanish origin of the Irish, citing as well Alcuin's comment to Charlemagne,
in which the Irish are called Egyptians (128). The comparative perspective of the book is notable and would appeal to a cultural nationalist:
"Celtic mythology is not copied from Greek mythology. It is based upon
conceptions originally identical with those from which Greek mythology
is derived, but has developed the fundamental elements of the myth in a
manner of her own, which is as independent as it is original" (165). And
again, "Ireland . . . borrowed nothing from Greece. The characteristics
common to Irish and to Greek mythology come from an old foundation
of Graeco-Celtic legends anterior to the separation of the two races" (69).
These views are not unique to d'Arbois de Jubainville, but he gives a clear
formulation of a position that facilitates the correlation of the two mythologies, even as it validates both.[16]

16. In d'Arbois de Jubainville's Les Celtes depuis les temps les plus anciens
Joyce might have found a detailed account of the Phoenician influence on the Ibe-
rian peninsula (chs. 10, 18); in view of theories about the Spanish origin of the
Irish, this discussion supports the kinds of views put forth by Vallencey, for example.

The authority of d'Arbois de Jubainville would have been recommended to Joyce in several instances. Although publication of *The Irish
Mythological Cycle* by the *United Irishman* in 1901–2 may have brought
this scholar to Joyce's attention initially, announced as it was by a generous tribute to d'Arbois de Jubainville (*United Irishman* 26 Oct. 1901)
and followed by an interview with him as the series was in progress
(*United Irishman* 11 Jan. 1902), when Joyce was in Paris in 1902–3 he
would also have heard about d'Arbois de Jubainville's lectures and publications, if not through general intellectual circles, then from J. M.
Synge, who had attended some of those lectures. The writings of d'Arbois
de Jubainville would have served Joyce as an ideal critical entry to the
original Celtic texts in translation and would have provided him with a
less narrowly nationalistic perspective on early Irish literature than that
promulgated by Irish cultural nationalism. The Continental perspective
of such scholars as d'Arbois de Jubainville as well as those trained in such
a perspective (like Synge) is reflected in Joyce's use of early Irish literature.
What can be seen as a revisionist use of Irish myth in Joyce's writings or
a demythologizing of Irish literature may be in the first instance an application of a Continental perspective on Celtic literature. This perspective on Irish literature was reinforced by the philological framework for
Celtic studies that Joyce encountered in Zurich (discussed below). Because Joyce had access to the complete run of d'Arbois de Jubainville's
Cours de la littérature celtique in Zurich as well as in Paris, any reading
in this author's monographs during Joyce's early years could have been
followed up at the period he was writing *Ulysses*.

The Voyage of Bran

One of the most influential publications about early Irish literature at the
turn of the century was the edition of *Imram Brain* by Kuno Meyer. Published in two volumes in 1895 and 1897 by David Nutt under the title
The Voyage of Bran, the book includes Meyer's editions and translations
of texts with parallels to *The Voyage of Bran*, as well as two essays by
Alfred Nutt, "The Happy Otherworld" in the first volume and *The Celtic
Doctrine of Re-birth*, which constitutes the whole of the second. The
prima facie relation of the themes and imagery of *Ulysses* to Meyer's
book have been traced, particularly in the construction of Molly's Gi-

braltar and in the doctrine of metempsychosis that underlies the mythic framework of Joyce's book.

Moreover, the ideas in Nutt's critical essays would have buttressed d'Arbois de Jubainville's views of the happy otherworld and reincarnation and shapeshifting as discussed in *The Irish Mythological Cycle*. Nutt, like the French scholar, uses a comparative method, focusing in the first essay on the relationship of Greek concepts of the happy otherworld to similar Irish concepts; he concludes that the Irish idea of the happy otherworld is closest to that of the Greeks. In a similar fashion, his essay on the doctrine of rebirth or metempsychosis compares Greek and Celtic ideas of rebirth, stressing their differences but concluding that they derive from common ideas, with the Celtic texts representing a more ancient layer of ideation. Nutt's essays are important not merely for their content related to the themes and motifs of *Ulysses* but also for the methodology, the enterprise of welding together Irish and Greek myth found also in *Ulysses*.

Some of the observations Nutt makes about the Irish happy otherworld are particularly interesting in relation to *Ulysses*. Nutt slyly contends that "quatrain 41 of Bran's Voyage gives a picture of the island Elysium from which one gathers that it must have resembled Hampstead Heath on an Autumn Bank Holiday evening. The trait is not confined to Bran's Voyage. Unlimited love-making is one of the main constituents in all the early Irish accounts of Otherworld happiness" ("Happy Otherworld," 290–91). Nutt continues, "At a later stage of national development the stress laid upon this feature puzzled and shocked" (291). Clearly the sexual component of Joyce's otherworld has antecedents that had been noted in the critical literature of his day. In a discussion of the adventure of Loegaire mac Crimthainn, Nutt also observes that in this story, as in *The Sickbed of CuChulainn*, there are the motifs of "the wife who mourns the lost lover, but returns, not unwillingly, to the husband who willingly takes her back" (184). With some modification this could be a description of the emotional trajectory of *Ulysses*.

Concluding that the concept of the Irish happy otherworld is "substantially pre-Christian" (331), Nutt takes the view that it is "untouched by ethical speculation" (cf. 309). He notes, too, that some texts "humanise the Otherworld by minimising as much as possible the differences between its inhabitants and mortal men" (184), thus providing another link with the naturalized presentation in *Ulysses* of the otherworld as Gibraltar. Nutt notes also that presentations of the otherworld share a common literary method, not unrelated to the techniques in the final episode of *Ulysses*: "There is the same fondness for detail, the same richness of colour, the same achievement of effect by accumulation rather than by selection of images" (223). Finally, Nutt contends that "one poem, the Odyssey, . . . supplies parallels to all the salient traits of the Irish conception of the Happy Otherworld" (261). This comment may be seen as an invitation to overlay the Greek tale with an Irish mythological component.

Nutt's essay *The Celtic Doctrine of Re-birth* is equally provocative. There is important material in the essay related to the motif of metempsychosis in *Ulysses*; moreover, Nutt makes observations about Irish literature as a whole that are of interest in relation to Joyce's works. For example, he discusses the humorous tone of the stories, regarding "the Rabelaisian, Aristophanesque element" in *The Second Battle of Mag Tuired*, for example, "not as accidental and secondary, but as primary and essential"; he sees it as Dionysiac (180). Nutt discusses the cyclical and episodic nature of Irish narrative (192) as well as the euhemerization that pervades Irish myth (cf. 196). Equally important is Nutt's emphasis on the mythic nature of Irish literary tradition, a contention that may shed light on Joyce's own purposes for using narrative structured by myth:

We may again find in Greece at once a parallel and a contrast to the development of mythic literature in Ireland. Down to a certain period, alike the substance and the animating spirit of Greek literature are almost wholly drawn from the mythology, and down to that period the literature is national, accessible to, shared in, and understanded [*sic*] of all. . . . In Ireland there is nothing corresponding to the great break at the close of the fifth century B.C. between the Greek thinker and artist and the traditional mythology; the Irish man of letters never outgrew his archaic ideal. (202–3)

As even this brief discussion illustrates, *The Voyage of Bran* represents the nexus of several essential elements in *Ulysses*: the outlines of the Irish otherworld (including its free sexual mores), the theme of metempsychosis, the juxtaposition of Greek and Irish myth, a delineation of the humor in Irish myth, the humanization of the otherworld and the euhemerization of myth, and the validation of mythos as a vehicle of national unity. It seems likely that Joyce became acquainted with the study before he left Ireland in 1904, but it is difficult to document that Joyce actually read Nutt's essays and Meyer's translations of the early Irish texts pertaining to the other-world and metempsychosis. It is probable nonetheless that Joyce had read these volumes and been influenced by them, as the textual parallels with *Ulysses* are so extensive that they suggest Joyce had a more detailed knowledge of the volumes than the retailing of these texts in conversation and popular culture would have provided. Though *The Voyage of Bran* was not available in Zurich, it was to be found in Paris, where Joyce wrote the last episode of *Ulysses*, which shows the closest affinities to Meyer's publication; it is possible that Joyce reviewed the book at that time.

Táin Bó Cúailnge

Close parallels between *Táin Bó Cúailnge* and *Ulysses* make it virtually certain that Joyce had read a version of this tale by the time he was writing *Ulysses*. As one of the longest of the early Irish narratives and the one most often—and most easily—compared to other European epics, it was an important tale for Irish cultural nationalists; thus, even without the textual evidence in Joyce's work, there would be prima facie reason to believe that he was familiar with the story. Although it is easy to identify popular refractions of the tale that Joyce knew, such as the version in Gregory's *Cuchulain of Muirthemne*, there is reason to believe Joyce had read a version of the story in an extended or scholarly translation.

The elements of the tale that are most important for *Ulysses* have already been discussed in the earlier chapters. The "Pillow-talk" introduction to the version of *Táin Bó Cúailnge* in the Book of Leinster offers a perspective on Leopold Bloom's qualities as husband and hero, and his lack of jealousy is appropriately compared with the same quality in Ailill, Medb's spouse, in that story. Medb's imperious actions in *Táin Bó Cúailnge* and her sexual, dominating nature set a context for evaluating Molly's characteristics, lifting Joyce's portrait out of the realistic and personal realms and giving it a mythic and cultural context. Medb is in many ways the prototype of the Sovereignty figures found in early Irish literature, and her urination in *Táin Bó Cúailnge*, particularly in the final scenes, is the mythic model for Molly's own release of waters.

This early Irish story is also used extensively in *Finnegans Wake*: Kelleher has argued that "the single heroic tale that is most extensively employed in the *Wake* is an episode from the *Táin Bó Cuailnge*," the fight between CuChulainn and his foster brother FerDiad ("Identifying the

Irish Printed Sources" 170). The tale provides the architectonics for the fight between two brothers that runs through much of *Finnegans Wake*, the conflict between Shem and Shaun in all their various personae; the medieval story is a paradigm of "the high tragedy of the hero who must, in order to fulfil his duty and save his own people, fight and kill the friend dearest to his heart and who therefore fights reluctantly and wins with sorrow" (Kelleher, "Identifying the Irish Printed Sources" 172). Even in the early Irish tale, the pattern of a fight between brothers appears in a trifold repetition. It is obvious why Joyce picks up this element in his own history of Ireland, for internecine warfare and betrayal are the leitmotifs of Irish history, and these are in fact the very reasons that this central episode of *Táin Bó Cúailnge* became a lasting part of Irish oral tradition, surviving to the present century. Kelleher details the shapeshifting that Joyce's heroes undergo as they play out their conflict, taking such forms as Buckley and the Russian general, Butt and Taff; and he argues as well that CuChulainn's secret weapon, the *gaí bulga*, also makes many metamorphic appearances in Joyce's text (172–75).

In settling on a source for Joyce's use of *Táin Bó Cúailnge* in *Finnegans Wake*, Kelleher argues that Joyce needed a version of the text that included an episode (the Dolb and Indolb scene) that forms a triplet of battling pairs and that occurs only in two late manuscripts; thus, he indicates that refractions such as that of Gregory are not sufficient, for they do not include the action in question. He suggests that Joyce used Joseph Dunn's 1914 English version, *The Ancient Irish Epic Tale Táin Bó Cúalnge*, which, though based on the Book of Leinster text, supplements that version with episodes from other manuscripts. The problem with this suggestion is twofold: first, there is no evidence that Joyce had access to this publication on the Continent; second, Dunn's version, like all the English translations of *Táin Bó Cúailnge*, mutes some of the elements of the early Irish text that have important affinities to Joyce's own works, namely the sexual, scatological, grotesque, and humorous facets of *Táin Bó Cúailnge* (Tymoczko, "Translating the Old Irish Epic"; "Strategies"; "Translating the Humour").

The presupposition behind Kelleher's suggestion is that Joyce was limited to consulting an English translation of *Táin Bó Cúailnge*, though in suggesting that Joyce used other German materials for *Finnegans Wake* (174–75), Kelleher clearly acknowledges that Joyce's German was more than up to the task of using a German version. The question of Joyce's source for *Táin Bó Cúailnge* becomes much more interesting when we allow for the possibility that Joyce depended on French and German translations, which were not constrained by the demands of Irish cultural nationalism and hence were much more able to provide Joyce a view of Irish tradition congenial to his tastes, values, and interests. If we look to publications in languages other than English, a more plausible text for Joyce to have depended on than Dunn's translation is Ernst Windisch's 1905 edition of the Book of Leinster version of *Táin Bó Cúailnge*, published with German translation as a supplementary volume to the series *Irische Texte* and entitled *Die altirische Heldensage Táin Bó Cúalnge nach dem Buch von Leinster, in Text und Uebersetzung mit einer Einleitung.*

Windisch's text is based on the Book of Leinster manuscript, which gives the "Pillow-talk" introduction to the story, yet it also includes all the variants from the eighth-century version of the story preserved in the Book of the Dun Cow as well as variants from later manuscript versions of the tale; thus, it contains the fights by three sets of brothers (550–63), which Joyce used in *Finnegans Wake*, as well as all the humorous and sexual elements of *Táin Bó Cúailnge* that have left traces in *Ulysses*. Windisch's edition of *Táin Bó Cúailnge* was in fact the most complete available in any language at the period, and his translation, like those of P. W. Joyce, reflects adequately the formal qualities of early Irish narrative, including variations in prose and poetry, alternations in register and tone, and the like, as well as the details of the contents, unconstrained by censure from Irish nationalism. Not only does Windisch's text provide the content needed for Joyce's use of *Táin Bó Cúailnge* in *Finnegans Wake*, but it also acts as an excellent template for an understanding of early Irish narrative as a whole, providing Joyce the materials excised from most versions circulated in Ireland at the turn of the century. The great advantage of seeing Windisch as Joyce's source for his knowledge of *Táin Bó Cúailnge* is that there is also clear evidence that Joyce had access to the volume: it was part of the collection in Zurich's Zentralbibliothek, where Joyce worked daily while he was writing the bulk of *Ulysses*, but Dunn's version of the *Táin* was not.

Summary

It would be easy to continue this survey of publications on early Irish history and literature that contributed either directly or indirectly to

Joyce's treatment of the Irish materials in his narratives. Although in some cases we have as evidence that he read certain books only implicit similarities between his works and the monographs in question, it is also difficult to rule out most literature on the topic; and the range of materials canvassed in oral culture and in popular digests, to which Joyce was therefore exposed at second hand, is very wide indeed. The publications surveyed above, therefore, do not in any way exhaust the scholarly materials that lie behind Joyce's use of Irish myth in *Ulysses*. It is, for example, probable that at certain points in his life he had read some of the more scholarly publications devoted to early Irish history and literature: journals such as *Revue celtique* and *Zeitschrift für celtische Philologie*, the early publications of Eugene O'Curry and John O'Donovan, the editions of the indefatigable Whitley Stokes, or the work of such German philologists as Ernst Windisch. Joyce's mythic method makes tracing the particulars of his reading difficult and in fact superfluous: though he might have gone on to read the edition and translation of *The Midnight Court* published in *Zeitschrift für celtische Philologie* in 1905, his exposure to the outlines of the text in the detailed summary carried by *Dana* would have sufficed for the subtext from Merriman in the Nighttown episode of *Ulysses*.

The books surveyed here represent central materials that inform Joyce's work: they do not simply contribute to his knowledge of the particulars of Irish tradition; they shape his understanding of and perspective on the traditional history and literature of his country. I have chosen to focus on materials that bring together text and criticism in order to account not only for the surfacing in *Ulysses* of motifs from early Irish history and literature but also for Joyce's own vision of those materials, an outlook that distinguishes his work from that of other writers of the Irish literary revival, even as his enterprise of using early Irish history, literature, and myth continues the program of Irish cultural nationalism in the early decades of the twentieth century.

iii. Ideas in general circulation from monographs

Many of the ideas in general circulation in the popular press, discussed in the last chapter, are also to be found in books related to early Irish literature that Joyce may have consulted. Indeed, in many cases the discussions in the popular press are outgrowths of ideas put forward in the first instance in books or in scholarly publications. Thus, for example, the comparisons of Greek and Irish myth, literature, and culture found in the periodicals surveyed in the last chapter have many counterparts in book-length studies, including the works of d'Arbois de Jubainville, which return again and again to the topic, and Meyer's *Voyage of Bran*, particularly in Nutt's essays on metempsychosis and the happy other-world. Another early and important discussion of the question is Alfred Nutt's 1900 publication entitled *Cuchulainn, the Irish Achilles*, which predicates CuChulainn as the Irish parallel to the Greek hero and sets a pattern for the reclamation of early Irish heroism by Irish cultural and military nationalism. Nutt's study of CuChulainn is cited repeatedly by later writers, and his ideas come to be the common coin of the movement. Such examples could be multiplied, but it is clear enough that Joyce's con-flation of Irish and Greek myth in *Ulysses* has a larger context in Irish intellectual history, as indicated by both the popular press and more scholarly discussions.

Monographs are even more detailed about the relation of the Irish to various other cultures than the popular press can be. Thus, for example, the theory of the Spanish origin of Irish culture was discussed by many of the historians, as well as by literary historians such as d'Arbois de Ju-bainville; as early as 1861 Eugene O'Curry referred to the Milesian con-quest of Ireland as a "Spanish colonization" (446). In the same way, the impetus to localism discussed in the last chapter was fueled by material published in book-length studies. Knowledge of Irish sites and localities, as well as of Irish topography, rested upon the Ordnance Survey in the first instance as well as upon P. W. Joyce's many publications related to placelore and toponymy. In the sphere of scholarly publications interest in the topic is reflected also in Edmund Hogan's 1910 publication entitled *Onomasticon Goedelicum locorum et tribuum Hiberniae et Scotiae* and in the publication of the metrical dindsenchas by Edward Gwynn in the Todd Lecture Series. In the critical literature the topographical element in Irish literature is discussed in such sources as Eleanor Hull's *Text Book of Irish Literature* (1: 101 ff.).[17] Though in general there is a great deal of

---

17. Although there is no evidence that Joyce knew Hull's *Text Book*, her work is a very convenient summary of received knowledge at the period she was writ-ing. The book had been reviewed favorably and recommended by *Sinn Féin* (1 Dec. 1906), and it was brought out by David Nutt as part of his series of Celtic

continuity between the ideas discussed in the popular press and the ideas developed in more scholarly publications, some of the intellectual context for *Ulysses* is best indicated by examples taken from monographs.

The role of the Irish fili

In a famous lecture to the Irish Literary Society entitled "Irish Literature: Its Origin, Environment, and Influence," George Sigerson had said, "If our nation is to live, it must live by the energy of intellect. . . . Whilst wealth of thought is a country's treasure, literature is its articulate voice" (114). Published in 1894 along with Douglas Hyde's speech "The Necessity for De-Anglicizing Ireland" and two lectures by Charles Gavan Duffy calling on Irishmen to write books, Sigerson's lecture helped to set the tone and program for the Irish literary revival. The search for a way to write books that would both help the nation live and at the same time de-anglicize Ireland inevitably turned attention to the early Irish fili, the native practitioner of Irish literature. A considerable amount of information was available about the role and nature of the fili, and this information was promulgated in scholarly, literary, and popular contexts. Thus, for example, in *Introduction à l'étude de la littérature celtique*, the first volume of the *Cours de littérature celtique*, d'Arbois de Jubainville had included nine chapters on the poets, principally the poets in Ireland. Various roles and functions of the poets in Ireland are discussed, including the functions of creating satire, telling stories, and passing judgment; the role of history, law, and divination in the poet's work is also presented. The grades, privileges, and schools of the poets are discussed, and information about the tale lists and genres of tales is provided. The book also contains five chapters on bards and eighteen chapters on druids.

This is just one of many discussions of the topic available at the time, albeit an early one. In his *Social History of Ancient Ireland* of 1903, which appeared during the time Joyce was studying Irish and involved in reading books about Irish literature, P. W. Joyce covered much the same ground as d'Arbois de Jubainville had, stressing the existence of lay schools, the long period of study required in bardic schools, and the im-

---

publications; thus, it would have had wide appeal in Ireland. Hull herself follows the work of P. W. Joyce. For all these reasons, then, her work is representative of the sort of material that would have influenced Joyce.

portance of annals, histories, genealogies, and placelore to the poet's work. The soothsaying and divination of the *fili* is presented. The book was discussed and recommended in the periodical literature of the time, as mentioned above; the contents would also have been circulated orally, at least in part. The material was summarized for the 1906 publication of P. W. Joyce's *Smaller Social History of Ancient Ireland* and distilled yet again in the 1907 *Story of Ancient Irish Civilisation*. Eleanor Hull, who indicates her indebtedness to P. W. Joyce, devotes two chapters to the poets and the druids in her 1904 *Pagan Ireland*, stressing the knowledge of the future that both classes of learned men were to possess. She also has chapters on the poets and the bards in her *Text Book of Irish Literature*, where she states that

the file is, in fact, the spiritual leader of the people; at once their Law-giver, Magician, and Man of Wisdom. . . . His poetic gifts . . . were exercised rather in uttering charms and incantations than in composing poetry for amusement; or else in putting into use the terrible faculty for satire. . . . In addition, the laws, genealogies, records of the tribes, and other matters belonging to the kingdom, were guarded and recited by the file. (1: 181–82)

She discusses the topographical, genealogical, and historical content the poets were to master, as well as the ancient esoteric bardic language. In George Sigerson's *Bards of the Gael and Gall*, which also received wide attention, many of the same points are covered. The list of books presenting information about the filid could be extended, but the essential point is that such information was widespread in Ireland at the turn of the century, and it is alluded to as well in the popular press.

Not only was the fili discussed in scholarly and popularized sources, but the writers of the Irish literary revival had assimilated many of the concepts pertaining to the fili and had made them their own. The mysticism of such figures as Yeats and A. E. was shaped in part by the knowledge of the visionary role of the Irish fili, and to some extent each models his role as poet on that earlier pattern. Yeats spells out his mystic revelations in *A Vision*; A. E. is an apologist for the poet's being a seer, having visions, and using dreams in *The Candle of Vision*, and he details one of his own visions in *The Avatars*. Although these latter works cannot be the source of similar ideas in *Ulysses*, since they either appear after *Ulysses* or are too late to have made much impact on its overall structure, the same conceptions can be traced implicitly and explicitly in the earlier works of Yeats and A. E.; the convergence of their thought illustrates the currency of such ideas in Ireland at this period among the writers using English as their literary language.

Irish formalism

However much disagreement there was about the nature of a national Irish literature in English, there was widespread understanding at the turn of the century that formalism was characteristic of the early Irish literary tradition. Book after book, article after article stressed this point to the general and scholarly reader alike. It was widely known that Ireland had been one of the seats of learning in Europe during the early Middle Ages, and it was understood that during this period Ireland had cultivated literature to a great degree. Calling Ireland "the Mother of Literatures," Sigerson was a proponent of the position that Ireland's literary interests in turn initiated much of European literary development (*Bards of the Gael and Gall* 107).

There are many allusions in the popular press to the complexity of Irish meters listed and exemplified in the early Irish metrical tracts, many of which had either been discussed or published by 1912.[18] These scholarly editions and commentaries had in turn been digested in more general publications; there are, for example, descriptions of the Irish syllabic meters in Eleanor Hull's *Text Book* (1: 234–37; cf. Sigerson, "Irish Literature" 72ff., and Hyde, *Gaelic Literature* 173–74, quoted in *U* 9.96–99). In his *Smaller Social History* P. W. Joyce summarized the metrical complexity as follows: "The classification and the laws of Irish versification were probably the most complicated that were ever invented: indicating on the part of the ancient Irish people, both learned and unlearned, a delicate appreciation of harmonious combinations of sounds" (215). Johann Caspar Zeuss and his followers had claimed that rhyme was an invention of the Old Irish poets, and this view was promulgated by Sigerson and other writers, including P. W. Joyce.[19] It became a topos of nationalist literary history to stress the intricacies of Irish rhyme (e.g., Sigerson, "Irish Literature" 75–78). Moreover, P. W. Joyce claimed that "rhyme

18. See Best, *Bibliography* (1913) 52–54.
19. See Sigerson, "Irish Literature" 77ff., and P. W. Joyce, *Smaller Social History* 215. Cf. E. Hull, *Text Book* 1: 219–37.

was brought to far greater perfection in Irish than in any other language" (*Smaller Social History* 216), and Sigerson generalized that the Irish had sharper sound discrimination than most peoples ("Irish Literature" 77ff.). Sigerson also compared the Irish grace in poetry to the intricacy of the Book of Kells; it was essential to learn Irish, for it was agreed that the metrical complexity of Irish verse could not be reproduced in English translation (*Bards of the Gael and Gall* 23), a point that Douglas Hyde took up in his *Love Songs of Connacht* (iv).[20]

Irish poetry was seen as difficult not only because of its metrical intricacy but also because of its deliberate obscurity. The arcane language of the poets had been discussed in various publications, including Eleanor Hull's *Text Book* (1: 184). Elsewhere we find descriptions of the most archaic Irish poetry, the passages of obscure poetry called *rosc*. Sigerson analyzes rosc as rhythmical though unrhymed verse designed to express or to stir up vehement enthusiasm and claims it is the first example of blank verse (*Bards of the Gael and Gall* 25); Hull characterizes rosc as a declamatory, alliterative blank verse where changes of meter correspond to changes of idea (*Text Book* 1: 202–4).

The formal intricacy of the early Irish narratives is discussed by many authors. The system of narrative prose interspersed with poetry is delineated, and various authors attempt to give a systematic account of the formal variation. As early as 1894 P. W. Joyce had taken the following position on the mixture of forms:

In many of the prose tales the leading characters are often made to express themselves in verse, or some striking incident of the story is repeated in a poetical form. Not unfrequently the fragments of verse introduced into a prose tale are quotations from an older poetical version of the same tale; and hence it often happens that while the prose may be plain enough, the poetry is often archaic and obscure. (*Old Celtic Romances* iv–v)

Later Eleanor Hull explained that the poems frequently take "the form of dialogue" and that they are "fitly introduced at points of special pathos or passion" (*Text Book* 1: 219). These and other discussions of the mixed prose and poetry came to be repeated in popular periodicals as well.

---

20. Note that Hyde's book is mentioned in *Ulysses* in the library episode (9.93–94), and Joyce owned it in 1920 (Ellmann, *Consciousness of Joyce* 113; Gillespie #226). The impact of Hyde's volume is beyond the scope of this discussion, spawning as it did the Anglo-Irish idiom and having a tremendous influence on most of the major writers of the Irish literary revival.

Irish prose stylistics was also discussed. In lecturing about early Irish literature, Sigerson had cautioned against the assumption that there was one Irish style: "As in other countries, there were not one but many styles, differing with the subject, the writer, and the age" ("Irish Literature" 71). Eleanor Hull analyzed three levels of style in the prose tales: a rough-hewn, abrupt style in the archaic tales of the early period; a more elaborated style of the tales from the eighth to tenth centuries; and a tedious alliterative style of the narratives from the eleventh and succeeding centuries (*Text Book* 1: 94–95). Yet P. W. Joyce could generalize about the earlier prose narratives and pick a translation strategy accordingly: "The originals are in general simple in style; and I have done my best to render them into simple, plain, homely English" (*Old Celtic Romances* vii).

This sampling of contemporary views on the formal properties of Irish literature indicates that many of the features of Irish literature that have here been traced in *Ulysses* were explicitly acknowledged in the cultural milieu that formed Joyce. The awareness of and pride in Irish formalism are a backdrop for the formalism in both Yeats's poetry and Joyce's prose, and their common emphasis of the formal aspects of literature must be seen as in part an outgrowth of the way in which each positioned himself as a writer of Irish literature in English.[21]

The tone of Irish narrative

One of the explosive issues related to the reclamation of early Irish literature for the purposes of cultural nationalism was the dissonance between the content of the literature and the proprieties of late Victorianism. This issue was debated hotly in public lectures, and reflections of the public discussion are found both in the popular press and also in positions taken in the monographs of the time. Because the moral purity of the Irish had become a central tenet of Irish nationalism (cf. W. Thompson 10ff.), the reception of the sexual and moral aspects of early Irish literature and culture was particularly charged. The way in which these issues filtered into general cultural life in Ireland in Joyce's youth is captured in the discussion between Stephen and Madden in *Stephen Hero*

21. Later Irish writers such as Austin Clarke and Flann O'Brien go even further in the direction of transposing Irish metrics or formal characteristics into English writing.

about the moral quality of the Irish peasant compared with that of the English city dweller; Madden's final defense of the Irish is that the Irish peasants "are noted for at least one virtue all the world over," to which Stephen retorts that they are chaste only "because they can do it by hand" (55). The irony of elevating the Irish because of their sexual purity is taken up again in *A Portrait of the Artist* when Davin tells Stephen about his encounter with a peasant woman who, half undressed when he knocks at her cottage door, invites him to stay the night as her husband is away; for Stephen "the figure of the woman in the story stood forth . . . as a type of her race and his own . . . a woman without guile, calling the stranger to her bed" (182–83). Here Stephen turns the moral platitudes of Irish nationalism on their head: it is natural sexual freedom, not chastity, that epitomizes the race.

Such women are found aplenty in the early literature, and although Joyce was comfortable with these mores, his views were not shared by many. In a public lecture Robert Atkinson had charged early Irish literature with being indecorous and unsavory, a charge that was reported and discussed widely in the press. Many of the popular periodicals followed up on the issues raised by Atkinson, and Kuno Meyer took up the job of defending the literature from Atkinson's charges. Among others, the *Irish Catholic* covered the controversy, citing at length a lecture by Meyer on 5 April 1902:

The stream of Irish literature ran deep and broad, and if in its course it carried along with it some earthy matter, such slight admixture did not affect the general purity of its waters, from which none need hesitate to drink deeply. The literature of no nation was free from occasional grossness, and considering the great antiquity of Irish literature and the primitive line which it reflected, what would strike an impartial observer was not its license or coarseness, but rather the noble, lofty, and tender spirit which pervaded it.

The article continues, "The testimony of a scholar of Dr. Meyer's attainments far outweighs the allegations of the Atkinsons and their ilk."

The issues were taken up in book-length studies also. Thus, for example, P. W. Joyce summarizes in his *Smaller Social History*:

As to the general moral tone of the ancient Irish tales, it is to be observed that in all early literatures, Irish among the rest, there is much plain speaking of a character that would now be considered coarse, and would not be tolerated in our present social and domestic life. But on the score of morality

and purity the Irish tales can compare favourably with the corresponding literature of other countries; and they are much freer from objectionable matter
than the works of many of those early English and continental authors which
are now regarded as classics. (237)

P. W. Joyce's tactic here, like that of Meyer, is a clever one; indeed, he is
correct that there is nothing more scandalous in Irish literature than in
Chaucer or the French fabliaux, to name examples that immediately
come to mind; it is an argumentative strategy that James Joyce would
have appreciated. In his even shorter treatment of Irish culture in *The
Story of Ancient Irish Civilization*, P. W. Joyce quotes Whitley Stokes and
Kuno Meyer justifying the moral tone of the tales, particularly considering their context and antiquity (80–82). It is not that P. W. Joyce denies
the sexual content or the grotesque in the stories, but merely that, like
Meyer, he claims this material has a larger context in which the functions
of the fili dominate; a not dissimilar argument was made in the 1933
Woolsey decision rejecting the charges of pornography made against
Ulysses (*JJ*2 666–67).

In her treatment of the same subject Eleanor Hull takes a slightly more
anthropological view. After saying that the artificial tone and highly
wrought manners and moralities of Arthurian literature are absent from
the early Irish tales, she continues: "We see the champions as we can actually conceive them to have lived in an early pre-Christian age. Their
barbarities are described without a shade of disgust; their chivalries are
the outcome of a natural fairness and fineness of mind, and are not the
product of a courtly attention to an exterior code of morals" (*Text Book*
1: 90). She concludes that the tales are purely and frankly pagan.

In addition to defending the early Irish tales from attacks on their
moral character, books on early Irish literature try to define the special
characteristics that distinguish the literature. Hull (*Text Book* 1: 92), for
example, characterizes the stories as having a dramatic quality, and in her
view the variation in the stylistics is an essential element in their dramatic
quality. Hull's assessment of the texts includes a catalogue of their weak-
nesses: the tales, she says, are often "wandering and wild"; they "abound
in repetitions and exaggerations"; their "sense of proportion and balance" is often obscured by minute descriptions (*Text Book* 1: 96). Finally,
critical studies acknowledge the humor of the early literature. Although
some writers are at pains to reject the humor—seeing it, for example, as
a late addition by Christian scribes (Henderson, introduction), others de-

fend the humor. Hull is one of the latter; she discusses the humor of the Ulster Cycle in general and *Táin Bó Cúailnge* in particular (*Text Book* 1: 48–51) and concludes: "Connected with this dramatic quality, and largely contributing to it, is the strong sense of humour observable in the tales. . . . Everywhere [the humour] lightens and relieves the tedium of the recital. This quality is especially Irish; the Arthurian romance is deficient in humour, hence a certain monotony of repetition which is conspicuously absent from the Irish tales" (*Text Book* 1: 92–93). Nutt's validation of the humor in the stories has already been considered, including his comparison of this facet of Irish literature with Dionysiac aspects of Greek literature.

All of these features of the tone of early Irish literature, an understanding of which became part of the cultural debate in Ireland at the turn of the century, clearly relate to the tone of *Ulysses*. Some readers—including perhaps James Joyce—might have considered that Irish literature had the virtues of its defects.

The position of women in early Irish literature

The status of women in pre-Christian and precolonial Ireland was topical at the turn of the century in Ireland, in part because of the wave of feminism in the British Isles associated with the drive for women's suffrage and in part because of the generalized interest in social reform that was ancillary to the mounting desire for national independence in Ireland.[22] In popular culture the manifestation of this interest was manifold. A series of lectures on early Irish historical and legendary women was sponsored by Inghinidhe na hÉireann, the women's organization associated with Cumann na nGaedhael. The lectures, which covered Saint Brigit, Macha, Medb, Gráinne Ní Mháille, and Emer, were summarized or even given in extenso in the periodical literature, notably the *United Irishman*.[23] In these lectures Irish women were represented as having a high estate, being independent and often aggressive, having the choice of a spouse, and being able to divorce. Some of the character of this discourse

22. See B. Scott, esp. 1–54. Periodicals such as the *United Irishman* also carried occasional articles discussing the desideratum of freeing women as the nationalist movement freed Ireland.

23. See accounts of these speeches in the *United Irishman* 8 Dec. 1900, 5 Jan. 1901, 5 Oct. 1901, 23 Nov. 1901, and 11 Oct. 1902/1 Nov. 1902, respectively.

was probably influenced by Maud Gonne, a liberated woman par excellence for the period. Gonne delivered a lecture on Medb that stressed Medb's warlike nature and sexual liberation, traits that Gonne herself reified and that she generalized to all early Irish women. It is typical of the atmosphere of the time that Gonne played the title role in the first series of performances of Yeats's *Cathleen ni Houlihan*.

In more scholarly publications and monographs, the same views are projected about women, and the general belief was that Ireland's women had a strong social position. P. W. Joyce maintained that in most respects women were on a level with men (see, e.g., *Smaller Social History* 284), and such authors as Eleanor Hull and Alice Stopford Green concurred. Hull devotes an entire chapter of her *Pagan Ireland* to the position of women, maintaining that women took an active part in warfare, that they were nurses and doctors, that they were proud and formidable in words as well as deeds. Her summary of the position of women in *A Text Book of Irish Literature* represents views known and shared by nationalists at the time:

The Irish women belong to an heroic type. They are often the counsellors of their husbands and the champions of their cause; occasionally, as in Maeve's case, their masters. They are frequently fierce and vindictive, but they are also strong, forceful, and intelligent. In youth they possess often a charming gaiety; they are full of clever repartee and waywardness and have a delightful and careless self-confidence. (1: 78)

The position of Irish women was a nationalist point of pride; as Alice Stopford Green observed in 1912, "We are often told that the civilization of a people is marked by the place of its women: a rule by which the Irish stand high" (100).[24] Views such as these underlie Synge's views about women in the Ulster Cycle: "Most of the moods and actions that are met with are more archaic than anything in the Homeric poems, yet a few features, such as the imperiousness and freedom of the women, seem to imply an intellectual advance beyond the period of Ulysses" ("Epic of Ulster" 368–69). One of the most important publications fueling this discourse was Heinrich Zimmer's "Der kulturgeschichtliche Hintergrund in

24. These elements of Irish nationalism coalesced with views promulgated by Ferrero in which the relations of the sexes are an index to national temperament; cf. Manganiello (ch. 2) for a full discussion of Ferrero's influence on Joyce. The theme is explored both in "Two Gallants" and in *Ulysses* in rather different ways.

der Erzählungen der alten irischen Heldensage." Zimmer details the independence and assertiveness of the female characters in early Irish narratives, noting that their behavior is uncharacteristic of Aryan culture; he
concludes that the Irish culture has sustained non-Aryan influences that
have changed basic elements of the culture. These views Joyce would have
found congenial with his theories of Ireland's mixed racial heritage and
of Semitic affinities or influences; it is significant that Zimmer's treatise
was part of the collection in Zurich's Zentralbibliothek.

The social position of women in these scholarly and popular analyses
is to a large extent derived from the literary representation of females,
including goddesses, and the role of mortal women in literature was connected in turn with the mythology as it was understood at the time.[25] The
importance of the goddesses in early Celtic literature is repeated over and
over again, and conclusions are drawn from the myth about social roles.
With such views widespread and in a sense normative, it is perhaps not
surprising that historical women such as Maud Gonne and Constance
Markiewicz were involved in militant action, and the dominant traits in
Molly's character are completely in the literary tradition as it was understood at the time in popular and scholarly publications alike. Molly's sexual and personal assertiveness are to be read as positive features within
the constructs of Irish nationalist views about women. Eleanor Hull's
summary of Irish women could be a description of Molly, explaining
many of her characteristics and actions, right down to her advocacy of
Bloom to his boss (18.510).

The folding over of past and present:
the coming of the avatars

Hugh Kenner takes the view that "it was surely at the behest of talk in
Dawson Chambers about metempsychosis . . . and by analogy with
Maud Gonne as Helen returned that [Joyce] conceived Bloom as unwit-
ting Ulysses" (*Joyce's Voices* 61). Though this may be a factor in the con-

25. The hypotheses here are obviously questionable; it is not always possible
to extrapolate from myth to social circumstance, as myth can act as compensatory gratification for a culture. See Preston, introduction. Early Irish literature is
particularly complicated in these regards because most of the supernatural figures
have been euhemerized and it is difficult to unravel the mythological from the
historical; see Mac Cana, "Aspects of the Theme"; Tymoczko, "Unity and Duality."

struction of the mythic substructure of *Ulysses*, the matter is more complicated. In chapter 2 I argued that metempsychosis is the central feature from myth in *Ulysses*, linking, among other things, the major figures with the principal characters of the *Odyssey* and also with the mythic types of *The Book of Invasions*. Implicit in the structure of the book is that the Irish characters are avatars returned to earth; these avatars in turn foreshadow possibilities for the new Irish state. Even this suggestion of Irish avatars returned to earth was in circulation in Ireland at the turn of the century. The idea is most clearly represented in the writings of the mystic A. E., notably in his *Candle of Vision*, published in 1918. In this book A. E. speaks of his own visions, and he says that only one vision of his has been prophetic, a vision of an avatar, a child of destiny (98–101). Speaking primarily of mantic roles, he says "the powers which were present to the ancestors are establishing again their dominion over the spirit" (151). The essays in this collection, based in part on ideas from Eastern religion, anticipate his 1933 publication *The Avatars: A Futurist Fantasy*, in which the spiritual transfiguration of Ireland is envisioned as coming from the converse of human characters with the avatars of the otherworld.

Although *The Avatars* itself cannot have influenced *Ulysses*, it seems likely, particularly in view of A. E.'s essays in *The Candle of Vision*, that the ideas themselves had been in circulation before 1933. In his introduction to *The Avatars* A. E. writes somewhat apologetically of his book: "*The Avatars* has not the spiritual gaiety I desired for it. The friends with whom I once spoke of such things are dead or gone far from me. If they were with me, out of dream, vision and intuition shared between us, I might have made the narrative to glow. As it is, I have only been able to light my way with my own flickering lantern" (vii). These friends with whom he once spoke about such ideas would have included Yeats and Augusta Gregory (who by 1933 was dead); but it must be remembered that for years A. E.'s house was the gathering place of the Dublin literati and that "the friends with whom [he] once spoke of such things" formed a large circle. They may even have included Joyce, who by 1933 had gone far from George Russell.

Yeats, too, uses ideas close to these both in *A Vision*, where the great characters of Irish myth serve as prototypes of the various states of the soul, and also in such poems as "Crazy Jane on the Mountain":

> Last night I lay on the mountain
> (Said Crazy Jane)
> There in a two horsed carriage
> That on two wheels ran
> Great bladdered Emer sat,
> Her violent man
> Cuchulain, sat at her side,
> Thereupon,
> Propped upon my two knees,
> I kissed a stone;
> I lay stretched out in the dirt
> And I cried tears down.
>
> (*Poems* 582)

Here the idea is used somewhat bitterly and ironically, for it is the lack of the presence of the avatars on this earth that leads to Jane's lying down and crying, and it is the comparison between the greats of the past and the paltry minds and bodies of the present that Yeats uses to express his disenchantment with the "filthy modern tide."

In *Ulysses* Joyce's use of the avatars also has considerable irony from the viewpoint of A. E.'s vision, in which contact with the avatar results in mystical experiences and "a spiritual wonder" (*Avatars* 136). In *Ulysses* the avatars may result in renewal in Ireland, but the renewal is resolutely human, ordinary, physical, as well as moral and spiritual, though in directions far from the values of A. E. In this irony is encapsulated Joyce's relationship with the Anglo-Irish literary revival, for he has taken one of the ideas of the movement, followed through on it literally, and, because of his own values and perspectives, changed it utterly, giving a result that appears to subvert the original intent of the literary revival.

iv. Zurich

A fundamental question remains about Joyce's use of early Irish literature and history in *Ulysses*: was Joyce's knowledge of early Irish myth and literature acquired principally before he left Ireland in 1904, or did he deepen his understanding of Irish literature and history in significant ways after 1904? The question has implications for the way in which we perceive the early Irish elements in *Ulysses*: Joyce's mythic structures will be interpreted quite differently if it is assumed, on the one hand, that he had access to texts and critical material about early Irish culture for verification of details and other purposes while he was writing *Ulysses*, or if it is assumed, on the other hand, that he relied almost exclusively on knowledge gained more than a decade earlier. Is the broad but schematized use of Irish myth in Joyce's work attributable primarily to his mythic method itself and thus comparable to his treatment of other mythologies in *Ulysses*, or is it attributable in a significant degree to Joyce's isolation from Irish myth after 1904, to his working largely from memories of texts, conversations, speeches, and the like, many years after the fact when those memories may themselves have become somewhat vague?

On the whole, evidence suggests that even after leaving Ireland, Joyce continued to deepen his knowledge of early Irish myth and literature. As noted above, he continued to receive the *United Irishman* and thereafter *Sinn Féin* for some years, and the educative function of these newspapers would have provided Joyce with materials during the years between 1904 and 1914. Moreover, Joyce would to some extent have been brought au courant with developments in the field of Irish literature during his visits to Ireland in 1909 and 1912. These were years when Kuno Meyer was director of the School of Irish Learning in Dublin and when he and others kept the topics of early Irish literature and myth in the domain of public discourse through lectures and statements in the popular press as well as through their teaching. The prestigious and scholarly Irish journal *Ériu* was making accessible many texts of early Irish literature.[26] Anglo-Irish writers, including Yeats, also kept early Irish material in circulation; during the years between 1904 and 1912 Yeats produced two of his Cu-Chulainn plays (*On Baile's Strand* and *The Green Helmet*) as well as his *Deirdre*.

While Joyce was in Trieste, he used early Irish history and literature in several ways, notably for his Trieste lectures and also for the architectonics of "The Dead." In discussing Joyce's use of *The Destruction of Da Derga's Hostel* in "The Dead," Kelleher takes up the possibility that Joyce called on his memory for his knowledge of Irish myth in that story:

26. *Ériu* was begun in 1904; the early volumes were edited principally by Kuno Meyer in association with various other scholars including Carl Marstrander, Osborn Bergin, and R. I. Best, and the first two volumes were reviewed favorably in *Dana*.

It may rightly be objected that at the time Joyce was working on the story in Trieste his letters indicate that he had very few Irish books or maps with him. Moreover, he complained in a letter of 1906 that Dublin was already growing hazy in his memory. I doubt it ever really grew hazy. I doubt that his memory, particular and capacious as a bard's, ever relinquished anything once learned from books, from observation, or from his father whose knowledge of Dublin was as intimate and curious as his own. ("Irish History" 431)

Budgen also comments on Joyce's prodigious memory of written text (*Making of "Ulysses"* 176–77; cf. Power, *From the Old Waterford House* 66–67). If we take the position that Joyce, like the ancient Irish poets, was able to retain copious and detailed memories indefinitely, then his need to consult books to refresh and sharpen his understandings about early Irish matters is moot. This, however, is a large and ultimately unnecessary assumption.

It is clear that once located in Paris, a major center of Celtic studies where d'Arbois de Jubainville had been professor, Joyce would have had access to virtually any text or critical book on early Irish literature that he cared to work with, but by the time he was in Paris the broad mythic structures linking *Ulysses* to early Irish literature had been set. It is precisely during the period that *Ulysses* was taking shape in Zurich, therefore, that Joyce would have consulted Irish mythic materials to greatest effect, for he arrived in Zurich in June 1915, just as he was beginning on the third episode, and he left in October 1919 as he was about to begin "Nausicaa" (*JJ*2 383, 469, 473).

Though in Trieste, as Kelleher points out, Joyce had access to few Irish books, necessitating requests to his Aunt Josephine for Irish materials, in Zurich Joyce found a different set of resources, extensive materials that make it unnecessary to suppose that Joyce was dependent on either his personal library or his memory of texts read long since for his use of Irish myth in *Ulysses*. Joyce worked almost daily, as is well known, in the Zentralbibliothek, a library formed when voters of the canton and city determined in 1914 to merge the relatively recent Kantonsbibliothek (founded 1835) with the older Stadtbibliothek (founded 1629). The former, housed in the Predigerchor, served also as the library of the University of Zurich. Though the Zentralbibliothek existed on paper from 1914, it was only in March 1917 that the new construction for the joint facilities was opened; until that date Joyce would have used the several reading rooms of the original foundations.

German philology was at its height during the second half of the nineteenth century and the early decades of the twentieth, and German philologists were at the forefront of Celtic studies, partly in virtue of the fact
that Celtic languages and Celtic evidence are central to the enterprises of
comparative philology and to the construction of the Indo-European hypothesis. The University of Zurich had an excellent faculty with philological interests. Not surprisingly, then, since it served the research needs
of the university and a public interested in philological questions, the
Zentralbibliothek in Joyce's day had a small but distinguished Celtic
collection to which Joyce as reader had ready access. Examination of
the collection of the Zentralbibliothek indicates that even had Joyce
known nothing of early Irish literature and culture before he went to Zurich in 1915, *he would have found in the Zentralbibliothek all the source
texts required to furnish the Irish architectonics* in *Ulysses* discussed
above.

The library subscribed to the major scholarly journals of the period,
including *Revue celtique* (1870–1934). The library received as well several series, among them the Todd Lecture Series and the series of texts
edited by Whitley Stokes and Ernst Windisch under the title *Irische Texte
mit Uebersetzungen und Wörterbuch*, which had as a supplementary volume Windisch's 1905 edition and translation of *Táin Bó Cúailnge*. The
holdings included the entire run of d'Arbois de Jubainville's *Cours de littérature celtique*. These series and periodicals form the backbone of the
Zurich collection of Celtic publications (as they do of any collection of
early Celtic materials, for that matter) and provide most of the materials
needed for the study of early Irish literature.[27]

Joyce found an extensive collection of monographs on early Irish language and literature in the Zentralbibliothek as well. The German scholars are, not surprisingly, best represented. Philological texts included J. K.
Zeuss, *Grammatica Celtica* (2 vols., 1853 and 1871); publications by

27. Not all the early publications on Irish history and literature currently in
the Zentralbibliothek were part of the collection when Joyce was working on
Ulysses. Gaps in the holdings were filled in during the 1940s and 1950s at the
request of Julius Pokorny, then professor in Zurich. Thus, the library currently
holds *Ériu* (1904–) as well as an incomplete run of *Zeitschrift für celtische Philologie* (1899–); R. I. Best's *Bibliography of Irish Philology and Printed Irish Literature* (1913) was apparently added to the collection in 1947–48 when Best's
second bibliographical volume was purchased. I am indebted to Georg Bührer for
clarifying accession dates here and elsewhere.

Heinrich Zimmer; philological works by Whitley Stokes, including his *Three Irish Glossaries* (1863); philological studies by d'Arbois de Jubain-ville, Joseph Vendryes (notably *De hibernicis vocabulis quae a Latina lingua originem duxerunt*, 1902), and Holger Pedersen, among others;[28] John O'Donovan's *Grammar of the Irish Language* (1845); Ernst Windisch's *Kurzgefasste Irische Grammatik* (1879); early linguistic studies by Rudolf Thurneysen, including his *Handbuch des Alt-Irischen* (1909), which remains in its English translation (*A Grammar of Old Irish*, 1946) the standard grammar of Old Irish; and publications by Julius Pokorny. Significantly, the library also owned Charles Vallancey's *Essay on the Antiquity of the Irish Language* as well as his *Grammar of the Iberno-Celtic or Irish Language*.[29]

In addition to the series of editions and texts listed above, literary publications included editions by Kuno Meyer, such as his publications on early Irish poetry, his Fenian text *Cath Finntrága* (1885), and his editions brought out by the Todd Lecture Series, which include *The Triads of Ireland*, *The Instructions of Cormac Mac Airt*, and the early Fenian texts in the volume *Fianaigecht*; Whitley Stokes's editions of religious literature, including *Saltair na Rann* (1883), *The Calendar of Oengus* (1880), and *Lives of Saints from the Book of Lismore* (1890). The library also owned Thurneysen's *Sagen aus dem alten Irland* (1901); Carl Marstrander's *Fleadh Dúin na nGéadh ocus Cath Muighe Ráth* (1910); and Eleanor Hull's *Poem-book of the Gael* (1913). The library had purchased some Modern Irish materials, among them Edward Walsh's *Irish Popular Songs with English Metrical Translations* (1847).

Publications owned by the Zentralbibliothek on early Irish history and culture are extensive and too numerous to detail here. They include volumes in d'Arbois de Jubainville's twelve-volume *Cours*, Alexander Bugge's *Contributions to the History of the Norsemen in Ireland* (1900), the edition of the laws by John O'Donovan, and Zimmer's important study of the role of women in Irish literature, "Der kulturgeschichtliche

28. Joyce's comments to Larbaud about the Latin borrowings in Irish may reflect a familiarity with Vendryes's work; see *Letters* 1: 217–18.
29. The library currently owns James Midgley Clark's *Vocabulary of Anglo-Irish* (1917) as well as P. W. Joyce's *English as We Speak It in Ireland* (1910), both of which contain useful materials for an author representing characters who speak an Anglo-Irish dialect; however, these works were acquired only in the 1930s.

Hintergrund in den Erzählungen der alten irischen Heldensage." Many of
the important collections and studies of placelore were represented in the
collection when Joyce used the Zentralbibliothek. These works included
the volumes of Edward Gwynn's publication of the dindsenchas in the
Todd Lecture Series that appeared before 1919. P. W. Joyce's publications
on placelore were also represented, with the first two volumes of his *Origin and History of Irish Names of Places* and two copies of *Irish Local
Names Explained* as part of the collection.[30]

The current author/title card catalogue of the Zentralbibliothek was
begun in 1898 as a unified catalogue of various libraries in Zurich, principally the Kantonsbibliothek and the Stadtbibliothek; initially cataloguing the new acquisitions of the several libraries, it was funded by the canton but organized by the staff of the Stadtbibliothek. Only gradually did
the card catalogue become a comprehensive listing of the holdings. For
more than two decades, including the period when Joyce read in the library, it was used in conjunction with catalogues of the several institutions; these catalogues were kept in the form of volumes, like those of the
catalogue of the British Library. The subject catalogue (*Schlagwort-
katalog*), a pioneering effort in Swiss library science, was organized in the
first decade of the twentieth century originally for the Stadtbibliothek but
soon encompassed the Kantonsbibliothek as well; following American
practices, it was a card catalogue based on a system of subject categories
developed under the guidance of the library director, Hermann Escher,
who was interested in making the library more available to the nonspe-
cialist but serious reader. In advance of its time in European libraries, this
efficient system would have made it very easy for a reader like Joyce to
identify and call for publications about Irish material owned by the library. During the period 1915–19, when Joyce was working in the library, there were subject entries under "Irische" and "Irland" as well as
"Keltische" and "Kelten." These subjects were in turn subdivided; under
"Irische," for example, there were such divisions as "Irische Sprache," and
the subdivisions of "Irland" included "Flora," "Fauna," "Geschichte,"
and so forth. Joyce could also, of course, have looked for the publications
of specific authors such as d'Arbois de Jubainville in the author/title catalogues.

30. Volume 3 of *Origin and History* was acquired in 1954 at the instance of
Pokorny.

The collection of Irish materials in Zurich is important as much for what it does not contain as what it does contain. Because the holdings were acquired to serve the interest in philology in the German culture area and at the University of Zurich in particular, the collection of Irish materials is strongest in early Irish language, literature, history, and culture rather than in Modern Irish materials or literature in Anglo-Irish, specifically the writings of the Anglo-Irish literary revival. In Ireland cultural nationalism embraced Old and Middle Irish, Modern Irish, and Anglo-Irish writings related to Irish material, but in Zurich the primary interest was in Old and Middle Irish language and literature, which are of greater significance than Modern Irish for the Indo-European hypothesis and comparative historical linguistics. In this regard the bibliographical emphasis in Zurich is very different from library collections of Irish materials that Joyce had used in Ireland. In Zurich Joyce found neither Douglas Hyde's publication of Modern Irish poetry, *Love Songs of Connacht* (1893), nor books by A. E.; these omissions would have been unlikely in an Irish library of comparable size.[31]

The Zurich library also made available, not unnaturally, a different set of authors from those generally found in English-language libraries. German and French authors are best represented in the Zurich Irish collection, with the English authors primarily those working within the tradition of German philology. Thus, the library contains important books by such scholars as Zeuss, Zimmer, Windisch, Thurneysen, and d'Arbois de Jubainville; authors writing in English are more restricted, with Stokes and Meyer being notable exceptions that prove the rule. No Sigerson is to be found, and little P. W. Joyce.[32]

The emphasis in the Zentralbibliothek was on scholarly publications rather than popular ones, in part because it is by statute a research library. The library has very few of the popularizations, retellings, and translations that were part of the program of Irish cultural nationalism. A striking example is the absence of Augusta Gregory's *Cuchulain of*

31. The library later purchased A. E.'s *Collected Poems* (1920) and Douglas Hyde's *Beside the Fire*, but it contained nothing by either of these authors while Joyce was in Zurich during World War I.

32. As noted above, some of P. W. Joyce's monographs were part of the Zurich collection, but it would appear that James Joyce knew this author primarily from his Irish days. P. W. Joyce's *Social History of Ancient Ireland* is part of the collection at present, but the library owns the third edition, issued in 1920; hence the book was not available to Joyce while he was working on *Ulysses* in Zurich.

Muirthemne, the book Yeats called in his preface "the best that has come out of Ireland in my time"; it is virtually inconceivable that an Irish library interested in the cultural revival would have failed to purchase this text.[33] Critical texts and commentaries aimed at a more general audience are likewise missing: the library contains neither Eleanor Hull's *Text Book* nor Douglas Hyde's *Literary History of Ireland*, a book that likewise had great currency in Ireland. In Zurich, therefore, a more scholarly view of Irish myth, literature, and history was thrust upon Joyce, a view to which he had probably been exposed briefly during his stay in Paris in 1902–3; the philological framework for Irish studies stressed texts and translations rather than retellings and popular refractions. Though even scholarly sources at times omit some of the most sexually explicit passages of Irish literature, by and large the Irish materials available to Joyce in Zurich were the raw texts with very literal translations showing both the texture of the language and the formal properties of the narratives, as well as a relatively candid view of the contents.

An important and for Joyce probably fortunate gap in the Zurich holdings is the lack of any English-language translation of *Táin Bó Cúailnge*. The library later acquired John Strachan and J. G. O'Keeffe's *"Táin Bó Cúailnge" from the Yellow Book of Lecan* (1904–12) as a supplementary volume to *Ériu*, but it does not own the various truncated translations of the text by such people as Winifred Faraday. In particular, the library does not hold Joseph Dunn's 1914 translation. For *Táin Bó Cúailnge* Joyce would have had to rely on Ernst Windisch's comprehensive 1905 German edition and translation of the text, issued as a supplementary volume to the series *Irische Texte* and owned by the Zentralbibliothek, as noted earlier. Acquaintance with Windisch's text would have been a happy chance for Joyce, because in English-language translations *Táin Bó Cúailnge* was severely circumscribed and bowdlerized; since the text was presented as the national epic by nationalists, nothing offending nationalist sensibilities was tolerated in translation. Windisch, by contrast, is motivated by philological interests; his text is complete and the translation transposes the formal properties of the text, the humor,

33. The Zentralbibliothek now owns the 1926 editions of Gregory's *Cuchulain of Muirthemne* and *Gods and Fighting Men*, acquired when the Anglo-Irish literary revival had become a literary phenomenon worth collecting in its own right.

the sexual and scatological aspects, the redundancies and absurdities. In-sofar as Molly is reminiscent of Medb, she is closer to the Medb of Win-disch's *Táin Bó Cúailnge* and translation than to the Medb of any English translation Joyce might have read.

The wealth of materials related to early Irish literature, history, and language in Zurich's Zentralbibliothek illustrates again the overdetermi-nacy of Joyce's knowledge of these subjects. He had become acquainted with materials related to Irish history and literature used in *Ulysses* be-fore he left Ireland in 1904; in addition the publications he needed for his treatment of Irish myth in *Ulysses*—even the flamboyant texts and theories of Vallancey—were at hand in the libraries he used in Zurich.[34] Moreover, though the Zurich collection of Irish materials is not, strictly speaking, essential as a repository of sources for the Irish myth in *Ulys-ses*, the affinities between the configuration of the Zentralbibliothek's Irish holdings and Joyce's treatment of Irish myth, which transcends the constraints of Irish nationalism, suggest that the library's collection influ-enced Joyce's thinking about his country's traditions. Because of both the composition of the collection of books pertaining to Celtic language and literature and the accessibility of that collection, in part by virtue of a superior catalogue system, few libraries in Europe and the British Isles would have been better than Zurich's Zentralbibliothek for Joyce to have pursued his interests in early Irish literature, history, and language.

v. Oral sources in Zurich

In the previous chapter I stressed the importance of oral culture for Joyce's knowledge of Irish tradition. From his father's stories and place-lore, to the circulation of ideas among students and Irish intellectuals, to his contacts with Synge and other figures of the Anglo-Irish revival, to his interchange with his brother Stanislaus, we can trace a steady flow of con-versational information to James Joyce, some of which had central im-

---

34. A major gap in the collection in the Zentralbibliothek is Meyer's *Voyage of Bran*. Joyce must have known this study either directly or through oral sources before he left Ireland in 1904. He would also have been able to consult it when he arrived in Paris in 1919, where the Celtic holdings were more extensive than those of Zurich and where he composed Molly's episode, in which the concept of the happy otherworld is refracted.

portance for his understanding of Irish literature, myth, and history. The
influence of oral culture on Joyce did not cease when he went to Zurich.

Fritz Senn has illuminated the curious anachronism in *Ulysses* in
which Haines credits "professor Pokorny of Vienna" with the view that
Irish myth has no trace of hell (10.1076–85). As Senn has pointed out,
in 1904 Julius Pokorny was seventeen, a student himself rather than professor ("No Trace of Hell"). Yet in fact Pokorny did hold these views,
though they were not published until 1923, a year after *Ulysses* itself appeared in print. Pokorny himself believed that Joyce had either heard lectures Pokorny delivered in Ireland in 1912 or that Joyce had heard about
the content of these lectures from a third party.

Yet all of this speculation overlooks the obvious: that Joyce was working on *Ulysses* for four years in a city which was part of the culture area
dominated by German philology and in which ideas of scholars like Pokorny (who was teaching in nearby Vienna) were circulating. In the case
of Pokorny's views about Irish myth cited in *Ulysses*, the conclusion
seems inescapable that Joyce had learned of Pokorny's views through oral
channels, but it may be more reasonable to suppose that Pokorny's views
circulated in Zurich in the intellectual life that Joyce participated in at a
critical time in his artistic growth, the very time when he was writing
Ulysses, than to imagine that Joyce was dependent on contact with Ireland for those views.

At the very least, in Zurich Joyce would have become aware through
oral channels of the difference in approach between German philological
methods and the nationalist filter of Irish culture in Ireland. The anach-
ronistic attribution of views about the Irish otherworld to Pokorny in
Ulysses suggests that Joyce learned specifics as well as generalities about
Pokorny's views on early Irish culture while he was in Zurich, either directly through lectures or written sources or indirectly through third parties. I am suggesting that the reference to Pokorny in *Ulysses* is Joyce's
way of giving tribute to what he had learned of Irish literature and culture
in his Zurich days as much as anything else; it is, of course, also a way
of making Haines a fool. The details of what Joyce picked up through
conversation in Zurich are irretrievable; but it is significant that in
Haines's remark Pokorny is credited with views that indicate the early
Irish were resolutely non-Christian—views Joyce would have taken up
with some satisfaction.

vi. Conclusion

Compared to his contemporaries in Ireland, Joyce emerges as a person with substantial interests in the history and literature of Ireland. His interest in Irish as a language went beyond the rather pallid Gaelic League program, and it is clear from his acquisition of Irish dictionaries later in life that this interest in Irish persisted. His discernment related to Irish culture is indicated in his interest in and valuation of the writings of P. W. Joyce and others whose treatments of Irish literature, history, and culture are distinguished in comparison with the sentimentalized and circumscribed fare of the Irish cultural nationalists. The likelihood that Joyce used Windisch's edition and translation of *Táin Bó Cúailnge*, his unfavorable review of Augusta Gregory's *Poets and Dreamers*, his use of d'Arbois de Jubainville, as well as other evidence discussed above, all corroborate this supposition.

Although Joyce owned some key books about Irish history and literature, he did not depend on his personal library for his resources in this area during the time he was composing *Ulysses*. An analysis of the books he collected before 1920—his so-called Trieste library—indicates that only 4 percent of the books were related to Irish culture and history (Gillespie 17).[35] Together with the slim evidence for the use of specific books on Irish history and literature, these data support the suggestion that Joyce's Irish architectonics and poetics result from his general knowledge gained in Ireland, from popular sources read in Ireland and abroad, and from library resources that he had at his disposal in Zurich and Paris.

Joyce was exposed to a very broad view of Irish culture during his lifetime. Raised in Ireland, he was introduced early in his life to many aspects of early Irish myth and literature, as well as to Modern Irish as a language and to Irish history. Initially these subjects were presented to him through the veil of cultural nationalism, and he learned of them largely through popularizations of various sorts, though he also undertook study of Irish as a language in a more serious way. As early as 1902, when Joyce went to Paris, he would have met with a different view of Celtic and Irish studies: a more scholarly view, but one influenced as well by French nationalisms and sep-

---

35. Note, however, that a similar percentage of the library is in political science (3 percent) and the social sciences (2 percent), yet Manganiello has demonstrated the significant role that politics plays in Joyce's work and thought.

aratisms. This exposure to a different way of regarding early Irish material was probably reinforced for Joyce by his contact with J. M. Synge, who was himself sensible of the limitations of Irish nationalist refractions of the early texts. Later Joyce lived and worked in Zurich, manipulating Irish myth and literary texts as he wrote *Ulysses* in an environment where the German philological perspective on those same materials was dominant.

For Joyce these alternative perspectives on Irish tradition broke the stranglehold of parochial and proprietary Irish nationalism on Irish literature. Joyce's attitude toward Irish myth and his use of it in *Ulysses* show influences other than those of the Irish revival and reflect in part Continental views emphasizing a comparative Indo-European perspective. Although a comparative perspective was sometimes adopted by cultural nationalists—the Gael-and-Greek brief discussed above, for example—the method was for nationalists primarily a means of validating Irish culture and literature. The Continental philological tradition was more dispassionate about features of the tradition that violated dominant values, mores, and literary standards, using a comparative framework to situate Irish literature as a whole within the Indo-European tradition. The European context for Irish culture that Joyce met in both Paris and Zurich comes to fruition in Joyce's appreciation and use of Irish material in both *Ulysses* and *Finnegans Wake*, a use that is more extensive and more various than that of most of his contemporaries among the writers of the Anglo-Irish literary revival. Joyce is more able, as argued above, to transpose and reanimate, among other things, the humor, the sexuality, the ironies, the genres, and the formal properties of early Irish literature.

The comparative framework implicit in the program of German philology and historical linguistics, particularly in investigations of Indo-European culture and linguistics, to which Joyce was exposed in Zurich sets an intellectual context for Joyce's coordination of Greek, Irish, and other mythologies in *Ulysses*. A recognition of the implicit comparatism in *Ulysses* in turn illuminates ways in which *Finnegans Wake* is a logical extension of Joyce's earlier work. That Zurich and the Zentralbibliothek played an important role in Joyce's ability to see Irish tradition whole, to use Irish myth in ways that are less tainted and parochial than are those of his nationalist Irish contemporaries (including W. B. Yeats), can hardly be doubted. To these influences we also owe a partial debt for Joyce's brilliant experimentations with form in the second half of *Ulysses* as well as in *Finnegans Wake*.

Chapter 9

Finit

CLOV: *(fixed gaze, tonelessly)* Finished, it's finished,
nearly finished, it must be nearly finished.
(Pause)
Grain upon grain, one by one, and one day, suddenly,
there's a heap, a little heap, the impossible heap.

Samuel Beckett, *Endgame*

As critics have noted, in the closing paragraphs of *Ulysses* Molly's memories of kissing Mulvey under the Spanish wall merge with her memories of the lovemaking with Bloom on Howth Head.[1] The undifferentiated "he" of her interior monologue is the pivot word causing the two scenes to merge:

the sun shines for you he said the day we were lying among the rhododendrons on Howth head in the grey tweed suit and his straw hat the day I got him to propose to me yes first I gave him the bit of seedcake out of my mouth and it was leapyear like now yes 16 years ago my God after that long kiss I near lost my breath yes he said I was a flower of the mountain . . . and Gibraltar as a girl where I was a Flower of the mountain yes when I put the rose in my hair like the Andalusian girls used or shall I wear a red yes and how he kissed me under the Moorish wall and I thought well as well him as another and then I asked him with my eyes to ask again (18.1571–1605)

Here the first *he* refers to Bloom, but the *he* kissing her under the Moorish wall is Mulvey, and she is back to Bloom as she thinks "as well him

---

1. Ellmann, *Ulysses on the Liffey* 171–72, gives a good discussion of this scene.

as another" for her first lovemaking and for marriage. In the process Ireland and Gibraltar as the Irish otherworld also merge: the rhododendrons and sunny day on Howth Head become the flowers and sun of Gibraltar.

The moment distills several mythic strands from Irish tradition. The scene reveals Molly as Sovereignty figure: flower of the mountain, rose of Ireland, the eternal *puella senilis* transformed once again. The passage brings to a close the Sovereignty theme sounded at the opening of the book and simultaneously celebrates the union of the Sovereignty with sacral king. The moment also represents the coming together of Milesian and Spanish woman on a height—a prominence to be identified symbolically as *the height* in *The Book of Invasions* from which Ireland is to be sighted. At the same time there is a cresting and focusing of the otherworld imagery in the text. In the interweaving of these central mythic themes from Irish literature, Joyce gives us at once a view of the possibilities for the renewal of the Irish people in the new Ireland of 1922 and also a glimpse of what the new Ireland itself might become. As Ireland merges textually with Gibraltar-cum-otherworld, Joyce suggests a vision for the new Ireland in terms of the Irish otherworld: a beautiful land where music and poetry are in the air, where love and sexuality exist without sin, where sectarian differences cause no conflict, where there is peace. Joyce's overlaying of Gibraltar with Howth Head suggests an Ireland made in the image of the ancient Irish ideal of the otherworld. To be sure, there are some whimsical touches here, particularly the climatic ones; but the vision Joyce holds out is still compelling, particularly in this era of Irish sectarian and political turmoil, in an era that has seen the renewal of the commitment to the legislation of Catholic morality. The possibilities Joyce holds out are in fact the ancient ideals that have dominated the Irish imagination since time immemorial and that continue to have relevance and power—the ideal of a nourishing island, full of pleasure, peace, freedom, tolerance, health, beauty, life rather than death.

In giving a vision of Ireland's future possibilities in 1922, Joyce reenacts the ancient role of the Irish poet: he is the fili, the seer, who reveals for the community not only the normative values of the present but the direction of the future. His sight is inner sight, second sight, sight of the mind rather than sight of the eye: sight gained from afar, in Trieste-Zurich-Paris, rather than from the streets of Dublin. The vision is made possible by perspective, including a comic perspective that sets things in their proper proportions. There is no attempt to proselytize: it is sufficient to promulgate the vision in view of "the futility of triumph or protest or vindication: the inanity of extolled virtue: the lethargy of nescient matter: the apathy of the stars" (17.2224–26). The moment was a brief one for Joyce; vision as invitation in *Ulysses* gives way to a more somber mood, a less than open sense of the future in *Finnegans Wake*. But that is another story, with Joyce assuming different aspects of the role of *fili*.

The elements of otherworld imagery that Joyce uses in episodes 15 and 18 of *Ulysses*, the climax and the *clou* of the book respectively, should cause critics to be cautious. In chapter 4 I explored briefly the ways in which the semiotics of gender in Irish tradition is at variance with the semiotics of gender in dominant Western thought. The otherworld strands of "Circe" and "Penelope" illustrate that the semiotics of Irish tradition varies with respect to more than just gender: the semiotics of *underworld*, *ghost*, *trial*, *king*, *midnight*, *entrapment*, and *rescue* are different as well. And there are *flower*, *rose*, *mountain*, *tower*, *warmth*, *island*, *voyage*, *drink*, *kiss*, which also resonate with their own meanings in Irish culture. One is tempted to play with Saussure's famous distinction between *langue* and *parole* and to say that in the case of Joyce and his critics, the *parole* is the same, but the *langue* is different. Joyce's actual utterances, his performance speech, could emerge from the critics' language, yet because Joyce's abstract linguistic system is different by virtue of his being Irish, communication breaks down.[2] But if the Irish language and the Irish literary tradition make Joyce's words remote, what hope is there of understanding his texts without understanding the Irish substratum? Until his language is understood, his words will remain opaque, impenetrable. There are texts, subtexts, and contexts to be mastered.

How is it that Joyce can smoothly dovetail his central mythic structures from Irish tradition—the material from *The Book of Invasions*, the Sovereignty theme, the otherworld imagery and plotting—so seamlessly

---

2. For a brief summary of Saussure, see Aitchison 30, 39–40.
Wall (17; cf. 17–20), speaking of homonyms, notes, "One of the hidden difficulties of the Anglo-Irish dialect is the fact that it contains a considerable number of words which are not the English words they appear to be." Thus, the linguistic problems that a speaker of standard English will have in decoding Anglo-Irish are complex and occur on several levels.

at the end of the book and, in fact, throughout? It is tempting to take the romantic's way out and say that Joyce is able to knit together his Irish themes—and, indeed, his mythic themes as a whole—through genius. But in the case of the Irish material there is another factor: the coherence of a tradition that remained rooted, operative, and largely intact into the twentieth century. In an integrated tradition the individual elements will be compatible with each other, will buttress and reinforce each other, will cohere because they are inscribed in a larger whole. Ireland's political history has been one of bitter oppression and dispossession, particularly since the seventeenth century, but this same bitter legacy ironically preserved its mythic system to the modern era. The political oppression that made it illegal to print books in Irish, to educate the young in Irish, to exercise Irish Catholicism or to have Catholic seminaries in Ireland—this same oppression meant also that Ireland had the longest manuscript tradition and the most vigorous oral tradition in Western Europe. It has been said that Ireland never experienced the Renaissance. Manuscripts were copied in the nineteenth century as they had been in the Middle Ages, yet even this was a marginal way of preserving the tradition. For most of the Irish, an illiterate population, Irish literature and Irish tradition were passed from generation to generation as human traditions have been since the dawn of human history: mouth to ear, orally, by the master teller and keeper of lore. In 1935 there were more unrecorded folktales—and a more extensive living oral tradition—in the tiny rocky parish of Carna in West Galway than in all the rest of Western Europe (Ó Súilleabháin, *Folktales of Ireland* xxxvii). The oral tradition and its isolation from the dominant discourse of Western literary movements preserved Ireland's language, its imagery, its symbols. The bitter political legacy of Ireland contributed as well to the preservation of Ireland's myth and traditional tales.

This rooted tradition, a tradition that in certain remarkable ways survived and sustained the transition from Irish to English,[3] was a reason that Yeats turned to Ireland rather than England when he wanted to develop a mythic verse drama. In an article entitled "The Dramatic Movement" in the December 1904 issue of *Samhain*, Yeats inveighed against

---

3. Though much survived into English, the oral literature and traditional customs preserved in the Irish-speaking areas of Ireland are, not surprisingly, considerably richer.

the English censorship laws that forbade the dramatization of biblical subjects:

And yet it is precisely these stories of The Bible that have all to themselves, in the imagination of English people, especially of the English poor, the place they share in this country with the stories of Fion and of Usheen and of Patrick.

Milton set the story of Sampson into the form of a Greek play, because he knew that Sampson was, in the English imagination, what Herakles was in the imagination of Greece. . . . An English poet of genius once told me that he would have tried his hand in plays for the people, if they knew any story, the censor would pass, except Jack and the Bean Stalk. (8)

In Ireland, by contrast, the traditional mythos was alive and was known to the audience, known in some cases all too well. Running afoul of the nationalist sensitivities in *The Countess Cathleen*, Yeats realized: "In using what I considered traditional symbols I forgot that in Ireland they are not symbols but realities" (*Autobiography* 252). This is the culture that formed Joyce, the culture from which his own mythic method springs.

Joyce's culture provided him an autonomous mythos, articulated, ancient, coherent, complex, that had lived on to his own time. The mythos was embedded in a larger system of symbols and signs, encoded in a native language, which had bequeathed many of those same symbols, as it had bequeathed elements of phonology, morphology, syntax, and lexis, to Anglo-Irish culture.[4] In turn there was a native poetics for writers to draw upon, a poetics autonomous of the poetics of English and European literature, but a poetics that had in some respects—in its aesthetic of the comic, for example—been generalized in Anglo-Irish cultural domains. During his artistic development Joyce learned how to use these cultural materials in his own work. The sophisticated use of personal names and place names referring to the Irish god of the dead in *Dubliners*, the framework from *The Destruction of Da Derga's Hostel* in "The Dead," the otherworld and Sovereignty elements in *A Portrait of the Artist*, and the Sovereignty imagery in *Exiles* all show a growing interest in Irish mythos and a growing mastery of the ability to transpose the material into an English-language literary context, as well as an ability to meld Irish elements with myth and symbols from other strands of Western culture.

---

4. On aspects of the influence of Irish on Anglo-Irish dialects, see Van Hamel, "Anglo-Irish Syntax," and P. W. Joyce, *English as We Speak It*.

Joyce's mobilization of all these native resources is clear in *Finnegans Wake*, and the analysis of *Ulysses* undertaken in this volume shows the extent to which the trajectory is traceable in Joyce's central literary work.

The value and potential of Joyce's cultural heritage is virtually inconceivable to those who have been formed by most other Western literary traditions. Almost without exception the rest of the West—most of literate Europe and English-speaking America—has lost its living, autonomous mythic heritage (or heritages, to speak more properly). There have been attempts to revive a native mythos (Wagner), or to use folklore for these purposes (the brothers Grimm), or to raise native legends to international stature (Goethe's *Faust*); some of these attempts have been notably productive. But by and large, literate Westerners have replaced the native mythos of their particular cultures with classical and Christian myth learned at school and church. For his European readers who depended on such transplanted and grafted mythic systems, Joyce was willing to speak the international language of Greek mythology; his methods show his appreciation of the principles of comparative mythology both in his ability to strip a myth to its skeletal outline, its fabula, and in his conflation of similar mythic patterns from varied sources. For readers who didn't participate in his living Irish mythic tradition, Joyce provided European parallels to and justifications for the native Irish symbols and myths: not only is the voyage of Ulysses invoked in parallel with *The Book of Invasions*, but for the Sovereignty imagery, the figures of Ann Hathaway (9.180ff.) and Xanthippe (9.234) are raised as ersatz archetypes, making Bloom as an uxorious man a sort of Shakespearean Socrates.

Yet these cerebral invocations fail fully to convince: they come from Joyce's brain, not his blood. It may be the sense of the artificial clinging to the Homeric scaffolding that caused Pound to dismiss it as *affaire de cuisine* ("James Joyce et Pécuchet" 91; cf. "Ulysses" 406). The Irish mythic elements operate on a different level: still vital, they are the ineluctable modality of the mythic. It is the Irish mythic subtext that makes Molly come alive: not her Penelope's weaving and unweaving of words, but her associations as Sovereignty with fruits, flowers, otherworld imagery, sexual vitality and dominance. One needs to understand the cultural grid supporting the mythos to appreciate Joyce's creation fully; the unfamiliar reader is like an observer at an African masked ritual, where, as Germaine Dieterlen has observed, "the details of a mask, which are understood in all their significance only by the initiated, are related to mythical events, expressed in artistic language. The mythical element is hidden, and at the same time given expression, by the artist's skill, for the symbolism of the mask exists on several levels" (quoted in Lommel 42). At such a ritual onlookers participate to the extent of their knowledge (Lommel 44), and so it is in the case of Joyce's mythic method. Yet even readers outside the Irish tradition feel the power of the living Irish myth in his work, as the critical passion over Molly indicates.[5] At the same time, not understanding the cultural context of Joyce's symbology and myth, critics do not always read the signs correctly, even when they feel the power of the patterns Joyce draws on. The attempt to realign such misreadings—by providing some of the knowledge possessed by the initiates, as it were—has provided points of departure for a new critique in this book.

Joyce is a writer between literary traditions. The Irish tradition is a divided tradition, even, as Joyce himself puts it, "divided against itself" (*CW* 185); to be an Irish writer is to be heir of two languages, two poetics, two literary traditions, two literary histories. Literary traditions are systems embedded in turn in larger cultural systems, including political, economic, religious, and aesthetic systems.[6] An Irish writer, or any writer in a divided tradition, inherits more than one set of cultural norms and develops, as any minority writer must, a multicultural perspective. When cultural systems—literary systems in particular—interface, certain predictable results follow, results that reflect gradients of cultural prestige, power, and dominance (Even-Zohar 45–94). An Anglo-Irish writer such as Joyce is himself the locus of a polysystems interface: he moves between cultural systems and literary systems, and, like any other writer, between subsystems as well; encoding, decoding, recoding, and code switching become facts of artistic life.

The position of Anglo-Irish literature at the beginning of the twentieth century was complex because it was a subsystem of English (language)

---

5. Shechner (196) says that most criticism of the last episode of *Ulysses* is best understood as "an open letter to Molly, for much that is puzzling as literary analysis makes abundant sense as courtship or masculine protest," a comment not irrelevant to his own analysis.

6. Or rather a literary tradition is a polysystem, a system composed in turn of subsystems: a system of poetics, a system of mythologies, a system of literary patronage, a system of literary practitioners, and so forth. See Even-Zohar 1–44.

literature yet as an internally organized literary system was becoming increasingly dependent on Irish (language) literature and culture. In Ireland literary works written in English and Irish were becoming (and still remain) symbiotic to a large extent. The process was not, however, a simple exchange of literary materials; in most cases, the gradients of power, prestige, and cultural and political dominance operated in the process to privilege elements of the English literary system. Thus, Irish content (e.g., Irish myth and Irish history) was incorporated into English-language literature in Ireland, and at the same time more fundamental English literary elements, such as the system of genres or poetic conventions as well as cultural values, remained in place and even spread to literature in Irish.[7]

Joyce did not primarily aspire to succeed within the English literary system. Unlike his older Irish contemporaries who wrote in English—Wilde, Shaw, and Yeats, for example—and unlike other members of the Irish literary revival—Gregory or even A. E.—he did not look immediately to London as the center of literary activity and patronage and as the standard by which his success as a writer would be judged. When he left Ireland, deciding that a writer could not work there, he went to the Continent, not London. Joyce was intent on creating an Irish literature in English, not on succeeding as an English writer. For Joyce, Irish literature was a subsystem of world literature rather than a branch of English literature. By locating himself on the Continent rather than in England, by turning to an international patronage system, and by retaining his own focus on Ireland, he positioned himself to remain an Irish writer, even if an Irish writer in exile.[8]

---

7. The trajectory of much literature in Irish in the twentieth century has been in this direction: English genres such as the novel, for example, have become privileged. This is the context out of which emerges Stephen's bitter comment (borrowed from Wilde) about Irish art: "the cracked lookingglass" of a servant is its symbol (*U* 1.146). This statement obviously compresses criticism of the dominant aesthetic of realism and a bitter cultural and political commentary. The Irish artist is the servant of two masters—one English and one Italian—and Irish art mirrors the worlds of the two masters even as it attempts to reflect the artist's own face. The cracked mirror may also refer obliquely to Ireland's divided tradition, Irish culture overlaid by the colonizers' culture, resulting in a shearing and doubling of perspectives that further complicate the artistic task.

8. See Manganiello, esp. 41, 43, 56. Hunt (2) claims that within a European context the Irish genius can escape from provincialism on the one hand and the pervasive influence of England on the other and argues that the Irish national theater emerged from such a European context; although Joyce would have agreed with the premise, he would probably have disagreed with Hunt's conclusions

In the first decades of the twentieth century, Continental artists were turning to "primitive" cultures for new models in the visual and plastic arts. In African art and Cycladic art, among others, such artists as Picasso, Braque, Modigliani, Arp, and Giacometti found ways to break out of the constraints of European realism and at the same time to extend the formal experiments of the impressionists and postimpressionists. Using iconography and forms from other cultures, such artists challenged the artistic idioms of their time and attempted to expand the repertory of Western art. Their work signals an appreciation of the iconographic and hieratic; stimulated by artistic works of other cultures, they inject the grotesque and the humorous, and in some cases a certain raw sexuality, into the visual and plastic arts of Europe. They show an interest in the symbolic rather than the realistic, setting the stage for the major movements of Western visual arts in the first half of the twentieth century, attempting to challenge the very language of art as well as the worldview encoded in the conventions of Western art. They were joined in this enterprise by artists working in other media as well—musicians such as Stravinsky and Ravel, for example, who turned to African rhythms to remake the musical idiom of their day.

Joyce used Irish literature and myth for many of the same artistic reasons as his contemporaries used African or prehistoric art forms.[9] His purposes are not those of a simple nativism; there is a sophisticated modernist and even postmodernist usage of many qualities of Irish literature that runs contrary to the dominant poetics of his time. In *Ulysses* Irish literary materials are used to challenge English and European literary premises and conventions—including the conventions of genre, of subject matter and artistic domain, of artistic function—and to transcend those conventions. Joyce was able to use Irish literature in this fashion in part because the Irish literary tradition was to a great extent still a medieval tradition: in virtue of its political and religious history, Ireland had in some essential ways missed both the Renaissance and the Reformation.[10]

---

about the dramatic movement itself. Deane writes, "Joyce was always to be the Irish writer who refused the limitations of being Irish; the writer of English who refused the limitations of being an English writer" (100).

9. Loss, *Joyce's Visible Art*, discusses various other ways in which Joyce's literary work relates to modernism in the visual arts. See also Frank.

10. This is a factor in the medievalism of Joyce's thought, which is usually attributed primarily to his Catholicism and his training by the Jesuits; on Joyce's medievalism, see Mercier, "James Joyce as Medieval Artist," and Eco. His medievalism was discussed by early critics as well, including Gilbert and Levin.

The hieratic characters of the medieval Irish sagas, like the portraits in the Book of Kells or the figures of primitive cultures that inspired Joyce's contemporaries, are intended to impress and overwhelm the audience; realism gives way to decorative and symbolic impulses that heighten the figural impact. Those same characters are presented humorously, becoming grotesques to the modern sensibility; but the humor and the grotesque figuration serve larger purposes in commenting on and affirming the life cycle of humanity, in promulgating and questioning values. As with other medieval works, in Irish literature there is little boundary between the secular and the sacred; symbolic and mythic elements do not preclude humor and sexuality. Many of these elements continued in an unbroken tradition in Irish literature to Joyce's own time. As Yeats observed, in Ireland in the twentieth century the symbols were still alive. Joyce's characters, in *Ulysses* notably Molly and Leopold, recapitulate these features: they work within the mode of realism, but through their Irish mythic dimension the characters impose themselves upon the reader as hieratic figures. Joyce develops his characters with humor, pushing them to the limit as grotesques, ultimately exposing yet affirming the underpinnings of life. In Joyce's *Ulysses*, in medieval literature, and in primitive art as well, these characteristics are healing; they lead to an acceptance of life and to generativity.

This is one sense in which the material in *Ulysses* signifies and has meaning. Though Joyce eschews didacticism and polemic, though his art remains static rather than kinetic, and though the book is not univocal, the Irish mythic framework presents possibilities and opens the world. Here Harry Levin's observation that Joyce's affinities are with Dante and the medieval iconographers remains useful; Joyce evokes the past to illuminate the present ("Editor's Introduction" 14). Yet it is his medievalism of form, not just of content, that distinguishes Joyce from many of his contemporaries who attempted to inject the content of Irish mythos into the dominant conventions of an English-language literature, for Joyce also uses Irish literature to challenge the substance of narrative and of language itself. Using literary forms and genres from his native tradition, he shatters the confines of both epic and novel, breaking the boundaries of high and low art, mixing genres and styles, to make room for a modernist sensibility and a modernist vision of the world. The freedom of narrative convention that Joyce claims enables him to call attention to the question of convention per se, just as contemporary artists do in the visual and plastic arts by borrowing the conventions of primitive art.

There is a self-reflexive quality in *Ulysses* that derives in part from Joyce's use of elements appropriated from Irish literary tradition. Unlike some of his contemporaries Joyce does not merely set the primitive and noncanonical against the canonical; by melding the classical myth of Ulysses with the "primitive" Irish myths of *The Book of Invasions*, the Sovereignty, and the Irish otherworld, he asserts that the values found in the noncanonical Irish myth can be reconciled with the canonical and be equated with aspects of mainstream Western culture that have been submerged by other dominant strands of the poetics. Joyce brilliantly models a change in poetics—and by extension, a change in worldview—that results from reordering hierarchies, privileging new aspects of art, reorganizing culture, adopting the nonlinear and nonrational forms of Irish literature.

It is thus on many levels ironic that it has become a *topos* to ask of *Ulysses*, "If Joyce wished to base his narrative on an ancient legend, why did he turn to Greek rather than Gaelic tales?" (Kiberd, "Bloom the Liberator" 3), and it is finally too simple to juxtapose Joyce with Yeats, as modernist versus revivalist, as so many critical studies do.[11] Joyce's writing is so extensive and so various that it is possible, even easy, to construct a reading in which one discerns a "modernist" repudiation of Ireland's literary tradition. But the situation is much more complicated, as revisionist work on Joyce makes plain. In *Ulysses* not only does Joyce use a system of Irish myths, but he writes in an Irish narrative mode. There is an Irish literary discourse in *Ulysses*, as there is in *Finnegans Wake* and (as we are coming to understand) his early work as well, permeating content and form.

At the same time Joyce's use of his literary tradition is a paradox, for it is true that he repudiates—or perhaps *rewrites* is a more accurate term—the orthodox refraction of Irish literature.[12] He does so, however, in order to revive a more penetrating version of the past than the one that

---

11. In light of the Irish literary discourse in *Ulysses*, the kinds of rather conventional dichotomies set up by such authors as Flanagan and Kearney—and repeated so often as givens—need to be reexamined.

12. For the argument that Joyce repudiates the militaristic cult of Cu-Chulainn, see Kiberd, "Bloom the Liberator."

cultural nationalism had promulgated. To use Irish literature this way, Joyce had to redefine it for himself, reimage it against the conventional, stereotyped, and univocal definition that Irish nationalist politics and Anglo-Irish literature had given it. Joyce wrote to "shock his compatriots into a deeper awareness of their self-deceptions" (Kiberd, "Bloom the Liberator" 3) but also to awaken them to a deeper awareness of their Irish identity. In the process he not only outraged the British and the world with the ordinariness of Bloom's dailiest of days (cf. Kiberd, "Bloom the Liberator" 4) but also struck a blow with sensibilities that can be traced to Ireland's heroic-comic literary tradition. Joyce transformed English from "an imperial humiliation" to "a native weapon" (Heaney 40), and he wrested English-language literature out of the possession of the English, thereby paving the way for other twentieth-century postcolonial writers, whatever their language.

Joyce's Irish discourse is complex. Often what is taken as demythologizing (cf. Benstock) actually follows the early Irish texts themselves with their louse-ridden, humorous, and grotesque heroes. Vivian Mercier (*Irish Comic Tradition* 246) reminds us that Gaelic literature revels in exposing to ridicule its greatest heroes: Finn, CuChulainn, and Saint Patrick himself. Joyce redefines Irish heroism in *Ulysses* and *Finnegans Wake* so as to challenge the received idea of heroes, but at the same time he embraces the Irish mythic heritage with its life-affirming sexual heroics, its commitment to Hebraism and Hellenism, its double vision of life. His view of the literary tradition to be revived was different, broader than that of most of his contemporaries, though Synge stands as an exception here. But Joyce's appreciation of his Irish literary heritage included its form as well as its content and values, its poetics as well as its language.

There is a vertical dimension to Joyce's Irish discourse—the restating and re-presenting of earlier texts—but there is a horizontal dimension also—the intertwining of various Irish myths, fusing and linking them with myths from other textual traditions.[13] Thus, the Irish literary elements sustain both paradigmatic and syntagmatic analyses. Although this study has been concerned primarily with delineating areas of Joyce's Irish intertextuality, it has also emphasized the significance and implication of his quotations and his use of Irish texts within *Ulysses*. If in Joyce's works there is no attempt to sustain a continuous link between past and present

---

13. See Topia on some theoretical aspects of intertextuality in Joyce's work.

(Kearney 12) and no attempt to establish a monocular view of the past, there is nevertheless a paradigm of the metempsychosis—as well as the recycling and reawakening—of Irish tradition across gaps in space and time. The past is reawakened in the present, reinscribed within "the now, the here, through which all future plunges to the past" (9.89). At times Joyce's Irish discourse contains tensions and contradictions, and at times it runs counter to other domains of discourse. This is Joyce's favorite posture; as Richard Ellmann has written of Joyce's method in *Ulysses*, "Whenever confronted by a choice between two possible things to include, Joyce chose both" (*Ulysses on the Liffey* 34). Joyce's voices overlap and contradict themselves. Although such contradictions have bothered critics, neither Joyce nor his personae were troubled by such scruples (Anderson 62–63; cf. *U* 1.517), and these very contradictions are part of his method.[14]

Having removed himself to the Continent, Joyce did not escape the problems of working between literary systems. Paradoxically, he multiplied the number of literary systems within which his own art evolved: he became situated not simply between English and Irish literatures but also in the web connecting German, French, Italian, Latin, Greek, Norwegian, and Swedish literatures as well. In short, he became an Irish writer working amidst the literary systems of Europe. In trying to evolve an autonomous position as an Irish writer, he had to come to terms not just with his divided tradition but with the position of his art within Western art as a whole. T. S. Eliot saw the use of myth in *Ulysses* as a discovery, a way of structuring the chaotic and formless experience of twentieth-century life. This is, of course, one function of the myth in Joyce's work, but it is not the central feature. Joyce's mythic method does serve to organize and structure the multifarious materials he includes in his narrative, but it also serves to make connections, to establish equivalences, to coordinate—and also to disrupt connections, to deny likeness, to establish differences and conflicts. It is, among other things, a way of reconciling the early Irish texts to the literary polysystem that is its new context or, to turn the matter inside out, a way of positioning Joyce's own mythic work within a number of literary systems in which it can be situated. Joyce's works, *Ulysses* and *Finnegans Wake* in particular, are par-

---

14. Topia claims, for example, that in "Cyclops" Joyce uses this type of contradiction to dissolve all possibility of "the unified real in fiction" (124).

adigmatically Irish books that take their place in an international literary polysystem.

Before the twentieth century a mythic work was essentially a retelling or re-creating of an established myth. The myth was the surface of the narrative, and the significance was the subtext that emerged from the implicit comparison of the established myth with the particular manipulation of the story at hand. While this type of mythic retelling has continued in the twentieth century, another mythic method has emerged as an outgrowth of the nineteenth-century developments in comparative mythology. In this second paradigm the myth itself is stripped to its essential outline and comes to be seen as the substructure lying behind a variety of surface manifestations: the myth also becomes the subtext and the means by which the surface tale signifies. Throughout the nineteenth century this new meaning of myth emerged in varied fields. In studies of folklore and oral tradition the new approach to mythos culminated in works such as *The Types of the Folktale* by Antti Aarne and Stith Thompson, which organizes the oral stories collected in decades of field research throughout the Indo-European culture area into 2,340 traditional narrative patterns; these basic patterns in turn illuminate the functions and forms of any individual telling of a tale. The same trajectory can be traced in comparative mythology, where *The Golden Bough* of Sir James Frazer represents another type of culminating effort. In the field of comparative mythology the discernment of underlying common patterns was used to illuminate the meaning of specific manifestations of myths in varied cultural contexts or even to reconstruct mythic patterns.[15]

At the turn of the century the methods of comparative mythology were particularly important in Celtic studies, for mythic substructures often must be used to explicate or make sense of Celtic texts that are fragmentary or have a confused surface. In studies of Irish literature in particular, the method was most useful, even perhaps essential, in establishing patterns in a mythology that was in many ways opaque as a closed circle of texts. A millennium of euhemerization and disambiguation had blurred the mythic basis of the tales (Tymoczko, "Unity and Duality"), which could be reappropriated only through a comparative examination. Such an approach, illustrated by the work of Henri d'Arbois de Jubainville or

---

15. In the work of Georges Dumézil and others this effort continues; see Littleton for an overview and an assessment.

Alfred Nutt, had permeated Irish culture during Joyce's youth and had become part of intellectual discourse.

The extension of the methods of comparative mythology and folklore to the creation of literary works was pioneered by Joyce, though he was not the sole practitioner of these techniques.[16] Eliot himself in *The Waste Land* depends on comparative mythology, using the fabula, the basic pattern behind the myth, rather than the surface of the myth, to achieve his ends; lest we miss his deep structures, Eliot provides footnotes to spell out the patterns we need in order to understand the meaning of his poem. Joyce has dispensed with footnotes, though through the works of Stuart Gilbert and Frank Budgen he has given us authorized guidebooks to elements of the mythic subtext of *Ulysses*. These guides have been only partial, for the methods of comparative mythology that Joyce implicitly depends on in *Ulysses* permit the tale to be both an odyssey and an imram, or an odyssey and a taking of Ireland—or, for that matter, to be also a peripatetic retelling of Dante's *Commedia*, Shakespeare's *Hamlet*, and Goethe's *Faust*.

The coordination and conflation of myths, the comparative mythic method that lies behind *Ulysses*, is hinted at in *Dubliners* and found in a sophisticated form as early as *A Portrait of the Artist*, where Irish otherworld imagery and Christian eschatology are integrated with the Daedalus and Icarus myths, to name but the obvious. In *Ulysses* this comparative mythic method is used to correlate not only Irish and Greek myth but also English, Italian, and German myth. Joyce's eclectic use of myth in *Ulysses* is a partial response to the complex literary and cultural relations he had developed; in seeking to move to an autonomous position as an Irish writer, to move out of the conflicting demands of his divided tradition, Joyce ended up positioning himself in the midst of even more literary systems. In *Ulysses* Joyce's response to his complex literary situation presages the mythic method of *Finnegans Wake*; in a sense *Finnegans Wake* is the logical extension of the methodology of *Ulysses*, necessitated by Joyce's situation as an Irish writer seeking to make a place for an Irish idiom in the literatures and languages of Europe. At the same time Joyce's mythic method contributes to the openness and indeterminacy of his texts.

16. For a recent discussion of Joyce's mythic method, see Palencia-Roth ch. 3, esp. 185ff. See also Kenner, *Pound Era*, esp. 33, 146–47, 169–70.

When Joyce was writing *Ulysses*, there were (as there still are) severe problems in knowing how to read early Irish literature. By the time *Ulysses* was written, most of the raw data (the texts) had been available for years in scholarly English, French, and German editions with facing translations, but still there was no comfortable way to receive this literature in an English-language context and in the context of Irish nationalism. It had to be adapted in various ways, refracted, before it could become integrated and culturally useful. Like many other Irish writers of his time, Joyce acts as a kind of translator of Irish literature into the English literary system. Theorists have shown that translations can have a number of positions and can serve many functions within literary systems; for example, they can be subordinated to the poetics of the time, or they can be used to change the dominant poetics. Translation becomes prestigious when a literature is young, weak, or in crisis, as literature in Ireland was at the turn of the century, for translated works can be used to remake the literary center and to forge a new poetics. At such times the blurring of translation and literary production often occurs, and creative writers become translators. The phenomenon of pseudotranslation can even emerge: a literary work that purports to be a translation but that in fact has no original. Yeats, in his manipulations of Irish myth in "The Song of the Wandering Aengus" or *Deirdre*, is Yeats as mythmaker or Yeats as pseudotranslator. But at such times translations can also masquerade as original works.[17]

Many of the innovative formal elements in *Ulysses* are related to the Irish literary system, including aspects of the system that caused reception problems in an English literary context: the "subliterary" genres, including senchas; the mixed tone of Joyce's epic; the hyperbole and grotesque; the narrative gaps and blurred margin. Joyce found a way to use these "difficult" formal aspects of Irish literature to challenge the poetics of his time, "translating" (in the etymological sense) them into English in his own literary work in *Ulysses*. As a translator he is of a class with Pound, who used his literary translations from medieval poetry and Chinese poetry to change the direction of twentieth-century poetry. Joyce's innovations in narrative are not unlike Yeats's innovations in drama, wherein

---

17. Even-Zohar (45–51) discusses these theoretical issues. Case studies can be found in Hermans and in Lefevere and K. D. Jackson. On the importance of translation to the modernists, see Kenner, *Pound Era*, esp. 150, 170.

ritualistic drama, specifically Noh theater, is "translated" into an English literary context, for the purposes of shifting the theatrical conventions of the time toward a symbolic and universalized nonrepresentational drama.

But there are two differences. Unlike Pound, Joyce is translating Irish literary techniques, Irish poetics, and parameters of the Irish literary system *that are his own cultural heritage* and that emanate from a linguistic tradition Joyce could claim as that of his ancestors; these literary features are translated into English-language writing, underscoring again Joyce's identity as an Irish writer and linking his enterprise to the work of postcolonial writers. It is as if Joyce had learned how to read and appreciate early Irish literature for himself and in the process of coming to terms with his own reception of it had learned useful things about how to *write* twentieth-century literature, specifically twentieth-century narrative. He is a translator of the methods of one side of his divided tradition into the other side of the tradition: he undertakes this translation endeavor in part to renew Irish literature and culture as a whole.

The second difference is that Joyce obscures the fact that he is translating. Why does he do so? It is a given that any translator must limit the amount of unfamiliar material translated into the receptor system; otherwise, the information load of the text will become unmanageable for readers. To be sure, information load was not the primary concern of the man who wrote *Finnegans Wake*, and even *Ulysses* is overwhelming in the quantity of its information to most readers the first time through. Still, Joyce may have kept the Irish mythic patterns beneath the text, latent, without even the exiguous sign of a title to point to the mythic substructure and without an authorized vade mecum to the Irish myth analogous to Gilbert's study of the Greek myth, partly in order to permit the receptor audience to approach the unfamiliar Irish material without becoming alienated. Most English translators of Irish literature foreground the content but assimilate the form to English poetics and to English value structures as a way of avoiding an information overload. Joyce submerges the content of the material, making it latent rather than overt, just as he does with classical myth, but he privileges the poetics and values of his Irish sources. Like Hyde, Yeats, A. E., Synge, and Gregory, Joyce was working "to de-Anglicize, to de-provincialize Ireland and to make it live again in all its individuality as a Celtic country, different in race, in traditions, in ancestral glories from the neighbouring island that had looked, not only across, but down on it for so long" (Reynolds 383): he simply works in a different way. In *Ulysses* Joyce reanimates aspects of Irish form and creates an Irish style, but he consigns the Irish content to silence.

Thus, the Irish literary discourse in *Ulysses* became a kind of secret subtext for which Joyce gave no key, no Linati scheme. Joyce is using a minority-culture myth for dominant-culture audiences. There is a wonderful irony in the history of the reception of Joyce's *Ulysses* when it is seen in the context of the history of the Irish literary revival: whereas Synge was denounced in 1903 by nationalists for presenting in *The Shadow of the Glen* "a crude version pretending to be Irish of the Greek story of the Widow of Ephesus" (quoted in Hunt 49), in *Ulysses* Joyce presented to his international readers an Irish story pretending to be Greek. In a sense Joyce sardonically turned the tables on the nationalist critics and is only now being caught at his game. Phillip Herring has suggested that Joyce remembered Arthur Griffith's attacks on Synge and wished to anticipate similar objections from the Irish nationalist quarter (*Joyce's "Ulysses" Notesheets* 73), but one could as well say that Joyce is having a joke all around, recognizing that when a comparative perspective is applied to myth and when old tales are stripped to the fabula, most stories, including the tale of the Widow of Ephesus and the imram, are found to be international. It is the surface of the tale that is local, and the form of a literary tradition—its styles, as Joyce said to Power—that distinguishes the writing of one nation from another. As Frank O'Connor observed, "Joyce had a mania for mystification, and he even amused himself by mystifying those he enlightened" (20). Likewise, Stanislaus Joyce's insistence that the architectonics of *Ulysses* are Irish (*Recollections of James Joyce* 19) suggests that Joyce's brother knew the truth of the Irish subtext and that Joyce himself was entirely conscious of the Irish elements.

The explanation of Joyce's reticence about his Irish architectonics also has to do in part with his view of himself and his own artistic creativity. When Yeats died, Joyce conceded that Yeats was a greater writer than he was: it was Yeats's imagination that always dazzled him (*JJ*2 660–61); about himself he said he had "a grocer's assistant's mind" (*JJ*2 28). He attributed much of his creativity to others: the humor of *Ulysses* was his father's (*JJ*2 22), and he thought that three-quarters of his books were written by his friends. His styles were known and discovered, obscure only to his fellow tradesmen (*Letters* 1: 167). He felt that with himself the thought was always simple (*JJ2* 476). He was sensible of owing debts to others—the stream-of-consciousness technique, for example—but obscured his sources, citing European sources rather than ones closer to home, attributing the technique to Dujardin when he might as well have credited his brother Stanislaus (*MBK* 16; *JJ2* 133). Some of Joyce's posture results from his view of the role of the artist; in *Stephen Hero* (25) Joyce has Stephen take the position that the beauty of verse consists as much in the concealment as in the revelation of construction. However, this use of borrowed materials rather than created ones also underlies the motif of his alter ego in *Finnegans Wake*: Shem is a sham and a plagiarizer.[18] As Ellmann notes, "Inspired cribbing was always part of James's talent; his gift was for transforming material, not for originating it" (*MBK* 19). And it was useful for Joyce to obscure the Irish elements he had borrowed: in terms of the patronage he sought, it was in fact utterly self-serving to obscure his Irish sources and to differentiate himself from the other writers of the Anglo-Irish literary revival. Cribbing from an oppressed and despised (in the Anglophile world) literary tradition was risky business. While Joyce was in exile, silence and cunning were essential in building his reputation as a revolutionary international writer.

Jean-Paul Sartre has said that criticism is a constitutive dimension of a work and that it includes the image of the audience for whom it is written (see Eagleton 84). Joyce understood this necessity, and he promoted critical refractions of his work that facilitated its reception with the only audience that would ultimately support him as an artist: an international avant-garde audience. In a sense there are actually two implied audiences in *Ulysses*: an Irish audience and an international audience. The Irish reader is embedded in the Irish mythic and formal structure of the book and in the minutely realistic surface; the international reader is embedded in the structure of the book taken from international mythologies and international literary formalism. Joyce promoted a critical reception "constitutive of the text" for his international readers rather than for the Irish audience perhaps because he expected that his Irish readers would pick up the mythic substratum without a metatextual guide: certainly the

18. Stephen is also presented as a plagiarist in *Ulysses* (see R. Adams 121ff.; Schutte, esp. 47ff.), and in Nighttown Bloom himself is accused of the same crime (15.822).

Joyce also refused to acknowledge any debt to Freud and Jung; see, for example, B. Scott 117; *JJ2* 634; cf. *JJ2* 436.

audiences at the early performances of the Irish dramatic movement needed no guide to the symbolic underpinnings of the plays. There was little way Joyce could have foreseen either the isolation of *Ulysses* from an Irish audience or the extent to which the international critical refraction of *Ulysses* would dominate the perception of *Ulysses* even in Ireland itself.

Irish literature was not only instrumental but essential in Joyce's discovery process, which led to the reformulation of the novel, and in his strategy for executing this program. Irish literature is thus germane to the entire development of narrative in this century. This will not be entirely welcome news to all readers interested in Joyce: it's daunting to contemplate the necessity of learning about an obscure and difficult branch of literature. Still, there it is: *Ulysses* is an Irish book, its title notwithstanding, and in order to apprehend it, the reader must understand the Irish elements. In Stephen Dedalus's Aristotelian aesthetic there are three principal qualities of beauty: *integritas, consonantia, claritas,* or "wholeness," "harmony," and "radiance." *Ulysses* is not just an Irish book; it is a beautiful Irish book. The argument drawn out in the previous chapters has been designed to show the *integritas* of *Ulysses* as a piece of Irish literature, the way in which as an *Irish* book it is *one* thing: it has wholeness. Ireland's native and ancient literary tradition, a tradition with both mythic and poetic aspects, is the foundation for the *consonantia* of *Ulysses*: the fact that it is "complex, multiple, divisible, separable, made up of its parts and their sum, harmonious"; the fact that the various elements—the mythic systems and the formal elements—cohere and reinforce each other. The *claritas* of *Ulysses* as an Irish book, its radiance, can be "apprehended luminously by the mind" (*PA* 211–13) only after the other two qualities have been perceived.

Ireland's divided tradition at the beginning of the century was emblematic of oppression and exploitation, but at this remove it has become a symbol of the fracturing and fragmentation of all of modern life. All of us, even those who are not Irish, in some sense hail from divided traditions in which there are many slippages, not least the fracture between present and past. The analogue to our own divided traditions epitomized in the divided tradition of Ireland is one reason the Irish writers speak so powerfully to the modern age: Seamus Heaney's fractured farm is our own home. Yet in writing about Yeats and Joyce, Thomas Kinsella has claimed that there are differences between these Irish writers: "Yeats stands for the Irish tradition as broken; Joyce stands for [it] as continuous, or healed—or healing—from its mutilation" ("Irish Writer" 65). Joyce's achievement in *Ulysses*, in his Irish *Ulysses*, is the writing of an Irish book that translates Irish poetics and Irish myth into an English-language work, fusing the two halves of his divided tradition, and in turn remaking both English literature and world literature; this achievement is a major reason why it can be said that Joyce represents the Irish tradition healed or healing. This is the power of much postcolonial literature: not simply the lure of the exotic, though there is some of that, even in *Ulysses*, but the modeling of the fracturings of experience and the repair of those fracturings, if only in the literary domain.

How does Joyce's Irish discourse relate to the difficulty—or uncertainty and indeterminacy—of Joyce's texts? In *Ulysses* Joyce establishes the mythic framework from the title forward for the Greek structures, from the opening words for the Irish. By the end of the first episode the mythic themes of a second chosen people, of dispossession, of failure of the land, and of the wasting of the *puella senilis* have been established, to be resolved only at the end with the homecoming of Bloom and the epiphany of Molly. Joyce also opens an Irish poetic structure with the first word of *Ulysses*, closing that structure only with the last letter of the text. Irish literature is part of Joyce's primary reference system, like the reference system of Dublin's geography (Hart and Knuth 18). Thus, a knowledge of Irish myth, symbols, and poetics explains much in *Ulysses* and all Joyce's work, resolving the level of difficulty in Joyce's texts attributable to Irish cultural specificity; such difficulties arise when the shared literary and cultural heritage of one time and place are unfamiliar to readers of another time and place because of the difference in cultural heritage.[19] Joyce understood the perils, and in *Stephen Hero* he has Stephen tell Cranly: "What we symbolise in black the Chinaman may symbolise in yellow: each has his own tradition. Greek beauty laughs at Coptic beauty and the American Indian derides them both" (212).

Yet the very naming of the elements of Irish mythos and poetics in

19. These sorts of difficulties George Steiner calls "contingent difficulty" and "modal difficulty"; see also the discussion in Herring, *Joyce's Uncertainty Principle* 77–96.

Joyce's texts, while resolving one level of difficulty, brings with it more fundamental levels of difficulty and uncertainty.[20] When mythic patterns are evoked, even through the allusive and partial method characteristically used by Joyce, the text offers an "interpretive summons," as Bert States, writing on Beckett, has put it; this interpretive summons is similar to those of medieval figural representations.[21] Beckett, writing on Proust in words that could apply to either *Ulysses* or *Finnegans Wake*, represents the situation as follows:

The identification of immediate with past experience, the recurrence of past action or reaction in the present, amounts to a participation between the ideal and the real, imagination and direct apprehension, symbol and substance. Such participation frees the essential reality that is denied to the contemplative as to the active life. What is common to present and past is more essential than either taken separately. . . . Thanks to this reduplication, the experience is at once imaginative and empirical, at once an evocation and direct perception, real without being merely actual, ideal without being merely abstract, the ideal real, the essential, the extratemporal. But if this mystical experience communicates an extratemporal essence, it follows that the communicant is for the moment an extratemporal being. (*Proust* 55–56)

Thus, although the repetition of patterns—traditional mythic patterns in Joyce's case—brings with it an invitation to interpret, it makes possible no determinate rational response; rather, it permits only analogy, possibility, perhaps. The indeterminacy of the reader's response is augmented by Joyce's conflation of various mythic patterns and his reliance on myth as the understructure of the tale rather than its surface. As the mythic systems double each other in *Ulysses*, the ambiguity deepens. In the first

20. Herring, *Joyce's Uncertainty Principle* 77–102, partially following Steiner, discusses various levels of uncertainty or difficulty that cannot be resolved: tactical, ontological, and gnomonic difficulties that are part of the openness of Joyce's texts.

21. I am indebted here to the line of argument developed by States in *The Shape of Paradox* 14–27. Certain similarities between Beckett's mythic writing and Joyce's use of myth suggest literary filiation.

Thornton, "Allusive Method in *Ulysses*," stresses the importance of understanding allusions in *Ulysses* since they are an "integral and organic" element in the text. Thornton sees allusions functioning as analogies inviting inexhaustible comparison and contrast and also evoking patterns of history or art that are held up against the present. Herring, *Joyce's Uncertainty Principle* (esp. 87–92), discusses gnomonic figurations in Joyce's texts that the reader is invited to finish, figurations that juxtapose present form with implied form.

See also L. Thompson 29–30; Frank 59–60; Seward 218.

edition the ambiguity began with the cover itself, whose blue and white evoked not only the Greek flag but the old nationalist colors of Ireland during the Stuart period.

Myth—particularly myth that has its origin in religious myth, as many of the Irish patterns do—also has elements of what Schopenhauer sees as the allegorical nature of religion:

Before the people truth cannot appear naked. A symptom of this *allegorical* nature of religions is the *mysteries*, to be found perhaps in every religion, that is, certain dogmas that cannot even be distinctly conceived, much less be literally true. In fact, it might perhaps be asserted that some absolute inconsistencies and contradictions, some actual absurdities, are an essential ingredient of a complete religion; for these are just the stamp of its *allegorical* nature, and the only suitable way of making the ordinary mind and uncultured understanding *feel* what would be incomprehensible to it, namely that religion deals at bottom with an entirely different order of things. . . . In the presence of such an order the laws of this phenomenal world, according to which it must speak, disappear. (2: 166)

To these inconsistencies of religion we can juxtapose Joyce's relentless breaks in the surface realism of *Ulysses* that signal the presence of Irish myth: Stephen, Bloom, and Molly as anomalous immigrants yet prototypical Dubliners; the improbability of all their natures, particularly those of Bloom and Molly;[22] the "hallucinatory" quality of the events in Nighttown; the ahistoricity of Molly's Gibraltar. These fields of inconsistency signal the great Irish myths structuring *Ulysses: The Book of Invasions*, the Sovereignty myth, and the Irish otherworld. These breaks in the surface realism tell the reader to seek another level of meaning; they are correlates to the mysteries of religious myth and religious thought; they recreate a numinous framework for interpretation. Such difficulties cannot be resolved in terms of a rational or stipulative language.

Thus, the identification of Irish mythos in Joyce's work does not lead to closed readings of *Ulysses*; it points once again to the openness of the narrative. Joyce's medievalism consists of more than an ordering principle borrowed from Scholasticism.[23] Through such features as nominal real-

22. Herring, *Joyce's Uncertainty Principle* 205–6, discusses the paradoxical and indeterminate nature of the characters; cf. 92–101. Cf. French 258–59.

23. Eco argues that Joyce relies on the *cosmogonic* structure of medieval thought in juxtaposition to the chaos of modern experience.

ism and pseudohistory, multiple point of view encoded in multiple styles, and a perspective on the comic that denies the excluded middle, in the second half of *Ulysses* in particular—the half most indebted to medieval Irish literature—Western rational discourse is exploded. In turn, a medieval mythic consciousness is embedded in the literary modes and forms imported from early Irish literature that move the text toward openness. Joyce uses the openness at the heart of mythic consciousness—a mythic consciousness alive in medieval Irish literature and even in early twentieth-century Irish culture—to mirror the essential openness of life: not just of modern life, but of life.

Works Cited

Abbreviations

AIT	Cross and Slover, *Ancient Irish Tales*
AT	Aarne and Thompson, *Types of the Folktale*
CW	James Joyce, *Critical Writings*
D	James Joyce, *Dubliners*
DIL	*Dictionary of the Irish Language*
E	James Joyce, *Exiles*
*JJ*2	Ellmann, *James Joyce*, 2d ed.
MBK	Stanislaus Joyce, *My Brother's Keeper*
OED	*Oxford English Dictionary*
PA	James Joyce, *A Portrait of the Artist*
SH	James Joyce, *Stephen Hero*
U	James Joyce, *Ulysses*

Aarne, Antti, and Stith Thompson. *The Types of the Folktale: A Classification and Bibliography*. 2d revision. Helsinki: Academia Scientiarum Fennica, 1961.

Achebe, Chinua. *Things Fall Apart*. 1958. London: Heinemann, 1986.

Adams, Michael. *Censorship: The Irish Experience*. University: U of Alabama P, 1968.

Adams, Robert Martin. *Surface and Symbol: The Consistency of James Joyce's "Ulysses."* New York: Oxford UP, 1962.

A. E. [George Russell]. *The Avatars: A Futurist Fantasy*. London: Macmillan, 1933.

——. *The Candle of Vision*. London: Macmillan, 1918.

——. *Deirdre: A Legend in Three Acts*. Irish Drama Series 4. Chicago: De Paul U, 1970.

Aitchison, Jean. *General Linguistics*. London: English Universities P, 1972.

All Ireland Review (Kilkenny).

Anderson, Chester G. *James Joyce and His World*. London: Thames and Hudson, 1967.

Anouilh, Jean. *Antigone*. Paris: La Table Ronde, 1946.

Arbois de Jubainville, Henri d'. *Les Celtes depuis les temps les plus anciens jusqu'en l'an cent avant notre ère*. Paris: Albert Fontemoing, 1904.

———. *La civilisation des Celtes et celle de l'épopée homérique*. Vol. 6 of *Cours de littérature celtique*. Ed. d'Arbois de Jubainville. Paris: Albert Fontemoing, 1899.

———. *Le cycle mythologique irlandais et la mythologie celtique*. Vol. 2 of *Cours de littérature celtique*. Ed. d'Arbois de Jubainville. Paris: Ernest Thorin, 1884.

———. *Études sur le droit celtique*. Vols. 7–8 of *Cours de littérature celtique*. Ed. d'Arbois de Jubainville. Paris: Thorin et Fils, 1895.

———. *Introduction à l'étude de la littérature celtique*. Vol. 1 of *Cours de littérature celtique*. Ed. d'Arbois de Jubainville. Paris: Ernest Thorin, 1883.

———. *The Irish Mythological Cycle and Celtic Mythology*. 1884. Trans. R. I. Best. Dublin: O Donoghue, 1903.

———. *Principaux auteurs de l'antiquité à consulter sur l'histoire des celtes depuis les temps les plus anciens jusqu'au règne de Théodose Ier, essai chronologique*. Vol. 12 of *Cours de littérature celtique*. Ed. d'Arbois de Jubainville. Paris: Thorin et Fils, 1902.

———, ed. *Cours de littérature celtique*. 12 vols. Paris: Ernest Thorin; Albert Fontemoing; Thorin et Fils, 1883–1902.

Arbois de Jubainville, Henri d', with Georges Dottin, Maurice Grammont, Louis Duran, and Ferdinand Lot, trans. *L'épopée celtique en Irlande*. Vol. 5 of *Cours de littérature celtique*. Ed. d'Arbois de Jubainville. Paris: Ernest Thorin, 1892.

Arnold, Matthew. *Culture and Anarchy*. *Culture and Anarchy, With Friendship's Garland and Some Literary Essays*. Ed. R. H. Super. Vol. 5 of *The Complete Prose Works of Matthew Arnold*. Ann Arbor: U of Michigan P, 1965. 85–256.

———. "On the Study of Celtic Literature." *Lectures and Essays in Criticism*. Ed. R. H. Super with the assistance of Sister Thomas Marion Hoctor. Vol. 3 of *The Complete Prose Works of Matthew Arnold*. Ann Arbor: U of Michigan P, 1962. 291–386.

Atherton, James S. *The Books at the Wake: A Study of Literary Allusions in James Joyce's "Finnegans Wake."* London: Faber, 1959.

Bakhtin, M. M. *The Dialogic Imagination*. 1981. Trans. Caryl Emerson and Michael Holquist. Austin: U of Texas P, 1990.

Bal, Mieke. *Narratology: Introduction to the Theory of Narrative.* 1980. Trans. Christine van Boheemen. Toronto: U of Toronto P, 1985.

Baumgarten, Rolf. *Bibliography of Irish Linguistics and Literature, 1942–71.* Dublin: Dublin Institute for Advanced Studies, 1986.

Beckett, Samuel. *Endgame.* New York: Grove, 1957.

———. *Proust.* 1931. New York: Grove, n.d. [1957].

———. *Waiting for Godot.* New York: Grove, 1954.

Bell-Villada, Gene H. *García Márquez: The Man and His Work.* Chapel Hill: U of North Carolina P, 1990.

Benstock, Bernard. "A Setdown Secular Phoenish: The Finn of *Finnegans Wake.*" 1978. Rpt. in Hederman and Kearney, *Crane Bag Book* 172–77.

Benstock, Shari, and Bernard Benstock. *Who's He When He's at Home: A James Joyce Directory.* Urbana: U of Illinois P, 1980.

Bérard, Victor. *Les Phéniciens et l'Odyssée.* 2 vols. Paris: Librairie Armand Colin, 1902–3.

Bergin, Osborn, and R. I. Best, eds. and trans. "Tochmarc Étaíne." *Ériu* 12 (1938): 137–96.

Bernal, Martin. *Black Athena.* Vol. 1. New Brunswick: Rutgers UP, 1987.

Bessai, Diane E. "'Dark Rosaleen' as Image of Ireland." *Éire-Ireland* 10.4 (1975): 62–84.

———. "Who Was Cathleen Ni Houlihan?" *Malahat Review* 42 (1977): 114–29.

Best, Richard Irvine. *Bibliography of Irish Philology and Manuscript Literature; Publications 1913–1941.* Dublin: Dublin Institute for Advanced Studies, 1942.

———. *Bibliography of Irish Philology and of Printed Irish Literature.* Dublin: National Library of Ireland, 1913.

Bettelheim, Bruno. *The Uses of Enchantment: The Meaning and Importance of Fairy Tales.* 1976. New York: Vintage-Random, 1977.

Binchy, Daniel A. "The Linguistic and Historical Value of the Irish Law Tracts." *Proceedings of the British Academy* 29 (1943): 195–227.

Bowen, Charles. "Great-Bladdered Medb; Mythology and Invention in the *Táin Bó Cúailnge.*" *Éire-Ireland* 10.4 (1975): 14–34.

———. "A Historical Inventory of the *Dindshenchas.*" *Studia Celtica* 10–11 (1975–76): 113–37.

Bowen, Zack. *Musical Allusions in the Works of James Joyce: Early Poetry through "Ulysses."* Albany: SUNY P, 1974.

———. *"Ulysses" as a Comic Novel.* Syracuse: Syracuse UP, 1989.

Breatnach, R. A. "The Lady and the King: A Theme of Irish Literature." *Studies* 42 (1953): 321–36.

Bromwich, Rachel, ed. and trans. *Trioedd Ynys Prydein, The Welsh Triads.* Cardiff: U of Wales P, 1961.

Brown, Stephen J. M. *The Press in Ireland: A Survey and a Guide.* 1937. New York: Lemma, 1971.

Budgen, Frank. *Further Recollections of James Joyce.* 1955. Rpt. in Budgen, *James Joyce and the Making of "Ulysses,"* 314–28.

———. *James Joyce and the Making of "Ulysses."* 1934. Bloomington: Indiana UP, 1960.

Bugge, Alexander. *Contributions to the History of the Norsemen in Ireland.* Christiania: J. Dybwad, 1900.

Campbell, Joseph. *The Hero with a Thousand Faces.* 1949. Bollingen Series 16. Princeton: Princeton UP, 1972.

Card, James V. D. "A Gibraltar Sourcebook for 'Penelope.'" *James Joyce Quarterly* 8 (1970–71): 163–75.

Carney, James. *The Irish Bardic Poet.* Dublin: Dolmen, 1967.

Cave, Richard Allen. "Staging the Irishman." *Acts of Supremacy: The British Empire and the Stage, 1790–1930.* By J. S. Bratton, Richard Allen Cave, Brendan Gregory, Heidi J. Holder, and Michael Pickering. Manchester: Manchester UP, 1991. 62–128.

Chanady, Amaryll Beatrice. *Magical Realism and the Fantastic: Resolved Versus Unresolved Antinomy.* New York: Garland, 1985.

An Claidheamh Soluis (Dublin).

Clark, Barrett H. *European Theories of the Drama.* 1918. New York: Crown, 1957.

Clark, James Midgley. *The Vocabulary of Anglo-Irish.* St. Gallen: Zollikofer, 1917.

Clark, Rosalind. *The Great Queens: Irish Goddesses from the Morrígan to Cathleen Ní Houlihan.* Gerrards Cross: Colin Smythe, 1991.

Collier, William Francis. *History of Ireland for Schools.* London: Marcus Ward, 1886.

Colum, Padraic, ed. *An Anthology of Irish Verse.* 1922. New York: Liveright, 1948.

Connellan, Owen, ed. and trans. *Imtheacht na Tromdháimhe, The Proceedings of the Great Bardic Institution.* Transactions of the Ossianic Society 5. 1860. New York and London: Johnson Reprint, 1972.

Connolly, Thomas Edward. *The Personal Library of James Joyce: A Descriptive Bibliography. University of Buffalo Studies* 22.1 (1955); Monographs in English 6.

Corkery, Daniel. *The Hidden Ireland: A Study of Gaelic Munster in the Eighteenth Century.* 1924. Dublin: Gill and Macmillan, 1975.

Cross, Tom Peete. *Motif-Index of Early Irish Literature.* Indiana U Publications, Folklore Ser. 7. Bloomington: Indiana UP [1952].

Cross, Tom Peete, and Clark Harris Slover, eds. *Ancient Irish Tales.* 1936. New York: Barnes and Noble, 1969.

Daily Express (Dublin).

Dana (Dublin).

Deane, Seamus. *Celtic Revivals: Essays in Modern Irish Literature 1880–1980.* 1985. London: Faber, 1987.

Delargy, James H. "The Gaelic Story-Teller." *Proceedings of the British Academy* 31 (1945): 3–46.

De Vere, Aubrey. *The Foray of Queen Maeve and Other Legends of Ireland's Heroic Age.* London: K. Paul, Trench, 1882.

Dictionary of the Irish Language, Based Mainly on Old and Middle Irish Materials. Compact ed. Dublin: Royal Irish Academy, 1983.

Dillon, Myles. "The Archaism of Irish Tradition." *Proceedings of the British Academy* 33 (1947): 245–64.

———. *The Cycles of the Kings.* London: Oxford UP, 1946.

———. *Early Irish Literature.* Chicago: U of Chicago P, 1948.

———. *There Was a King in Ireland.* Austin: U of Texas P, 1971.

Dillon, Myles, and Nora K. Chadwick. *The Celtic Realms.* London: Weidenfeld and Nicolson, 1967.

Dinneen, Patrick S. *Foclóir Gaedhilge agus Béarla, An Irish-English Dictionary.* Rev. ed. 1927. Dublin: Irish Texts Society, 1965.

———. *A Smaller Irish-English Dictionary for the Use of Schools.* 1910. Dublin: Irish Texts Society, 1923.

Dublin Evening Mail (Dublin).

Dublin Penny Journal (Dublin).

Duffy, Charles Gavan. "The Revival of Irish Literature." *The Revival of Irish Literature and Other Addresses.* By Charles G. Duffy, George Sigerson, and Douglas Hyde. London: T. Fisher Unwin, 1894. 1–60.

Duggan, G. C. *The Stage Irishman: A History of the Irish Play and Stage Characters from the Earliest Times.* 1937. New York: Benjamin Blom, 1969.

Dunn, Joseph, trans. *The Ancient Irish Epic Tale Táin Bó Cúalnge: The Cualnge Cattle-raid.* London: David Nutt, 1914.

Eagleton, Terry. *Literary Theory: An Introduction.* Oxford: Blackwell, 1983.

Eco, Umberto. *The Aesthetics of Chaosmos: The Middle Ages of James Joyce.* 1962. Trans. Ellen Esrock. 1982. Cambridge: Harvard UP, 1989.

Edel, Doris. "The Catalogues in *Culhwch ac Olwen* and Insular Celtic Learning." *Bulletin of the Board of Celtic Studies* 30 (1983): 253–67.

Eglinton, John [W. K. Magee]. "Irish Books." *Anglo-Irish Essays*. Dublin: Talbot, 1917. 79–89.

Eliot, T. S. "*Ulysses*, Order, and Myth." 1923. Rpt. in *James Joyce: Two Decades of Criticism*. Ed. Seon Givens. New York: Vanguard, 1948. 198–202.

———. *The Waste Land*. 1922. Rpt. in *The Complete Poems and Plays, 1909–1950*. New York: Harcourt, 1952. 37–55.

Ellis-Fermor, Una. *The Irish Dramatic Movement*. 1939. London: Methuen, 1967.

Ellmann, Richard. *The Consciousness of Joyce*. Toronto and New York: Oxford UP, 1977.

———. *James Joyce*. 1959. 2d ed. New York: Oxford UP, 1982.

———. *Ulysses on the Liffey*. New York: Oxford UP, 1972.

Evans, E. Estyn. *Irish Folk Ways*. London and Boston: Routledge, 1957.

Evening Telegraph (Dublin).

Even-Zohar, Itamar. *Polysystems Studies*. *Poetics Today* 11.1 (1990): special issue.

Ferrer, Daniel. "Circe, Regret, and Regression." *Post-Structuralist Joyce: Essays from the French*. Ed. Derek Attridge and Daniel Ferrer. Cambridge: Cambridge UP, 1984. 127–44.

Flanagan, Thomas. "Yeats, Joyce, and the Matter of Ireland." *Critical Inquiry* 2 (1975): 43–67.

Flower, Robin. *The Irish Tradition*. Oxford: Oxford UP, 1947.

Foley, John Miles. "Reading the Oral Traditional Text: Aesthetics of Creation and Response." *Comparative Research on Oral Traditions: A Memorial for Milman Parry*. Ed. Foley. Columbus: Slavica, 1987. 185–212.

Frank, Joseph. "Spatial Form in Modern Literature." 1945. Rpt. in *The Widening Gyre: Crisis and Mastery in Modern Literature*. New Brunswick: Rutgers UP, 1963. 3–62.

Frazer, James George. *Adonis, Attis, Osiris: Studies in the History of Oriental Religion*. 2 vols. Vol. 4 of *The Golden Bough: A Study in Magic and Religion*. 1906. 3d ed. 1914. New York: Macmillan, 1935.

Frazier, Adrian. *Behind the Scenes: Yeats, Horniman, and the Struggle for the Abbey Theatre*. Berkeley and Los Angeles: U of California P, 1990.

Freeman's Journal (Dublin).

French, Marilyn. *The Book as World: James Joyce's "Ulysses."* Cambridge: Harvard UP, 1976.

Friel, Brian. *Translations*. London: Faber, 1981.

Garvin, John. *James Joyce's Disunited Kingdom and the Irish Dimension*. Dublin: Gill and Macmillan, 1976.

Gifford, Don, with Robert J. Seidman. *"Ulysses" Annotated: Notes for James*

Joyce's "Ulysses." 2d ed. Berkeley and Los Angeles: U of California P, 1988.

Gilbert, Stuart. *James Joyce's "Ulysses": A Study.* 1930. New York: Vintage-Random, 1955.

Gillespie, Michael Patrick. *James Joyce's Trieste Library: A Catalogue of Materials at the Harry Ransom Humanities Research Center, The University of Texas at Austin.* Austin: U of Texas, 1986.

Giraudoux, Jean. *La guerre de Troie n'aura pas lieu.* Vol. 6 of *Le théâtre complet de Jean Giraudoux.* Neuchâtel: Ides et Calendes, 1946.

Gorman, Herbert S. *James Joyce: A Definitive Biography.* London: John Lane, Bodley Head, 1941.

Gray, Elizabeth A., ed. and trans. *Cath Maige Tuired, The Second Battle of Mag Tuired.* Naas: Irish Texts Society, 1982.

Grayson, Janet. "'Do You Kiss Your Mother?': Stephen Dedalus' Sovereignty of Ireland." *James Joyce Quarterly* 19 (1982–83): 119–26.

Green, Alice Stopford. *The Old Irish World.* Dublin: M.H. Gill, 1912.

Greene, David H., and Edward M. Stephens. *J.M. Synge, 1871–1909.* New York: Macmillan, 1959.

Gregory, Augusta. *Our Irish Theatre: A Chapter of Autobiography by Lady Gregory.* 1913. New York: Oxford UP, 1972.

———, trans. *Cuchulain of Muirthemne.* 1902. New York: Oxford UP, 1973.

———, trans. *Gods and Fighting Men.* 1904. Gerrards Cross: Colin Smythe, 1970.

———, trans. *Poets and Dreamers: Studies and Translations from the Irish.* Dublin: Hodges, Figgis, 1903.

Groden, Michael. *"Ulysses" in Progress.* Princeton: Princeton UP, 1977.

Gross, John. *James Joyce.* New York: Viking, 1970.

Gwynn, Edward J., ed. and trans. *The Metrical Dindshenchas.* 5 vols. Todd Lecture Series 8–12. Dublin: Hodges, Figgis, 1903–35.

———, ed. and trans. *Poems from the Dindshenchas.* Todd Lecture Series 7. Dublin: Royal Irish Academy House, 1900.

Haley, Gene Clifford. "The Topography of the *Táin Bó Cúailnge.*" Diss. Harvard U, 1963.

Harris, William. *The History and Antiquities of the City of Dublin from the Earliest Accounts: Compiled from Authentick Memoirs, Offices of Record, Manuscript Collections, and Other Unexceptionable Vouchers.* Dublin: Laurence Flinn, James Williams, 1766.

Hart, Clive, and Leo Knuth. *A Topographical Guide to James Joyce's "Ulysses."* 1975. Rev. ed. Colchester: Wake Newslitter, 1981.

Hayman, David. "The Empirical Molly." Staley and Benstock, *Approaches to "Ulysses"* 103–35.

———. "Forms of Folly in Joyce: A Study of Clowning in *Ulysses*." *ELH* 34 (1967): 260–83.

Heaney, Seumas. "The Interesting Case of John Alphonsus Mulrennan." *Planet: The Welsh Internationalist* 41 (Jan. 1978): 34–40.

Hederman, Mark Patrick, and Richard Kearney. "Editorial." 1978. Rpt. in Hederman and Kearney, *Crane Bag Book* 155–56.

———, eds. *The Crane Bag Book of Irish Studies (1977–81)*. Dublin: Blackwater, 1982.

Henderson, George, ed. and trans. *Fled Bricrend, The Feast of Bricriu*. London: Irish Texts Society, 1899.

Henry, R. M. *The Evolution of Sinn Fein*. New York: B. W. Huebsch, 1920.

Hermans, Theo, ed. *The Manipulation of Literature: Studies in Literary Translation*. London: Croom Helm, 1985.

Herr, Cheryl. *Joyce's Anatomy of Culture*. Urbana: U of Illinois P, 1986.

Herring, Phillip F. "The Bedsteadfastness of Molly Bloom." *Modern Fiction Studies* 15 (1969): 49–61.

———. *Joyce's "Ulysses" Notesheets in the British Museum*. Charlottesville: UP of Virginia, 1972.

———. *Joyce's Uncertainty Principle*. Princeton: Princeton UP, 1987.

———. "Toward an Historical Molly Bloom." *ELH* 45 (1978): 501–21.

Hillman, James. *The Dream and the Underworld*. New York: Harper, 1979.

Hodgart, Matthew J. C., and Mabel P. Worthington. *Song in the Works of James Joyce*. New York: Columbia UP, 1959.

Holloway, Joseph. *Joseph Holloway's Abbey Theatre: A Selection from his Unpublished Journal, Impressions of a Dublin Playgoer*. Ed. Robert Hogan and Michael J. O'Neill. Carbondale: Southern Illinois UP, 1967.

Hogan, Edmund. *Onomasticon Goedelicum locorum et tribuum Hiberniae et Scotiae*. Dublin: Hodges, Figgis, 1910.

Hone, Joseph. *W. B. Yeats, 1865–1939*. 1943. 2d ed. New York: St. Martin's, 1962.

Honton, Margaret. "Molly's Mistresstroke." *James Joyce Quarterly* 14 (1976–77): 25–30.

Hull, Eleanor. *Pagan Ireland*. Dublin: M. H. Gill, 1904.

———. *A Text Book of Irish Literature*. 2 vols. London: David Nutt, 1906–8.

———, ed. and trans. *The Poem-book of the Gael*. London: Chatto and Windus, 1912.

———, trans. *The Cuchullin Saga in Irish Literature*. London: David Nutt, 1898.

Hull, Vernam, ed. and trans. *Longes Mac n-Uislenn, The Exile of the Sons of Uisliu.* New York: MLA, 1949.

Hunt, Hugh. *The Abbey: Ireland's National Theatre, 1904–1979.* New York: Columbia UP, 1979.

Hutton, Mary A., trans. *The Táin: An Irish Epic Told in English Verse.* Dublin: Maunsel, 1907.

Hyde, Douglas. *A Literary History of Ireland from Earliest Times to the Present.* London: T. F. Unwin, 1899.

———. "The Necessity for De-Anglicising Ireland." *The Revival of Irish Literature and Other Addresses.* By Charles G. Duffy, George Sigerson, and Douglas Hyde. London: T. Fisher Unwin, 1894. 115–61.

———. *The Story of Early Gaelic Literature.* London: T. Fisher Unwin, 1895.

———, ed. and trans. *Beside the Fire: A Collection of Irish Gaelic Folk Stories.* London: David Nutt, 1890.

———, ed. and trans. *Abhráin Grádh Chúige Connacht or Love Songs of Connacht.* 1893. Shannon: Irish UP, 1969.

Hyman, Louis. *The Jews of Ireland.* Shannon: Irish UP, 1972.

Ibsen, Henrik. *The Master Builder: A Play in Three Acts.* Trans. Edmund Gosse and William Archer. London: William Heinemann, 1893.

Irish Catholic (Dublin).

Irish Daily Independent and Daily Nation (Dublin).

Irish Field and Gentleman's Gazette (Dublin).

Irish Homestead (Dublin).

Irisleabhar na Gaedhilge, The Gaelic Journal (Dublin).

Irish Times (Dublin).

Iser, Wolfgang. *The Implied Reader: Patterns of Communication in Prose Fiction from Bunyan to Beckett.* 1972. Baltimore: Johns Hopkins UP, 1983.

Jackson, Kenneth. *The Oldest Irish Tradition: A Window on the Iron Age.* Cambridge: Cambridge UP, 1964.

Jameson, Fredric. "Modernism and Imperialism." *Nationalism, Colonialism, and Literature.* By Terry Eagleton, Fredric Jameson, and Edward W. Said. Minneapolis: U of Minnesota P, 1990. 43–66.

Jarman, A. O. H. "The Delineation of Arthur in Early Welsh Verse." *An Arthurian Tapestry.* Ed. Kenneth Varty. Glasgow: British Branch of the International Arthurian Society, 1981. 1–21.

Joyce, James. *Critical Writings.* Ed. Ellsworth Mason and Richard Ellmann. New York: Viking, 1959.

———. *Dubliners: Text, Criticism, and Notes.* Ed. Robert Scholes and A. Walton Litz. New York: Viking, 1969.

———. *Exiles.* New York: Viking, 1951.

——. *Finnegans Wake.* New York: Viking, 1939.

——. *Letters of James Joyce.* Vol. 1. Ed. Stuart Gilbert. 1957. Reissued with corrections. New York: Viking, 1966. Vols. 2 and 3. Ed. Richard Ellmann. New York: Viking, 1966.

——. *A Portrait of the Artist as a Young Man: Text, Criticism, and Notes.* Ed. Chester G. Anderson. New York: Viking, 1968.

——. *Stephen Hero.* Ed. John J. Slocum and Herbert Cahoon. 1944. New York: New Directions, 1963.

——. *Ulysses: A Critical and Synoptic Edition.* Ed. Hans Walter Gabler, with Wolfhard Steppe and Claus Melchior. 3 vols. New York and London: Garland, 1986.

——. *Ulysses: The Corrected Text.* Ed. Hans Walter Gabler et al. New York: Random, 1986.

Joyce, Patrick Weston. *A Child's History of Ireland.* London: Longmans Green, 1897.

——. *A Concise History of Ireland from the Earliest Times to 1837.* Dublin: M. H. Gill, 1893.

——. *English as We Speak It in Ireland.* Dublin: M. H. Gill, 1910.

——. *The Geography of the Counties of Ireland with a General Description of the Country.* London: George Philip, 1883.

——. *A Grammar of the Irish Language.* 1878. Dublin: Educational Co. of Ireland, 1920.

——. *An Illustrated History of Ireland.* Dublin: Educational Co. of Ireland, 1919.

——. *Irish Local Names Explained.* Dublin: McGlashan and Gill, n.d.

——. *Irish Peasant Songs in the English Language.* Dublin: M. H. Gill, 1906.

——. *The Origin and History of Irish Names of Places.* 3 vols. 1869, 1870, 1913. 3d ed. Dublin: McGlashan and Gill, 1920.

——. *A Short History of Ireland from the Earliest Times to 1608.* London: Longmans and Green, 1893.

——. *A Smaller Social History of Ancient Ireland.* Dublin: M. H. Gill, 1906.

——. *A Social History of Ancient Ireland.* 2 vols. London: Longmans and Green, 1903.

——. *The Story of Ancient Irish Civilisation.* Dublin: M. H. Gill, 1907.

——. *The Wonders of Ireland and Other Papers on Irish Subjects.* Dublin: M. H. Gill, 1911.

——, ed. and trans. *Forus Feasa air Éirinn, Keating's History of Ireland.* Dublin: M. H. Gill, 1880.

———, trans. *Old Celtic Romances*. 1879. 2d ed. London: David Nutt, 1894.

Joyce, Stanislaus. *My Brother's Keeper: James Joyce's Early Years*. Ed. Richard Ellmann. 1958. London: Faber, 1982.

———. *Recollections of James Joyce*. 1941. Trans. Ellsworth Mason. New York: James Joyce Society, 1950.

Joyce, Stephen J. "The Private Lives of Writers." *New York Times Book Review* 31 Dec. 1989: 2.

Kain, Richard M. *Fabulous Voyager: James Joyce's "Ulysses."* Chicago: U of Chicago P, 1947.

———. "Motif as Meaning: The Case of Leopold Bloom." Staley and Benstock, *Approaches to "Ulysses"* 61–102.

Kearney, Richard. *Transitions: Narratives in Modern Irish Culture*. Dublin: Wolfhound, 1988.

Keating, Geoffrey. *Foras Feasa ar Éirinn, The History of Ireland*. Ed. and trans. Patrick S. Dinneen. 4 vols. London: Irish Texts Society, 1902–14.

Kelleher, John V. "Humor in the Ulster Saga." *Veins of Humor*. Ed. Harry Levin. Harvard English Studies 3. Cambridge: Harvard UP, 1972. 35–56.

———. "Identifying the Irish Printed Sources for *Finnegans Wake*." *Irish University Review* 1.2 (1971): 161–77.

———. "Irish History and Mythology in James Joyce's 'The Dead.'" *Review of Politics* 27.3 (1965): 414–33.

———. "The Táin and the Annals." *Ériu* 22 (1971): 107–27.

Kelly, Fergus, ed. and trans. *Audacht Morainn*. Dublin: Dublin Institute for Advanced Studies, 1976.

Kenner, Hugh. *Joyce's Voices*. Berkeley and Los Angeles: U of California P, 1978.

———. "The Look of a Queen." *Woman in Irish Legend, Life, and Literature*. Ed. S. F. Gallagher. Totowa, N.J.: Barnes and Noble, 1983.

———. "Molly's Masterstroke." *James Joyce Quarterly* 10 (1972): 19–28.

———. *The Pound Era*. 1971. Berkeley and Los Angeles: U of California P, 1974.

———. "The Rhetoric of Silence." *James Joyce Quarterly* 14 (1977): 382–94.

———. *"Ulysses."* 1980. London, Boston, and Sydney: George Allen and Unwin, 1982.

Kiberd, Declan. "Bloom the Liberator." *TLS* 3 Jan. 1992: 3–6.

———. "The Fall of the Stage Irishman." *The Genres of the Irish Literary Revival*. Ed. Ronald Schleifer. Norman, Okla.: Pilgrim, 1980. 39–60.

Kimpel, Ben. "The Voices of *Ulysses*." *Style* 9 (1975): 283–319.

Kinsella, Thomas. "The Irish Writer." *Davis, Mangan, Ferguson? Tradition and the Irish Writer.* By W. B. Yeats and Thomas Kinsella. Dublin: Dolmen, 1970. 57–70.

——, trans. *The Táin.* 1969. London and New York: Oxford UP, 1970.

Knott, Eleanor, and Gerard Murphy. *Early Irish Literature.* London: Routledge, 1966.

Lamb, Charles. *The Adventures of Ulysses.* London: T. Davison, 1808.

Lawrence, Karen. *The Odyssey of Style in "Ulysses."* Princeton: Princeton UP, 1981.

Leader (Dublin).

Lee, Joseph J. "Women and the Church since the Famine." *Women in Irish Society: The Historical Dimension.* Ed. Margaret Mac Curtain and Donncha Ó Corráin. Dublin: Arlen House, 1978. 37–45.

Lefevere, André. "Literary Theory and Translated Literature." *Dispositio* 7 (1982): 3–22.

Lefevere, André, and Kenneth David Jackson, eds. *The Art and Science of Translation. Dispositio* 7 (1982): special issue.

Levin, Harry. "Editor's Introduction." *The Portable James Joyce.* New York: Viking, 1947.

——. *James Joyce: A Critical Introduction.* 1941. Rev. ed. New York: New Directions, 1960.

Littleton, C. Scott. *The New Comparative Mythology.* 1966. Rev. ed. Berkeley and Los Angeles: U of California P, 1973.

Litz, A. Walton. *The Art of James Joyce: Method and Design in "Ulysses" and "Finnegans Wake."* London: Oxford UP, 1961.

——. "The Genre of *Ulysses.*" *The Theory of the Novel.* Ed. John Halperin. New York: Oxford UP, 1974. 109–120.

Lommel, Andreas. *Masks: Their Meaning and Function.* 1970. Trans. Nadia Fowler. New York: McGraw-Hill, 1972.

Lord, Albert B. *The Singer of Tales.* 1960. Cambridge: Harvard UP, 1964.

Loss, Archie K. *Joyce's Visible Art: The Work of Joyce and the Visual Arts, 1904–1922.* Ann Arbor: UMI Research Press, 1984.

Loth, J. *La métrique galloise.* Vols. 9–11 of *Cours de littérature celtique.* Ed. Henri d'Arbois de Jubainville. Paris: Thorin et Fils, 1900–1902.

——, trans. *Les Mabinogion traduits en entier pour la première fois en français.* Vols. 3–4 of *Cours de littérature celtique.* Ed. Henri d'Arbois de Jubainville. Paris: Ernest Thorin, 1889.

Macalister, R. A. S., ed. and trans. *Lebor Gabála Érenn, The Book of the Taking of Ireland.* 5 vols. Dublin: Irish Texts Society, 1938–56.

Macalister, R. A. S., and John MacNeill, eds. and trans. *Leabhar Gabhála, The Book of Conquests of Ireland: The Recension of Micheál Ó Cléirigh.* Dublin: Hodges, Figgis, 1916.

MacBride, Maud Gonne. *A Servant of the Queen*. 1938. Woodbridge, Suffolk: Boydell, 1983.

Mac Cana, Proinsias. "Aspects of the Theme of King and Goddess in Irish Literature." *Études celtiques* 7 (1955): 76–114; 7 (1956): 356–413; 8 (1958): 59–65.

———. *Celtic Mythology*. London: Hamlyn, 1970.

———. *The Learned Tales of Medieval Ireland*. Dublin: Dublin Institute for Advanced Studies, 1980.

———. "The Sinless Otherworld of *Immram Brain*." *Ériu* 27 (1976): 95–115.

McCarthy, Patrick A. "Joyce's Unrealiable Catechist: Mathematics and the Narration of 'Ithaca.'" *ELH* 51 (1984): 605–18.

MacKillop, James. *Fionn mac Cumhaill: Celtic Myth in English Literature*. Syracuse: Syracuse UP, 1986.

MacManus, Seumas. *The Story of the Irish Race: A Popular History of Ireland*. 1921. New York: Devin-Adair, 1944.

Mac Neill, Máire. *The Festival of Lughnasa*. London: Oxford UP, 1962.

Magee, W. K. *See* Eglinton, John.

Manganiello, Dominic. *Joyce's Politics*. Boston: Routledge, 1980.

Marcus, Philip L. *Standish O'Grady*. Lewisburg, Penn.: Bucknell UP, 1971.

Marstrander, Carl, ed. and trans. "The Deaths of Lugaid and Derbforgaill." *Ériu* 5 (1911): 201–18.

———, ed. *Fleadh Dúin na nGéadh ocus Cath Muighe Ráth*. Christiania: J. Dybwad, 1910.

Maturin, Charles Robert. *Melmoth the Wanderer*. 1820. 3 vols. London: Richard Bentley and Son, 1892.

Mayhew, Henry. *London Labour and the London Poor*. 1861–62. 4 vols. New York: Dover, 1968.

Mercier, Vivian. *The Irish Comic Tradition*. 1962. London, Oxford, and New York: Oxford UP, 1969.

———. "James Joyce as Medieval Artist." 1978. Rpt. in Hederman and Kearney, *Crane Bag Book* 161–67.

Merriman, Brian. *The Midnight Court*. Ed. and trans. Patrick C. Power. Cork: Mercier, 1971.

———. "*Cuirt an mheadhóin oidhche*." Ed. and trans. Ludwig Chr. Stern. *Zeitschrift für celtische Philologie* 5 (1905): 193–415.

Meyer, Kuno, ed. and trans. *Cath Finntrága, or The Battle of Ventry*. Oxford: Clarendon, 1885.

———, ed. and trans. *Fianaigecht*. Todd Lecture Series 16. Dublin: Hodges, Figgis, 1910.

————, ed. and trans. *The Instructions of King Cormac Mac Airt*. Todd Lecture Series 15. Dublin: Hodges, Figgis, 1909.

————, ed. and trans. *The Triads of Ireland*. Todd Lecture Series 13. Dublin: Hodges, Figgis, 1906.

————, ed. and trans. *The Voyage of Bran Son of Febal to the Land of the Living*. 2 vols. London: Grimm Library, 1895–97.

Murphy, Gerard. *Early Irish Metrics: Eighth to Twelfth Century*. Dublin: Royal Irish Academy and Hodges, Figgis, 1961.

————, ed. and trans. *Early Irish Lyrics*. Oxford: Oxford UP, 1956.

Nagy, Joseph Falaky. *The Wisdom of the Outlaw: The Boyhood Deeds of Finn in Gaelic Narrative Tradition*. Berkeley and Los Angeles: U of California P, 1985.

Nilsen, Kenneth. "Down among the Dead: Elements of Irish Language and Mythology in James Joyce's *Dubliners*." *Canadian Journal of Irish Studies* 12 (1986): 23–34.

Nutt, Alfred. *The Celtic Doctrine of Re-birth*. Vol. 2 of Meyer, *Voyage of Bran*.

————. *Cuchulainn, the Irish Achilles*. 1900. New York: AMS, 1972.

————. "The Happy Otherworld." Meyer, *Voyage of Bran* 1: 101–331.

O'Brien, Darcy. "Some Determinants of Molly Bloom." Staley and Benstock, *Approaches to "Ulysses"* 137–55.

O'Brien, M. A., ed. *Corpus Genealogiarum Hiberniae*. Dublin: Dublin Institute for Advanced Studies, 1962.

O'Casey, Sean. *Juno and the Paycock*. *Collected Plays*. London: Macmillan, 1957. 1: 1–89.

Ó Cathasaigh, Tomás. "The Semantics of 'Síd.'" *Éigse* 17 (1977–78): 137–55.

O'Connor, Frank. "Joyce and Dissociated Metaphor." *The Mirror in the Roadway: A Study of the Modern Novel*. New York: Knopf, 1956. 295–312.

O'Curry, Eugene. *Lectures on the Manuscript Materials of Ancient Irish History*. Dublin: James Duffy, 1861.

O'Donovan, John. *A Grammar of the Irish Language*. Dublin: Hodges and Smith, 1845.

————, ed. and trans. *Ancient Laws of Ireland*. 6 vols. Ed. W. M. Hennessy, W. N. Hancock, Thaddeus O'Mahony, A. G. Richey, Robert Atkinson. Dublin: H. M. Stationery Office, 1865–1901.

————, ed. and trans. *Annala Ríoghachta Éireann, Annals of the Kingdom of Ireland by the Four Masters, from the Earliest Period to the Year 1616*. 7 vols. Dublin: Hodges and Smith, 1848–1851.

O'Flaherty, Roderic. *Ogygia, or a Chronological Account of Irish Events*. 1685. Trans. James Hely. Dublin: W. M'Kenzie, 1793.

O'Grady, Standish. *History of Ireland: The Heroic Period*. 2 vols. London: Sampson Low, 1878–80.

———. "Introduction of the Bardic History of Ireland." *Selected Essays and Passages*. Dublin: Talbot, n.d. 23–51.

O'Growney, Eugene. *Simple Lessons in Irish*. 3 vols. Gaelic League Series. Dublin: M. H. Gill, 1894–96.

O Hehir, Brendan. *A Gaelic Lexicon for "Finnegans Wake" and Glossary for Joyce's Other Works*. Berkeley and Los Angeles: U of California P, 1967.

Ó hEochaid, Seán, Máire Mac Neill, and Séamus Ó Catháin. *Síscéalta ó Thír Chonaill, Fairy Legends from Donegal*. Dublin: Comhairle Bhéaloideas Éireann, University College, 1977.

Ó Máille, Tomás. "Medb Chruachna." *Zeitschrift für celtische Philologie* 17 (1928): 129–46.

O'Neill, Joseph, ed. and trans. "Cath Boinde." *Ériu* 2 (1905): 173–85.

O'Rahilly, Cecile, ed. and trans. *Táin Bó Cúalnge from the Book of Leinster*. Dublin: Dublin Institute for Advanced Studies, 1967.

O'Rahilly, Thomas F. *Early Irish History and Mythology*. Dublin: Dublin Institute for Advanced Studies, 1946.

Ó Súilleabháin, Seán [Sean O'Sullivan]. *A Handbook of Irish Folklore*. 1942. Detroit: Singing Tree, 1970.

———, trans. *The Folklore of Ireland*. London: B. T. Batsford, 1974.

———, trans. *Folktales of Ireland*. Chicago: U of Chicago P, 1966.

O'Sullivan, Sean. *See* Ó Súilleabháin, Seán.

Ó Tuama, Seán, ed., and Thomas Kinsella, trans. *An Duanaire: An Irish Anthology, 1600–1900: Poems of the Dispossessed*. Philadelphia: U of Pennsylvania P, 1981.

Palencia-Roth, Michael. *Myth and the Modern Novel: García Márquez, Mann, and Joyce*. New York and London: Garland, 1987.

Patch, Howard Rollin. *The Other World According to Descriptions in Medieval Literature*. Cambridge: Harvard UP, 1950.

Petrie, George. "On the History and Antiquities of Tara Hill." *Royal Irish Academy Transactions* 18, part 2 (1837): 25–232.

Piggott, Stuart. *The Druids*. 1968. Harmondsworth: Penguin, 1974.

Pound, Ezra. "James Joyce et Pécuchet." *Polite Essays*. 1937. Freeport, N.Y.: Books for Libraries, 1966. 82–97.

———. "Ulysses." *Literary Essays of Ezra Pound*. Ed. T. S. Eliot. London: Faber, 1954. 403–9.

Power, Arthur. *Conversations with James Joyce*. Ed. Clive Hart. New York: Harper, 1974.

———. *From the Old Waterford House*. London: Mellifont, n.d. [1944].

Preston, James J., ed. *Mother Worship: Theme and Variations.* Chapel Hill: U of North Carolina P, 1982.

Raleigh, John Henry. *A Chronicle of Leopold and Molly Bloom.* Berkeley and Los Angeles: U of California P, 1977.

Rees, Alwyn, and Brinley Rees. *Celtic Heritage: Ancient Tradition in Ireland and Wales.* 1961. London: Thames and Hudson, 1975.

Reynolds, Lorna. "The Irish Literary Revival: Preparation and Personalities." *The Celtic Consciousness.* Ed. Robert O'Driscoll. 1981. New York: George Braziller, 1982. 383–99.

Robinson, Fred Norris. "Satirists and Enchanters in Early Irish Literature." *Studies in the History of Religions presented to Crawford Howell.* Ed. David Gordon Lyon and George Foot Moore. New York: Macmillan, 1912. 95–130.

Roche, Anthony. " 'The Strange Light of Some New World': Stephen's Vision in *A Portrait.*" *James Joyce Quarterly* 25 (1988): 323–32.

———. "The Two Worlds of Synge's *The Well of the Saints.*" *The Genres of the Irish Literary Revival.* Ed. Ronald Schleifer. Norman, Okla.: Pilgrim, 1980. 27–38.

Rose, Danis, and John O'Hanlon, eds. "Commentary." *The Lost Notebook: New Evidence on the Genesis of "Ulysses."* By James Joyce. Edinburgh: Split Pea, 1989. xi–xxxvii.

Ross, Anne. *Pagan Celtic Britain.* 1967. London: Cardinal, 1974.

Russell, George. *See* A. E.

Scholes, Robert, and Richard M. Kain, eds. *The Workshop of Daedalus: James Joyce and the Raw Materials for "A Portrait of the Artist as a Young Man."* Evanston: Northwestern UP, 1965.

Scholes, Robert, and Robert Kellogg. *The Nature of Narrative.* 1966. London, Oxford, New York: Oxford UP, 1968.

Schopenhauer, Arthur. *The World as Will and Representation.* Trans. E. F. J. Payne. 1958. 2 vols. New York: Dover, 1966.

Schutte, William M. *Joyce and Shakespeare: A Study in the Meaning of "Ulysses."* New Haven: Yale UP, 1957.

Schutte, William M., and Erwin R. Steinberg. "The Fictional Technique of *Ulysses.*" Staley and Benstock, *Approaches to "Ulysses"* 157–78.

Scott, Bonnie Kime. *Joyce and Feminism.* Bloomington: Indiana UP, 1984.

Scott, Robert Douglas. *The Thumb of Knowledge in Legends of Finn, Sigurd, and Taliesin: Studies in Celtic and French Literature.* New York: Institute of French Studies, 1930.

Seidel, Michael. *Epic Geography: James Joyce's "Ulysses."* Princeton: Princeton UP, 1976.

Senn, Fritz. "'He Was Too Scrupulous Always': Joyce's 'The Sisters.'" *James Joyce Quarterly* 21 (1965): 66–72.

―――. "No Trace of Hell." *James Joyce Quarterly* 7 (1970): 255–56.

Seward, Barbara. *The Symbolic Rose*. New York: Columbia UP, 1960.

Shaw, Bernard. *Arms and the Man*. *Complete Plays with Prefaces*. New York: Dodd, Mead, 1962. 3: 123–96.

―――. *John Bull's Other Island*. *Complete Plays with Prefaces*. New York: Dodd, Mead, 1962. 2: 503–611.

Shechner, Mark. *Joyce in Nighttown: A Psychoanalytic Inquiry into "Ulysses."* Berkeley and Los Angeles: U of California P, 1974.

Sigerson, George. *Bards of the Gael and Gall*. 1897. Dublin: Talbot, 1925.

―――. "Irish Literature: Its Origins, Environment, and Influence." *The Revival of Irish Literature and Other Addresses*. By Charles G. Duffy, George Sigerson, and Douglas Hyde. London: T. Fisher Unwin, 1894. 61–114.

Sinn Féin (Dublin).

Sjoestedt, Marie-Louise. *Gods and Heroes of the Celts*. 1940. Trans. Myles Dillon. 1949. Berkeley: Turtle Island Foundation, 1982.

Skeat, Walter William. *An Etymological Dictionary of the English Language*. Oxford: Clarendon, 1882.

Slotkin, Edgar. "Evidence for Oral Composition in Early Irish Saga." Diss. Harvard U, 1977.

Staley, Thomas F., and Bernard Benstock, eds. *Approaches to "Ulysses": Ten Essays*. Pittsburgh: U of Pittsburgh P, 1970.

States, Bert O. *The Shape of Paradox: An Essay on "Waiting for Godot."* Berkeley and Los Angeles: U of California P, 1978.

Steinberg, Erwin R. "James Joyce and the Critics Notwithstanding, Leopold Bloom Is Not Jewish." *Journal of Modern Literature* 9 (1981–82): 27–49.

Steiner, George. "On Difficulty." *On Difficulty and Other Essays*. New York: Oxford UP, 1978. 18–47.

Stewart, Bruce. "Adamology." 1978. Rpt. in Hederman and Kearney, *Crane Bag Book* 193–204.

Stokes, Whitley, ed. and trans. *Cóir Anmann (Fitness of Names)*. Vol. 2 of *Irische Texte mit Uebersetzungen und Wörterbuch*, ser. 3. Ed. Whitley Stokes and Ernst Windisch. Leipzig: S. Hirzel, 1897.

―――, ed. and trans. "The Death of Crimthann Son of Fidach, and the Adventures of the Sons of Eochaid Muigmedon." *Revue celtique* 24 (1902): 190–203.

―――, ed. and trans. "The Destruction of Da Derga's Hostel." *Revue celtique* 22 (1901): 9–61, 165–215, 282–329, 390–437; 23 (1902): 88.

————, ed. and trans. *Lives of Saints from the Book of Lismore*. Oxford: Clarendon, 1890.

————, ed. and trans. *On the Calendar of Oengus*. Dublin: Royal Irish Academy, 1880.

————, ed. and trans. "The Prose Tales in the Rennes Dindsenchas." *Revue celtique* 15 (1894): 272–336, 418–84; 16 (1895): 31–83, 135–67, 269–312.

————, ed. and trans. *The Saltair na Rann*. Oxford: Clarendon, 1883.

————, ed. and trans. "The Second Battle of Moytura." *Revue celtique* 12 (1891): 52–130, 306–8.

————, ed. and trans. *Three Irish Glossaries*. London: Williams and Norgate, 1862.

————, ed. and trans. "Tidings of Conchobar Mac Nessa." *Ériu* 4 (1910): 18–38.

Stokes, Whitley, and Ernest Windisch, eds. and trans. *Irische Texte mit Uebersetzungen und Wörterbuch*. Ser. 2, 3, 4. Leipzig: S. Hirzel, 1884–1909.

Stoppard, Tom. *Travesties*. New York: Grove, 1975.

Strachan, John, and J. G. O'Keeffe, eds. and trans. *The Táin Bó Cúailnge from the Yellow Book of Lecan: With Variant Readings from the Lebor na Huidre*. 1904–12. Dublin: Royal Irish Academy, 1967.

Sultan, Stanley. *Eliot, Joyce, and Company*. New York: Oxford UP, 1987.

Synge, J. M. *J. M. Synge, Collected Works*. Gen. ed. Robin Skelton. 1962–68. 4 vols. Gerrards Cross: Colin Smythe, 1982.

————. "An Epic of Ulster." *Collected Works*. Vol. 2, *Prose*. Ed. Alan Price. 367–70.

————. *The Playboy of the Western World*. *Collected Works*. Vol. 4, *Plays, Book 2*. Ed. Ann Saddlemyer. 51–175.

————. *The Shadow of the Glen*. *Collected Works*. Vol. 3, *Plays, Book 1*. Ed. Ann Saddlemyer. 29–59.

Tarzia, Wade. "No Trespassing: Border Defence in the *Táin Bó Cuailnge*." *Emania* Autumn 1987: 28–33.

Thompson, Lawrance R. *A Comic Principle in Sterne-Meredith-Joyce*. Oslo: U of Oslo British Institute, 1954.

Thompson, Stith. *Motif-Index of Folk-Literature*. Rev. ed. 6 vols. Bloomington: Indiana UP, 1955–58.

Thompson, William Irwin. *The Imagination of an Insurrection: Dublin, Easter 1916: A Study of an Ideological Movement*. 1967. New York: Harper, 1972.

Thom's Official Directory of the United Kingdom of Great Britain and Ireland. Dublin: Alex Thom and Company, 1904.

Thornton, Weldon. *Allusions in "Ulysses": An Annotated List.* 1961. Chapel Hill: U of North Carolina P, 1968.

————. "The Allusive Method in *Ulysses.*" Staley and Benstock, *Approaches to "Ulysses"* 235–48.

Thurneysen, Rudolf. *A Grammar of Old Irish.* Rev. ed. Trans. D. A. Binchy and Osborn Bergin. 1946. Dublin: Dublin Institute for Advanced Studies, 1961.

————. *Handbuch des Alt-Irischen, I. Teil Grammatik.* Heidelberg: C. Winter, 1909.

————, ed. "Zu Irischen Texten. III. Cath Maige Turedh." *Zeitschrift für celtische Philologie* 12 (1918): 401–6.

————, trans. *Sagen aus dem alten Irland.* Berlin: Wiegandt und Grieben, 1901.

Topia, André. "The Matrix and the Echo: Intertextuality in *Ulysses.*" *Post-Structuralist Joyce: Essays from the French.* Ed. Derek Attridge and Daniel Ferrer. Cambridge: Cambridge UP, 1984. 103–25.

Tristram, Hildegard L. C. "Why James Joyce Also Lost His 'Brain of Forgetting': Patterns of Memory and Media in Irish Writing." *Anglistentag 1988 Göttingen.* Ed. Heinz-Joachim Müllenbrock and Renate Noll-Wiemann. Tübingen: Max Niemeyer, 1989. 220–233.

Tymoczko, Maria. "Amateur Political Theatricals, *Tableaux Vivants,* and *Cathleen ni Houlihan.*" *Yeats Annual* 10 (1993): 33–64.

————. "Animal Imagery in *Loinges Mac nUislenn.*" *Studia Celtica* 20–21 (1985–86): 145–66.

————. " 'The Broken Lights of Irish Myth' ": Joyce's Knowledge of Early Irish Literature." *James Joyce Quarterly* 29 (1992): 763–74.

————. " 'Cétamon': Vision in Early Irish Seasonal Poetry." *Éire-Ireland* 18.4 (1983): 17–39.

————. "Knowledge and Vision in Early Welsh Gnomic Poetry." *Proceedings of the Harvard Celtic Colloquium* 3 (1983): 1–19.

————. "Molly's Gibraltar and the Morphology of the Irish Otherworld." *Irish University Review* 20 (1990): 264–81.

————. "The Personal Names in the Ulster Sagas: A Tool for Understanding the Development of the Cycle." Diss. Harvard U, 1973.

————. "Sovereignty Structures in *Ulysses.*" *James Joyce Quarterly* 25 (1988): 445–64.

————. "Strategies for Integrating Irish Epic into European Literature." *Dispositio* 7 (1982): 123–40.

————. "Symbolic Structures in *Ulysses* from Early Irish Literature." *James Joyce Quarterly* 21 (1984): 215–30. Also in *James Joyce and His Contemporaries*. Ed. Diana A. Ben-Merre and Maureen Murphy. New York: Greenwood, 1989.

————. "Translating the Humour in Early Irish Hero Tales: A Polysystems Approach." *New Comparison* 3 (1986–87): 83–103.

————. "Translating the Old Irish Epic *Táin Bó Cúailnge*: Political Aspects." *Pacific Quarterly Moana* 8.2 (1983): 6–21.

————. "Unity and Duality: A Theoretical Perspective on the Ambivalence of Celtic Goddesses." *Proceedings of the Harvard Celtic Colloquium* 5 (1985): 22–37.

————, trans. *Two Death Tales from the Ulster Cycle: "The Death of CuRoi" and "The Death of CuChulainn."* Dublin: Dolmen, 1981.

Unkeless, Elaine. "The Conventional Molly Bloom." *Women in Joyce.* Ed. Suzette Henke and Elaine Unkeless. Urbana: U of Illinois P, 1982: 150–68.

————. "Leopold Bloom as a Womanly Man." *Modernist Studies* 2 (1976): 35–44.

United Irishman (Dublin).

Vallancey, Charles. *An Essay on the Antiquity of the Irish Language.* 1772. Dublin: R. Marchbank, 1781.

————. *An Essay on the Primitive Inhabitants of Great Britain and Ireland. Proving from History, Language, and Mythology that they were Persians or Indosythae composed of Scythians, Chaldeans and Indians.* Dublin: Graisberry and Campbell, 1807.

————. *A Grammar of the Iberno-Celtic or Irish Language.* Dublin: R. Marchbank, 1773.

————. *Prospectus of a Dictionary of the Language of the Aire Coti or Ancient Irish, Compared with the Language of the Cuti or Ancient Persians, with the Hindoostanee, the Arabic and Chaldean Languages.* Dublin: Graisberry and Campbell, 1802.

————. *A Vindication of the Ancient History of Ireland.* Dublin: Luke White, 1786.

Van Hamel, A. G. "An Anglo-Irish Syntax." *Englische Studien* 45 (1912): 272–92.

Vendryes, Joseph. *De hibernicis vocabulis quae a Latina lingua originem duxerunt.* Paris: C. Klincksieck, 1902.

Voelker, Joseph C. "'You Think Its the Vegetables': Aristotle, Aquinas, and Molly Bloom." *Modern British Literature* 1 (1976): 35–45.

Walkowitz, Judith R. "Male Vice and Female Virtue: Feminism and the Politics of Prostitution in Nineteenth-Century Britain." *Powers of Desire: The*

Politics of Sexuality. Ed. Ann Snitow, Christine Stansell, and Sharon Thompson. New York: Monthly Review Press, 1983. 419–38.

Wall, Richard. *An Anglo-Irish Dialect Glossary for Joyce's Works.* Gerrards Cross: Colin Smythe, 1986.

Walsh, Edward. *Irish Popular Songs with English Metrical Translations.* Dublin: McGlashan, 1847.

Waters, Maureen. *The Comic Irishman.* Albany: SUNY P, 1984.

Watkins, Calvert. "Indo-European Metrics and Archaic Irish Verse." *Celtica* 6 (1963): 194–249.

Weekly Freeman (Dublin).

Weston, Jessie. *From Ritual to Romance.* Cambridge: Cambridge UP, 1920.

Wilde, Oscar. *The Importance of Being Earnest.* Ed. Russell Jackson. London: Ernest Benn, 1980.

———. *The Letters of Oscar Wilde.* Ed. Rupert Hart-Davis. New York: Harcourt, 1962.

Williams, Ifor. *Lectures on Early Welsh Poetry.* Dublin: Dublin Institute for Advanced Studies, 1944.

Williams, J. E. Caerwyn, and Patrick K. Ford. *The Irish Literary Tradition.* Cardiff: U of Wales P, 1992.

Williams, Raymond L. *Gabriel García Márquez.* Boston: Twayne, 1984.

Wilson, Edmund. *The Portable Edmund Wilson.* Ed. Lewis M. Dabney. New York: Viking and Penguin, 1983.

Windisch, Ernst. *Kurzgefasste Irische Grammatik mit Lesestücken.* Leipzig: S. Hirzel, 1879.

———, ed. and trans. *Die altirische Heldensage Táin Bó Cúalnge nach dem Buch von Leinster, in Text und Uebersetzung mit einer Einleitung.* Leipzig: S. Hirzel, 1905.

Yeats, W. B. *The Autobiography of William Butler Yeats.* New York: Macmillan, 1953.

———. *The Celtic Twilight.* 1892. Gerrards Cross: Colin Smythe, 1981.

———. *A Critical Edition of Yeats's "A Vision" (1925).* Ed. George Mills Harper and Walter Kelly Hood. London: Macmillan, 1978.

———. *The Poems, A New Edition.* Ed. Richard J. Finneran. New York: Macmillan, 1983.

———. *The Variorum Edition of the Plays of W. B. Yeats.* Ed. Russell K. Alspach assisted by Catharine C. Alspach. New York: Macmillan, 1966.

———, ed. *Fairy and Folk Tales of the Irish Peasantry.* 1888. Rpt. in *Fairy and Folk Tales of Ireland.* Gerrards Cross: Colin Smythe, 1988. 3–294.

Younger, Calton. *Arthur Griffith.* Dublin: Gill and Macmillan, 1981.

Zeuss, Johann Caspar. *Grammatica Celtica.* 2 vols. Leipzig and Berlin, 1853–71.

Zimmer, Heinrich. *The Celtic Church in Britain and Ireland.* Trans. A. Meyer. London: David Nutt, 1902.

————. "Der kulturgeschichtliche Hintergrund in den Erzählungen der alten irischen Heldensage." *Sitzungsberichte der königlich preussischen Akademie der Wissenschaften,* Philosophisch-historischen Classe 1911, 174–227.

Index

Compositor:	Wilsted & Taylor Publishing Services
Text:	10/14 Sabon
Display:	Sabon

.

Lightning Source UK Ltd.
Milton Keynes UK
UKHW010858180721
387318UK00001B/45

9 780520 330238